THE INSIDER'S GUIDE TO U.S. COIN VALUES 20TH EDITION

THE INSIDER'S GUIDE
TO U.S. COIN VALUES

SCOTT A. TRAVERS

20TH EDITION

House of Collectibles
New York Toronto London Sydney Auckland

All rights reserved. Published in the United States by House of Collectibles, an imprint of The Random House Audio Publishing Group, a division of Random House, Inc., New York and in Canada by Random House of Canada Limited, Toronto.

 House of Collectibles and colophon are registered trademarks of Random House, Inc.

Some of the material in this book appeared previously in *One-Minute Coin Expert®, 6th Edition,* by Scott A. Travers (House of Collectibles, 2007).

RANDOM HOUSE is a registered trademark of Random House, Inc.

This book is available for special discounts for bulk purchases for sales promotions or premiums. Special editions, including personalized covers, excerpts of existing books, and corporate imprints, can be created in large quantities for special needs. For more information, write to Random House, Inc., Special Markets/Premium Sales, 1745 Broadway, MD 3-1, New York, NY 10019 or e-mail specialmarkets@randomhouse.com.

Please address inquiries about electronic licensing of reference products for use on a network, in software or on CD-ROM to the Subsidiary Rights Department, Random House Reference, fax 212-572-6003.

Visit the Random House Web site: www.randomhouse.com

Printed in the United States of America

Twentieth Edition: November 2012

10 9 8 7 6 5 4 3 2 1

ISBN: 978-0-375-72370-4
ISSN: 1530–7727

ON THE COVER: This stunning coin, produced by the U.S. Mint in 2009, is a replica of the Ultra High Relief 1907 double eagle, or $20 gold piece, designed by famed sculptor Augustus Saint-Gaudens. It was struck in limited numbers for sale to collectors at a premium price above its gold content. *(Photo courtesy U.S. Mint)*

To my parents

CONTENTS

ACKNOWLEDGMENTS

I especially appreciate the knowledge and advice given to me by so many persons during the preparation of this book. Given the uncertain nature of some of the issues addressed, this book is really a consensus of opinion of many of the contributors consulted. Those contributors are:

John Albanese; David T. Alexander; Jonathan Auerbach; Richard A. Bagg; Dennis Baker; Q. David Bowers; H. Robert Campbell; Jeanne Cavelos; Mike Chipman; William L. Corsa, Sr.; John W. Dannreuther; Beth Deisher; Thomas K. DeLorey; Silvano DiGenova; Shane Downing; Al Doyle; Bill Fivaz; Leo Frese; Michael Fuljenz; David L. Ganz; Salvatore Germano; Marcy Gibbel; William T. Gibbs; Lindsey Glass; Ira Goldberg; Ron Guth; David Hall; James L. Halperin; David C. Harper; Dorothy Harris; Michael R. Haynes; Leon Hendrickson; Brian Hendelson; Robert L. Hughes; Steve Ivy; R. W. Julian; Christine Karstedt; Melissa Karstedt; Jim Kingsland; Charles H. Knull; Timothy J. Kochuba; Chester L. Krause; David W. Lange; Julian Leidman; Robert J. Leuver; Kevin J. Lipton; Steve Markoff; Steve Mayer; Raymond N. Merena; Bob Merrill; Amy Metsch; Lee S. Minshull; Maren Monitello; Richard Nachbar; John Pasciuti, Sr.; Martin Paul; Donn Pearlman; Ed Reiter; Robert S. Riemer; Brandi Robinson; Maurice H. Rosen; Deborah G. Rosenthal; Mark D. Rosenthal; Tom Russell; Howard Ruff; John Sack; Stephen H. Spahn; Mark Salzberg; Helena Santini; Hugh Sconyers; Michael W. Sherman; Jeff Shoop; John Slack; Harvey Stack; Michael J. Standish; Kari Stone; Barry Stuppler; David Sundman; Rick Sundman; Marilyn Van Allen; Armen Vartian; Fred Weinberg; Leigh H. Weiss; Bob Wilhite; Mark Yaffe; Marc D. Zand, and Keith M. Zaner.

John Albanese reviewed the manuscript and approved the prices for rare gold coins.

Michael R. Fuljenz of Universal Coin & Bullion in Beaumont, Texas, updated the values for gold dollars through double eagles. He is one of the nation's highest-profile and most esteemed gold coin authorities. His contributions, like the metal itself, glitter.

Robert W. Julian compiled the mintage figures for the modern coins, and updated the mintage numbers for earlier issues, too. His contributions were extraordinary.

Jim Kingsland served as my mentor at all hours of the day and night and provided invaluable facts about gold and silver.

Amy Metsch, editorial director at Random House Digital Publishing, recognized the need for this book and lent her wisdom and genius to the project.

Maren Monitello, editorial manager at Random House Digital Publishing, edited the book and used her extraordinary skill to transform it into an electronic masterpiece. She also added brilliance and wit to the published work.

Ed Reiter served as my numismatic editor and carefully reviewed and assisted in revising the finished manuscript.

Maurice H. Rosen was of supreme importance in his assistance in understanding market psychology and issues relating to the performance of gold. He also provided virtually all of the statistical matter for chapter 9, and, consequently, should be considered for a great honor—a Nobel Prize in Economics would be appropriate.

Marilyn Van Allen and Keith Zaner compiled many of the photographs and coin prices.

Scott A. Travers
travers@USGoldExpert.com
New York
November 2012

INTRODUCTION

When times are hard, as they have been in recent years, smart people turn to hard assets. Precious metals and rare coins are among the assets they turn to the most, and with the greatest confidence.

Coins made of gold and silver provide a double-strength dose of financial protection, combining the potent wealth-preserving qualities of both precious metals and collectible coinage. And both of these ingredients have been extremely active in recent years.

The Insider's Guide to U.S. Coin Values, 20th Edition is also a blend, combining the best elements of two time-tested bestsellers, *The Insider's Guide to U.S. Coin Values* and *One-Minute Coin Expert*®—both of which have been mainstays on coin collector's bookshelves for upwards of two decades. Separately, over the years, they have answered two questions inevitably asked by collectors ranging all the way from neophytes to numismatic veterans: "What's it worth?" and "How can I get the most—in terms of both pleasure and profit—from this hobby?" Together, in this single fact-filled volume, they now pack an even more powerful punch, delivered in a 1-2 combination.

Since 1991, *One-Minute Coin Expert*® has given readers vital information on how to get the most out of coin collecting and investing, showing them how to demystify the marketplace and master the art of buying and selling coins. Since 1992, *The Insider's Guide to U.S. Coin Values* has provided them with timely, accurate data on what their coins—and coins they're thinking of purchasing—are worth. Its price valuations are based on my experience as a major market

1913 Liberty head nickel worth at least $3.5 million dollars that was found at the bottom of a closet in the summer of 2003. (Photo courtesy Donn Pearlman)

1804 silver dollar that sold for $4,140,000 in 1999. (Photo courtesy Auctions by Bowers and Merena, Inc.)

insider, plus input from other top coin experts across the country—and its mintage listings have proven so precise that Congress has used them in preference to the numbers supplied by the U.S. Mint.

Gold and silver have soared to unprecedented heights in recent years, as people around the globe have rushed to find safe haven for their assets at a time when stocks, bonds, housing and other traditional bulwarks were being swept up by an economic tsunami. In just five years, from March 2007 to February 2012, the price of gold rose more than two and a half times, from $654.80 to $1,723.10. During the same period, silver made a similar leap, from $13.15 to $33.69. And these huge gains lifted the coin market, too.

Coins containing gold and silver have enjoyed healthy price increases simply as pieces of metal, reflecting the higher value of their precious metal content. More than 10,000 valuations in *The Insider's Guide to U.S. Coin Values, 20th Edition* had to be revised just because of changes in coins' intrinsic worth, and many were further refined to account for market changes in their numismatic value.

The hobby's base already has been expanded tremendously by the 50-state Washington quarters, which have captured the attention of millions of noncollectors and converted many into hobbyists. So for now, good values still appear within the reach of almost everyone.

At times, the only reach needed is into your pocket or purse. Coins worth hundreds—even thousands—of dollars can be found in otherwise ordinary pocket change. True, it doesn't happen every day. But bettors don't hit the lottery very often either, and that doesn't stop them from playing their numbers religiously week after week. You're much more likely to find a valuable coin in pocket change than you are to win a bundle in the lottery. And the cost—just the face value (or spending value) of the coin—is cheaper by a long shot than what people spend on lottery games.

The Insider's Guide to U.S. Coin Values will tell you how to maximize your chances to reap big profits from *your own* small change. It also will provide you with all the tools you need to buy and sell coins effectively, shrewdly—and profitably—in the bustling coin marketplace, an international network of dealers, collectors, and investors where rare cents are no penny-ante proposition and scarce nickels and dimes are much more than merely a five-and-ten-cent business. By following a series of quick, easy steps, you'll soon be able to transform your coin collection into a healthy bankroll of that other highly popular form of money—the kind you spend!

While certainly important, profit is just one reason why millions of people all around the world collect coins. The hobby is richly rewarding in other ways, as well.

Pick up an old coin and you're literally holding history in your hand. Coins are mirrors of the civilizations that issued them, and they frequently furnish fascinating insights into the life and times of those who made them.

They're more than just mirrors, of course: They're tangible mementos of the cultures in which they were produced; in fact, they're among our most important links with some of mankind's greatest, most glorious eras. The temples of ancient Athens have vanished or lie in ruins, but many lovely coins endure as tangible reminders of the grandeur that was Greece.

Coins are also tiny works of art. Although they may be only millimeters wide, many are exquisitely beautiful and their owners take great pride in possessing and displaying them.

Collectors enjoy assembling sets of coins. Finding a coin you need—whether in pocket change, a piggy bank, or even a dealer's display case—is a source of satisfaction and even exhilaration. It's just like digging up buried treasure.

Coin collecting didn't come into its own as a pastime for the masses until relatively recently. At one time, it was known as "The Hobby of Kings" because only noblemen had the time and money to indulge in it. During the last few decades, interest and involvement in this stimulating pastime have multiplied geometrically, and "The Hobby of Kings" has now become "The King of Hobbies" instead.

The coin market, too, has undergone major changes in recent years. A generation ago, it was populated almost exclusively by mom-and-pop dealers and small collectors. But now, well-heeled investors have joined the hunt, altering the ground rules fundamentally and raising the stakes—and many of the prices—enormously.

Coin collecting still holds great appeal for small collectors; it's avidly pursued by multitudes of people—including several million Americans—in virtually every age group and income bracket. This widespread demand provides a solid base for the coin market, serving as an important underpinning for the price structure. Today, however, rare coins are no longer mere collectibles. In a word, they have become an *investment*—an investment whose returns can be spectacular.

Investors' interest in coins peaked in the late 1980s, when several Wall Street firms became active, aggressive participants in the coin market. Unfortunately, that involvement proved to be premature. Coin prices soared initially amid the euphoria generated by these new "players," but after the frenzy subsided, price levels also fell back. Far from being a source of concern, this represented a wonderful opportunity: The lower prices made the market even more attractive for potential investors.

The coin market has grown not only in size but also in sophistication. For example, a 70-point grading system is now used to denote coins' "condition," or state of preservation. The number 70 refers to a coin which is perfect— which has no nicks or scratches and never has been passed from hand to hand. As a coin goes from hand to hand, the metal wears down and that coin loses detail which can never be recovered. Coins that have lost this detail are said to be "circulated."

The market's greater complexity is evident, as well, from the way coins are now bought and sold. Dealers conduct transactions on computerized trading networks; and neighborhood coin shops, while far from extinct, are dwarfed today by large, high-profile dealerships with international clienteles and multimillion-dollar inventories and sales. In other ways, however, buying and selling coins is really simpler—for those who know what they're doing and where they're going.

Some people have trouble telling the difference between coins which have no scratches, and have not been spent, and other coins which have passed through many hands and been worn down. "Certification" services give people an impartial opinion as to how worn—or how new—a coin is. These organizations seal each coin in a special plastic holder designed so the coin cannot be easily removed. A paper insert stating the service's grading is sealed inside this holder with the coin. Any attempt to remove the coin or insert, or to change the grading on the insert, can be easily detected.

Independent grading services have removed much of the guesswork—and much of the risk—from buying and selling coins. A number of certified coins are so widely accepted, in fact, that many dealers feel comfortable making offers for them on a sight-unseen basis. Although most buyers now prefer to look at coins first, and purchase them on a sight-seen basis, the sight-unseen concept has made it possible for even neophytes to participate successfully in the coin market.

The ability to grade coins accurately is partly a science, partly an art. *You* don't need to be an expert grader; the grading services' expertise provides you with a fine security blanket. Still, you should equip yourself with a fundamental knowledge of what's involved—and once understood, the elements are simple.

The Insider's Guide to U.S. Coin Values makes them even simpler by showing you an easy, enjoyable way to determine the grade of a coin by reviewing its key components.

Like any investment field, the rare coin market goes up and down. And how you "play the game" goes a long way toward determining how much money you make. *The Insider's Guide to U.S. Coin Values* gives you a big head start and an inside track. Knowledge is the key. Many current players lack the knowledge they need to be successful—but after reading this book, you'll be ready to compete like a seasoned veteran.

The Insider's Guide to U.S. Coin Values will tell you what to look for. Whether you're simply a casual accumulator—someone who pulls odd-looking coins out of pocket change and sticks them away in a drawer—or a high-powered investor who buys expensive coins for thousands of dollars apiece, this book will give you all the information you need to maximize your return on the time and money you spend.

I'll tell you how to cash in your profits when the coin market is strong. And I'll also explain how to ride out the storm comfortably when hard times hit.

The Insider's Guide to U.S. Coin Values provides you with a maximum of information in a minimum of time. I'll give you a simple, straightforward blueprint of how the market works and how it can be made to work for you, enabling you to turn your small change into big money.

I'll start by explaining why people save coins, and examine the four different categories into which most of these people fall. Then I'll tell you more about coins in general, including how to spot the mint marks on U.S. coins—small symbols that can add enormous value.

In Chapter Two, I'll give you a checklist of valuable coins that can and do appear in ordinary pocket change. Then, in Chapter Four I'll tell you about still other worthwhile coins that won't be in your pocket change but may very well turn up around your home—perhaps in a cigar box or dresser drawer. Chapter Four encompasses twenty years of price guide experience by incorporating 136,000 coin values.

Once you know which dates and mint marks to look for, I'll take you on a guided tour of the coin market, showing you what makes it tick and how you can get the edge on everyone else when buying or selling coins. I'll make you an instant expert not only on grading coins but also on trading them. And I'll tell you how to spot the coins with the greatest potential—the ones that are likely to go up in value faster and farther than all the rest. I'll even give you a secret list of my personal Top Twelve recommendations.

Coins and precious metals are closely interrelated. I'll show you just how they work together, and how this can provide you with golden opportunities to pocket sizable profits.

You'll learn how to spot bargains . . . how to pick coins that will rise in value quickly . . . how to grade coins . . . how to buy and sell . . . how to understand market psychology . . . how to protect your investments from the tax man. In short, you'll learn how to play this intriguing, potentially lucrative money game—and how to win!

CHAPTER 1

YOU CAN BE AN EXPERT

This is a book on how to become an expert on coins.

Expertise on coins can take many forms. It can mean becoming adroit at checking pocket change for coins that will bring you a financial windfall. It also can mean becoming astute at spending money on coins, whether you're reaching into your pocket for one hundred dollars to buy a rare coin, or even reaching deep into your bank account for many thousands of dollars to spend on extremely rare coins in hopes of achieving a profit.

Whatever your degree of involvement, this book will make you an expert. And if you become an expert, you can profit from rare coins at every level of involvement, regardless of whether current market conditions are good or bad.

At one time or another, possibly without even realizing it, just about everyone thinks about coins as an investment. It happens, for example, when a really old coin turns up in your change or in your travels, or when you get a coin that just doesn't look right—one, for example, on which the date and some of the words are misprinted.

Many of us have had this experience. And when it happens, we invariably want to know two things: What's it worth, and will I make more money if I sell it now or later?

You don't have to wait for scarce and valuable coins to come along; you can go looking for them. And you can make money by buying and selling scarce coins. Many such coins today are authenticated and graded by independent experts and then encased in special plastic holders. This process assures the buyer that the grade, or level of preservation, is being properly stated by the seller. "Certified" coins change hands readily on nationwide trading networks and greatly enhance the appeal of rare coins to traditional investors.

I've come up with simple, easy-to-follow guidelines that will take you step by step through the process of identifying good values at all levels of the coin-buying spectrum. Follow these steps and you'll not only know what to look for, but also what to do with the coins once you have them.

Coins go up and down in value frequently; the coin market has peaks and valleys. But I'll show you how to make money in all kinds of markets—when coins are red-hot and also when prices are in a tailspin. That, after all, is the sign of a real expert: knowing how to thrive whether the coin market is rallying or is in one of its characteristic cyclical downturns.

WHY PEOPLE ACQUIRE COINS

People save coins for a number of different reasons. Some find them appealing as miniature works of art. Others are intrigued by the rich historical significance they possess. Many simply enjoy the challenge of pursuing something rare, elusive, and valuable. And, not least of all, many are attracted by the marvelous track record rare coins have achieved as good investments. Obviously, a great many people collect rare coins for *all* these different reasons, to a greater or lesser degree.

Finding something valuable is understandably thrilling, and many scarce coins do turn up in ordinary pocket change. I'll furnish a list of such coins in Chapter Two. Realistically, though, many rare coins have to be purchased.

Billions of dollars are spent on rare coins every year, and U.S. coins are by far the biggest segment of that market. In large part, that's because Americans account for the single biggest group of collectors in the world, as well as being among the most affluent. But other factors also have a bearing. For one thing, U.S. coins require less in-depth knowledge than ancient coins or international coins from the modern era. For another thing, the U.S. coin market is an easy-entry, easy-exit field with no regulation by the government—and many entrepreneurs find this appealing.

THE COIN BUYER SPECTRUM

The rare coin market is really a spectrum of different kinds of buyers. While one group of buyers may have different motivations from other groups, all are integral parts of the overall market—and all, in a real sense, are interdependent.

We can better understand who buys and saves coins, and why, by looking at the following graphic.

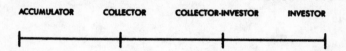

Accumulators   Accumulators are people who save coins haphazardly, without a particular pattern or plan of action. Many are undoubtedly attracted by the same positive qualities that motivate collectors and investors: the physical appeal of the coins and the notion of selling them for a profit, for example. But these objectives are only vaguely defined.

An accumulator may have sugar bowls or jars filled with coins, but they're probably not arranged in any special order and he probably doesn't have a very good idea what they're worth—even though some of them may be worth a great deal.

Collectors   In theory, a collector is someone who purchases coins with no regard at all for their profit potential—someone who is motivated strictly by such factors as aesthetics and historical significance. If a collector purchased a coin for $100 and its value went up to $1,000, he wouldn't even consider selling that coin, since he wouldn't have any interest in the coin's financial aspects. Theoretically, a collector also wouldn't concern himself with how much he had to pay to obtain a coin.

Collectors enjoy assembling coins in sets, and they strive for completeness in those sets. Lincoln cents with wheat stalks on the reverse were issued, for example, from 1909 to 1958. A collector would be interested in putting together representative Lincoln cents from each of those years so that she would have a complete set. Some collectors also like to assemble "type" collections, consisting of one coin from each of a number of different series. A twentieth-century type set of U.S. coins, for instance, would include one example of every different U.S. coin issued since 1901. A "type" coin is a representative example of a major coin variety but not a rare date of that variety.

Investors   On the other end of the spectrum, at the right-hand side of our graphic, is the investor. Unlike the collector, the investor pays close attention to inflation, interest rates, the size of the money supply—and, in short, the economic justification for purchasing rare coins. The quintessential investor, in fact, would be concerned *only* with profit, and not at all with coins' aesthetics and history.

Collector/Investors   In practical terms, no one is ever a totally solid collector or solid investor. Even the most dedicated collectors can't be completely oblivious to the cost and the value of their coins. And even the most profit-oriented investor can't completely ignore the intangible allure of beautiful coins.

The collector/investor combines the best of both worlds. This is a person who buys coins not only for their cultural, historical, and artistic appeal, but also to make a profit. The collector/investor represents a new breed of coin buyer, and a very healthy one.

OLD-TIME COLLECTING

Years ago, many people set aside interesting coins: circulated coins they found in pocket change, rolls of brand new coins they obtained at face value from the bank, or possibly government proof sets they purchased for modest premiums from the Mint. These coins may not have been particularly valuable at the time, but over the years coin collecting has evolved from a small hobby into a big business. And today, these tiny treasures may very well command enormous premiums.

As with anything else, it's a matter of supply and demand. Many of these coins, rolls, and proof sets have been in small supply since the day they were made. But years ago, the number of collectors was also relatively small, so demand for these coins remained at moderate levels. That served to hold down their prices.

Coin collecting became much more popular in the early 1960s. Thousands and thousands of newcomers started looking for low-mintage coins in their pocket change; many would go to the bank and get rolls of coins every week, then take them home and pick out the scarcer pieces. During that period, many people also began to purchase proof sets from the government every year. The expansion continued and accelerated during the 1970s and into the 1980s.

THE COMING OF THE INVESTOR

Investors began to enter the coin market in large numbers in the mid to late 1970s. The timing was no accident: Coins, like precious metals, have come to be viewed as hedges against economic calamities, and the late 1970s were years of unusual turbulence economically. Inflation was on the rise and many people were skeptical of the government's ability to control it. They also were wary of conventional investments such as stocks.

Driven by these fears, many turned to tangible assets and diverted large sums of money into gold, silver, and other such investments—including coins. Some combined their interest in coins and precious metals by buying *bullion coins*. These are coins whose value goes up or down in accordance with the value of the metal they contain—usually gold or silver. We'll discuss these in greater detail in a later chapter.

During the period ending in early 1980, the coin market experienced the most tremendous boom it has ever enjoyed.

THE GROWTH OF COLLECTING/INVESTING

As the number of collectors and investors expanded, so did the demand for better-date coins. The results were entirely predictable: As market demand increased for a fixed (and small) supply, prices began to escalate dramatically. At the same time, more and more people began to approach rare coins as both a collecting outlet and an investment.

Many collector/investors are baby boomers grown up: people who possibly started collecting coins when they were twelve or thirteen years old and built a solid foundation, then took a hiatus to pursue other interests such as college, courtship, and careers. Many of these collector/investors returned to the field in the mid to late 1980s and returned with a vengeance, bringing with them not only their strong foundation in coins but also finely honed minds and high incomes—testaments to their high degree of success at institutions of higher learning and in their careers.

These people are buying coins like there's no tomorrow. They have substantial sums of money at their disposal and they're savoring the chance to spend it on desirable coins. They appreciate every aspect of coins, including the one which can benefit *your* pocketbook: the financial aspect.

Collector/investors have added to the market's volatile nature—its suscepti-bility to going up or down in value very quickly.

Collectors and investors—and collector/investors—come in different degrees. Many, for example, would fall between the *Collector* and *Collector/Investor* locations on our graphic. The coin buyer spectrum is broad, diverse, and continuous, and buyers can be found across that spectrum.

THREE KINDS OF RARE COINS

For the purposes of this book, there are basically three different kinds of valuable coins.

"Cigar-box rarities" probably wouldn't be found in pocket change. Many are coins that aren't being minted anymore. But most people have such coins sitting around the house, or know of a friend or relative who does. Often, they've been handed down by relatives who found them—or maybe even purchased them—years ago. If so, they may be quite valuable. Many coins that were looked upon as common fifty years ago, or even twenty-five years ago, are worth large sums of money in the current marketplace.

There's an excellent chance that some of these scarce coins—coins that have become quite valuable over the years—may be sitting in *your* attic, or perhaps in a jewelry case in the back of a dresser drawer. Perhaps your father put them there many years ago, when they were still regarded as not of great consequence, then forgot them. Or maybe they've been handed down through generations that go back even farther.

PROOF SETS AND MINT SETS

A proof set is a group of specimen-quality coins, usually bearing a uniform date and housed in protective packaging. Proof coins are made by taking special, highly polished coin blanks and striking them several times with highly polished dies. These are considered the highest-quality coins available. The United States Mint offers proof sets for sale to the public every year.

A mint set, by contrast, consists of business-strike coins: the kind that are produced for circulation. A mint set contains one example of each different coin struck for circulation in any given year by each of the different mints. The coins in such a set may have been chosen carefully, but they're business strikes just the same.

Normally, a proof set costs more than a mint set when purchased from the government and also has higher value in the resale market. However, on occasion a mint set may be more valuable in the resale market than the corresponding proof set for that year. This may happen, for example, if the mint set contains a coin that wasn't actually made for general use. Since the mint set then contains the only circulation-quality example, that coin and that set will command an added premium.

MINT MARKS AND HOW TO LOCATE THEM

Many coins' values are enhanced by the presence of *mint marks*. These are little letters denoting the mint facility where the coins were manufactured.

During its earliest years, the United States Mint had only one production plant—in Philadelphia—and so there was no need to identify the source of any coins. As the nation grew and coinage requirements rose, branch mints were established in cities around the country. Each of these branches placed a mint mark on its coins to distinguish them readily from those being made at other mints.

Following are the letters used on U.S. coins to denote branch mints:

C—Charlotte, North Carolina (1838–1861, gold coins only)
CC—Carson City, Nevada (1870–1893)
D—Dahlonega, Georgia (1838–1861, gold coins only)
D—Denver (1906 to date)
O—New Orleans (1838–1909)
S—San Francisco (1854 to date)
W—West Point, New York (1984 to date)

Throughout most of U.S. history, coins produced at the main mint in Philadelphia carried no mint mark. Their origin was denoted by the *absence* of any such mark. In recent years, however, a small P has been placed on most coins produced in Philadelphia. This practice began in 1979, when the P mint mark was used on the Susan B. Anthony dollar. The following year, it was added to all other coins with one exception: No P has been used on Lincoln cents.

A Philadelphia mint mark was used one other time. During World War II, nickel was urgently needed for war-related purposes, so from 1942 through 1945 the Mint used a substitute alloy without any nickel in making five-cent pieces. The emergency alloy's components were copper, silver, and manganese. To denote this change in composition, the Mint placed large mint marks above Monticello's dome on the coins' reverse—including a large, slender P on non-nickel "nickels" produced during those years in Philadelphia. (The reverse of a coin is what is commonly known as the "tails" side and carries the monetary value of the coin. The obverse or "heads" side commonly carries a portrait and the year of the coin's issue.)

On nineteenth-century coins, the mint mark was usually placed at the base of the reverse, below the wreath or eagle depicted on that side. Mint marks' locations have varied a great deal more on twentieth-century coins, and some coins have carried them in several different places at different times.

Here's a checklist of where to look for mint marks on some of the coins you're most likely to encounter in current pocket change or older hoards:

- Lincoln cent (1909 to date)—below the date.

- Indian Head cent (1859–1909)—below the wreath (mint marks appear only on coins dated 1908 and 1909).

- Jefferson nickel (1938 to date)—on the reverse, to the right of Monticello, on most dates from 1938 to 1964; above Monticello on war nickels from 1942 to 1945; below the date from 1968 to the present.

- Buffalo nickel (1913–1938)—on the reverse, below the words *FIVE CENTS*.

- Liberty Head nickel (1883–1912)—on the reverse, to the left of the word *CENTS* (mint marks appear only on coins dated 1912).

- Roosevelt dime (1946 to date)—on the reverse, to the left of the torch's base, from 1946 to 1964; above the date from 1968 to the present.

- "Mercury" dime (1916–1945)—on the reverse, to the left of the fasces (the symbolic bundle of rods).

- Barber dime (1892–1916)—below the wreath.

- Washington quarter (1932 to date)—below the wreath from 1932 to 1964; to the right of George Washington's pigtail from 1968 to the present.

- Standing Liberty quarter (1916–1930)—to the left of the date. (*NOTE:* The M to the right of the date is not a mint mark; it stands for Hermon MacNeil, the coin's designer.)

- Barber quarter (1892–1916)—below the eagle.

• Kennedy half dollar (1964 to date)—to the left of the eagle's tail feathers in 1964; below John F. Kennedy's neck from 1968 to the present.

• Walking Liberty half dollar (1916–1947)—on the front, below *IN GOD WE TRUST*, in 1916 and 1917; on the reverse, above and to the left of *HALF DOLLAR*, from 1917 to 1947 (1917 examples come in both varieties).

• Barber half dollar (1892–1915)—below the eagle.

• Anthony dollar (1979–1981)—above Susan B. Anthony's right shoulder.

• Eisenhower dollar (1971–1978)—below Dwight D. Eisenhower's neck.

• Peace silver dollar (1921–1935)—on the reverse, below the word *ONE*.

• Morgan silver dollar (1878–1921)—below the wreath.

• Saint-Gaudens $20 gold piece (1907–1933)—above the date.

• Liberty Head $20 gold piece (1850–1907)—below the eagle.

Now that you have some idea of where you fall on the collector/investor spectrum and the different types of coins that are available to you, it's time to take a closer look at the coins you already have—in your pocket change.

CHAPTER 2

A FORTUNE IN POCKET CHANGE

A penny saved isn't always a penny earned. It can be *thousands* or *millions* of pennies earned if the penny in question is rare.

A client of mine discovered this recently when he looked through a box of old coins in the attic of his grandmother's home. Included in that hoard were several Lincoln cents dated 1909. They turned out to be extremely scarce coins worth hundreds of dollars apiece—yet they had been pulled out of pocket change many years before. Thus, the initial "investment" had been just a penny apiece.

That wasn't *all* my client found. Altogether, that box of coins probably contained only a few hundred dollars in face value—but because some of the coins were rare and especially well preserved, the tiny keepsakes were worth more than *a quarter of a million dollars* as collector's items. And they hadn't cost a penny more than "face" when the grandmother and other family members set them aside.

This experience is hardly an isolated case. Over the years, untold thousands of people have come across valuable coins in their pockets or purses, or set aside coins for sentimental reasons and learned later to their amazement that those coins had soared in value as collectibles.

MISSTRIKES AND MINT MARKS

Sometimes the value of such coins stems from the fact that they are "misstrikes": coins with obvious errors that somehow eluded detection at the mint where they were made. Other times, they're valuable because they display an important identifying mark, such as a mint mark. As I explained in Chapter One, coins produced at certain mints are stamped with little letters denoting the place of manufacture. Coins made at the Denver Mint have a small letter D, while those produced at the San Francisco Mint have an S.

Worth $200. *1970 Roosevelt dime struck off-center and too many times at the Denver Mint.* (*Photo courtesy* Coin World)

The presence—or absence—of a mint mark can sometimes make a difference of hundreds or thousands of dollars in the value of certain coins. Those 1909 Lincoln cents found by my client, for instance, had a small letter S under the date. That means they were made at the San Francisco Mint. They also had the letters V.D.B. at the base of the reverse, or "tails" side. These are the initials of Victor D. Brenner, the artist who designed the Lincoln cent. Without the S mint mark and the initials of the designer, those pennies would be worth just two or three dollars apiece. Those letters were missing on most of the Lincoln cents produced in 1909. Only a few displayed them—and with coins as with anything else, value is determined by supply and demand. The supply of these coins is small, the demand is great, and therefore the value is high.

Worth $1,000. *1909-S V.D.B. Lincoln cent received in change at a supermarket.* (*Photo courtesy* Coin World)

Most of these 1909-S V.D.B. cents were put away years ago by collectors. But some turn up in ordinary pocket change even now. A few years ago, a hospital employee in Los Angeles got an unusual cent in change at a local supermarket. She showed it to a friend at the hospital, seventy-nine-year-old Sid Lindenbaum, who worked there as a volunteer. Lindenbaum, a longtime coin collector, looked at the strange cent under a magnifying glass—and sure enough, it had both the S and the V.D.B.

"Miracles can still happen!" Lindenbaum exclaimed in an interview with a newspaper reporter. "I've been collecting coins for over sixty years and this is a first."

The coin had some wear, but wasn't in bad condition considering its age— two years older than Lindenbaum himself. Buying one would have cost the veteran hobbyist a couple of hundred dollars. Doing the right thing, he compensated his friend and both shared the joy of the occasion.

"I paid her more than she ever dreamt a Lincoln penny could possibly be worth, and she was as deliriously happy as I was," Lindenbaum told the reporter.

Some coins are valuable because they *lack* a mint mark. A case in point occurred in 1982, when the Philadelphia Mint made a small number of dimes without the mint mark P which normally appears just above the date on coins from that mint. Because of that omission and the scarcity of these dimes, collectors soon began to bid up the price. If one of these coins shows up in your change next time you go to the store, put it in a safe place: It's worth at least $50—and possibly several times more, depending on what condition it's in.

PROFITABLE MISTAKES

"Mint errors"—oddball coins—make great conversation pieces, and finding one can sometimes be the next best thing to digging up buried treasure.

Consider these examples:

- In 1955, odd-looking cents began appearing in upstate New York and New England. The date and lettering on the "heads" side of these coins (the side called the "obverse" by collectors) had a double image—a sort of shadow effect. Thousands of these pennies popped up in people's change.

At that time, cigarettes cost eighteen cents a pack and people who bought them in vending machines would insert twenty cents and get their two cents change tucked inside the cellophane in the pack. On occasion, both these coins would be double-

Worth $1,000. *1955 doubled-die Lincoln cent, a mint error. This example is circulated or worn. (Photo courtesy* Coin World*)*

image cents. Lots of people saved them as curiosities—and today they're glad they did: These 1955 "doubled-die" cents, as collectors call them, are now worth almost $400 even in used condition. Brand new, they're worth well over $1,000 apiece.

• In 1972, similar double-image cents began turning up in the East, especially in and around Philadelphia. These weren't quite as obvious as the ones from 1955, and they seemed to be somewhat more numerous. Nonetheless, they were soon bringing premiums of well over $100 apiece. Some show up in pocket change even now—and when they do, they're readily salable to dealers and collectors for $50 to $200, depending on how well preserved they are.

Worth $300. *1972 doubled-die Lincoln cent, a mint error. This example is new and has not been spent. Notice the prominent doubling of the letters, as the close-up indicates. (Photo courtesy* Coin World*)*

Worth $100. *1995 doubled-die Lincoln cent, a mint error. Doubling is most visible on LIBERTY, and IN GOD WE TRUST, shown here blown up. (Photo courtesy Heritage Auctions)*

- In 1995, thousands of Lincoln cents minted in Philadelphia (without a mint mark) turned up with doubling on the obverse. The error is most obvious in the word *LIBERTY*. These coins were being sold for $40 or so by the end of the year. Values are highest in top mint condition. The gem pictured sold at auction for $120.

- In 1937, an especially fascinating error was discovered on certain Buffalo nickels. For those of you too young to remember them, let me explain that these well-loved coins had the portrait of an Indian on the "heads" side and a realistic likeness of a bison on the reverse.

On a small number of 1937 nickels made at the Denver Mint, the bison's right front leg appeared to be missing. These "three-legged" nickels became extremely popular with collectors, and remain in great demand to this day. You won't find Buffalo nickels in pocket change today, but chances are good that you—or a member of your family—may have a few stuck away in a dresser or desk. If so, check the dates and if you find any dated 1937, count the legs on the bison. A three-legged nickel can be worth many hundreds of dollars in top condition.

Worth $650. *1937 Buffalo nickel struck by the Denver Mint. The weakness of the right leg (left to you) has led to collectors calling this the "three-legged Buffalo." (Photo courtesy* Coin World)

LOW-MINTAGE COINS

In 1950, the government made only about two million Jefferson nickels at the branch mint in Denver. That's far below normal production levels. Each of these Denver nickels carried a small letter D just to the right of the building on the back of the coin (Monticello, the home of Thomas Jefferson). Collectors got wind that the nickels were scarce and rushed to their banks. They saved so many that hardly any entered circulation. Within a few years, these nickels were selling for $30 apiece. Some can still be found in circulation, and even in worn condition they're worth about $5 each.

Sometimes people put away coins from special years—years that have personal meaning to them, or years when new coins first appear. Many people saved Kennedy half dollars when those were first produced in 1964.

I know of one woman born in 1921 whose parents assembled a set of all the U.S. coins bearing that date. They did this soon after their child's birth, putting together the set from coins they obtained at their local bank—coins that had never been spent and were still mint fresh. Twenty-one years later, on their daughter's wedding day, they gave her the coins. As luck would have it, the mintage levels of most U.S. coins were unusually low during 1921. As a result, the coins in this set are extremely desirable to dealers and collectors. In fact, this meticulously preserved set—formed by noncollectors for a total of just a few dollars—is now worth more than $50,000. This felicitous set of coins, a birth memento that later became a wedding gift, is now a valued nest egg, helping to secure the woman's golden years.

PROOF SETS

Birth-year tributes are much more common now than they were back in 1921. But rather than obtaining ordinary coins from a bank, parents today frequently purchase current-year "proof sets" from the government or a coin shop.

The U.S. Mint makes two or three million proof sets every year. Each set contains special, high-quality examples of all the current coins—one example each of the cent, nickel, dime, quarter, and half dollar. These coins are produced by a painstaking process which gives them shimmering mirror-like surfaces and a frosty appearance on the high points. Each set is housed in a plastic presentation case suitable for display. Up to and including 1998, the cost of these sets was $12.50 apiece. In 1999, the Mint struck the first five statehood Washington quarters and included all five in the regular proof set, raising the issue price to $19.95. It also offered a five-coin proof set with only the quarters for $13.95.

Proof sets, too, contain mint errors now and then. And, when they do, the coins in question can be worth a lot of money.

As in the case of regular coins, the error often takes the form of a missing mint mark. That happened, for instance, in 1970, when someone forgot to stamp the letter S above the date on a small number of dimes produced for that year's proof sets. All the proof coins were made at the branch mint in San Francisco and should have carried the mint mark—but an estimated 2,200 dimes did not. Today, those dimes are worth $700 apiece.

A similar error occurred with nickels in 1971. In an estimated 1,655 proof sets that year, the Jefferson nickel was missing the S mint mark. Today, each one is worth close to $1,000.

Worth $1,500. *1971 no-S proof Jefferson nickel. All of the proof coins were struck in San Francisco and were supposed to have carried the S mint mark. (Photo courtesy* Coin World)

History has a way of repeating itself at Uncle Sam's mints. In 1983, the S turned up missing again on the dimes in a small number of proof sets. These mint errors are now bringing $200 to $300 apiece. And in 1990, the S was missing on Lincoln cents in 3,555 proof sets. One collector in Washington State bought four 1990 proof sets from the Mint and all four contained no-S cents. He sold the sets to a dealer for $1,400 apiece, or a total of $5,600—a very tidy return on his $44 investment. The near-perfect example shown here sold at auction in 2004 for $15,000, although most examples are worth a bit more than a third of that.

Worth $8,500. *1990 no-S proof Lincoln cent. Again, someone at the mint left off the S. It should have appeared just under the date. (Photo courtesy Heritage Auctions)*

One of the most desirable of these mint-error proof coins is the no-S proof dime of 1968. It's thought that fewer than five hundred examples of this coin were produced, and each has a market value of $8,000 to $16,000 at this writing.

Obviously, your chances of finding a $6,000 coin in pocket change, or in a low-cost proof set, are remote. But they're no more remote than your chances of scoring a $8,000 win in a lottery. And I'd be willing to bet you'll spend a lot less money—and have a lot more fun—seeking your fortune in pennies, nickels, and dimes than in random numbers.

A 1989 RARITY

Finding a rare coin in a proof set isn't quite the same as finding one in pocket change. You do have to spend a modest premium above the face value to get the proof set. But the thrill of discovery, the sense of satisfaction, and the joy of ownership are really no different at all. And the profits are equally real and equally high.

Proof sets aren't the only special coins sold to the public by the government. In recent years, the U.S. Mint has also made a number of "commemorative" coins—coins produced in honor of noteworthy people or events. In 1986, for example, the

Mint made three coins for the one hundredth anniversary of the Statue of Liberty. And in 1987, it produced two special coins as a two hundredth-birthday tribute to the nation's Constitution.

In 1989, the Mint produced three special coins to honor the U.S. Congress on its two hundredth anniversary. One of these, a silver dollar, was sold to collectors and other interested purchasers for $23 each. A few of the Congress silver dollars were found to have a seldom-seen error—and, as this is written, coins with this error are being bought and sold for prices in excess of $300 apiece.

The error involves a feature known as the "rotation" of the coin. On most U.S. coins, the "heads" and "tails" designs are engraved in diametrically opposite positions; when the obverse design is right side up, the reverse design is upside down. To see what I mean, take a quarter out of your pocket and hold it in your hand. Position it so that George Washington's portrait is right side up, with the date at the bottom. Flip the coin over, from north to south, and the eagle should be standing straight up. (If it isn't, you've got an error coin that may be worth a premium to collectors.)

On a small number of 1989 Congress silver dollars, the reverse is rotated 180 degrees from this normal position. If you flip one of *these* coins in the manner I just described, from north to south, it will look upside down.

This may not seem like much of an error to you, but many collectors view it as a great rarity and they're willing to pay a correspondingly great premium.

A VALUABLE 1997 NICKEL

Jefferson nickels are minted each year by the hundreds of millions. In 1997, however, the U.S. Mint made one kind of Jefferson nickel that was so scarce—and so highly desired by collectors—that within a matter of weeks it was being sold for several hundred dollars.

The Mint produced the unusual nickels as part of a special collector set honoring the U.S. Botanic Garden in Washington, D.C. The centerpiece of the set—ostensibly, at least—was a silver dollar bearing a design emblematic of the famous national garden. But the set—the Botanic Garden Coinage and Currency Set—also contained a crisp new $1 bill and a 1997 Jefferson nickel because the two presidents depicted on these pieces of money, George Washington and Thomas Jefferson, both were identified closely with horticulture. And while the silver dollar and the $1 bill could be obtained elsewhere as well, the nickel was a type available only as part of this special set.

The nickel was distinctive because of the way it was made: Unlike regular Jefferson nickels, which have a shiny appearance when they are new, this one exhibited a dull "matte" finish because the dies used to produce it were subjected to chemical treatment. Mint technicians applied a combination of aluminum oxide and silver dioxide to the dies, spraying them with this mixture under high pressure. The nickels made from these dies are readily identifiable—and since the Mint limited production to 25,000 Botanic Garden Coinage and Currency Sets, and the nickels could be obtained nowhere else, the 1997 "matte-finish" coin was viewed at once by collectors as an instant rarity—the lowest-mintage issue in the whole Jefferson series.

Worth $175. *1997 matte-finish Jefferson nickel from U.S. Botanic Garden Coinage and Currency Set. (Photo courtesy Heritage Auctions)*

As you might expect, the Botanic Garden set was also an instant sellout. All 25,000 sets were sold almost immediately, even though the Mint cut multiple orders to a maximum of five sets per customer. The lucky buyers got their sets for $36 apiece from Uncle Sam, and could have sold them for ten times that amount within days. As of June 2000, the matte-finish nickel was trading in the resale market for $175 or more, making it one of 1997's very best investments. Indeed, for those who bought it from the Mint, this curious five-cent piece was an even better buy than most stocks—and, at a time when bulls were running rampant on Wall Street, that was quite an accomplishment! The virtually flawless example pictured sold at auction in 2004 for $630.

A SCARCE 1998 HALF DOLLAR

In 1998 the U.S. Mint produced another "matte"-finish coin—this time a Kennedy half dollar. And like its Jefferson nickel counterpart from the previous year, it proved to be a winner for those who bought it.

The matte half dollar was offered to Mint customers as part of a two-coin "Kennedy Collectors Set," also including an uncirculated example of the 1998 Robert F. Kennedy silver dollar. The dollar was a one-year commemorative coin marking the 30th anniversary of Robert Kennedy's death. The Mint did not limit the number of sets it would produce, as it had done with the 1997 Botanic Garden set. However, it did establish a time limit, accepting only orders submitted by that date.

Orders were higher this time than they had been for the set containing the 1997 matte nickel—but not by very much. When the Mint announced that the all-but-final figure was approximately 62,000, the price of the set rose sharply in the secondary market. Within a short time, it was selling for more than twice its $59.95 issue price, and some were predicting it would go up considerably more. Like the matte nickel, this new half dollar became overnight the lowest-mintage coin in its series. And it has the added advantage of the Kennedy mystique: Admirers of John F. Kennedy, not only in this country but also around the world, have helped make the Kennedy half dollar one of the most popular of all U.S. coins.

THE 1943 'COPPER' CENT

One of the most famous of all U.S. coins is the 1943 bronze Lincoln cent—widely and inaccurately referred to by many laypersons as the 1943 "copper" cent. (The actual coinage metal, bronze, is an alloy of copper, tin, and zinc.) Millions of non-collectors—people who don't know the first thing about coin collecting—have heard about this coin, know it's worth a great deal of money, and have made at least a cursory attempt to locate one in their pocket change.

By 1943, World War II was at a crucial stage and the war effort permeated every aspect of American society. Coinage was no exception. Copper was urgently needed for battlefield uses, and to help conserve the supply of this critical metal the U.S. Mint suspended production of bronze ("copper") cents and made the coins instead from steel with a coating of zinc. These "white" cents proved unsuitable almost at once. For one thing, people confused them with the dime; for another, they rusted rapidly. As a result, they were minted for just that one year.

Official government records make no mention of regular bronze cents dated 1943; as far as the Mint was concerned, it never made any. However, it's well established that a few such coins—probably fewer than twenty—do exist. Apparently, a few bronze coin blanks were still in a hopper at the end of production in 1942 and somehow got stamped along with the new steel cents in 1943.

For many years, a story made the rounds that the Ford Motor Company would give a new car to anyone finding a 1943 "copper" cent. That story was unfounded, but anyone fortunate enough to find such a coin today could certainly parlay it into a new car. It wouldn't be surprising, in fact, to see the former owner of some 1943 bronze cents driving around today in a Jaguar or a Porsche. One of these coins, a 1943-D cent (struck at the Denver Mint) changed hands at a Beverly Hills, Calif., auction in February 2003 for $212,750—the highest price ever paid for any Lincoln cent. That nearly doubled the record set three years earlier, in February 2000, when a 1943-S bronze cent (struck at the San Francisco Mint) sold for $115,000 at a Los Angeles auction. The 1943-D specimen is the only "copper-alloy" 1943 cent known to have been made at the Denver Mint. It was authenticated by the Professional Coin Grading Service (PCGS), which certified it as Mint State-64 Brown—an unusually high level of preservation for a 1943 bronze cent. That same coin reportedly sold by private treaty in September 2010 for $1.7 million. Most of the examples that have come to light over the years have been in less-than-mint condition, indicating that these coins saw actual use in circulation. Ira Goldberg, a principal of the auction firm that conducted the February 2003 sale, Ira & Larry Goldberg Coins and Collectibles, said the coin originally belonged to the heirs of a Denver Mint employee. The same coin had brought $82,500 in its last previous sale, at an auction in May 1996, so its price level jumped more than two-and-a-half times in less than seven years—dramatic evidence of just how dynamic the market is for these famous mint errors.

As spectacular as those prices seemed at the time, as this book goes to press in November 2012, most of those values are up substantially.

The Philadelphia Mint produced the lion's share of the 1943 bronze cents—or at least those that have surfaced to date. As a result, specimens from that mint (distinguishable by the absence of any mint mark below the date) bring somewhat lower premiums than their scarcer "D" and "S" counterparts. But they, too, cost about the same as some very snazzy cars. At the same auction in February 2003 where the 1943-D cent broke the record, a 1943 Philadelphia specimen went for an impressive $97,750—to the very same buyer. That coin had been certified as MS-61 by PCGS.

Worth $165,000. *1943-S "copper" cent graded Mint State-61 Brown by NGC. (Photo courtesy Ira and Larry Goldberg Auctions, Beverly Hills, California)*

In December 1999, a different 1943 bronze cent from the Philadelphia Mint was sold in a private transaction for $112,500. That piece had been certified as MS-61 Red-Brown by ANACS. Some circulated specimens also came on the market that year—and did well enough to put their former owners in, say, a Lincoln Continental or a Cadillac. A Philadelphia piece graded Extremely Fine-40 changed hands for $32,200, and a 1943-S graded Very Fine-35 brought $51,750. I can vouch for the excitement surrounding the latter coin's sale, since I was in the gallery—bidding on the coin on behalf of a client—and ended up being the underbidder.

The flurry of excitement surrounding these rare wartime cents undoubtedly got a boost in February 1999 when the news media carried a report—which proved to be highly misleading—concerning the disappearance of a purported 1943 "copper penny" owned by an Idaho businessman. The man told The Associated Press that his wife had inadvertently spent the coin, which he said he had kept in plain view, in a dish atop his refrigerator, to avoid calling attention to it. The AP story was filled with inaccuracies, including a claim that the coin could be worth up to $500,000. Nonetheless, its wide dissemination triggered a wave of new public interest in the '43 bronze cent, helping pave the way for the round of record sales in the year that followed.

Worth $80,000. *1943-S "copper" cent graded VF-35 by PCGS. I was the underbidder on this coin when it sold at auction in August 1999. (Photo courtesy Q. David Bowers)*

A similar media report in January 2004 sparked another burst of excitement among the general public—but again the story had an unhappy ending. The protagonist this time was a Staten Island, New York man who claimed to have found a 1943 "copper" cent in his storage box. A local coin dealer apparently tested the coin with a magnet—and it passed. (Steel cents are attracted to a magnet, but bronze cents are not—and this man's coin was not attracted.) At this point, the man, who is not a collector, contacted both me and, at my recommendation, Asa Aarons, the award-winning consumer reporter for WNBC-TV in New York. I had appeared on television with Asa in a series about the 1943 "copper" cent after my firm brokered one for nearly $100,000. When the Staten Island man told me that his coin had passed the magnet test, I advised him to submit it to a certification service so that its authenticity could be verified. He replied that he wouldn't let the coin out of his sight.

When Asa Aarons learned that I was just leaving to attend the Florida United Numismatists (FUN) coin show in Orlando, Fla., and that the major certification services would also be participating in the show, he agreed to have the man take his coin to Orlando and let the experts examine it on the spot, while television cameras captured the instant drama. The TV people took the unusual step of reimbursing the man for his trip—in return they were able to cover the story, which they did for NBC affiliates from coast to coast.

Sadly, the coin turned out to be an impostor: Someone had taken a 1945 cent (which was made of copper alloy) and altered the "5" in the date to resemble a "3." Expert authenticator Miles Standish and his skilled team at the Professional Coin Grading Service needed only seconds to spot the alteration and pass the news along to the coin's now crestfallen owner. Instead of being rare and worth a small fortune, the coin was just an ordinary cent. But again, as in the Idaho case five years earlier, the story produced enormous publicity for the coin hobby in general and 1943 cents in particular. For days afterward, NBC affiliates continued to carry reports detailing the man's quest and his ultimate disappointment—and each time the story aired, the mystique of the *real* 1943 bronze cent became even more ingrained in the public's subconscious.

HOW TO TELL IF YOU HAVE A REAL BRONZE 1943 CENT

There are many, many fakes of the 1943 bronze cent—some produced initially as novelty items, others made with malice aforethought by con artists in hopes of victimizing the unwary. The most common fakes are copper-plated steel 1943 cents. As noted, these can be detected quite easily with a magnet: Being made of steel, they'll be attracted to the magnet, while genuine bronze cents will not. Simply applying a magnet to a 1943 cent will unmask the typical pretender, even though it may look very realistic to the naked eye.

Altered-date coins can be trickier to identify, as the man in New York discovered. In their effort to fleece unknowledgeable victims, fast-buck artists have tinkered with the dates of many cents that were bronze to begin with. Alterations are seen most frequently on cents made in 1945 and 1948, but also on those originally dated 1933 and 1953. In each of these cases, only one numeral had to be modified to change the date to 1943. Most of these alterations can be detected by examining a coin with a simple 5-power magnifying glass. For one thing, this will often reveal scratches on the surface, where the con artist applied a tool in reworking the metal. For another, the numerals in the date of a genuine 1943 cent are highly distinctive and differ significantly from those in many other dates, including 1945 and 1948. On a real 1943 cent, the "9" and "3" in the date are much longer than the "1" and "4." On both 1945 and 1948 cents, the last digit (either "5" or "8") is the same height as the "4." Similarly, the last "3" on 1933 cents is shaped much differently than the "3" on real 1943 cents, making it almost impossible to duplicate the appearance—even if the first "3" could be molded somehow into a convincing-looking "4." The 1953 cents have a "3" very much like those of 1943. But on all but the most professional alterations, scratches or other signs of finagling should be visible in the area where the "5" was changed to a "4."

Sophisticated fakes do exist. Fakes have been made, for instance, by using steel cents to produce new steel dies, then striking bronze cents with those dies. This technique would be impractical with any other cents, for copper is too soft for use in preparing dies. But, because of its hardness, the steel in the 1943 cent will withstand the pressure required to impart its image to another piece of steel. Counterfeits produced in this manner can be spotted by the softness—or "mushiness"—of elements in the design. The genuine 1943 bronze cents are exceptionally sharp; the Mint had to use extra pressure to bring up the design on the steel cents, so bronze cents struck under similar pressure have greater sharpness than normal bronze cents.

Because of the existence of so many fakes, some of which are good enough to fool even experienced collectors, it is imperative never to buy a 1943 bronze cent unless it has been authenticated and certified by a reputable third-party grading service. And if you should be fortunate enough to find one of these coins—or what *appears* to be one of these coins—you should have it certified immediately.

THE AURA OF THE 1943 CENTS

More than 60 years have passed since the 1943 bronze cents were produced, and since they presumably entered circulation. At this point, they have entered something else—the imagination of the American people—and achieved a status few, if any, other U.S. coins now enjoy: They are the stuff of legends. I have appeared frequently on Asa Aarons' consumer affairs segments on WNBC-TV News programs in New York, and on several occasions Asa and I have discussed the 1943 bronze cents—both genuine and fake. These segments have never failed to generate overwhelming response from the public. After several of these appearances, I created a number of web pages on wnbc.com, knbc.com and msnbc.com, and they all stirred tremendous interest. In fact, NBC's on-line services director told me that the weather was the only other subject that drew as much interest while the 1943 cents were on the Web sites for a period of over a year. My web work for NBC News was later given a "best mass-market web site" award.

1943 "copper" cent sold by the author's firm to a collector for nearly $100,000. This coin and Scott Travers were widely publicized on television for the sale.

The odds are long against finding a genuine bronze 1943 cent in your pocket change, or stashed away in a cubbyhole in that old desk in your attic. But it could happen—and the fact is, it *has* happened for other lucky people over the years.

OTHER WARTIME RARITIES

Oddball coins seem to be produced more frequently at times when the nation is at war. There are several reasons for this. The need to conserve strategic metals may lead to experimentation with new compositions—as happened with Lincoln cents in 1943—and this may result in unintended coinage consequences. Wartime economies may cause the Mint to stretch the normal working life of its equipment, including coinage dies, and this may lead to coins with weak strikes and other deficiencies. And skilled Mint technicians may be off fighting the war, leaving their jobs at the Mint in the hands of less experienced personnel, more prone to making mistakes that will turn up in the hands of John Q. and Jane Q. Public.

World War II gave rise to an unusually high number and variety of offbeat U.S. coins. All of the factors just mentioned contributed to this. Beyond these elements, though, the nation's coinage needs were exceptionally high; the war shoved the U.S. economy into high gear, and after more than a decade of unusually low Depression-era mintages, Americans needed new coins in unprecedented numbers. The conditions were ideal for mint-error coins, and the bumper crop that resulted has been a boon for collectors ever since.

The 1943 bronze cents are surely the most famous of the World War II mint errors, but they have some distinguished—and extremely valuable—company. Here are a few others that you should be on the lookout for when checking your pocket change or old accumulations:

• The 1942 "white-metal" Lincoln cent.

The experiments that resulted in the 1943 steel cents actually began in 1942, and during that year the Mint produced numerous test coins in various compositions—including not only new metals but also glass and Bakelite. Almost all of those die-trial pieces later were destroyed, but at least one is known to have escaped. The piece in question carries the same design as the regular Lincoln cent but is made of white metal.

In offering this coin for sale at an auction in August 1997, Heritage Numismatic Auctions of Dallas said that it has "almost the appearance of steel, being bright and nearly white . . ." Its actual composition had not yet been determined, but there can be no question about its value: The coin—believed to be unique—brought the eye-popping sum of $12,500 at the sale.

Worth $12,500. *Experimental 1942 white-metal Lincoln cent. (Photo courtesy Heritage Auctions)*

• The 1944 steel Lincoln cent.

Widespread public dissatisfaction with the "white"1943 cents prompted the Mint to abandon the experiment after just one year. When cent production resumed in 1944, the zinc-coated steel gave way to brass, an alloy very much like the previous bronze, containing copper and zinc but lacking tin. Just as wartime requirements had dictated the removal of copper a year earlier, war conditions now provided the needed raw material: The Mint obtained the brass from salvaged cartridge shell casings.

While millions of people know about the off-metal bronze cents of 1943, few are aware that similar minting mistakes occurred in 1944, this time in reverse. Small numbers of steel cent blanks remained in the pipeline at the start of 1944, and these were then struck with the new date. A few escaped detection and reached collectors' hands, and these now command substantial premiums.

Worth $15,000. *1944 zinc-coated steel Lincoln cent should have been struck in brass. (Photo courtesy Heritage Auctions)*

The 1944 steel cents have never captured the public's imagination in the same way as the 1943 "coppers," so they've trailed behind in value—but their market level has risen impressively through the years. In 1997, an AU-58 example from the Denver Mint brought $5,000 at a Heritage auction. By February 2003, the market had advanced to the point where two specimens in slightly lower grades both sold for more than six times that amount: A P-mint piece graded AU-55 by PCGS brought $31,050 and a 1944-D graded AU-53 by PCGS went for $35,650. As with the 1943 coppers, certification is a must when buying or selling these appealing mint errors.

Worth $20,000. *1944-D zinc-coated steel Lincoln cent. (Photo courtesy* Coin World.*)*

- Wartime Jefferson nickels struck on prewar planchets.

The Lincoln cent wasn't the only U.S. coin to undergo a change of composition during World War II. The Jefferson nickel got a make-over, too, and for much the same reason: Combat requirements led to the removal of nickel as a component of U.S. coinage. Up until 1942, the five-cent piece had been 75-percent copper and 25-percent nickel. Midway through production that year, the coin was changed to an alloy of 56-percent copper, 35-percent silver, and 9-percent manganese. This alloy would be retained through the end of 1945—and to underscore the change, the Mint placed a large mint mark above the portrait of Monticello, Thomas Jefferson's home, on each coin's reverse. A large "P" appeared on wartime Jefferson nickels from the Philadelphia Mint, coins which normally wouldn't have carried any mint mark at all.

Recently, a collector came across a 1944-P nickel made from the prewar alloy of 75-percent copper and 25-percent nickel. The coin had a large "P" above Monticello, suggesting along with its date that it should have been made of the substitute alloy, but tests confirmed that it was of standard composition. This coin, a circulated piece graded Very Fine-30, was offered for sale by Superior Stamp & Coin, but failed to attract the minimum required bid of $5,000. Still, it is clearly a major rarity and worth a pretty penny—in fact, many thousands of pretty pennies.

Worth $5,000. *1944-P Jefferson nickel of standard copper-nickel composition should have been struck in wartime alloy of copper, silver, and manganese. (Photo courtesy Superior Stamp & Coin)*

- The 1942-over-1 Mercury dimes.

The three silver U.S. coins—the half dollar, quarter, and dime—didn't get new alloys during World War II. It seems ironic today, with precious metal gone from our everyday coins, but while copper and nickel needed to be conserved to aid the war effort, silver was relatively plentiful, even being added to the nickel. As noted previously, however, the war affected coinage in other ways, as well, and one of those impacts—the stretching of Mint resources—probably was responsible for a fascinating and valuable error on a wartime U.S. dime.

In 1942, with a budget squeeze being applied, Mint technicians decided not to discard some of the dies used in the production of dimes dated 1941, as they would have done in normal times. Instead, they cut a "2" over the final "1" in the date. Since the dies were not yet worn out, this seemed like a good way to maximize their working life and thus save the government money. But people soon noticed the dimes produced with these dies, for the 1 was clearly visible under the 2. In fact, the date appeared to be 1942/1. The "overdate" dimes were quickly removed from circulation, and it soon became apparent that they were quite scarce. A superb example, graded Mint State-67 by the Professional Coin Grading Service, fetched $15,950 at a 1997 auction held by Superior Stamp & Coin. It would be hard to imagine a better return on any investment costing just ten cents!

Worth $22,500. *1942-over-1 Mercury dime, with the "2" engraved over the final "1" of "1941." (Photo courtesy Superior Stamp & Coin)*

1965 SILVER ROOSEVELT DIME

The U.S. Mint officially stopped the manufacture of silver Roosevelt dimes in 1964. So virtually every Roosevelt dime you find dated "1965" will not be silver;

it will be composed of copper and nickel "clad." This rare 1965 dime mistake is made of 90% silver and, as such, is one of only a few accounted for. You can tell silver from clad by examining the coin's edge: The rare silver coin has a silver edge; *the common clad coin has a strip of brown around the edge*. Experts believe that many hundreds of 1965 silver dimes were manufactured by mistake by the Mint, and are waiting to be discovered hiding in piggy banks and cookie jars. These coins, depending on their condition, can be valued up to $30,000 or more.

An ordinary-looking circulated 1965 *SILVER* Roosevelt dime just like the specimen shown here was found in pocket change by a reader of the book's fifth edition. He called me, and we had it authenticated and graded by the Professional Coin Grading Service (PCGS). After certification by PCGS, at my recommendation, he sold it at a public auction conducted by Heritage Auction Galleries, Dallas, TX for $8,912.50.

Worth up to $30,000. *1965 Silver Roosevelt dime. The U.S. Mint officially stopped manufacturing silver Roosevelt dimes in 1964. The National Star featured this coin and the author in a 2-page spread.*

CHECK THAT CHANGE!

Your chances of finding a 1943 copper cent or a 1909-S V.D.B. cent in pocket change are diminished by the fact that in 1959 the Lincoln cent's reverse got a new design. Since that time, the back of the coin has portrayed the Lincoln Memorial. With the passage of time, the earlier Lincoln cents—with two sheaves of wheat displayed on the reverse—have grown steadily harder to find in circulation. As a result, these "wheat-ears" cents are conspicuous when they do appear in change and therefore are quickly set aside. Likewise, a Buffalo nickel (three-legged or otherwise) would stand out from other coins if it showed up in circulation, and that reduces your chances of finding one of these.

There are many scarce and valuable coins waiting for lucky finders in cash drawers, sugar bowls, pockets, and purses today—but, for the most part, these are coins that blend in with the rest of our current coinage. Their basic design is the same, they're made of the same metal, and at first glance they don't look any different.

While they may *look* ordinary, these coins can often be like nuggets of high-grade gold for the prospectors lucky enough to find them.

To give you an idea of the quantity and diversity of these coins, I've compiled a list including some typical illustrations. I've limited this list to coins whose common counterparts are still routinely seen in circulation. It doesn't contain Buffalo nickels or pre-1959 Lincoln cents, for example, since those are seldom encountered anymore and any that did turn up—even common ones—would be set aside almost at once as curiosities. That, of course, would minimize the chances for finding pocket-change rarities of those types.

To readily identify some of the following coins, you may need a magnifying glass. But an inexpensive glass with 5-power magnification will do just fine.

Keep in mind that if you find one of these coins and offer it for sale to a dealer, he's likely to offer substantially less than its current list price. That, after all, is a retail price and dealers must purchase at wholesale in order to turn a profit.

Care to hold a personal treasure hunt? Here's a list of scarce coins—some worth hundreds of dollars—that might turn up in your pocket change today:

- The 1960 small-date Lincoln cents.

    Early in 1960, coin collectors noticed something strange about the new one-cent pieces coming out of the main mint in Philadelphia and the branch in Denver. The numbers in the date were perceptibly smaller on some of these cents than on others—and the "small-date" coins were significantly scarcer than those with larger numbers.

1960-D small- and large-date Lincoln cents. The close-up of the 6 on the left is the large date; the 6 on the right is the small date. The large date has the longer tail on the 6. (Photos courtesy Coin World)

As word of these "instant rarities" spread around the country, a coast-to-coast scavenger hunt ensued. The small-date cents from the Philadelphia Mint proved to be much more elusive than those from Denver. Before long, the price of these 1960-P cents (which carry no mint mark below the date) jumped to $400 for a roll of fifty coins. That's $8 apiece—a very tidy profit for those who obtained these coins at face value. The Denver small-date cents (with a D below the date) rose as high as $20 a roll, or 40 cents apiece, which is also nothing to sneeze at and also a nice return for those who invested just a penny and a little time.

The premiums on these coins have dropped with the passage of time. Still, both will bring you considerably more than a penny for your thoughts if you're fortunate enough to find them in circulation. The 1960-P small-date cent is now worth between $1 and $2 each, depending on its condition, while the 1960-D is worth between a nickel and a dime.

How can you tell a "small date" from a "large date"? The photos make the distinction clear. Take special note of the 6 on the small-date cent: It looks somewhat squashed and has a shorter upward tail than its large-date counterpart. Also, in the small date, the numbers seem farther apart. And the top of the 1 lines up with the top of the 9.

Cents in 1960 proof sets also came in both varieties, and again the small-date version was quite a bit scarcer. You'd have to pay about $25 today for a 1960 proof set with the small-date cent. That's $10 more than the price of the normal set with the large-date cent.

• The 1960-D cent with a small date punched over a large date.

   The cents of 1960 come in many varieties. This is one case where you'll need magnification. Under a glass, you'll note what appears to be slight double images in the numbers in the date. What you're actually seeing are numbers from both the "small date" and the "large date."

• The 1969-S doubled-die Lincoln cent.

   Earlier in this chapter, I wrote in some detail about the double-image cents made by mistake in 1955 and again in 1972 at the Philadelphia Mint. Those are coins you should always be alert for, since both command handsome premiums—and the 1972 cent, in particular, may very well appear in your pocket or purse someday. (The chances of discovering the 1955 cent are more remote since, as I noted earlier, the Lincoln cent's design was modified in 1959 and coins produced before that date are more likely to have been saved.)

While these are the best-known examples of "doubled-die" cents, they're not the only ones. Others exist—and some of these come with similarly fancy price tags.

One was made in 1969 at the San Francisco Mint (denoted by an S below the date). As with the 1955 and 1972 varieties, the features of this coin are doubled on only the obverse (or "heads" side). The date and inscriptions on this side of the coin display distinct doubling. You can see this much more readily under a magnifying glass, and I recommend that you buy one to assist you. It will come in handy not only in identifying doubled-die coins but also in spotting other mint errors and unusual varieties. A 5-power glass is fine for most such purposes, and you can obtain one for only a few dollars. You'll recoup this small investment with a single worthwhile find.

The 1969-S doubled-die cent would be a *very* worthwhile find: Well-known coin dealer Harry J. Forman of Philadelphia is paying between $100 and $200 for typical examples of this coin. And Forman says he would pay $1,000 for a really exceptional example.

- The 1970-S "Atheist" cent.

The motto *IN GOD WE TRUST* has appeared on U.S. coinage since 1864, when religious fervor born of the Civil War gave impetus to this and other expressions of the nation's collective belief in a supreme being. Not all coins carried the inscription right away; it didn't appear on the nickel, for example, until 1938. But it now has been a fixture on every U.S. coin for more than half a century.

The Lincoln cent has borne this familiar motto right from the start—since Abe Lincoln's penny first appeared on the scene in 1909. And the motto has a prominent place along the top of the obverse, right above Lincoln's head. There are, however, a few Lincoln cents on which the nation's trust in God is compromised. The result is both interesting and potentially profitable for lucky pocket-change treasure hunters.

The compromise occurs because of mint errors which cause part of the motto to be missing. The best-known example of this took place in 1970 at the San Francisco Mint. Part of the metal on one or more of the obverse cent dies—the pieces of metal used to strike the "heads" side of the cent—broke off that year along the upper edge. As a result, that portion of the coin was covered by a "cud," or small lump of metal, instead of getting the imprint of the design. (Since the die metal was missing, the metal in the coin blank simply expanded and filled the empty area.) As luck would have it, the cud completely obliterated the words *WE TRUST* in the motto. Enterprising dealers soon dubbed this the "Atheist cent."

At one time, there was a lively market for Atheist cents and a brand new example would fetch $20 or more. The market isn't as active today—but, even so, a nice Atheist cent will bring about $5. Keep in mind that the error occurred on San Francisco cents, which have an S mint mark below the date.

• The 1970-S small-date Lincoln cent.

Small-date and large-date cents turned up again in 1970—this time on coins from the San Francisco Mint (identified by an S below the date). As in 1960, they appeared on both regular cents and proofs. And, once more, the small-date coins proved to be scarcer and more valuable.

1970-S small- and large-date Lincoln cents. The small date on the right has the top of the 7 and the top of the 0 aligned. (Photos courtesy Krause Publications)

The 1970 small-date cents didn't create as much excitement initially as their predecessors had ten years earlier. But, while the 1960 coins have dipped in value with time, the 1970 versions appear to be getting more popular and desirable. That's because collectors have determined that fewer were made.

To get a 1970-S small-date cent from a coin dealer, you'd have to pay about $17 each for the "business strike"—the regular kind produced for circulation—and $65 for the proof. However, there's a much cheaper way to pick one up: Check the cents in that jar in your kitchen cupboard! You're not very likely to find one of the proofs; those were sold to collectors in custom-made plastic cases. But the regular kind may very well turn up. And, if it does, you've made yourself close to $20!

As with the 1960 small-date cents, it may take a little time before you can tell the "small" 1970 dates from the "large" ones. But knowing how to spot them is your edge! That's what gives you the inside track over people who don't know the difference. To the untrained eye, these coins—and the scarce 1960 coins, too—blend in with all the other Lincoln cents in a cookie jar or cigar box. The trick is to develop a *trained* eye. And it's really an easy trick.

Take a close look at the photos I've provided. Focus, in particular, on the 7 in each of the dates. In the large date, the tops of the 9 and the 0 are higher than the top of the 7. In the small date, the tops of all four numbers look uniform.

- The 1971-S cent with a doubled-die obverse (or "heads" side).

    This has been far less publicized than the 1972 doubled-die cent described earlier in this chapter, and apparently is far rarer.

- The 1972-D cent without the designer's initials V.D.B.

    Cents without the V.D.B. turned up in significant quantities starting in 1988. The same kind of error has also been discovered on 1972 cents minted in Denver (with a D below the date). These appear to be considerably rarer than those from the late 1980s.

- The 1979-D cent without the designer's initials FG.

    Frank Gasparro had a long and busy career at the U.S. Mint, where he was chief engraver for more than sixteen years. Besides designing the back of the Kennedy half dollar, he also created the Lincoln Memorial design used on the reverse of the current cent. And just as his initials have sometimes been omitted from Kennedy halves, they've also turned up missing on Lincoln cents. The letters "FG" are supposed to appear just to the right of the Lincoln Memorial's base. But in 1979, they were left off a few of the cents from the Denver Mint (identifiable by the D below the date).

- The 1980 D-over-S cent.

    From time to time, more than one mint mark shows up on a coin—not in different places, but with one super-imposed directly above the other. Sometimes this occurs because of misguided economy: In an effort to save a little money, an engraver at one of the mints may take an unused die made for use at the San Francisco Mint (with an S mint mark) and cut a D into the metal right above the S so the die can be used in Denver. Inevitably, an eagle-eyed collector will detect the original letter with a magnifying glass.

    "Over-mint-mark" and "overdate" varieties are not routine; this kind of sloppiness is discouraged at the Mint—and when it does take place, the coins that result are eagerly pursued by many collectors. That, in turn, gives them considerable value.

    Through the years, several such varieties have been found among Lincoln cents. Under a glass, you'll see that the D mint mark below the date is actually superimposed above an S. This coin is considered very scarce.

• The 1981 D-over-S cent.

The same thing happened again the following year. Only a microscopic trace remains of the original "S" mint mark.

• The 1982 small-date zinc cent.

Most people don't realize that the current one-cent piece is made almost entirely out of zinc. It looks very much like the "copper" cent of yesteryear, but that's because it's plated with pure copper. The core of the coin is 99.2 percent zinc.

The Mint made the change in 1982 because the price of copper had risen to the point where the cent's metal value was approaching its value as money. Zinc is not only cheaper than copper but also lighter-weight, so more coins can be made from the same number of pounds.

The cent had contained zinc for more than a century; from 1864 to 1962, the coin's composition had been bronze (an alloy of copper, tin, and zinc), and since 1962 it had been brass (copper and zinc but no tin). But, in both those alloys, copper accounted for 95 percent of the weight. The present cent, by contrast, is 97.5 percent zinc and just 2.5 percent copper.

During the changeover year of 1982, brass and zinc cents were both produced in very substantial numbers. Both were made at Philadelphia (no mint mark) and also at Denver (a D below the date). And, to make matters even more interesting, the date that year came in both large and small varieties.

In all, there are seven different 1982 cent varieties: large-date brass cents from both Philadelphia and Denver . . . small-date brass cents from Philadelphia . . . and large- and small-date zinc cents from both mints. For some reason, small-date brass cents weren't made at the Denver Mint—but that was the only missing combination.

None of these varieties turned out to be extremely scarce. But the small-date zinc cent from the Philadelphia Mint is elusive, and coin dealers who specialize in cents are currently paying $25 a roll (or 50 cents per coin) for this variety.

How can you tell the difference? It's relatively easy to distinguish the large date from the small; there's a sharp variation in size. Telling brass from zinc isn't quite so simple, since outwardly the zinc cent looks pretty much like the brass. People who handle coins on a regular basis find the brass cents noticeably heavier, but the difference may not be as apparent to those with less experience.

Until you gain the expertise and confidence to tell the coins apart without external help, I recommend the purchase of a simple scale. For a nominal cost, you can obtain a penny scale. With a brass cent, the indicator will dip; with a zinc cent, it will stay up.

- The 1983 doubled-die Lincoln cent.

In 1983, another double-image cent appeared. This time, however, the doubling was on the reverse. Find one of these and you'll be not only seeing double but sitting pretty: Brand new, this coin now retails for about $200—and even in worn condition it's worth between $50 and $100.

Worth $200. *1983 doubled-die Lincoln cent. This blow-up shows the doubled letters on the reverse that make this coin scarce and sought after. (Photo courtesy* Coin World*)*

Worth $100. *1984 doubled-die Lincoln cent. The doubled ear is visible on the blow-up. (Photo courtesy* Coin World*)*

One expert estimates that no more than 10,000 examples were produced. And most, he says, were released in the vicinity of Lancaster, Pennsylvania. Obviously, you should be especially watchful for this coin if you live within spending distance of that town.

• The 1984 cent without the initials FG.

This coin is similar to the 1979-D cent described a few paragraphs earlier. It's not a great rarity, but it's worth a modest premium to mint-error specialists.

• The 1984 cent with a doubled obverse.

This coin has attracted less publicity than the 1983 cent with the double-image reverse I just described. Nonetheless, it appears to be quite scarce; according to one expert, only about 2,000 have shown up. The doubling is clearest at Lincoln's ear and beard.

• Lincoln cents without the designer's initials V.D.B.

At the start of this chapter, I mentioned that some Lincoln cents derive substantial value from the presence of the letters V.D.B. As I explained, these are the initials of Victor D. Brenner, the artist who designed this durable coin. It now turns out that the *absence* of these initials can also give a coin added value.

Before reviewing the reason, let's go back to 1909, the year the Lincoln cent was introduced. Brenner's initials, along the lower edge on the coin's reverse, caught the eye of many sharp observers—and more than a few objected to the size of this "signature." So many complained, in fact, that the Mint removed the letters within a matter of weeks.

In 1918, the initials were restored—but in much smaller letters and in a location where they wouldn't be nearly as conspicuous: at the base of Abraham Lincoln's shoulder. They've remained there ever since—or rather, they're *supposed* to be there. In 1988, collectors discovered a number of newly minted cents on which the initials were missing. Apparently, someone at the Mint inadvertently removed them while polishing one of the dies (the pieces of steel that impart the design to a coin, very much like cookie cutters).

The same thing happened again in 1989 and 1990. Pull out your magnifying glass and see if *you* can find some. If you do, there are dealers who will pay you upwards of $5 each. Please note, however, that the premiums will apply only to coins in brand new condition or very nearly so. Once Lincoln cents circulate for a while, the letters V.D.B. tend to wear down and wear off, and those coins naturally don't command a premium based on the absence of the initials.

- The 1939 Jefferson nickel with a doubled reverse.

  Despite its age (more than fifty years old), this coin has a good possibility of turning up in pocket change. That's because Jefferson nickels still have the same design and metallic composition today as they did when they first came out in 1938. You'll notice the doubling especially in the words *FIVE CENTS* and *MONTICELLO*. (Don't expect to see a dramatic double image in the building; the doubling isn't that obvious.) This coin is worth $10 or more even in well-worn condition.

- The 1949 D-over-S Jefferson nickel.

  You'll certainly need a 5-power glass—and maybe even a 10-power glass—to pick out this rarity; after all, the letters are small and the people who cut the dies were trying to conceal the original mint mark. But, if you're successful in finding one of these coins, the reward can be great.

  The 1949 D-over-S nickel was struck at the Denver Mint with a die originally meant for San Francisco. Look very closely and you'll see part of the S directly below the D. You'll also see dollar signs, for this coin can be worth more than $100 in nice condition.

- The 1954 S-over-D Jefferson nickel.

  In 1954, the tables were turned: This time, a die made for Denver was recut for use in San Francisco. The S mint mark doesn't completely hide the original D—although, once again, you'll need a decent magnifying glass to detect this. The payoff this time will be a little less, since this coin appears to be more common. Even so, you'll pocket $10 or more—a lot more if the coin is unusually nice.

- The 1955 D-over-S Jefferson nickel.

  In 1955, operations were halted at the San Francisco Mint, not to be resumed for more than a decade. Thus, the temptation was particularly strong to pull an unused San Francisco die off the shelf when the need arose for an extra die in Denver. After all, there wouldn't be any more need for the die in San Francisco.

  Whatever the cause, the result was another crop of D-over-S nickels. These coins are approximately equal in scarcity and value to the S-over-D nickels from one year earlier.

- The 1964-D nickel with E PLURIDUS UNUM.

  E PLURIBUS UNUM ("Out of many, one") is a motto that has graced U.S. coins for nearly two centuries. Once in a while, production problems lead to misspelling of this inscription. That's what happened in 1964 with Jefferson nickels made at the Denver Mint (with a D just to the right of Monticello on the reverse). Heavy polishing of one or more of the dies caused the center of the letter "B" to be obliterated. As a result, the word looks like PLURIDUS instead of PLURIBUS. This isn't an extremely valuable error, but it's certainly an interesting one—and it does command a modest premium.

- The 1983-D nickel with a doubled reverse.

  Again, here's a coin with doubling of some of the features—this time on the reverse. The double image is relatively weak on this 1983 nickel from the Denver Mint (with a D just below and just to the left of the date on the "heads" side). Still, it's worth a premium to dealers and collectors who specialize in this type of error.

- The 1964 dime struck in copper-nickel.

  The rising price of silver forced the U.S. government to discontinue production of silver dimes and quarters starting in 1965. Since then, these coins have been made from an alloy of copper and nickel bonded to a core of pure copper. All dimes and quarters minted during 1964 were made of silver—or rather, they were *supposed* to have been. But experiments with the new "clad" coinage were already under way at that time, and somehow a few dimes dated 1964 were made of copper-nickel, rather than silver. These are extremely rare and quite valuable. Hint: Look for a coppery reddish line around the rim of the coin; if it's there, the chances are good that you've found a "clad" coin, rather than a silver one.

- The 1967 dime with a doubled obverse.

  Again, the Mint produced a coin with a double image, this time on the "heads" side. It's uncertain where this 1967 dime was produced; from 1965 through 1967, the Mint withheld mint marks in order to discourage hoarding of coins by speculators. In any event, the coin is quite scarce. The doubling is most apparent on the mottos and the date.

- The 1970-D dime with a doubled reverse.

  By 1970, mint marks had been restored—and a double-image error was in evidence once again. This 1970 dime from the Denver Mint (with a D just above the date) has doubling on the reverse.

• The 1982 no-P Roosevelt dime.

Up until recent years, coins that were made at the Philadelphia Mint almost never carried a mint mark. "P-mint" coins were distinguished not by a special letter, but rather by the *absence* of any such letter. But, since 1980, a tiny letter P has been stamped on all Philly coins except the cent.

Worth $150. *1982 no-P Roosevelt dime. (Photo courtesy Heritage Auctions)*

As you might expect, this has given rise to errors now and then when the P has been omitted. One such error occurred in 1982, when collectors began to notice Philadelphia dimes without the mint mark. This error proved embarrassing for the Mint—but make no mistake, it can be a real bonanza for people like you: A typical example will bring you between $25 and $100.

• The 1965 quarter struck in silver.

This is the flip side of the dime error I listed a few coins back. In that case, a 1964 dime was *supposed* to be silver but was made of copper-nickel instead. In 1965, all dimes and quarters were supposed to be made of copper-nickel—but a very small number of quarters got minted in silver by mistake. This is a rare and valuable coin. Unlike "clad" coins, it *won't* have a reddish line around the rim.

• The 1970 quarter with a doubled reverse.

Once more, a double-image error appeared in 1970—this time on quarters from the Philadelphia Mint (struck without a mint mark near the lower right corner of the "heads" side, behind George Washington's pigtail). The doubling is visible only on the coin's reverse, and you'll need a magnifying glass to detect it.

• The 1970-D quarter with a doubled reverse.

Double-image reverses turned up in 1970 on quarters from the Denver Mint as well (this time with a D mint mark behind Washington's pigtail). There are quite a few different varieties of this particular error.

• The 1977-D silver-clad quarter.

In 1975 and 1976, the Mint made special part-silver versions of the Washington quarter, Kennedy half dollar, and Eisenhower dollar. These were sold to collectors at a premium. Production of these 40-percent silver coins was discontinued after 1976—or rather, it was *supposed* to have been. But in 1977, a few quarters were made at the Denver Mint (with a D mint mark behind the pigtail) on leftover silver-clad (40-percent silver) coin blanks. These are extremely rare and valuable.

• The 1989 no-P Washington quarter.

The P mint mark went astray again in 1989 on a small number of quarters. (The mint mark should appear behind George Washington's pigtail, near the bottom of the obverse.) And this time the error drew national attention, thanks to a page one story in *The New York Times*.

As with several other important mint errors, this one turned up in the largest quantities in Pennsylvania, especially the Pittsburgh area. An obvious explanation is the fact that the Mint itself is in that state, and these are early stops in the distribution chain. Multiple findings also were reported in North Carolina.

Coin dealer Harry Forman, himself a Pennsylvanian, touted this coin on the television program "Hidden Rewards." A number of lucky viewers who checked their change afterward found "no-P" quarters and shipped them off to Forman to claim their rewards—which were no longer hidden. The longtime Philadelphia dealer has purchased dozens of these coins at prices ranging from $10 to $100 apiece.

• The 1961 half dollar with a doubled reverse.

At first glance, Franklin half dollars seem rather common. These coins, bearing Benjamin Franklin's portrait on one side and the Liberty Bell on the other, had relatively high mintages throughout their short life span, from 1948 through 1963. On closer inspection, however, some have odd features that set them apart. In 1961, for example, some Franklin halves were made with doubling on the reverse, especially in the letters of *E PLURIBUS UNUM*.

Worth $5,000. *1961 cameo proof Franklin half dollar with doubled lettering on the reverse. (Photo courtesy Heritage Auctions)*

One of these coins appeared in an auction conducted by Heritage Numismatic Auctions in August 1997. Besides having a doubled reverse, this coin was a cameo proof—a special collector coin with dramatic contrast between its frosty devices (or raised portions) and its mirror-like fields (or background areas). It also was in a very high level of preservation: Proof-67. The winning bidder paid $3,500 for this prize—a princely sum belying the Franklin half dollar's seeming commonness.

- The 1964 half dollar with a doubled obverse.

The Kennedy half dollar drew international attention when it first appeared in 1964, soon after the assassination of President John F. Kennedy. Admirers of the slain president—not only in the United States but all around the world—rushed to obtain examples of the coin as Kennedy mementos. Only sharp-eyed collectors noticed that some of those very first Kennedy half dollars had doubling on the obverse (or "heads" side). You may very well have one sitting in a drawer or cigar box even now!

- The 1964 half dollar with a doubled reverse.

Some 1964 Kennedy half dollars have doubling on the *reverse*, rather than the obverse. Get out your magnifying glass to look for this variety; it won't jump right out at you. But you'll spot it right away under the glass.

- The 1966 half dollar without the designer's initials FG.

The Lincoln cent isn't the only coin discovered on occasion without its designer's initials. Eagle-eyed hobbyists have discovered that on some Kennedy half dollars, the letters FG are missing from their designated spot just to the right of the eagle's tail near the base of the coin's reverse. These are the initials of Frank Gasparro, the engraver who designed this side of the coin.

As in the case of cents without the "V.D.B.," this omission resulted from overzealous polishing of one or more dies (the pieces of metal used to strike the coins).

This error has been discovered on coins from a number of years and from different mints. Most don't seem to be excessively rare, but the 1966 is one of the scarcest. Relatively few examples are known with this date.

Half dollars without the designer's initials are not world-class mint errors; some, in fact, might argue that the error is trivial. But don't let that discourage you from looking: If you find one, you can sell it to a small army of dedicated enthusiasts—including Harry Forman—for several dollars.

- The 1972-D half dollar without the designer's initials FG.

The letters FG are missing on a small number of 1972 Kennedy halves from the Denver Mint (with a D below JFK's neckline on the "heads" side). These 1972-D error coins appear to be much scarcer than later ones.

- The 1973 half dollar without the initials FG.

Here we go again! While you're checking Kennedy half dollars for Frank Gasparro's initials, make a special point of examining those dated 1973. This is another instance where some were made without them.

- The 1974-D half dollar with a doubled obverse.

Another double-image error occurred in 1974, this time on Kennedy half dollars from the Denver Mint (with a D below Kennedy's neckline on the "heads" side). The doubling occurs only on the obverse and is plainest on the mottos. This appears to be a rare variety.

- The 1982 Kennedy half dollar without the designer's initials.

The 1982 half dollar without the letters FG was the first to receive widespread publicity. Similar error coins had been known before that, but hadn't really attracted much attention. When the 1982 coins became popular, collectors took a closer look at earlier half dollars and discovered—or rediscovered—several others. At present, the 1982 is worth about $5.

- Wrong-planchet coins.

On rare occasions, a coin is struck in error on a planchet, or coin blank, intended for a different denomination. A planchet meant for a Washington quarter might be struck, for instance, with dies bearing the image of a Jefferson nickel. Such errors are extremely interesting, very scarce, and usually quite valuable.

At an auction in August 1997, Heritage Numismatic Auctions offered a Lincoln cent struck on a dime planchet. The error took place in 1968 at the San Francisco Mint—and to make matters even more interesting, this off-metal mistake was struck with highly polished dies meant for special collector coins called "proofs." The coin changed hands at the auction for $1,550.

Worth $1,550. *1968 Lincoln cent struck in error with proof dies on a dime planchet. (Photo courtesy Heritage Auctions)*

- Coins overstruck with features meant for other coins.

Every now and then, a coin turns up with extraneous design elements stamped on top of its regular features. In most cases, these will be elements from another coin of the same kind—parts of a Lincoln cent superimposed, for instance, on another Lincoln cent. These errors come about in various ways during the production process. A coin already struck may pass between the dies again, for example, and be stamped in a different position.

A highly unusual coin of this kind was offered for sale at Heritage's auction in August 1997. It was a Jefferson nickel where the second striking took place not only in a different position but on the opposite side. To heighten the intrigue, the basic coin was a 1973 nickel, but the overstriking was done with a die dated 1974. And the coin was discovered in a government "mint set" of uncirculated coins, where any such error should have been spotted even more readily by inspectors at the Mint. The coin brought $1,650 at the auction, proving again that finding the Mint's mistakes—often "buried" right in full view—can be very profitable for sharp-eyed treasure hunters.

Worth $3,500. *1973 Jefferson nickel overstruck with the design of a 1974 Jefferson nickel. (Photo courtesy Heritage Auctions)*

• Any silver coins.

In 1965, with silver rising in price, the U.S. Treasury sought and obtained permission from Congress to change the composition of the coins it was producing in that metal. Under the legislation, new dimes and quarters were made with no silver at all, while the half dollar's silver content was reduced. (In 1971, the last trace of silver was removed from that coin, too.)

As you might expect, the American public responded with a nationwide silver rush, pulling silver coins out of circulation. Within a few years, hardly any remained—and today, a silver coin is an uncommon sight indeed among the copper-nickel dimes, quarters, and halves in our pockets and purses.

But, while seldom seen, silver coins do turn up from time to time—and those who are actively *looking* for these coins are the ones most likely to *see* them. At one time, in the early 1980s, silver was worth about $50 an ounce. Its value has declined considerably since then. But, even so, any silver coin you find in pocket change will bring you a healthy profit. As this is written, silver bullion is valued at approximately $5 an ounce, so any "traditional" silver U.S. coin (with a silver content of 90 percent) will be worth about five times its face value. The value of silver coins, of course, goes up proportionally as silver itself rises in price.

COINS NOT TO LOOK FOR

Some coins that seem unusual when they turn up in pocket change are really not worth your time or trouble. Although they are not encountered every day, they are actually quite common and have little or no premium value as collectibles. These coins may bring a premium in higher Mint State grades, but in lesser condition they're worth very little.

Here are a few coins *not* to look for:

• Susan B. Anthony dollars.

Except for the scarce 1979 variety with the "clear-S" mint mark, Anthony dollars are generally worth no more than face value: one dollar each. It's true that these much disliked coins haven't been produced since 1981. However, the Mint pumped out almost 900 million examples in 1979 and 1980, many of which remain in government vaults.

• Eisenhower dollars.

A few of the Eisenhower dollars minted between 1971 and 1978 are in demand as collector's items. But, with these exceptions, "Ike" dollars are just about as common as the Susan B. Anthony dollars that took their place.

• Kennedy half dollars dated after 1970.

From 1964 to 1970, Kennedy half dollars contained silver. The amount of precious metal was reduced beginning in 1965—but, even so, Kennedy halves from any of these years have bonus value based on the price of silver. Since 1971, virtually all half dollars have been made of a copper-nickel alloy—the same one used to make quarters and dimes. The only exceptions were the special collector's items sold in conjunction with the nation's Bicentennial in 1975–76. These coins may not be encountered very often, but they're certainly worth saving.

• Business-strike Bicentennial coins.

While relatively small quantities of the three Bicentennial coins—the Washington quarter, Kennedy half dollar, and Eisenhower dollar—were struck in silver for sale to collectors at a premium, the vast majority of these coins are regular "business-strike" pieces made of copper-nickel alloy. These may catch your eye when they pop up in change now and then, but they're neither scarce nor valuable.

• "Wheat-ears" Lincoln cents.

As noted earlier, the reverse of the Lincoln cent underwent a design change in 1959. As a consequence, cents with the old design—featuring two simple wheat stalks on the reverse—gradually came to be less common in Americans' pocket change. Today, these "wheat-ears" cents are relatively scarce in circulation. But that doesn't mean they're scarce in an absolute sense: Many millions have been saved by collectors and hoarders. These coins do enjoy a very small premium; you could probably sell a roll of 50 common-date wheat-ears cents for a dollar or two. But that hardly justifies an all-out search for these coins.

• The 1974 aluminum cent.

Another coin you shouldn't bother looking for is the 1974 aluminum cent. In this case, however, it's not because the coin is unduly common: It is, in fact, a rarity which any red-blooded collector would love to own. There are two reasons not to bother looking: First, you almost certainly won't find one; and second, even if you did find one, Uncle Sam would seize it if he found out.

In the early 1970s, a growing shortage of cents—and the rising price of copper—prompted the U.S. Mint to explore alternative metals for our nation's lowest-value coin. It settled upon aluminum as the most likely substitute and actually proceeded with production of considerable quantities—reportedly in the neighborhood of 1 million pieces. But Congress declined to authorize this switch and the Mint was obliged to abandon the idea.

There was just one complication: During the time it was seeking support in Congress for the plan, the Mint sent samples of the new aluminum cents to various senators and congressmen—and some of these coins never found their way back. Even today, some are unaccounted for. However, Mint officials have made it clear that since the aluminum cents were never officially issued, any that might turn up would be subject to confiscation by the U.S. Secret Service.

LESS THAN MINT

Just as there are certain coins you shouldn't waste your time looking for in pocket change, there also are coins you shouldn't waste your money buying. Modern coins and coin sets sold at a premium by government or private mints are high on this list of items to avoid.

In recent years, the U.S. Mint has made and marketed dozens of commemorative coins. These are coins authorized by Congress to honor some special person, place, or event. Typically, they are produced in limited quantities and offered for sale at a premium many times their face value and also well above the value of the metal they contain (generally silver or gold). With few exceptions, these coins have been very poor performers in the resale market. They tend to fall in price after their initial sale by the Mint, and within a few years almost all have market values below their issue price—often well below. In part, this is because the issue prices usually include substantial surcharges earmarked for the benefit of organizations sponsoring these coinage programs. The United States Olympic Committee has been a beneficiary several times, for example.

If your purpose in buying coins is to realize a profit, you would be wise to steer clear of commemoratives when the U.S. Mint offers them for sale. For that matter, new-issue coins and coin sets sold by *any* mint—government or private, domestic or foreign—have amassed a poor track record, by and large, in recent years. The annual proof sets and "mint sets" sold by Uncle Sam are very much in the group of items to avoid. Like U.S. commemorative coins, they have tended to fall in value—often sharply—in the secondary market.

NEW YORK CITY TREASURE HUNTS

In late July 1997, thousands of coin collectors gathered in New York City for the annual midsummer convention of the American Numismatic Association, the world's largest coin club. To help generate interest in the show, rare Lincoln cents worth well over $100 apiece were spent at face value in New York City. Donn Pearlman, a nationally known broadcaster and public relations executive from Chicago, coordinated publicity for the show. The following is his account of how these "Coin Drops" were conducted.

One of the most successful public awareness campaigns to encourage people to look at their money was conducted in the summer of 1997 by the American Numismatic Association (ANA), Littleton Coin Co. of Littleton, New Hampshire, and House of Collectibles, publisher of this book. The project attracted

Scott Travers (left) is seen spending in change a 1909-S VDB Lincoln cent valued at $1,000, as camera crews from around the world film the April 2006 event in New York's Times Square. (Photo courtesy Donn Pearlman)

nationwide media coverage for the coin-collecting hobby and prompted people across the country to closely examine their pocket change in hopes of finding valuable pennies.

Four rare coins originally pulled from New York bus and subway fares a half-century ago were deliberately put back into circulation in the Big Apple to publicize the ANA's 106th Anniversary Convention and the so-called World's Fair of Money held in conjunction with it.

The coins, 1914-D Lincoln cents valued at $165 each and part of the nearly 23,000-coin "New York Subway Hoard," were donated to the ANA by Littleton. With radio, TV, and newspaper reporters on hand for the event, the first 1914-D cent was used by Scott A. Travers, the author of this book, to purchase a $1.50 loaf of bread from a street vendor near the New York Coliseum. A rare coin from a famous hoard was back in circulation in New York City for anyone to find and enjoy!

The Subway Hoard coins came from the estates of collector and part-time coin dealer George Shaw of Brooklyn and his brother-in-law, Morris Moscow, who worked for the New York Transit Authority from the 1940s to the 1960s. Moscow and other transit system employees would search through coins used by passengers to pay bus and subway fares, pull out rare pieces and replace them at face value with common coins.

"There were a total of forty-four 1914-D cents in that astounding hoard, many of them housed for decades in New York Transit Authority envelopes," said David M. Sundman, president of Littleton Coin Co. "We deliberately saved a few of these coins to help the ANA publicize its New York convention and encourage the public to carefully look at their pocket change."

Littleton began buying coins from the estates of Shaw and Moscow in 1991 and completed the final purchase in the summer of 1996.

"When we acquired the hoard, many of the coins were grouped by denomination, date, and mint mark in small New York City Transit Authority 'miscellaneous remittances' envelopes with Shaw's handwriting on the outside indicating the types and quantities of coins held inside," Sundman explained.

"Some coins, like the 1914-D cents, were sitting, undisturbed, in those tan-colored envelopes for more than forty years."

Many news stories about the coins described or pictured those envelopes, adding even more flavor to the history of the coins and the excitement of the hunt.

To mark the opening day of the ANA convention, U.S. Treasurer Mary Ellen Withrow spent a 1909-S V.D.B. Lincoln cent valued at $350 to purchase a pretzel from a Times Square street vendor.

The Coin Drops proved to be a very successful stunt, helping to publicize both the convention and the hobby. CNN broadcast video of the drops for days, and local TV and radio stations and newspapers provided extensive coverage.

Perhaps the most successful Coin Drops ever were when I spent three valuable pennies to help publicize National Coin Week 2006 and the publication of my new book, *The Coin Collector's Survival Manual, Fifth Edition.*

Dozens of media organizations attended the April 18, 2006, main event in New York's Times Square. The scene was orchestrated by genius publicist Donn Pearlman. I purchased a bottle of Poland Spring Water for $1 in change that included a circulated 1909-S V.D.B. Lincoln cent valued at $1,000. Later that day, I placed a lightly circulated 1908-S Indian head cent with a $200 value in the change I used to purchase a copy of *The New York Times.*

The hoopla began earlier, on April 12, 2006, when I purchased a $3 hot pretzel from a street vendor in front of the NASDAQ stock exchange. The coins I used to pay for it included a circulated 1914-D Lincoln cent worth $300.

NBC-TV's Today Show *interviewed Scott Travers and featured* The Coin Collector's Survival Manual *in July 2006.*

Throughout this transaction, my movements were being captured by a photographer from *The New York Times,* and a crowd of curious onlookers began to watch. When I finally took a bite out of the pretzel, after posing with it for 20 minutes, the impromptu audience burst into applause—not because I had spent such a valuable coin (for no one knew about that except for the photographer and me), but because I was eating the pretzel at long last.

I was invited to appear as a guest on many TV shows. Just to name a few, I appeared on ABC News, MSNBC, CNN, and in a related story about pennies on NBC-TV's *Today Show.* The Coin Drops were also featured by Reuters, the Associated Press, Univision, and elsewhere. An AOL-ABC News poll featured on the AOL welcome screen asked users if the Coin Drops would cause them to look more closely at their pocket change. Nearly 300,000 people responded and said that they would more carefully examine their change.

Apparently, not enough people examined their change, as there have been no reported finds of those three coins I spent in April 2006.

Clearly, there is romance and excitement connected with the notion of finding worthwhile coins in your pocket or purse. It's the age-old allure of buried treasure—and in those cases, it proved to be "buried" in plain sight!

THE 1913 LIBERTY HEAD NICKEL: FAMOUS AND WORTH A FORTUNE

The 1913 Liberty Head nickel has been described as the most famous coin in the world. It's certainly one of the most heavily promoted. And its 15 minutes of fame have stretched into the better part of a century—helped along the way by nationwide treasure hunts that firmly embedded the coin in the public's consciousness.

In 1996, a 1913 Liberty nickel became the first coin ever to sell for more than a million dollars at a public auction. In 2003, that same coin changed hands privately for about $3 million. Only five examples are known—and when one of them surfaced in 2003 after being missing for more than 40 years, it was greeted by collectors like a much beloved king returning home from exile.

If it were indeed a king, this coin almost surely would be an illegitimate one. From all indications, it was made surreptitiously and illegally—not by the U.S. Mint, but by a Mint employee after hours. There is no mention of the coin in official government records. As far as Uncle Sam was concerned, the Liberty Head series ended in 1912 and the only five-cent piece issued by the Mint in 1913 was the new Buffalo nickel. But it's easy to see how mischief could have happened.

Anticipating the change in design, the Mint had prepared dies for the 1913 Buffalo nickel. But just in case the transition encountered trouble, the Mint had also made dies for a 1913 coin of the old design. These were locked in a vault at the Philadelphia Mint, to be destroyed once the Buffalo coin went into production. Instead, at least five pieces—all of them proofs—were struck with the Liberty Head dies.

Seven years passed before the coins' existence came to light. Collectors first learned of them through an ad in the December 1919 issue of *The Numismatist*, the official monthly journal of the American Numismatic Association. The advertiser, Samuel W. Brown of North Tonawanda, N.Y., offered to pay "$500 cash" for any 1913 Liberty Head nickel—"in Proof condition, if possible." Soon afterward, Brown disclosed that he had purchased five such coins and sold them all—for $600 each—to Philadelphia coin dealer August Wagner.

Cynics had a field day when they learned that Samuel Brown had worked at the Philadelphia Mint from 1903 to 1913—and that he was thought to have had access to the 1913 Liberty nickel dies. The theory quickly arose—and persists to this day—that Brown himself struck the coins, or had an accomplice make them, and then held them secretly after leaving the Mint. It so happens that 1920, the year when he announced their "discovery," also marked the end of the seven-year statute of limitations for prosecuting anyone who might have struck and removed the coins illegally in 1913.

The Philadelphia dealer who bought the five nickels resold all of them to Col. Edward H.R. Green, son of Hetty Green, the eccentric financier known as the "Witch of Wall Street" and reputed to be the world's richest woman. Green kept them until his death in 1938, after which his collection was dispersed.

Green was a flamboyant collector—but the coins got their greatest exposure and promotion not from him but from B. Max Mehl, a high-profile Texas coin dealer who used the nickels to hype his own business in the 1930s and '40s. Mehl placed nationwide ads—in magazines, Sunday supplements and even matchbooks—offering to pay $50 each for any and all 1913 Liberty nickels. He knew that none would turn up (besides the original five, which were, of course, already accounted for)—but most people didn't, and so they searched their pocket change, hoping to claim the $50 bounty. The hobby got positive notice, Mehl got new customers and the 1913 nickels got a lasting reputation as really rare coins.

Worth at least $3.5 million. *1913 Liberty head nickel found at the bottom of a closet (Photo courtesy and copyright American Numismatic Association)*

MILLION DOLLAR OFFER UNCOVERS CLOSET RARITY

In May 2003, Bowers and Merena Auctions, at that time a Collectors Universe (Nasdaq CLCT) company in Mandeville, La., announced "a reward of at least $1 million" for the discovery and purchase of the "missing, fifth specimen" of the rare nickel. "In fact, we'll pay $10,000 just to be the first to see it," said the company's president, Paul Montgomery. The announcement was coordinated by the exceptionally gifted publicist, Donn Pearlman, president of Minkus & Pearlman in Las Vegas. It received extensive media coverage, including a front-page story in *USA Today*. Pearlman's skillfully executed media campaign sent millions of Americans rummaging through cigar boxes, desk drawers, and sugar bowls in search of the million-dollar coin.

Among those who stopped and took notice were members of George Walton's family. Unlike the other searchers, they found what Paul Montgomery was looking for—in a box at the bottom of a closet.

It turns out that the nickel, along with other coins, had been retrieved from the wreckage of the 1962 crash by Walton's sister, and that she had submitted it to a major New York coin firm, one of America's oldest and largest coin dealers, to check its authenticity. At that time, the family firm had apparently concluded that the coin was not authentic. The woman hadn't sought a second opinion, partly because she knew that her brother frequently carried not only the real 1913 nickel but also an excellent fake.

After the sister's death in 1992, the nickel was handed down to other family members, who set it aside and gave it little thought—until Montgomery's million-dollar offer. Through the years, it had remained in George Walton's original custom-made plastic holder, so it was protected from mishandling. But the sister had placed it in an envelope on which she had made a notation that this was an altered-date coin—so the family thought it had no special value.

The big "reward" had piqued the relatives' interest, and when they learned of the ANA exhibit reuniting the other four 1913 nickels in Baltimore, not far from where they lived in North Carolina, they decided to take their coin for that second opinion—just in case. After all, this was a chance not only to have the coin checked by top experts but also to have it compared with the four nickels acknowledged to be genuine.

The coin arrived in Baltimore literally on the eve of the convention—and soon became the talk of the show. A panel of experts studied the coin carefully, comparing each detail with the other four pieces, and came to the conclusion that this was indeed the missing fifth specimen. "We were like a bunch of schoolboys," Montgomery said, "because we solved the mystery."

The Waltons returned home from Baltimore $10,000 richer—for giving Bowers and Merena the first look at the coin—but with no definite plans for consigning it for sale and thereby claiming the million-dollar reward. Given the prices in recent sales of other 1913 Liberty Head nickels, the coin could bring more than two million dollars—a payoff truly worthy of a nationwide treasure hunt. Collectors Universe later sold the Bowers and Merena firm to Greg Manning Auctions, Inc. (Nasdaq GMAI).

Note: In May 2004, coin dealer Blanchard & Company sold the Olsen 1913 Liberty head nickel for $3 million.

UNCONVENTIONAL WISDOM

Serious numismatists—dedicated coin collectors—sometimes make light of "pocket-change rarities." A feeling exists within a certain segment of the hobby that coins found in ordinary pocket change are somehow less significant than beautiful, pristine pieces that never entered everyday circulation. With all due respect to those who hold this view, I feel that on the contrary, coins that have "been around" gain added appeal from having seen actual use.

Most coins (excluding proofs) are made to be spent, so these pieces have served their intended function. And while it's always exciting to own an exceptional coin, there's a special satisfaction—an undeniable thrill—in finding a worthwhile coin in circulation. It's very much like digging up buried treasure.

Pocket-change rarities may not have fancy pedigrees, but many do command fancy prices. And they're definitely out there, waiting to be found. Interesting and valuable coins are turning up in pocket change every day. And more will turn up tomorrow.

So start looking—and happy hunting!

CHAPTER 3

MAKING THE GRADE IN COINS

Coins are made to be spent. But collectors prefer coins that have never been spent at all—coins that are still as shiny and sharp as the day they left the mint—and they're willing to pay big premiums to obtain them.

"Quality" is a very important word in coin collecting today, and a very important word for you, as well, if you have any plans to buy or sell coins in today's marketplace. Buying the best will cost you more money, but you'll get more money back when you go to sell, and chances are, those high-quality coins will hold their value better in the meantime. Conversely, if you're thinking of selling any coins you already own, you'll find potential buyers placing heavy stress on the coins' condition.

The condition or "grade" of a coin—its level of preservation—has become a primary key in determining how much that coin is worth. A brand-new coin, one in what is called Mint State, or "uncirculated" condition, is often worth many times as much as another coin of the same type and date that has passed from hand to hand. What's more, there are nuances of "newness." Coins aren't looked upon as simply "new" or "used": Experts now recognize no fewer than eleven different grade levels within the Mint State range, and a shift of just one or two levels can mean a difference of many thousands of dollars in the value of a coin.

RECOGNIZED GRADING STANDARDS

The coin market's preoccupation with quality has led to the establishment of industry-wide standards for grading coins. These standards were promulgated in 1977 by the American Numismatic Association (ANA), the world's largest organization of coin collectors, and have come to be accepted and observed throughout the marketplace.

The system set up by the ANA rates coins on a scale of 1 to 70, with the numbers ascending as the level of quality rises. A coin graded 1 can barely be identified; if it were a Lincoln cent, for instance, you could tell that's what it was, but little more. A coin graded 70 would be positively perfect in every respect: a coin with no nicks, no flaws, no scratches, and no imperfections of any kind. It also wouldn't have the slightest bit of friction on its highest points from having been touched or passed from hand to hand.

"Uncirculated" becomes "circulated" if just two tiny letters are removed. It's similarly easy to transform a Mint State coin into something a little less than that—and a lot less valuable. Suppose you had a coin worth $5,000 to collectors because of its virtual perfection—a coin that looked as new as the day it left the mint because it had never been spent and its owners had never mishandled it even once. If you were to take a sweat-soaked finger and wipe it lightly over that coin, it wouldn't be considered Mint State anymore; experts would downgrade it all the way to About Uncirculated, a grade that corresponds to the number 58—perhaps 10 points lower on the scale. The real damage would show up on your ledger sheet, for the value of that coin might now be just a few hundred dollars—and possibly even less.

Even the slightest mishandling can damage a coin irreparably. And once a coin passes from hand to hand, the most exposed parts of the metal begin to wear down, causing the loss of detail—detail that can never be replaced.

The grade assigned to each coin includes not only a number but also a word description. That perfect coin, for instance, would be designated Mint State-70. If it were a proof, or specimen coin, its grade would be Proof-70. Proofs are graded separately from regular coins (also known as "business strikes"), but the same 1-to-70 scale is used.

The ANA may have standardized grading with its 1-to-70 scale, but it didn't invent the concept of using specific terms to describe a coin's condition. Long before the present system evolved, dealers and collectors were utilizing such adjectives as "good," "fine," "choice," and "gem" to characterize their coins. These adjectives provided a convenient kind of shorthand for long-distance buyers and sellers—mail-order coin dealers, for example. They could carry out transactions by telephone or mail with reasonable confidence because there was general agreement on the meaning of the basic grading terms. This type of confidence is important in the rare-coin business, for coins by their nature lend themselves well to long-distance sales. Coins are small, extremely portable, and often quite valuable, so deals involving very high values can be carried out easily through the mail, using registered mail to protect against possible loss.

THE ELEMENTS OF GRADING

A number of different elements help to determine the grade of a coin. It's beyond the scope of this book to examine these elements in detail, but a brief discussion will give you a general idea of what's involved.

When a professional numismatist—usually a coin dealer—looks at a coin, he focuses on several different factors, and all of these have a bearing on how he grades the coin. He checks, of course, to see if there is wear—and, if so, how much. He also looks for obvious imperfections such as cuts, scratches, or nicks: Smooth *surfaces* enhance a coin's appearance and its grade. With a Mint State coin, in particular, the expert puts great emphasis on the *strike*—the sharpness of detail imparted to the coin when it was made. He also takes into account the *luster* of the coin—the way it reflects light. Finally, he considers everything all together by gauging the coin's *eye appeal*. Sometimes a coin may seem to have much to recommend it in each of the individual categories but somehow comes up short when viewed as a whole.

THE MOST IMPORTANT GRADES

There may be 70 numbers on the ANA grading scale, but not all those numbers are created equal. The 11 grades at the top of the scale, those between 60 and 70, constitute the Mint State range, and this is where the action is in today's coin market. This is where we see the overwhelming majority of important coin transactions—those involving substantial amounts of money. This is also the area where accurate grading is most crucial and where the greatest potential exists for disputes and costly mistakes.

Mint State coins cannot have any wear; by definition, a coin cannot be uncirculated if it has entered circulation—that is to say, been passed from hand to hand—and suffered even the slightest loss of detail. Mint State coins can have flaws, but any such imperfections must have occurred at the mint. For example, they can have "bag marks" from coming into contact with other coins at the mint. They still would be considered Mint State coins, but the marks would reduce their grade.

In practice, few coins qualify for designation as Mint State-70. This is really more of a theoretical grade, a utopian goal that is constantly pursued but seldom attained. MS-69 and MS-68 are attainable, but only with great difficulty. To qualify for one of these grades, a coin must be free of all but the tiniest flaws.

Here are some of the most important grades in the current marketplace:

• **MS-67.** A coin in this grade can have one or two small defects that are visible under 5-power magnification. However, these would not be apparent to the naked eye and the coin would seem practically perfect upon first being viewed.

• **MS-65.** While clearly not perfect, a coin in this grade is still highly desirable. In fact, coins graded MS-65 fall just short of what is called "supergrade" status. They possess great appeal but are held back by a single minor blemish.

• **MS-63.** A coin in this grade is still desirable, but even the naked eye can detect some flaws. There may be an obvious bag mark, for example, or spots on the surface of the coin.

• **MS-60.** A coin graded MS-60 is uncirculated—but just barely. It hasn't been passed from hand to hand, so technically it doesn't have any wear. But it does have very obvious mint-made imperfections. These may include scratches, nicks, and even large gashes in prominent locations.

• **About Uncirculated.** This is the grading level just below the Mint State range. It has three main components: AU-58, AU-55, and AU-50. Coins graded AU-58 may have considerable eye appeal; in fact, they may be more attractive at first glance than many Mint State coins. However, closer scrutiny will reveal slight wear on the highest points. These coins have passed through people's hands—but only through a few.

• **Extremely Fine.** Next in line, as we move down the scale, are coins graded EF-45 and EF-40. These coins have light wear on their highest points, but overall they're still detailed and attractive.

• **Very Fine.** Coins graded VF-30 and VF-20 are moderately worn, but all their major features remain sharp.

• **Fine.** A coin graded Fine-12 has passed through many hands and emerged with moderate to heavy wear. However, the wear is even, and all the major features are still clearly discernible.

• **Very Good.** When we reach the grade of VG-8, we're obviously approaching the bottom of the scale. A coin in this grade is well worn. Its design remains clear, but it's flat and lacks details.

• **Good.** It soon becomes evident that this is not what the uninitiated have in mind when they say that their coins are "in good condition." Far from being desirable, G-4 coins are heavily worn. The design and inscriptions are still discernible; however, they're faint here and there.

• **About Good.** For all practical purposes, AG-3 is the lowest collectible grade—and most collectors shun it except in the case of scarce-date coins. On an AG-3 coin, the design remains visible only in outline and parts of the date and inscriptions are worn smooth.

For in-depth information on coin grading, I recommend that you read *Official Guide to Coin Grading and Counterfeit Detection* by the Professional Coin Grading Service (House of Collectibles).

CLEANING COINS

Uninformed individuals mistakenly believe that dark, dull, or damaged coins can be magically restored to something approaching their original brilliance through the application of baking soda and elbow grease. This is a disastrous misconception.

Never clean a coin. Far from enhancing the value of a coin, cleaning almost always diminishes—or destroys—whatever appeal that coin might have held for collectors. A coin that has been cleaned may look bright and shiny to the untrained eye, but under a magnifying glass its surfaces will reveal unsightly scratches. The friction involved in cleaning a coin wears down the metal on its surface. This actually lowers the grade of the coin. What's more, many collectors find cleaned coins repugnant and flatly refuse to put them in their collections.

There are ways of cleaning coins that minimize the damage; museums, for example, have experts who are skilled in removing foreign substances from coins. For everyone else, however, the message is clear. When it comes to your coins, "cleaning" is a very dirty word.

GRADING SERVICES

The so-called "good old days" may stir our sense of nostalgia, but the old days weren't always all that good. Consider what used to happen when people had valuable coins to sell.

There wasn't any system in place in those days to offer people guidance on how much their coins were worth. Experienced collectors knew where to turn; besides being knowledgeable themselves about coins, they also knew which coin dealers could be counted upon to render honest appraisals. But those unschooled in the ways of the coin world had no such protection. They ended up taking their coins to local coin shops and putting themselves, quite literally, at the dealers' mercy. And all too often, those dealers weren't merciful: They offered ridiculously low sums for coins that were actually rare and valuable, then, after buying the coins, turned around and sold them for huge profits.

Today there is a safety net for consumers—meaning you! Companies known as grading services provide impartial opinions on the grades of rare coins that are sent in to them for review. They don't come right out and say what your coins are worth, but since a coin's value is determined by its grade, it's a very simple matter to figure out the value once you know the grade. Those of you who dabble in the stock market are undoubtedly familiar with Moody's Investor Services, a company that offers independent ratings of stocks. The grading services play a similar role today in the coin market: They offer independent third-party opinions on the grades of the coins they examine, based upon the 1-to-70 scale.

Two top grading services are the Professional Coin Grading Service (PCGS), and the Numismatic Guaranty Corporation of America (NGC). For a fee of approximately $25 per coin, these companies will examine your coins, assign appropriate grades, then encapsulate each coin in a hard plastic holder along with an insert stating the grade. Coins in these holders are said to be "certified coins." They enjoy wide acceptance in the marketplace, and this will facilitate the sale of your coins for fair market prices.

When you think of it, $25 is a small price to pay for the peace of mind and protection you receive. As you can see from reading through this book, it's not at all impossible that you may have a coin worth many thousands of dollars. If you walk into a coin shop without first having that coin certified, you might receive a low-ball offer—and possibly even a rip-off offer. Once you get it certified, you'll know what it's worth and you can then deal from a position of strength in seeking a buyer. Furthermore, its status as a certified coin will make it much easier to sell.

Recently, consumers have gained a new layer of protection through the establishment of a company called the Certified Acceptance Corp. (CAC). This company evaluates coins already certified by PCGS or NGC and places a sticker on the holder of each coin which, in its opinion, fully merits the grade that was assigned—or perhaps an even higher grade. These stickers incorporate tamper-proof holograms, but there would be no advantage to removing them, for they serve to enhance the coins' market acceptance and can add significantly to their value. They also protect consumers from overpaying for coins that are "low-end" for the grade assigned—in other words, barely qualify.

Certified coins have never been bought and sold on a "one price fits all" basis. Certification does establish a higher price base, and does make coins more marketable. But dealers have always been willing to pay somewhat more for "sight-seen" coins—those they actually examine—than for "sight-unseen" coins, where they accept the accuracy of the grading without having a chance to look at the coins in advance. The reason is that even when two coins are both graded correctly, one may be "higher-end" for the grade than the other, and therefore worth a bigger premium.

CAC will not affix a sticker to a coin it considers "low-end"—and because of its consistency in applying this standard, it has achieved wide credibility, to the point where the top dealers now accept certified coins "vetted" by CAC as equivalent to "sight-seen" coins in quality. As a result, sight-unseen certified coins are bought and sold today as if they were sight-seen if they have been "stickered" by CAC. The fair market values in this book reflect what would be paid for PCGS or NGC sight-seen coins, or sight-unseen coins with CAC stickers.

CHAPTER 4

PUTTING A VALUE ON YOUR COINS

(Photos courtesy of Doug Plasencia, Stack's/Bowers Auctions.)

> *IMPORTANT NOTE:* Values for Mint State and Proof copper coins are for specimens that exhibit both *red* and *brown* color, except where indicated.

URGENT INFORMATION ON MINTAGE FIGURES

In the earliest days of the U.S. Mint, officials went out of their way to publicize the number of coins being struck, as it proved to the new nation that the institution was fulfilling its task. It was commonplace to find, for example, large Eastern newspapers reporting the monthly coinage figures from the Philadelphia Mint.

Three branch mints were opened in 1838, followed by others at irregular intervals, but the general procedure was the same as in the earlier days. There was, however, a major change in 1857 when the government changed the fiscal year to end on June 30 and required the mint service to follow suit. Because of this change, mintage figures were now given out to the public on a fiscal-year basis, and calendar-year figures were not published. In 1887, Mint director James P. Kimball, responding to numerous collector inquiries, ordered that the missing calendar-year figures for 1857–1886 be compiled and published for all to see. This was done, but a few errors crept in that were generally corrected by numismatic researchers in the 1960s, using materials in the National Archives. After 1887, the Mint Bureau published both calendar- and fiscal-year figures so that there was no longer any confusion.

The Mint did not generally publish proof mintage figures, and the records for such pieces do not exist for years prior to 1858. In the 1940s, the Mint Bureau finally published the relevant figures beginning with 1864; earlier years were later filled in by researchers. Due to a quirk in record keeping, minor proof statistics do not exist before 1878, but are well documented after that time.

In the twentieth century, the Mint Bureau was usually quite open with mintage figures. Until the early 1960s, numismatic publications normally reported coinage production figures on a monthly and yearly basis. The coin shortage of the 1960s ushered in a new era, however, and Mint officials began to release only annual totals (though this has been relaxed somewhat in recent years for the regular—noncommemorative—coinage).

Following are fair market values for U.S. coins issued from 1792 to the present. The coins are arranged from the smallest-value denomination (the half cent) through the highest (the $20 gold piece), with commemoratives and American Eagle bullion coins listed separately.

The values are provided in several different grades, or levels of preservation; the better the condition of a coin, the higher its value will be. In some cases, you will find only two or three grades listed for certain coins. It may be that these coins are normally encountered only in those grades; other times, they may have no special value except in the very highest grades.

You will find a number of listings for "overdates." These are coins on which one or more of the numbers in the date are engraved over other numbers. This was a common occurrence in the U.S. Mint's early years, when dies from prior years were reused—and the new dates were cut over the old ones—in order to save money. Dies are the pieces of metal used to stamp coins; you might think of them as being like the cookie cutters used to press designs into cookies.

The italicized numbers after the dates of certain coins denote the number of proofs—or specimen coins—that were struck in that year at that mint.

(NOTE: Bullion-sensitive coins priced in this book were based on spot metal prices of gold at $1,600 to $1,730 per ounce, silver at $25 to $35 per ounce, and platinum at $1,500 to $1,600 per ounce. These metal prices are extremely volatile and are outdated on publication. Consequently, transactions should be consummated only after consumers confirm the current respective metals price.)

HALF CENTS (1793–1857)

Liberty Cap Portrait (1793–1797)

Portrait Facing Left (1793)

	Mintage	Good-4	Fine-12	EF-40
1793	35,334	$3,500	$9,000	$30,000

Portrait Facing Right (1794–1797)

	Mintage	Good-4	Fine-12	EF-40
1794	81,600	$350	$1,000	$5,000
1795	139,690	425	900	4,500
1796 combined total.......	1,390			
1796 with pole............		20,000	35,000	70,000
1796 without pole.........		20,000	45,000	80,000
1797 combined total.......	127,840			
1797 plain edge...........		425	1,650	4,500
1797 lettered edge		2,500	6,000	32,500

Draped Bust Portrait (1800–1808)

	Mintage	Good-4	Fine-12	EF-40
1800	202,908	$75.00	$150	$600
1802 combined total.......	20,266			
1802/0 overdate with same reverse as 1800		27,500	40,000	200,000
1802/0 with new reverse ...		900	6,000	20,000
1803	92,000	75.00	180	1,000
1804 combined total.......	1,055,312			
1804 with "spiked" chin....		75.00	115	375
1804, all others		75.00	150	375
1805 combined total.......	814,464			
1805 with small 5 and stems		875	4,250	15,000

	Mintage	Good-4	Fine-12	EF-40
1805, all others		75.00	150	375
1806 combined total.	356,000			
1806 with small 6 and stems		225	720	3,650
1806, all others		75.00	150	375
1807	476,000	75.00	175	625
1808 combined total.	400,000			
1808 regular date		75.00	125	400
1808/7 overdate		175	650	3,900

Classic Head Portrait (1809–1836)

	Mintage	Good-4	Fine-12	EF-40	Proof-63
1809 combined total	1,154,572				
1809 regular date.		$65.00	$125	$225	
1809/6 overdate.		65.00	125	300	
1810.	215,000	65.00	100	1,000	
1811.	63,140	400	2,000	6,000	
1825.	63,000	100	180	275	
1826.	234,000	65.00	125	200	
1828 combined total	606,000				
1828 with 13 stars		65.00	100	150	
1828 with 12 stars		65.00	100	375	
1829.	487,000	65.00	90.00	150	
1831 original.	2,200	7,000	12,500	25,000	
1831 restrike with large berries (proof only) . .	*unknown*	—	—	—	$8,500
1831 restrike with small berries (proof only) . .	*unknown*	—	—	—	15,000
1832.	51,000	65.00	75.00	85.00	
1833.	103,000	65.00	75.00	90.00	
1834.	141,000	65.00	75.00	90.00	
1835.	398,000	65.00	75.00	90.00	
1836 original (proof only)	*unknown*	—	—	—	7,700
1836 restrike (proof only)	*unknown*	—	—	—	25,000

Coronet Portrait (1840–1857)

	Mintage	Good-4	Fine-12	EF-40	Proof-63
1840–1848 original (proof only)	unknown	—	—	—	$4,850
1840–1848 restrike (proof only)	unknown	—	—	—	4,850
1849 large date.	39,364	$65.00	$80.00	$150	

	Mintage	Good-4	Fine-12	EF-40	Proof-63
1849 small date original (proof only)	unknown	—	—	—	4,600
1849 small date restrike (proof only)	unknown	—	—	—	4,700
1850.................	39,812	65.00	80.00	110	
1851.................	147,672	65.00	85.00	125	
1852 restrike (proof only)	unknown	—	—	—	3,900
1853.................	129,694	65.00	80.00	100	
1854.................	55,358	65.00	90.00	125	
1855.................	56,500	65.00	90.00	125	
1856.................	40,430	65.00	90.00	125	
1857.................	35,180	65.00	90.00	125	

LARGE CENTS (1793–1857)

Flowing Hair Portrait (1793)

Chain on Reverse (1793)

	Mintage	Good-4	Fine-12	EF-40
1793 combined total.......	36,103			
1793 with AMERICA spelled out		$7,000	$22,500	$68,500
1793 with AMERICA abbreviated AMERI................		12,000	25,000	92,500

Wreath on Reverse (1793)

	Mintage	Good-4	Fine-12	EF-40
1793 combined total.......	63,353			
1793 with vine and bars on edge		$2,000	$5,500	$15,500
1793 lettered edge		2,100	6,000	16,000
1793 with strawberry leaves above the date	4 known	150,000		(unknown in higher grades)

Liberty Cap Portrait (1793–1796)

	Mintage	Good-4	Fine-12	EF-40
1793	11,056	$8,000	$14,000	$150,000
1794 combined total.......	918,521			
1794 with same head as 1793		1,500	3,200	14,000
1794 with new head		500	775	4,000
1794 with stars on the reverse		15,000	35,000	300,000
1795 lettered edge	37,000	500	900	4,500
1795 plain edge...........	501,500	500	775	4,000
1795 Jefferson head		20,000	65,000	150,000
1796	109,825	325	900	4,200

Draped Bust Portrait (1796–1807)

	Mintage	Good-4	Fine-12	EF-40
1796 combined total.......	363,375			
1796 with same reverse as 1794		$250	$900	$4,200
1796 with regular 1796 reverse		120	600	3,500
1796 with same reverse as 1797		170	650	2,750
1796 with LIBERTY spelled LIHERTY..............		290	1,350	7,500
1797 combined total.......	897,510			
1797 with gripped edge		150	500	2,800
1797 plain edge...........		120	400	2,850
1797 with new reverse and stems on wreath		150	350	1,700
1797 with new reverse and no stems		130	600	4,300
1798 combined total.......	1,841,745			
1798 with old hairstyle.....		125	300	1,700
1798 with new hairstyle....		100	250	1,500
1798 with same reverse as 1796		100	650	5,250
1798/7 overdate		145	575	4,300
1799 regular date (mintage included with 1798)		1,800	8,500	
1799/8 overdate (mintage included with 1798)		2,200	8,000	
1800 combined total.......	2,822,175			
1800 regular date		100	200	1,550
1800/1798 overdate with old hairstyle..............		125	300	3,400
1800, 80/79 overdate with new hairstyle...............		115	250	1,850
1801 combined total.......	1,362,837			
1801 with regular reverse ..		100	170	1,100

	Mintage	Good-4	Fine-12	EF-40
1801 with fraction 1/000 ...		110	250	1,650
1801 with fraction 1/100 over 1/000		125	270	1,900
1801 with 3 errors (1/000, only one stem and IINITED instead of UNITED)		180	850	6,500
1802 combined total.......	3,435,100			
1802 with regular reverse ..		90.00	200	900
1802 with no stems on wreath		90.00	200	950
1802 with fraction 1/000 ...		100	180	1,000
1803 combined total.......	3,228,191			
1803 small date		100	150	900
1803 large date with small fraction		7,000	17,000	65,000
1803 large date with large fraction		85.00	370	2,750
1803 with no stems on wreath		110	240	1,500
1803 with fraction 1/100 over 1/000		110	240	1,500
1804 (mintage included with 1803)		750	6,500	20,000
1805	941,116	100	180	950
1806	348,000	110	225	2,600
1807 combined total.......	829,221			
1807 with small fraction....		50.00	175	1,250
1807 with large fraction		50.00	200	1,000
1807/6 overdate with small 7		2,550	12,000	75,000
1807/6 overdate with large 7		55.00	170	975

Classic Head Portrait (1808–1814)

	Mintage	Good-4	Fine-12	EF-40
1808	1,007,000	$55.00	$325	$1,350
1809	222,867	130	475	2,700
1810 combined total.......	1,458,500			
1810 regular date		55.00	250	1,150
1810/09 overdate		65.00	315	1,500
1811 combined total.......	218,025			
1811 regular date		100	400	1,800
1811/0 overdate		85.00	450	4,300
1812	1,075,500	55.00	240	1,100
1813	418,000	65.00	300	1,500
1814	357,830	50.00	300	1,150

Coronet Portrait (1816–1857)

	Mintage	Good-4	Fine-12	EF-40	AU-55	MS-63
1816..................	2,820,982	$20.00	$30.00	$100	$225	$400
1817 combined total	3,948,400					
1817 with 13 stars		20.00	30.00	100	200	400
1817 with 15 stars		22.00	35.00	150	300	800
1818..................	3,167,000	20.00	35.00	100	200	375
1819 combined total	2,671,000					
1819 regular date.......		20.00	35.00	100	200	375
1819/8 overdate........		22.00	35.00	110	250	400
1820 combined total	4,407,550					
1820 regular date......		20.00	30.00	110	240	375
1820/19 overdate.......		22.00	35.00	120	275	400
1821..................	389,000	50.00	75.00	375	1,750	—
1822..................	2,072,339	20.00	35.00	125	325	550
1823 combined total	68,061					
1823 regular date.......		75.00	150	1,000	4,000	—
1823/2 overdate........		75.00	150	850	2,500	—
1824 combined total	1,193,939					
1824 regular date.......		20.00	30.00	250	1,250	2,350
1824/2 overdate........		25.00	75.00	500	1,750	—
1825..................	1,461,100	20.00	30.00	125	375	800
1826 combined total	1,517,425					
1826 regular date.......		20.00	30.00	110	350	700
1826/5 overdate........		25.00	75.00	225	900	1,800
1827..................	2,357,732	20.00	30.00	100	200	350
1828 combined total	2,260,624					
1828 small date		21.00	30.00	47.50	375	800
1828 large date.........		20.00	30.00	45.00	350	775
1829 combined total	1,414,500					
1829 with medium letters		21.00	30.00	150	2,250	—
1829 with large letters ..		20.00	30.00	100	200	350
1830 combined total	1,711,500					
1830 with medium letters		30.00	100	275	2,500	—
1830 with large letters ..		20.00	30.00	100	200	350
1831..................	3,359,260	20.00	30.00	100	200	350
1832..................	2,362,000	20.00	30.00	100	200	350
1833..................	2,739,000	20.00	30.00	100	200	350
1834 combined total	1,855,100					
1834 with small 8, large stars and medium letters		20.00	30.00	100	200	350
1834 with large 8, small stars and medium letters		20.00	30.00	100	200	350
1834 with large 8, large stars and medium letters		175.00	300	925	3,000	—
1834 with large 8, large stars and large letters .		20.00	35.00	110	500	—
1835 combined total	3,878,400					
1835 with same head as 1834...............		21.00	35.00	120	240	400
1835 with same head as 1836................		20.00	30.00	110	220	425
1836..................	2,111,000	20.00	30.00	100	200	375
1837..................	5,558,300	20.00	30.00	100	200	350

	Mintage	Good-4	Fine-12	EF-40	AU-55	MS-63
1838.................	6,370,200	20.00	30.00	100	200	350
1839 combined total	3,128,661					
1839 with regular head ..		20.00	30.00	100	200	375
1839 with "silly" head ...		22.00	35.00	120	400	1,100
1839 with "booby" head .		20.00	35.00	100	300	850
1839/6 overdate........		300	700	3,850	20,000	—
1840 combined total	2,462,700					
1840 regular date.......		20.00	30.00	65.00	125	325
1840 with small 18 over large 18		20.00	30.00	90.00	200	375
1841.................	1,597,367	20.00	30.00	65.00	130	350
1842.................	2,383,390	20.00	30.00	65.00	125	300
1843 combined total	2,425,342					
1843 with small head and small letters		20.00	30.00	65.00	125	300
1843 with small head and large letters		22.00	35.00	120	400	800
1843 with large head and large letters		22.00	30.00	75.00	130	350
1844 combined total	2,398,752					
1844 regular date.......		20.00	30.00	65.00	125	300
1844/81 error		22.00	35.00	150	450	—
1845.................	3,894,804	20.00	30.00	65.00	125	300
1846 combined total	4,120,800					
1846 regular date.......		20.00	30.00	60.00	120	285
1846 small date		20.00	30.00	57.50	110	280
1847 combined total	6,183,669					
1847 regular date.......		20.00	30.00	57.50	110	280
1847 with 7 over small 7 .		22.00	30.00	90.00	250	
1848.................	6,415,799	20.00	30.00	75.00	125	300
1849.................	4,178,500	20.00	30.00	75.00	125	300
1850.................	4,426,844	20.00	30.00	57.50	110	300
1851 combined total	9,889,707					
1851 regular date.......		20.00	30.00	52.50	110	300
1851/81 error		20.00	30.00	90.00	180	375
1852.................	5,063,094	20.00	30.00	52.50	100	275
1853.................	6,641,131	20.00	30.00	52.50	100	275
1854.................	4,236,156	20.00	30.00	52.50	100	275
1855 combined total	1,574,829					
1855 with slanting 5 and knob on ear		15.00	20.00	60.00	110	285
1855, all other		10.00	20.00	52.50	100	275
1856.................	2,690,463	10.00	20.00	52.50	100	275
1857 combined total	333,456					
1857 small date		26.00	45.00	65.00	125	300
1857 large date........		25.00	40.00	60.00	120	325

FLYING EAGLE CENTS (1856–1858)

	Mintage	Good-4	Fine-12	EF-40	AU-55	MS-63	MS-65	Proof-65
1856 pattern	1,000	$5,800	$9,000	$12,000	$15,000	$17,000*	$75,000*	$35,000
1857	17,450,000	30.00	50.00	150	175	650	4,200	37,500
1858 combined total ...	24,600,000							
1858 with small letters .		30.00	50.00	150	175	650	4,200	37,500
1858 with large letters .		30.00	50.00	150	175	650	4,200	37,500
1858/7 overdate		100	150	775	1,500	8,000	75,000	

*Grading services no longer recognize business strikes.

INDIAN HEAD CENTS (1859–1909)

Copper-Nickel Composition (1859–1864)

Wreath on Reverse Without Shield (1859)

	Mintage	Good-4	Fine-12	EF-40	AU-55	MS-63	MS-65	Proof-65
1859 ...*800*..........	36,400,000	$12.00	$20.00	$100	$150	$500	$3,500	$8,000

Wreath and Shield on Reverse (1860–1909)

	Mintage	Good-4	Fine-12	EF-40	AU-55	MS-63	MS-65	Proof-65
1860 ...*1,000*	20,566,000	$12.00	$20.00	$75.00	$110	$200	$950	$4,500
1861 ...*1,000*	10,100,000	20.00	35.00	100	200	250	1,500	16,000
1862 ...*550*..........	28,075,000	10.00	20.00	30.00	60.00	150	1,100	3,000
1863 ...*460*..........	49,840,000	10.00	20.00	30.00	60.00	150	1,100	3,200
1864 ...*370*..........	13,740,000	20.00	35.00	100	200	165	1,350	4,000

Bronze Composition (1864–1909)

	Mintage	Good-4	Fine-12	EF-40	AU-55	MS-63	MS-65	Proof-65
1864 combined total ...	39,233,714							
1864 with no L ..*150* ..		$8.00	$20.00	$50.00	$100	$150	$350	$6,000
1864 with L on headdress ...*20* ...		50.00	125	300	375	500	1,500	225,000
1865 ...*500*	35,429,286	8.00	20.00	35.00	50.00	110	875	2,000
1866 ...*725*..........	9,826,500	40.00	75.00	200	300	400	1,250	1,700
1867 ...*625*..........	9,821,000	40.00	75.00	200	300	400	1,250	1,500
1868 ...*600*..........	10,266,500	40.00	75.00	200	300	400	1,000	1,500
1869 combined total ...	6,420,000							
1869 regular date ..*600*	80.00	300	400	500	700	1,500	1,600	
1869/9 overdate	100	300	675	1,000	1,500	2,500		
1870 ...*1,000*	5,275,000	50.00	300	500	650	800	1,500	1,600
1871 ...*960*..........	3,929,500	75.00	300	600	650	800	3,500	1,600
1872 ...*950*..........	4,042,000	85.00	300	600	900	900	3,750	1,900
1873 combined total ...	11,676,500							
1873 with closed 3 ..... *1,100*		40.00	100	200	400	800	1,400	1,100
1873 with open 3		20.00	50.00	175	300	400	1,000	

	Mintage	Good-4	Fine-12	EF-40	AU-55	MS-63	MS-65	Proof-65
1873 with double letters on LIBERTY		250	1,000	3,000	7,000	19,500	75,000	
1874 ... *700*	14,187,500	15.00	40.00	100	150	300	750	1,000
1875 ... *700*	13,528,000	15.00	50.00	100	150	300	950	1,800
1876 ... *1,150*	7,944,000	30.00	75.00	200	250	300	1,250	1,400
1877 ... *900*	852,500	875	1,650	2,250	3,300	5,000	14,000	12,750
1878 ... *2,350*	5,799,850	30.00	60.00	200	400	600	1,000	600
1879 ... *3,200*	16,231,200	8.00	15.00	100	175	200	400	550
1880 ... *3,955*	38,964,955	3.00	7.50	25.00	75.00	150	375	550
1881 ... *3,575*	39,211,575	3.00	7.50	25.00	75.00	200	375	550
1882 ... *3,100*	38,581,100	3.00	7.50	25.00	75.00	200	375	550
1883 ... *6,609*	45,598,109	3.00	7.50	25.00	75.00	200	375	550
1884 ... *3,942*	23,261,742	3.25	7.50	25.00	80.00	200	500	550
1885 ... *3,790*	11,765,384	6.00	12.00	50.00	90.00	250	750	550
1886 ... *4,290*	17,654,290	3.50	20.00	150	225	300	1,500	550
1887 ... *2,960*	45,226,483	2.00	5.00	50.00	70.00	125	400	550
1888 combined total ...	37,494,414							
1888 regular date .. *4,582*		2.00	6.00	20.00	50.00	125	900	600
1888/7 overdate		1,800	6,500	20,000	30,000	92,500	—	
1889 ... *3,336*	48,869,361	2.00	5.00	17.50	20.00	90.00	500	550
1890 ... *2,740*	57,182,854	2.00	5.00	17.50	20.00	90.00	375	550
1891 ... *2,350*	47,072,350	2.00	5.00	17.50	20.00	90.00	375	550
1892 ... *2,745*	37,649,832	2.00	5.00	17.50	20.00	90.00	375	550
1893 ... *2,195*	46,642,195	2.00	5.00	17.50	20.00	90.00	500	550
1894 ... *2,632*	16,752,132	4.00	12.00	27.50	80.00	125	425	550
1895 ... *2,062*	38,343,636	1.50	5.00	17.50	20.00	80.00	250	550
1896 ... *1,862*	39,057,293	1.50	5.00	16.00	20.00	80.00	250	550
1897 ... *1,938*	50,466,330	1.50	5.00	16.00	20.00	80.00	250	550
1898 ... *1,795*	49,823,079	1.50	5.00	16.00	20.00	80.00	250	550
1899 ... *2,031*	53,600,031	1.50	5.00	10.00	25.00	70.00	250	550
1900 ... *2,262*	66,833,764	1.50	5.00	7.50	25.00	55.00	240	550
1901 ... *1,985*	79,611,143	1.50	5.00	7.50	25.00	55.00	240	550
1902 ... *2,018*	87,376,722	1.50	5.00	7.50	25.00	55.00	240	550
1903 ... *1,790*	85,094,493	1.50	5.00	7.50	25.00	55.00	240	550
1904 ... *1,817*	61,328,015	1.50	5.00	7.50	25.00	55.00	240	550
1905 ... *2,152*	80,719,163	1.50	5.00	7.50	25.00	55.00	240	550
1906 ... *1,725*	96,022,255	1.50	5.00	7.50	25.00	55.00	240	550
1907 ... *1,475*	108,138,618	1.50	5.00	7.50	25.00	55.00	240	550
1908 ... *1,620*	32,327,987	1.50	5.00	7.50	25.00	57.50	245	550
1908-S	1,115,000	100	150	200	300	400	800	
1909 ... *2,175*	14,370,645	20.00	25.00	30.00	50.00	60.00	275	550
1909-S	309,000	600	650	900	1,200	1,500	1,750	

LINCOLN CENTS (1909–PRESENT)

Wheat-Ears Reverse (1909–1958)

Bronze Composition (1909–1942)

	Mintage	Good-4	Fine-12	EF-40	AU-55	MS-63	MS-65	Proof-65
1909 with initials V.D.B. on back . *420* ..	27,994,580	$10.00	$20.00	$25.00	$28.00	$30.00	$50.00	$12,900
1909-S V.D.B.	484,000	875	1,000	1,500	1,600	4,000	5,500	
1909 without initials *2,198*	72,700,420	5.00	6.00	10.00	15.00	22.50	48.00	800

	Mintage	Good-4	Fine-12	EF-40	AU-55	MS-63	MS-65	Proof-65
1909-S	1,825,000	100	125	300	325	500	950	
1910 .... *2,405*	146,798,813	.75	.90	4.00	10.00	45.00	100	700
1910-S	6,045,000	20.00	25.00	50.00	80.00	120	700	
1911 .... *1,733*	101,176,054	.75	3.00	10.00	15.00	32.50	600	700
1911-D	12,672,000	8.00	15.00	50.00	75.00	95.00	800	
1911-S	4,026,000	50.00	60.00	75.00	100	220	2,000	
1912 .... *2,145*	68,150,915	2.00	3.50	15.00	30.00	35.00	200	950
1912-D	10,411,000	10.00	12.00	75.00	100	150	1,200	
1912-S	4,431,000	20.00	25.00	75.00	100	150	1,800	
1913 .... *2,848*	76,529,504	.75	1.75	20.00	50.00	75.00	250	800
1913-D	15,804,000	3.00	5.00	50.00	65.00	150	900	
1913-S	6,101,000	8.50	15.00	22.50	45.00	210	900	
1914 .... *1,365*	75,237,067	1.00	1.20	8.00	12.50	75.00	100	1,000
1914-D	1,193,000	200	350	900	2,200	3,500	12,000	
1914-S	4,137,000	20.00	20.00	75.00	90.00	360	2,000	
1915 .... *1,150*	29,090,970	5.00	10.00	60.00	80.00	120	300	1,200
1915-D	22,050,000	1.00	5.00	15.00	25.00	110	300	
1915-S	4,833,000	7.00	20.00	50.00	75.00	500	850	
1916 .... *1,050*	131,832,627	1.00	3.00	4.00	8.00	27.50	100	2,500
1916-D	35,956,000	1.00	3.00	20.00	50.00	100	700	
1916-S	22,510,000	1.00	4.00	20.00	50.00	120	1,800	
1917	196,429,785	1.00	3.00	20.00	27.50	30.00	100	
1917-D	55,120,000	1.00	3.00	20.00	30.00	120	650	
1917-S	32,620,000	1.00	3.00	25.00	40.00	130	900	
1918	288,104,634	1.00	3.00	25.00	27.50	40.00	175	
1918-D	47,830,000	1.00	3.00	30.00	40.00	110	400	
1918-S	34,680,000	1.00	3.00	30.00	45.00	130	1,900	
1919	392,021,000	.85	2.00	20.00	22.50	45.00	50.00	
1919-D	57,154,000	1.00	3.00	30.00	50.00	85.00	450	
1919-S	139,760,000	.90	2.75	30.00	40.00	75.00	800	
1920	310,165,000	.75	2.75	30.00	20.00	40.00	40.00	
1920-D	49,280,000	1.00	2.75	30.00	40.00	90.00	350	
1920-S	46,220,000	1.00	2.75	30.00	40.00	110	1,650	
1921	39,157,000	1.00	2.75	35.00	40.00	75.00	100	
1921-S	15,274,000	1.25	2.75	35.00	150	250	900	
1922-D combined total .	7,160,000							
1922-D		10.00	20.00	50.00	100	175	400	
1922 Plain (strong reverse without D) ..		600	1,000	3,000	5,000	50,000	75,000	
1923	74,723,000	1.00	2.00	8.00	12.00	22.50	1,600	
1923-S	8,700,000	3.00	7.00	50.00	125	375	2,100	
1924	75,178,000	1.00	.75	10.00	25.00	45.00	100	
1924-D	2,520,000	40.00	50.00	100	125.00	375	1,250	
1924-S	11,696,000	2.00	5.00	30.00	75.00	190	1,500	
1925	139,949,000	.90	2.00	5.00	8.00	20.00	50.00	
1925-D	22,580,000	1.00	2.00	15.00	25.00	90.00	500	
1925-S	26,380,000	1.00	2.00	12.00	25.00	150	2,050	
1926	157,088,000	1.00	2.00	5.00	7.00	17.50	25.00	
1926-D	28,020,000	2.00	3.00	10.00	12.00	100	600	
1926-S	4,550,000	10.00	18.00	25.00	100	190	8,500	
1927	144,440,000	.90	2.50	6.00	10.00	17.50	50.00	
1927-D	27,170,000	1.00	2.00	5.00	10.00	70.00	350	
1927-S	14,276,000	3.00	5.00	10.00	25.00	130	1,400	
1928	134,116,000	1.00	2.00	5.00	10.00	17.50	100	
1928-D	31,170,000	1.00	2.00	5.00	10.00	52.50	200	
1928-S	17,266,000	1.00	5.00	12.00	25.00	110	500	
1929	185,262,000	.90	3.00	5.00	10.00	90.00	200	
1929-D	41,730,000	1.00	3.00	5.00	10.00	30.00	100	
1929-S	50,148,000	1.00	3.00	3.25	6.00	17.50	100	
1930	157,415,000	1.00	2.00	3.00	6.00	10.00	110	
1930-D	40,100,000	1.00	3.50	4.00	6.00	27.50	100	
1930-S	24,286,000	1.00	4.00	6.00	7.00	25.00	75.00	
1931	19,396,000	1.25	4.00	8.00	12.00	75.00	100	
1931-D	4,480,000	10.00	20.00	25.00	75.00	200	500	
1931-S	866,000	150	180	200	225	300	475	
1932	9,062,000	5.00	10.00	30.00	35.00	60.00	100	

	Mintage	Good-4	Fine-12	EF-40	AU-55	MS-63	MS-65	Proof-65
1932-D	10,500,000	2.00	5.00	30.00	30.00	50.00	150	
1933	14,360,000	2.00	5.00	30.00	30.00	50.00	150	
1933-D	6,200,000	6.00	7.00	30.00	30.00	50.00	175	

(NOTE: Mint State and Proof values are for Lincoln cents 1934 to present exhibiting full red color.)

	Mintage	Fine-12	EF-40	AU-55	MS-60	MS-63	MS-65	Proof-65
1934	219,080,000	$.15	$.50	$1.00	$2.50	$5.00	$25.00	
1934-D	28,446,000	.25	1.00	7.50	17.50	27.50	85.00	
1935	245,388,000	.15	.50	.85	1.50	2.50	20.00	
1935-D	47,000,000	.15	.50	1.25	2.50	5.00	30.00	
1935-S	38,702,000	.25	1.00	5.00	7.50	12.50	125	
1936 ...5,569	309,632,000	.10	.50	.85	1.50	3.00	25.00	$1,100
1936-D	40,620,000	.15	.50	1.00	1.75	3.25	25.00	
1936-S	29,130,000	.20	.60	1.25	2.00	3.50	27.00	
1937 ...9,320	309,170,000	.10	.40	.75	1.25	2.25	10.00	200
1937-D	50,430,000	.15	.45	.85	2.00	3.00	12.00	
1937-S	34,500,000	.15	.45	.85	1.75	3.25	9.50	
1938 ...14,734	156,682,000	.10	.30	.75	1.50	2.50	6.25	110
1938-D	20,010,000	.20	.50	1.00	2.25	3.50	8.50	
1938-S	15,180,000	.30	.60	1.10	2.40	3.75	30.00	
1939 ...13,520	316,466,000	.10	.25	.50	.75	1.25	6.00	100
1939-D	15,160,000	.45	.75	1.50	2.50	3.50	11.00	
1939-S	52,070,000	.15	.35	.75	1.25	1.75	15.00	
1940 ...15,872	586,810,000	.10	.20	.35	.70	1.10	8.00	100
1940-D	81,390,000	.10	.20	.40	.75	1.25	4.50	
1940-S	112,940,000	.10	.20	.50	.80	1.35	6.00	
1941 ...21,100	887,018,000	—	.15	.25	.65	1.00	3.50	100
1941-D	128,700,000	—	.15	.75	2.00	2.75	7.50	
1941-S	92,360,000	—	.15	.90	2.25	3.00	20.00	
1942 ...32,600	657,796,000	—	.10	.20	.50	.75	2.50	105
1942-D	206,698,000	—	.10	.25	.60	.90	3.50	
1942-S	85,590,000	—	.15	.90	3.50	5.25	50.00	

Zinc-Coated Steel Composition (1943)

	Mintage	Fine-12	EF-40	AU-55	MS-60	MS-63	MS-65	Proof-65
1943	684,628,670	$.10	$.25	$.50	$.75	$1.00	$3.50	
1943-D	217,660,000	.10	.25	.50	.85	1.50	10.00	
1943-S	191,550,000	.15	.45	.75	1.25	2.25	15.00	

Bronze* Composition (1943 Mint Error)

	Mintage	Fine-12	EF-40	AU-55	MS-60	MS-63	MS-65	Proof-65
1943	14	$42,000	$60,000	$100,000	$140,000	—	—	
1943-D	2	—	—	225,000	—	1,700,000	—	
1943-S	7	60,000	70,000	115,000	130,000	—	—	

*1943 Bronze ("copper" or brown in color) Lincoln cents are extremely rare, and these listed mintages are merely estimates that are subject to change. Zinc-coated steel ("white" or "silver" in color) cents that were copper plated outside the Mint are not valuable. 1943 cents that appear to be bronze but are attracted to a magnet are zinc-coated steel cents that carry the lower value. In order to command these values, the coin must be authenticated by a third-party grading and authentication service.

Brass Composition (1944–1946)

	Mintage	Fine-12	EF-40	AU-55	MS-60	MS-63	MS-65	Proof-65
1944	1,435,400,000	—	$.10	$.15	$.35	$.60	$1.25	
1944-D combined total	430,578,000							
1944-D regular mint mark		—	.10	.15	.40	.90	1.50	$1.50
1944-D/S Variety 1 (more obvious)		$75.00	150	375	500	800	5,000	

	Mintage	Fine-12	EF-40	AU-55	MS-60	MS-63	MS-65	Proof-65
1944-D/S Variety 2		60.00	120	300	400	600	3,000	
1944-S	282,760,000	—	.10	.15	.40	.80	1.50	
1945	1,040,515,000	—	.10	.15	.40	.80	1.50	
1945-D	266,268,000	—	.10	.15	.40	.80	1.50	
1945-S	181,770,000	—	.10	.15	.40	.80	1.50	
1946	991,655,000	—	.10	.15	.40	.80	1.50	
1946-D	315,690,000	—	.10	.15	.40	.80	1.50	
1946-S	198,100,000	—	.10	.15	.40	.80	1.50	

Bronze Composition (1947–1962)

	Mintage	Fine-12	EF-40	AU-55	MS-60	MS-63	MS-65	Proof-65
1947	190,555,000	—	$.10	$.15	$.40	$.80	$1.50	
1947-D	194,750,000	—	.10	.15	.40	.80	1.50	
1947-S	99,000,000	—	.10	.15	.40	.85	1.60	
1948	317,570,000	—	.10	.15	.40	.80	1.50	
1948-D	172,637,500	—	.10	.15	.40	.80	1.50	
1948-S	81,735,000	—	.10	.15	.40	.85	1.75	
1949	217,775,000	—	.10	.15	.40	.75	1.50	
1949-D	153,132,500	—	.10	.15	.40	.75	1.75	
1949-S	64,290,000	—	.15	.20	.75	1.25	4.00	
1950 ...51,386	272,635,000	—	.10	.15	.40	.85	1.25	$50.00
1950-D	334,950,000	—	.10	.15	.40	.75	1.10	
1950-S	118,505,000	—	.10	.15	.40	.80	1.20	
1951 ...57,500	284,576,000	—	.10	.15	.40	.90	1.50	40.00
1951-D	625,355,000	—	.10	.15	.25	.60	.90	
1951-S	136,010,000	—	.10	.15	.35	.75	1.75	
1952 ...81,980	186,775,080	—	.10	.15	.25	.60	.90	29.00
1952-D	746,130,000	—	.10	.15	.25	.60	.75	
1952-S	137,800,004	—	.10	.15	.35	1.00	2.25	
1953 ...128,800	256,755,000	—	.10	.15	.25	.60	.70	25.00
1953-D	700,515,000	—	.10	.15	.25	.60	.70	
1953-S	181,835,000	—	.10	.15	.25	.75	1.00	
1954 ...233,300	71,640,050	—	.15	.25	.35	.65	1.25	10.00
1954-D	251,552,500	—	.10	.15	.20	.30	.40	
1954-S	96,190,000	—	.15	.20	.25	.50	.75	
1955 combined total ...	330,580,000							
1955 regular date .378,200		—	.10	.15	.20	.25	.35	12.00
1955 with doubled-die obverse		1,300	2,000	2,500	4,000	12,000	40,000	
1955-D	563,257,500	—	.10	.15	.20	.25	.35	
1955-S	44,610,000	—	.20	.40	.60	.75	1.00	
1956 ...669,384	420,745,000	—	—	—	.15	.20	.30	2.50
1956-D	1,098,201,100	—	—	—	.15	.20	.30	
1957 ...1,247,952	282,540,000	—	—	—	.15	.20	.30	2.00
1957-D	1,051,342,000	—	—	—	.15	.20	.30	
1958 ...875,652	252,525,000	—	—	—	.15	.20	.30	2.25
1958-D	800,953,300	—	—	—	.15	.20	.30	

Lincoln Memorial Reverse
(1959–Present)

Bronze Composition (1959–1962)

	Mintage	EF-40	AU-55	MS-60	MS-63	MS-65	Proof-65
1959 ..... *1,149,291* ...	609,715,000	—	—	—	$.10	$.20	$1.50
1959-D	1,279,760,000	—	—	—	.10	.20	
1960 combined							
total	1,691,602	586,405,000					
1960 with large date		—	—	—	.10	.20	1.25
1960 with small date		$.75	$.90	$1.50	2.00	3.00	12.50
1960-D combined							
total	1,580,884,000						
1960-D with large date ...		—	—	—	.10	.20	
1960-D with small date ..		.10	.15	.20	.30	.40	.50
1961 ..... *3,028,244* ...	753,345,000	—	—	—	.10	.15	1.00
1961-D	1,753,266,700	—	—	—	.10	.15	
1962 ..... *3,218,019* ...	606,045,000	—	—	—	.10	.15	1.00
1962-D	1,793,148,400	—	—	—	.10	.15	

Brass Composition (1963–1982)

	Mintage	EF-40	AU-55	MS-60	MS-63	MS-65	Proof-65
1963 ..... *3,075,645* ...	754,110,000	—	—	—	—	$.10	$1.00
1963-D	1,774,020,400	—	—	—	—	.10	
1964 ..... *3,950,762* ...	2,648,575,000	—	—	—	—	.10	1.00
1964-D	3,799,071,500	—	—	—	—	.10	
1965	1,497,224,900	—	—	—	—	.15	
1966	2,188,147,783	—	—	—	—	.15	
1967	3,048,667,100	—	—	—	—	.15	
1968	1,707,880,970	—	—	—	—	.20	
1968-D	2,886,269,600	—	—	—	—	.10	
1968-S ..... *3,041,506* ...	258,270,001	—	—	—	—	.15	1.00
1969	1,136,910,000	—	—	—	—	.30	
1969-D	4,002,832,200	—	—	—	—	.10	
1969-S combined							
total. ... *2,934,631* ...	544,375,000	—	—	—	—	.15	1.00
1969-S with full doubled-							
die obverse		—	—	—	$17,000	—	
1970	1,898,315,000	—	—	—	—	.20	
1970-D	2,891,438,900	—	—	—	—	.10	
1970-S combined							
total ... *2,632,810* ...	690,560,004						
1970-S with small date ...	$17.50	$22.50	$32.50	50.00	90.00	150	
1970-S with large date ...		—	—	—	—	.15	1.00
1970-S with small date and a							
full doubled-die obverse					10,500	29,000	
1971	1,919,490,000	—	—	—	—	.20	
1971-D	2,911,045,600	—	—	—	—	.20	
1971-S ..... *3,220,733* ...	525,133,459	—	—	—	—	.15	1.00
1972 combined total	2,933,255,000						
1972 regular date		—	—	—	—	.10	
1972 with doubled-die							
obverse		175	190	275	325	680	
1972-D	2,665,071,400	—	—	—	—	.10	
1972-S ..... *3,260,996* ...	376,939,108	—	—	—	—	.15	1.00
1973	3,728,245,000	—	—	—	—	.10	
1973-D	3,549,576,588	—	—	—	—	.10	

	Mintage	EF-40	AU-55	MS-60	MS-63	MS-65	Proof-65
1973-S .... *2,760,339* ...	317,177,295	—	—	—	—	.15	1.00
1974	4,232,140,523	—	—	—	—	.10	
1974-D	4,235,098,000	—	—	—	—	.10	
1974-S .... *2,612,568* ...	409,426,660	—	—	—	—	.15	1.00
1975	5,451,476,142	—	—	—	—	.10	
1975-D	4,505,275,300	—	—	—	—	.10	
1975-S (proof only)	*2,845,450*	—	—	—	—	—	3.00
1976	4,674,292,426	—	—	—	—	.10	
1976-D	4,221,592,455	—	—	—	—	.10	
1976-S (proof only)	*4,149,730*	—	—	—	—	—	1.50
1977	4,469,930,000	—	—	—	—	.10	
1977-D	4,194,062,300	—	—	—	—	.10	
1977-S (proof only)	*3,251,152*	—	—	—	—	—	1.50
1978	5,558,605,000	—	—	—	—	.10	
1978-D	4,280,233,400	—	—	—	—	.10	
1978-S (proof only)	*3,127,781*	—	—	—	—	—	2.00
1979	6,018,515,000	—	—	—	—	.10	
1979-D	4,139,357,254	—	—	—	—	.10	
1979-S combined total							
(proof only)	*3,677,175*						
1979-S with clogged S ...		—	—	—	—	—	2.00
1979-S with clear S		—	—	—	—	—	6.00
1980	7,414,705,000	—	—	—	—	.10	
1980-D	5,140,098,660	—	—	—	—	.10	
1980-S (proof only)	*3,544,806*	—	—	—	—	—	1.25
1981	7,491,750,000	—	—	—	—	.10	
1981-D	5,373,235,677	—	—	—	—	.10	
1981-S (proof only)	*4,063,083*	—	—	—	—	—	1.25
1982 combined total							
....	10,712,525,000						
1982 with small date		—	—	—	—	.15	
1982 with large date		—	—	—	—	.10	
1982-D with large date ...		—	—	—	—	.10	
1982-S (proof only)	*3,857,479*	—	—	—	—	—	1.50

Copper-Plated Zinc Composition
(1982–Present)

	Mintage	EF-40	AU-55	MS-60	MS-63	MS-65	Proof-65
1982 mintage included							
in combined total							
1982 with small date ...		—	—	—	—	$.60	
1982 with large date ...		—	—	—	—	.40	
1983 combined total ...	7,752,355,000						
1983 with regular reverse		—	—	—	—	—	$.10
1983 with doubled-die reverse		$90.00	$105	$125	$225	300	
1983-D	6,467,199,428	—	—	—	—	.10	
1983-S (proof only)	*3,279,126*	—	—	—	—	—	3.00
1984 combined total ...	8,151,079,000						
1984 with regular obverse		—	—	—	—	—	.10
1984 with doubled-die							
obverse		50.00	60.00	100	150	200	
1984-D	5,569,238,906	—	—	—	—	.10	
1984-S (proof only)	*3,065,110*	—	—	—	—	—	4.00
1985	5,648,489,887	—	—	—	—	.10	
1985-D	5,287,399,926	—	—	—	—	.10	
1985-S (proof only)	*3,362,821*	—	—	—	—	—	2.75
1986	4,491,395,493	—	—	—	—	.10	
1986-D	4,442,866,698	—	—	—	—	.10	
1986-S (proof only)	*3,010,497*	—	—	—	—	—	7.00
1987	4,682,466,931	—	—	—	—	.10	
1987-D	4,879,389,514	—	—	—	—	.10	
1987-S (proof only)	*3,792,233*	—	—	—	—	—	2.75
1988	6,092,810,000	—	—	—	—	.10	
1988-D	5,253,740,443	—	—	—	—	.10	
1988-S (proof only)	*3,262,948*	—	—	—	—	—	4.00
1989	7,261,535,000	—	—	—	—	.10	

	Mintage	EF-40	AU-55	MS-60	MS-63	MS-65	Proof-65
1989-D	5,345,467,111	—	—	—	—	.10	
1989-S (proof only)	3,215,728	—	—	—	—	—	4.00
1990	6,851,765,000	—	—	—	—	.10	
1990-D	4,922,894,533	—	—	—	—	.10	
1990 without S mint mark							
(proof only)	3,555	—	—	—	—	—	7,850
1990-S (proof only)	3,296,004	—	—	—	—	—	6.00
1991	5,165,940,000	—	—	—	—	.10	
1991-D	4,158,442,076	—	—	—	—	.10	
1991-S (proof only)	2,867,787	—	—	—	—	—	6.75
1992	4,648,905,000	—	—	—	—	.10	
1992-D	4,448,673,300	—	—	—	—	.10	
1992-S (proof only)	4,176,544	—	—	—	—	—	5.00
1993	5,684,705,000						
1993-D	6,426,650,571						
1993-S (proof only)	3,360,876	—	—	—	—	—	5.00
1994	6,502,060,896	—	—	—	—	.10	
1994-D	7,132,975,896	—	—	—	—	.10	
1994-S (proof only)	3,212,792	—	—	—	—	—	5.75
1995 combined total	6,412,481,352	—	—	—	—	.10	
1995 with doubled-die							
obverse		—	5.00	10.00	25.00	50.00	
1995-D	7,129,601,352	—	—	—	—	.10	
1995-S (proof only)	2,796,345	—	—	—	—	—	5.75
1996	6,613,919,215	—	—	—	—	.10	
1996-D	6,512,249,215	—	—	—	—	.10	
1996-S (proof only)	2,925,305	—	—	—	—	—	5.75
1997	4,622,800,000	—	—	—	—	.10	
1997-D	4,576,555,000	—	—	—	—	.10	
1997-S (proof only)	2,788,020	—	—	—	—	—	5.75
1998	5,032,200,000	—	—	—	—	.10	
1998-D	5,225,200,000	—	—	—	—	.10	
1998-S (proof only)	2,965,503	—	—	—	—	—	5.75
1999	5,237,600,000	—	—	—	—	.10	
1999-D	6,360,065,000	—	—	—	—	.10	
1999-S (proof only)	2,454,319	—	—	—	—	—	5.75
2000	5,503,200,000	—	—	—	—	.10	
2000-D	8,774,220,000	—	—	—	—	.10	
2000-S (proof only)	3,186,300	—	—	—	—	—	5.75
2001	4,959,600,000	—	—	—	—	.10	
2001-D	5,374,990,000	—	—	—	—	.10	
2001-S (proof only)	2,293,200	—	—	—	—	—	5.75
2002	3,260,800,000	—	—	—	—	.10	
2002-D	4,028,055,000	—	—	—	—	.10	
2002-S (proof only)	3,210,674	—	—	—	—	—	5.75
2003	3,301,002,555	—	—	—	—	.10	
2003-D	3,549,002,555	—	—	—	—	.10	
2003-S (proof only)	3,362,834	—	—	—	—	—	5.75
2004	3,379,600,000	—	—	—	—	.10	
2004-D	3,456,400,000	—	—	—	—	.10	
2004-S (proof only)	2,992,069	—	—	—	—	—	5.75
2005	3,935,600,000	—	—	—	—	.10	
2005-D	3,764,450,500	—	—	—	—	.10	
2005-S (proof only)	3,273,000	—	—	—	—	—	5.75
2006 ....4,290,000,000—		—	—	—	.10		
2006-D ....3,944,000,000—		—	—	—	.10		
2006-S (proof only)	3,054,436	—	—	—	—	—	5.75
2007	3,762,400,000	—	—	—	—	.10	
2007-D	3,638,800,000	—	—	—	—	.10	
2007-S (proof only)	2,563,563	—	—	—	—	—	5.75
2008	2,569,600,000	—	—	—	—	.10	
2008-D	2,849,600,000	—	—	—	—	.10	
2008-S (proof only)	2,145,904	—	—	—	—	—	5.75
Birth and Childhood in Kentucky							
2009	284,400,000	—	—	—	—	.10	
2009-D	350,400,000	—	—	—	—	.10	
2009-S (proof only)	2,172,373	—	—	—	—	—	5.75

	Mintage	EF-40	AU-55	MS-60	MS-63	MS-65	Proof-65
Formative Years in Indiana							
2009	376,000,000	—	—	—	—	.10	
2009-D	363,600,000	—	—	—	—	.10	
2009-S (proof only)	2,172,373	—	—	—	—	—	5.75
Professional Life in Illinois							
2009	316,000,000	—	—	—	—	.10	
2009-D	336,000,000	—	—	—	—	.10	
2009-S (proof only)	2,172,373	—	—	—	—	—	5.75
Presidency							
2009	129,600,000	—	—	—	—	.10	
2009-D	198,000,000	—	—	—	—	.10	
2009-S (proof only)	2,172,373	—	—	—	—	—	5.75
2010	1,963,630,000	—	—	—	—	.10	
2010-D	2,047,200,000	—	—	—	—	.10	
2010-S (proof only)		—	—	—	—	—	5.75
2011	2,402,400,000	—	—	—	—	.10	
2011-D	2,536,140,000	—	—	—	—	.10	
2011-S (proof only)		—	—	—	—	—	5.75
2012		—	—	—	—	.10	
2012-D		—	—	—	—	.10	
2012-S (proof only)		—	—	—	—	—	5.75
2013		—	—	—	—	.10	
2013-D		—	—	—	—	.10	
2013-S (proof only)		—	—	—	—	—	5.75
2014		—	—	—	—	.10	
2014-D		—	—	—	—	.10	
2014-S (proof only)		—	—	—	—	—	5.75

TWO-CENT PIECES (1864–1873)

	Mintage	Fine-12	EF-40	AU-55	MS-60	MS-63	MS-65	Proof-65
1864 combined total	19,822,500							
1864 with small motto		$250	$600	$900	$800	$900	$2,800	$75,000
1864 with large motto *100*		25.00	40.00	75.00	90.00	140	600	2,000
1865 ... *500*	13,639,500	25.00	40.00	75.00	90.00	140	600	950
1866 ... *725*	3,176,275	25.00	40.00	75.00	90.00	140	650	1,000
1867 ... *625*	2,938,125	25.00	50.00	75.00	90.00	140	650	1,000
1868 ... *600*	2,803,150	30.00	75.00	90.00	125	175	750	1,000
1869 combined total	1,545,900							
1869 regular date *600*		40.00	45.00	150	190	225	700	1,000
1869/8 overdate	300	500	1,500	—	—	—		
1870 ... *1,000*	860,250	50.00	100	175	300	675	850	1,000
1871 ... *960*	720,290	70.00	150	200	420	600	1,000	1,000
1872 ... *950*	64,050	600	900	1,100	2,000	3,000	6,000	1,350
1873 closed 3 (proof only)	600	—	—	—	—	—	—	2,750
1873 open 3 (proof only)	500	—	—	—	—	—	—	4,500

SILVER THREE-CENT PIECES
(1851–1873)

	Mintage	Good-4	Fine-12	EF-40	AU-55	MS-63	MS-65	Proof-65
1851	5,447,400	$25.00	$50.00	$60.00	$200	$275	$1,350	
1851-O	720,000	28.00	60.00	175	400	450	3,250	
1852	18,663,500	25.00	60.00	90.00	200	275	1,350	
1853	11,400,000	25.00	60.00	90.00	200	275	1,350	
1854	671,000	30.00	60.00	150	300	575	4,000	$40,000
1855	139,000	35.00	60.00	250	350	1,250	10,500	18,000
1856	1,458,000	30.00	60.00	175	400	500	4,000	16,000
1857	1,042,000	30.00	60.00	175	400	600	4,000	13,000
1858	1,604,000	30.00	60.00	175	400	585	3,000	6,000
1859 . . . 800	364,200	30.00	60.00	175	400	600	1,000	2,400
1860 . . . 1,000	286,000	30.00	60.00	175	375	600	1,000	4,250
1861 . . . 1,000	497,000	30.00	60.00	175	375	600	1,000	2,100
1862 combined total . . .	343,000							
1862 regular								
date . 550		30.00	60.00	175	375	500	1,050	1,600
1862/1 overdate		40.00	70.00	175	400	550	1,050	
1863 combined								
total . 460	21,000							
1863 regular date		300	375	425	600	1,000	2,300	1,600
1863/2 overdate		400	500	1,000	2,000	2,200	2,500	4,800
1864 . . . 470	12,000	350	375	425	750	1,000	1,900	1,600
1865 . . . 500	8,000	300	500	550	750	1,100	2,000	1,600
1866 . . . 725	22,000	300	400	500	750	1,000	1,800	1,600
1867 . . . 625	4,000	350	500	600	750	1,050	2,600	1,600
1868 . . . 600	3,500	350	500	600	750	1,600	5,200	1,600
1869 combined								
total . 600	4,500							
1869 regular date		350	500	650	750	1,150	2,800	1,600
1869/8 overdate		—	—	—	—	—	—	5,000
1870 . . . 1,000	3,000	350	500	650	750	1,100	2,000	1,600
1871 . . . 960	3,400	350	500	650	750	1,100	1,800	1,600
1872 . . . 950	1,000	375	500	675	775	1,550	2,800	1,600
1873 closed 3								
(proof only) . . 600 . .		—	—	—	—	—	—	2,500

NICKEL THREE-CENT PIECES
(1865–1889)

	Mintage	Good-4	Fine-12	EF-40	AU-55	MS-63	MS-65	Proof-65
1865 . . . 500	11,381,500	$15.50	$17.50	$40.00	$50.00	$150	$900	$5,500
1866 . . . 725	4,800,275	15.50	17.50	40.00	50.00	150	700	1,550
1867 . . . 625	3,914,375	15.50	17.50	40.00	50.00	150	700	1,550
1868 . . . 600	3,251,400	15.50	17.50	40.00	50.00	150	700	1,550
1869 . . . 600	1,603,400	15.50	17.50	40.00	50.00	150	700	1,550
1870 . . . 1,000	1,334,000	16.00	18.25	45.00	60.00	150	700	1,550
1871 . . . 960	603,040	16.00	18.25	45.00	55.00	200	900	1,150
1872 . . . 950	861,050	16.00	18.25	45.00	55.00	175	900	1,000
1873 closed 3								
. . . . 1,100	388,900	16.00	18.00	45.00	55.00	180	950	1,050

	Mintage	Good-4	Fine-12	EF-40	AU-55	MS-63	MS-65	Proof-65
1873 open 3	783,000	16.00	18.00	45.00	55.00	180	950	1,050
1874 ... *700*	789,300	16.00	18.00	45.00	55.00	190	950	950
1875 ... *700*	227,300	20.00	25.00	45.00	55.00	200	950	1,550
1876 ... *1,150*	160,850	20.00	30.00	50.00	175	300	950	950
1877 (proof only)	*900*	1,000	1,050	1,100	1,175	1,200	—	2,500
1878 (proof only)	*2,350*	700	725	750	775	800	—	875
1879 ... *3,200*	38,000	60.00	90.00	100	125	375	900	600
1880 ... *3,955*	21,000	75.00	100	175	300	425	900	600
1881 ... *3,575*	1,077,000	15.50	20.00	40.00	40.00	150	700	550
1882 ... *3,100*	22,200	100	175	200	275	450	900	600
1883 ... *6,609*	4,000	220	260	340	400	650	4,400	750
1884 ... *3,942*	1,700	375	450	500	600	700	5,700	750
1885 ... *3,790*	1,000	425	600	675	725	750	5,000	750
1886 (proof only)	*4,290*	300	315	340	360	—	—	675
1887 combined								
total . *2,960*	5,001							
1887 regular date		250	400	425	500	750	900	675
1887/6 overdate (proof only)	—	—	—	—	—	—	—	775
1888 ... *4,582*	36,501	40.00	50.00	125	200	400	900	675
1889 ... *3,436*	18,125	85.00	150	200	225	350	700	675

HALF DIMES (1792)

	Mintage	Good-4	Fine-12	EF-40
1792	1,500	$60,000	$75,000	$110,000

HALF DIMES (1794–1873)
Flowing Hair Portrait (1794–1795)

	Mintage	Good-4	Fine-12	EF-40
1794	7,756	$1,200	$2,500	$8,000
1795	78,660	800	2,000	6,000

Draped Bust Portrait with Small Eagle on Reverse (1796–1797)

	Mintage	Good-4	Fine-12	EF-40
1796 combined total.......	10,230			
1796 regular date		$1,700	$3,500	$11,000
1796/5 overdate		2,000	3,500	11,000
1796 with LIBERTY spelled				
LIKERTY..............		1,700	3,500	12,000
1797 combined total.......	44,527			
1797 with 15 stars.........		925	1,750	8,000
1797 with 16 stars.........		925	1,750	8,000
1797 with 13 stars.........		1,800	2,700	10,500

Draped Bust Portrait with Heraldic Eagle on Reverse (1800–1805)

	Mintage	Good-4	Fine-12	EF-40
1800 LIBERTY	24,000	$1,000	$2,000	$7,000
1800 LIBEKTY	16,000	1,000	2,000	7,000
1801	27,760	1,000	2,200	8,000
1802	3,060	17,500	37,000	110,000
1803	37,850	1,000	2,000	7,000
1805	15,600	1,000	2,200	7,000

Capped Bust Portrait (1829–1837)

	Mintage	Good-4	Fine-12	EF-40	AU-55	MS-63
1829...................	1,230,000	$40.00	$75.00	$200	$250	$650
1830...................	1,240,000	40.00	75.00	200	250	650
1831...................	1,242,700	40.00	75.00	200	250	650
1832...................	965,000	40.00	75.00	200	275	675
1833...................	1,370,000	40.00	75.00	200	250	650
1834...................	1,480,000	40.00	75.00	200	250	650
1835...................	2,760,000	40.00	75.00	200	250	650
1836...................	1,900,000	40.00	75.00	200	500	650
1837 combined total	871,000					
1837 with small 5c......		50.00	85.00	250	600	2,250
1837 with large 5c		40.00	75.00	225	540	700

Seated Liberty Portrait (1837–1873)

Without Stars on Obverse (1837–1838)

	Mintage	Good-4	Fine-12	EF-40	AU-55	MS-63	MS-65
1837 combined total	1,405,000						
1837 with small date		$60.00	$75.00	$275	$800	$1,250	$3,700
1837 with large date		60.00	75.00	275	800	1,000	3,500
1838-O	70,000	100	275	900	1,200	8,000	30,000

With Stars on Obverse (1838–1859)

	Mintage	Good-4	Fine-12	EF-40	AU-55	MS-63	MS-65
1838 combined total	2,225,000						
1838 with regular stars ..		$20.00	$30.00	$90.00	$700	$700	$2,000
1838 with small stars		20.00	40.00	225	900	1,000	—
1839	1,069,150	20.00	30.00	90.00	300	700	2,000
1839-O	1,034,039	20.00	30.00	125	300	1,500	—
1840 without drapery from elbow	1,034,000	20.00	60.00	200	400	700	2,000
1840 with drapery from elbow	310,085	20.00	100.00	300	500	800	2,000

	Mintage	Good-4	Fine-12	EF-40	AU-55	MS-63	MS-65
1840-O without drapery from elbow	695,000	25.00	30.00	200	375	1,300	—
1840-O with drapery from elbow	240,000	45.00	175	550	1,900	4,000	—
1841	1,150,000	12.00	25.00	50.00	90.00	480	1,900
1841-O	815,000	15.00	25.00	90.00	300	1,500	4,000
1842	815,000	15.00	25.00	50.00	90.00	500	1,400
1842-O	350,000	25.00	30.00	500	1,000	1,100	17,500
1843	1,165,000	20.00	25.00	50.00	100	400	1,250
1844	430,000	20.00	25.00	50.00	100	400	1,250
1844-O	220,000	75.00	200	1,200	2,500	—	—
1845	1,564,000	20.00	25.00	50.00	80.00	400	1,250
1846	27,000	300	775	2,200	3,200	6,000	—
1847	1,274,000	20.00	25.00	50.00	125	400	1,250
1848 combined total	668,000						
1848 regular date		20.00	25.00	125	175	400	1,250
1848 with large date		20.00	50.00	125	200	1,300	—
1848-O	600,000	20.00	25.00	125	200	525	1,400
1849 combined total	1,309,000						
1849 with regular date ...		20.00	40.00	50.00	125	400	1,250
1849/6 overdate		20.00	25.00	200	300	700	—
1849/8 overdate		20.00	25.00	200	500	900	—
1850	955,000	20.00	25.00	50.00	150	400	1,250
1850-O	690,000	20.00	25.00	100	300	1,800	1,900
1851	781,000	20.00	25.00	50.00	125	400	1,250
1851-O	860,000	20.00	25.00	100	250	750	3,000
1852	1,000,500	20.00	25.00	50.00	150	400	1,250
1852-O	260,000	50.00	90.00	200	500	1,300	—
1853 without arrows	135,000	50.00	85.00	250	550	1,000	2,750
1853-O without arrows ..	160,000	250	400	1,650	3,000	9,000	35,000

With Arrows Beside the Date (1853–1855)

	Mintage	Good-4	Fine-12	EF-40	AU-55	MS-63	MS-65	Proof-65
1853	13,210,020	$15.00	$25.00	$50.00	$90.00	$500	$2,000	
1853-O	2,200,000	15.00	25.00	60.00	90.00	600	4,650	
1854	5,740,000	15.00	25.00	60.00	90.00	600	2,400	
1854-O	1,560,000	15.00	30.00	60.00	100	700	3,900	
1855	1,750,000	15.00	30.00	50.00	90.00	500	2,300	$20,000
1855-O	600,000	15.00	40.00	125	190	1,100	5,250	

Without Arrows Beside the Date (1856–1859)

	Mintage	Good-4	Fine-12	EF-40	AU-55	MS-63	MS-65	Proof-65
1856	4,880,000	$20.00	$25.00	$50.00	$200	$400	$1,500	
1856-O	1,100,000	20.00	25.00	100	250	1,000	2,000	
1857	7,280,000	20.00	25.00	50.00	150	300	1,500	$7,500
1857-O	1,380,000	20.00	25.00	60.00	200	600	1,400	
1858 combined total ...	3,500,000							
1858 regular date		20.00	25.00	50.00	150	400	1,500	5,000
1858 with inverted date underneath		50.00	75.00	200	300	800	1,800	
1858-O	1,660,000	20.00	25.00	125	200	800	2,200	
1859 combined total ...	340,000							
1859 with regular date .		20.00	25.00	125	150	600	1,900	4,500
1859-O	560,000	20.00	25.00	200	300	800	1,900	

With Motto on Obverse (1860–1873)

	Mintage	Good-4	Fine-12	EF-40	AU-55	MS-63	MS-65	Proof-65
1860 ... *1,000*	798,000	$18.00	$25.00	$35.00	$50.00	$300	$1,600	$2,500
1860-O	1,060,000	18.00	25.00	35.00	70.00	400	1,600	
1861 combined total ...	3,360,000							
1861 regular date								
..... *1,000*		18.00	25.00	35.00	60.00	300	1,400	2,000
1861/0 overdate		20.00	100	500	350	—	—	
1862 ... *550*	1,492,000	18.00	20.00	50.00	57.50	320	1,600	1,700
1863 ... *460*	18,460	225	400	485	750	1,150	1,800	1,800
1863-S	100,000	20.00	35.00	165	200	1,500	2,900	
1864 ... *470*	48,000	500	700	900	1,200	1,600	2,600	1,700
1864-S	90,000	75.00	160	600	750	900	3,500	
1865 ... *500*	13,000	350	500	925	1,000	1,500	3,500	1,900
1865-S	120,000	35.00	55.00	185	325	1,825	—	
1866 ... *725*	10,000	375	700	900	1,000	1,600	3,500	1,900
1866-S	120,000	30.00	75.00	200	300	1,300	5,000	
1867 ... *625*	8,000	500	900	1,000	1,275	1,400	—	1,800
1867-S	120,000	25.00	40.00	250	350	1,000	—	
1868 ... *600*	88,600	80.00	200	250	400	900	2,900	1,800
1868-S	280,000	20.00	25.00	30.00	50.00	90.00	900	—
1869 ... *600*	208,000	25.00	30.00	40.00	150	900	2,100	1,600
1869-S	230,000	25.00	35.00	50.00	75.00	90.00	500	—
1870 ... *1,000*	535,000	25.00	40.00	50.00	75.00	300	1,400	1,800
1870-S	1 known (graded MS-63)				1,250,000			
1871 ... *960*	1,873,000	25.00	40.00	50.00	60.00	300	1,400	1,700
1871-S	161,000	25.00	35.00	50.00	100	150	500	3,000
1872 ... *950*	2,947,000	25.00	35.00	45.00	60.00	300	1,800	1,700
1872-S combined total .	837,000							
1872-S with S inside the								
wreath		25.00	35.00	40.00	60.00	300	1,400	
1872-S with S below the								
wreath		25.00	35.00	40.00	60.00	300	1,400	
1873 ... *600*	712,000	25.00	35.00	40.00	60.00	300	1,875	1,650
1873-S	324,000	25.00	35.00	40.00	60.00	300	1,400	

NICKELS (1866–PRESENT)

Shield Portrait (1866–1883)

	Mintage	Good-4	Fine-12	EF-40	AU-55	MS-63	MS-65	Proof-65
1866 with rays between								
the stars *125*	14,742,375	$30.00	$45.00	$90.00	$125	$575	$2,500	$5,200
1867 with rays	2,018,975	40.00	50.00	115	225	275	5,600	90,000
1867 without rays . *625*	28,880,900	25.00	35.00	50.00	75.00	150	675	3,000
1868 ... *600*	28,816,400	25.00	35.00	50.00	75.00	150	675	1,500
1869 ... *600*	16,394,400	25.00	35.00	50.00	75.00	150	675	1,250
1870 ... *1,000*	4,805,000	35.00	40.00	50.00	75.00	150	2,000	1,550

	Mintage	Good-4	Fine-12	EF-40	AU-55	MS-63	MS-65	Proof-65
1871 ...*960*	560,040	75.00	135	250	275	300	2,000	1,250
1872 ...*950*	6,035,050	75.00	100	125	150	175	1,000	1,000
1873 with closed 3								
.....*1,100*	434,950	75.00	100	125	175	225	3,000	1,000
1873 with open 3	4,113,950	50.00	75.00	100	125	200	2,000	
1874 ...*700*	3,537,300	50.00	75.00	100	125	200	1,200	1,200
1875 ...*700*	2,086,300	50.00	75.00	100	125	200	3,000	1,800
1876 ...*1,150*	2,528,900	50.00	75.00	100	125	200	1,500	1,000
1877 (proof only)	*900*	—	—	—	—	—	—	2,750
1878 (proof only)	*2,350*	—	—	—	—	—	—	800
1879 ...*3,200*	25,900	350	400	500	600	650	2,000	675
1880 ...*3,955*	16,000	500	600	650	700	5,000	35,000	675
1881 ...*3,575*	68,800	500	750	900	1,000	1,100	1,500	675
1882 ...*3,100*	11,472,900	15.00	25.00	50.00	75.00	225	675	675
1883 combined total ...	1,456,919							
1883 regular date *.5,419*		15.00	20.00	35.00	75.00	180	675	675
1883/2 overdate		200	300	600	900	2,000	12,000	

Liberty Head Portrait (1883–1912)

	Mintage	Good-4	Fine-12	EF-40	AU-55	MS-63	MS-65	Proof-65
1883 without CENTS on reverse ...*5,219*	5,474,300	$5.00	$8.00	$10.00	$12.50	$40.00	$325	$600
1883 with CENTS *6,783*	16,026,200	12.00	30.00	50.00	62.50	80.00	575	500
1884 ...*3,942*	11,270,000	20.00	30.00	50.00	65.00	150	825	500
1885 ...*3,790*	1,472,700	500	800	975	1,200	2,000	10,000	600
1886 ...*4,290*	3,326,000	200	400	500	600	2,500	7,500	600
1887 ...*2,960*	15,260,692	15.00	40.00	50.00	75.00	175	575	500
1888 ...*4,582*	10,715,901	25.00	80.00	90.00	100	150	800	500
1889 ...*3,336*	15,878,025	10.00	25.00	50.00	100	175	575	500
1890 ...*2,740*	16,256,532	9.00	25.00	50.00	100	135	900	500
1891 ...*2,350*	16,832,000	9.00	25.00	50.00	100	125	800	500
1892 ...*2,745*	11,696,897	9.00	25.00	50.00	100	125	800	500
1893 ...*2,195*	13,368,000	9.00	25.00	50.00	100	100	800	500
1894 ...*2,632*	5,410,500	15.00	35.00	75.00	110	170	950	500
1895 ...*2,062*	9,977,822	9.00	25.00	40.00	57.50	100	975	500
1896 ...*1,862*	8,841,058	4.50	35.00	40.00	65.00	110	975	500
1897 ...*1,938*	20,426,797	2.50	10.00	40.00	75.00	90.00	975	500
1898 ...*1,795*	12,530,292	2.00	10.00	40.00	75.00	100	575	500
1899 ...*2,031*	26,027,000	1.25	10.00	40.00	75.00	100	575	500
1900 ...*2,262*	27,253,733	2.00	10.00	40.00	75.00	100	575	500
1901 ...*1,985*	26,478,228	2.00	10.00	40.00	75.00	100	575	500
1902 ...*2,018*	31,487,561	2.00	3.50	14.00	35.00	80.00	575	500
1903 ...*1,790*	28,004,935	2.00	3.50	14.00	35.00	80.00	575	500
1904 ...*1,817*	21,403,167	2.00	3.50	14.00	35.00	80.00	575	500
1905 ...*2,152*	29,825,124	2.00	3.50	14.00	35.00	80.00	575	500
1906 ...*1,725*	38,612,000	2.00	3.50	14.00	35.00	80.00	575	500
1907 ...*1,475*	39,213,325	2.00	3.50	14.00	35.00	80.00	575	500
1908 ...*1,620*	22,684,557	2.00	3.50	14.00	35.00	80.00	575	500
1909 ...*4,763*	11,585,763	2.00	4.00	16.00	40.00	100	600	500
1910 ...*2,405*	30,166,948	2.00	3.50	14.00	35.00	80.00	575	500
1911 ...*1,733*	39,557,639	2.00	3.50	14.00	35.00	80.00	575	500
1912 ...*2,145*	26,234,569	2.00	3.50	14.00	35.00	85.00	585	595
1912-D	8,474,000		3.00	15.00	37.50	75.00	170	600
1912-S	238,000	150	300	350	475	2,000	7,500	

	Mintage	Good-4	Fine-12	EF-40	AU-55	MS-63	MS-65	Proof-65
1913 (not an authorized Mint issue) .... 5 known	—	—	—	—	—	—		3,750,000*

*Proof-64

"Buffalo" Portrait (1913–1938)

Bison Standing on Mound (1913)

	Mintage	Good-4	Fine-12	EF-40	AU-55	MS-63	MS-65	Proof-65
1913 ... 1,520	30,992,000	$10.00	$20.00	$25.00	$30.00	$50.00	$175	$4,250
1913-D	5,337,000		18.00	20.00	50.00	65.00	90.00	300
1913-S	2,105,000		40.00	50.00	80.00	100.00	200.00	900

Bison Standing on Plain Line (1913–1938)

	Mintage	Good-4	Fine-12	EF-40	AU-55	MS-63	MS-65	Proof-65
1913 ... 1,514	29,857,186	$9.00	$10.00	$20.00	$25.00	$70.00	$300	$2,500
1913-D	4,156,000		100	200	280	300	700	1,600
1913-S	1,209,000		300	400	600	800	1,500	4,000
1914 ... 1,275	20,665,463	15.00	30.00	50.00	60.00	100	500	2,500
1914/3 overdate		175	400	1,000	2,000	8,000	25,000	
1914-D	3,912,000		100	200	350	425	725	2,000
1914-S	3,470,000		30.00	50.00	100	200	775	3,000
1915 ... 1,050	20,986,220	7.00	8.00	20.00	50.00	125	375	1,800
1915-D	7,569,000		30.00	50.00	105	200	1,100	3,250
1915-S	1,505,000		50.00	100	400	500	1,000	3,800
1916 ... 600	63,497,466	6.00	7.75	8.50	22.50	185.00	550	3,800
1916 with doubled obverse		3,000	9,000	22,000	44,000	170,000	350,000	
1916-D	13,333,000	20.00	30.00	100	125	900	3,250	
1916-S	11,860,000	12.00	25.00	80.00	175	975	3,000	
1917	51,424,019	8.00	10.00	20.00	50.00	200	600	
1917-D	9,910,000		25.00	75.00	130	300	1,100	4,000
1917-S	4,193,000		25.00	100	200	325	450	6,000
1918	32,086,314	8.00	10.00	12.50	75.00	250	1,800	
1918-D	8,362,000		30.00	75.00	250	375	1,800	5,000
1918/7-D overdate		1,400	1,850	13,750	27,500	86,000	385,000	
1918-S	4,882,000		14.50	52.50	140	400	1,840	38,000
1919	60,868,000	5.00	9.00	20.00	40.00	85.00	800	
1919-D	8,006,000		15.00	100	400	450	2,000	7,000
1919-S	7,521,000		9.00	50.00	250	475	2,000	23,500
1920	63,093,000	4.00	5.00	8.50	22.50	200	925	
1920-D	9,418,000		10.00	20.00	300	375	1,400	7,600
1920-S	9,689,000		5.00	12.00	200	400	2,000	42,000
1921	10,663,000	4.00	10.00	50.00	100	300	900	
1921-S	1,557,000		75.00	200	900	1,000	2,000	14,000
1923	35,715,000	2.00	3.00	10.00	40.00	100	600	
1923-S	6,142,000		8.00	25.00	250	500	1,000	12,000
1924	21,620,000	1.50	5.00	20.00	40.00	175	1,000	
1924-D	5,258,000		8.00	25.00	200	400	1,100	5,700
1924-S	1,437,000		10.00	100	1,200	2,000	3,800	14,000
1925	35,565,100	3.00	6.00	15.00	40.00	100	600	
1925-D	4,450,000		12.00	30.00	120	250	700	6,500
1925-S	6,256,000		5.00	20.00	190	300	2,000	68,000
1926	44,693,000	1.75	3.00	12.00	20.00	80.00	200	

	Mintage	Good-4	Fine-12	EF-40	AU-55	MS-63	MS-65	Proof-65
1926-D	5,638,000		10.00	15.00	175	300	600	6,000
1926-S	970,000	20.00	100	1,000	3,000	10,000	125,000	
1927	37,981,000	1.00	4.00	10.00	20.00	100	225	
1927-D	5,730,000		3.00	9.00	90.00	125	300	8,000
1927-S	3,430,000		1.75	4.00	90.00	200	2,000	25,000
1928	23,411,000	1.75	3.00	10.00	30.00	60.00	375	
1928-D	6,436,000		2.00	4.00	15.00	50.00	600	6,250
1928-S	6,936,000		2.00	6.00	13.50	30.00	600	9,000
1929	36,446,000	1.00	3.00	10.00	20.00	75.00	350	
1929-D	8,370,000		2.00	3.00	35.00	45.00	100	3,000
1929-S	7,754,000		1.50	3.00	14.00	30.00	80.00	500
1930	22,849,000	1.50	3.00	5.25	13.00	60.00	200	
1930-S	5,435,000		1.50	3.00	20.00	40.00	100	650
1931-S	1,200,000		15.00	20.00	30.00	50.00	100	300
1934	20,213,003	1.50	3.00	10.00	12.50	50.00	350	
1934-D	7,480,000		1.50	3.00	12.00	15.00	60.00	1,100
1935	58,264,000	1.50	3.00	10.00	20.00	50.00	100	
1935-D	12,092,000	1.50	4.00	12.00	100	200	900	
1935-S	10,300,000	1.50	4.00	10.00	25.00	100	200	
1936 . . . *4,420*	118,997,000	1.50	4.00	10.00	25.00	75.00	100	2,500
1936-D	24,814,000	1.50	4.00	10.00	25.00	50.00	100	
1936-S	14,930,000	1.50	4.00	10.00	11.00	50.00	100	
1937 . . . *5,769*	79,480,000	1.50	4.00	6.50	9.00	40.00	50.00	2,200
1937-D combined total .	17,826,000							
1937-D with normal reverse		1.50	2.00	3.25	8.00	22.50	50.00	
1937-D with 3-legged bison		600	1,000	1,275	1,500	5,000	30,000	
1937-S	5,635,000		1.50	5.00	10.00	20.00	50.00	60.00
1938-D combined total .	7,020,000							
1938-D with normal mint mark			1.50	3.00	5.00	7.50	17.50	60.00
1938-D/D		5.00	6.00	8.00	9.00	22.50	400	
1938-D/S			4.75	12.00	20.00	30.00	75.00	190

Jefferson Portrait (1938–Present)

	Mintage	Good-4	Fine-12	EF-40	AU-55	MS-63	MS-65	Proof-65
1938 . . . *19,365*	19,496,000	$.10	$.20	$.50	$.75	$1.50	$3.50	$35.00
1938-D	5,376,000	.50	.75	1.25	1.60	3.00	5.00	
1938-S	4,105,000	1.00	1.50	2.00	2.50	5.00	7.50	
1939 combined total . . .	120,615,000							
1939 with regular reverse *12,535*			.10	.20	.25	.50	1.00	30.00
1939 with double image on MONTICELLO and FIVE CENTS			5.00	9.00	35.00	50.00		
1939-D	3,514,000		2.00	3.00	3.75	7.50	25.00	50.00
1939-S	6,630,000		.25	.50	1.75	3.50	10.00	20.00
1940 . . . *14,158*	176,485,000	—	—	.10	.15	.75	1.25	30.00
1940-D	43,540,000	—	—	.20	.30	1.25	2.50	
1940-S	39,690,000	—	—	.15	.20	1.00	2.00	
1941 . . . *18,720*	203,265,000	—	—	.10	.15	.60	1.20	25.00
1941-D	53,432,000	—	—	.10	.20	1.00	2.00	
1941-S	43,445,000	—	—	.10	.20	1.10	2.25	
1942 . . . *29,600*	49,789,000	—	—	.10	.15	.60	1.20	20.00
1942-D	13,938,000	—	—	1.00	2.00	4.00	10.00	

Wartime Composition, Mint Mark Above Monticello (1942–1945)

	Mintage	Good-4	Fine-12	EF-40	AU-55	MS-63	MS-65	Proof-65
1942-P .. *27,600*	57,873,000	—	—	$2.00	$2.25	$3.00	$7.50	$90.00
1942-S	32,900,000	—	—	2.00	2.25	2.50	5.00	
1943-P combined total .	271,165,000							
1943-P regular date		—	—	2.00	2.25	2.50	4.00	
1943/2 overdate		—	—	90.00	150	350	1,000	
1943-D	15,294,000	—	—	2.00	2.25	2.50	4.50	
1943-S	104,060,000	—	—	2.00	2.25	2.50	4.00	
1944-P	119,150,000	—	—	2.00	2.25	2.50	4.00	
1944-D	32,309,000	—	—	2.00	2.25	2.50	4.00	
1944-S	21,640,000	—	—	2.00	2.25	2.50	4.50	
1945-P	119,150,000	—	—	2.00	2.25	2.50	4.00	
1945-D	37,158,000	—	—	2.00	2.25	2.50	4.00	
1945-S	58,939,000	—	—	2.00	2.25	2.50	4.00	

Regular Composition Returns (1946–Present)

	Mintage	Fine-12	EF-40	AU-55	MS-63	MS-65	Proof-65
1946	161,116,000	—	$.10	$.15	$.25	$.50	
1946-D	45,292,200	—	.15	.20	.35	.65	
1946-S	13,560,000	—	.20	.25	.40	.70	
1947	95,000,000	—	.10	.15	.25	.50	
1947-D	37,822,000	—	.15	.20	.35	.65	
1947-S	24,720,000	—	.15	.20	.35	.65	
1948	89,348,000	—	.10	.15	.25	.50	
1948-D	44,734,000	—	.15	.20	.35	1.00	
1948-S	11,300,000	—	.15	.20	.35	1.00	
1949	60,652,000	—	.10	.15	.25	.90	
1949-D combined total ..	36,498,000						
1949-D with regular mint mark		—	.15	.20	.30	.80	
1949-D/S		$17.50	60.00	75.00	200	350	
1949-S	9,716,000	.10	.20	.25	.45	1.00	
1950 ..... *51,386*	9,796,000	.10	.20	.25	.45	1.00	$40.00
1950-D	2,630,030	5.00	5.50	6.00	7.50	9.00	
1951 .... *57,500*	28,552,000	—	.10	.15	.25	.90	20.00
1951-D	20,460,000	—	.10	.15	.25	.90	
1951-S	7,776,000	.10	.15	.20	.35	1.25	
1952 .... *81,980*	63,988,000	—	.10	.15	.25	.50	19.00
1952-D	30,638,000	—	.15	.20	.35	1.00	
1952-S	20,572,000	—	.10	.15	.25	.60	
1953 ..... *128,800*	46,644,000	—	.10	.15	.25	.50	18.00
1953-D	59,878,600	—	.10	.15	.25	.50	
1953-S	19,210,900	—	.10	.15	.25	.60	
1954 .... *233,300*	47,684,050	—	.10	.15	.25	.50	10.00
1954-D	117,183,060	—	.10	.15	.25	.50	
1954-S combined total ...	29,384,000						
1954-S with regular mint mark			.10	.15	.25	.50	
1954-S/D		4.00	7.50	9.00	22.50	37.50	
1955 .... *378,200*	7,888,000	.10	.15	.20	.35	1.00	10.00
1955-D combined total ..	74,464,100						
1955-D with regular mint mark		—	.10	.15	.25	.50	
1955-D/S		5.00	10.00	15.00	35.00	60.00	
1956 ..... *669,384*	35,216,000	—	—	.10	.20	.30	6.00
1956-D	67,222,940	—	—	.10	.20	.30	
1957 ..... *1,247,952* ...	38,408,000	—	—	.10	.20	.30	4.00
1957-D	136,828,900	—	—	.10	.20	.30	
1958 ..... *875,652*	17,088,000	—	—	.15	.30	.40	5.00
1958-D	168,249,120	—	—	.10	.20	.30	
1959 ..... *1,149,291* ...	27,248,000	—	—	.10	.25	.35	4.00
1959-D	160,738,240	—	—	.10	.20	.30	
1960 ..... *1,691,602* ...	55,416,000	—	—	—	.10	.15	3.00
1960-D	192,582,180	—	—	—	.10	.15	

	Mintage	Fine-12	EF-40	AU-55	MS-63	MS-65	Proof-65
1961 . . . . . *3,028,144* . . .	73,640,100	—	—	—	.10	.15	2.50
1961-D	229,342,760	—	—	—	.10	.15	
1962 . . . . . *3,218,019* . . .	97,384,000	—	—	—	.10	.15	2.50
1962-D	280,195,720	—	—	—	.10	.15	
1963 . . . . . *3,075,645* . . .	175,776,000	—	—	—	.10	.15	2.50
1963-D	276,829,460	—	—	—	.10	.15	
1964 . . . . . *3,950,762* . . .	1,024,672,000	—	—	—	.10	.15	2.25
1964-D	1,787,297,160	—	—	—	.10	.15	
1965	136,131,380	—	—	—	.10	.15	
1966	156,208,283	—	—	—	.10	.15	
1967	107,325,800	—	—	—	.10	.15	
1968-D	91,227,880	—	—	—	.10	.15	
1968-S . . . . *3,041,506* . . .	100,396,004	—	—	—	.10	.15	1.00
1969-D	202,807,500	—	—	—	.10	.15	
1969-S . . . . *2,934,631* . . .	120,075,000	—	—	—	.10	.15	1.00
1970-D	515,485,380	—	—	—	.10	.15	
1970-S . . . . *2,632,810* . . .	238,832,004	—	—	—	.10	.15	1.60
1971	106,884,000	—	—	—	.25	.50	
1971-D	316,144,800	—	—	—	.10	.15	
1971-S combined total							
(proof only)	*3,220,733*						
1971-S with S		—	—	—	—	—	1.00
1971-S proof with no							
mint mark		—	—	—	—	—	700
1972	202,036,000	—	—	—	.10	.15	
1972-D	351,694,600	—	—	—	.10	.15	
1972-S (proof only)	*3,260,996*	—	—	—	—	—	1.10
1973	384,396,000	—	—	—	.10	.15	
1973-D	261,405,000	—	—	—	.10	.15	
1973-S (proof only)	*2,760,339*	—	—	—	—	—	1.20
1974	601,752,000	—	—	—	.10	.15	
1974-D	277,373,000	—	—	—	.15	.20	
1974-S (proof only)	*2,612,568*	—	—	—	—	—	1.35
1975	181,772,000	—	—	—	—	.10	
1975-D	401,875,300	—	—	—	—	.10	
1975-S (proof only)	*2,845,450*	—	—	—	—	—	1.60
1976	367,124,000	—	—	—	—	.10	
1976-D	563,964,147	—	—	—	—	.10	
1976-S (proof only)	*4,149,730*	—	—	—	—	—	1.40
1977	585,376,000	—	—	—	—	.10	
1977-D	297,313,422	—	—	—	—	.15	
1977-S (proof only)	*3,251,152*	—	—	—	—	—	1.50
1978	391,308,000	—	—	—	—	.10	
1978-D	313,092,780	—	—	—	—	.10	
1978-S (proof only)	*3,127,781*	—	—	—	—	—	1.60
1979	463,188,000	—	—	—	—	.10	
1979-D	325,867,672	—	—	—	—	.10	
1979-S combined total							
(proof only)	*3,677,175*						
1979-S with clear S		—	—	—	—	—	12.00
1979-S with clogged S . . .		—	—	—	—	1.50	
1980-P	593,004,000	—	—	—	—	.10	
1980-D	502,323,448	—	—	—	—	.10	
1980-S (proof only)	*3,554,806*	—	—	—	—	—	1.60
1981-P	657,504,000	—	—	—	—	.10	
1981-D	364,801,843	—	—	—	—	.10	
1981-S (proof only)	*4,063,083*	—	—	—	—	—	1.40
1982-P	292,355,000	—	—	—	—	.10	
1982-D	373,726,544	—	—	—	—	.10	
1982-S (proof only)	*3,857,479*	—	—	—	—	—	1.50
1983-P	561,615,000	—	—	—	—	.10	
1983-D	536,726,276	—	—	—	—	.10	
1983-S (proof only)	*3,279,126*	—	—	—	—	—	1.60
1984-P	746,769,000	—	—	—	—	.10	
1984-D	517,675,146	—	—	—	—	.10	
1984-S (proof only)	*3,065,110*	—	—	—	—	—	2.50
1985-P	647,114,962	—	—	—	—	.10	

	Mintage	Fine-12	EF-40	AU-55	MS-63	MS-65	Proof-65
1985-D	459,747,446	—	—	—	.10		
1985-S (proof only)	*3,362,821*	—	—	—	—		1.60
1986-P	536,883,483	—	—	—	.10		
1986-D	361,819,140	—	—	—	.10		
1986-S (proof only)	*3,010,497*	—	—	—	—		4.50
1987-P	371,499,481	—	—	—	.10		
1987-D	410,590,604	—	—	—	.10		
1987-S (proof only)	*3,792,233*	—	—	—	—		1.50
1988-P	771,360,000	—	—	—	.10		
1988-D	663,771,652	—	—	—	.10		
1988-S (proof only)	*3,262,948*	—	—	—	—		2.50
1989-P	898,812,000	—	—	—	.10		
1989-D	570,842,474	—	—	—	.10		
1989-S (proof only)	*3,215,728*	—	—	—	—		2.00
1990-P	661,636,000	—	—	—	.10		
1990-D	663,938,503	—	—	—	.10		
1990-S (proof only)	*3,299,559*	—	—	—	—		3.50
1991-P	614,104,000	—	—	—	.10		
1991-D	436,496,678	—	—	—	.10		
1991-S (proof only)	*2,867,787*	—	—	—	—		2.50
1992-P	399,552,000	—	—	—	.10		
1992-D	450,565,113	—	—	—	.10		
1992-S (proof only)	*4,176,544*	—	—	—	—		2.00
1993-P	412,076,000	—	—	—	.10		
1993-D	406,084,135	—	—	—	.10		
1993-S (proof only)	*3,360,876*	—	—	—	—		2.00
1994-P	723,370,896	—	—	—	.10		
1994-D	716,973,006	—	—	—	.10		
1994-S (proof only)	*3,212,792*	—	—	—	—		2.00
1994-P matte finish	167,703	—	—	—		50.00	
1995-P	775,197,352	—	—	—	.10		
1995-D	889,153,352	—	—	—	.10		
1995-S (proof only)	*2,796,345*	—	—	—	—		2.00
1996-P	830,785,215	—	—	—	.10		
1996-D	819,190,215	—	—	—	.10		
1996-S (proof only)	*2,925,305*	—	—	—	—		2.00
1997-P	470,972,000	—	—	—	.10		
1997-D	468,840,000	—	—	—	.10		
1997-S (proof only)	*2,788,020*	—	—	—	—		2.00
1997-P matte finish	25,000	—	—	—		225	
1998-P	688,292,000	—	—	—	.10		
1998-D	635,380,000	—	—	—	.10		
1998-S (proof only)	*2,965,503*	—	—	—	—		2.00
1999-P	1,212,000,000	—	—	—	.10		
1999-D	1,066,720,000	—	—	—	.10		
1999-S (proof only)	*2,454,319*	—	—	—	—		2.00
2000-P	846,240,000	—	—	—	.10		
2000-D	1,509,520,000	—	—	—	.10		
2000-S (proof only)	*3,934,000*	—	—	—	—		2.00
2001-P	675,704,000	—	—	—	.10		
2001-D	627,680,000	—	—	—	.10		
2001-S (proof only)	*3,186,300*	—	—	—	—		2.00
2002-P	539,280,000	—	—	—	.10		
2002-D	691,200,000	—	—	—	.10		
2002-S (proof only)	*3,210,674*	—	—	—	—		2.00
2003-P	442,842,555	—	—	—	.10		
2003-D	384,042,555	—	—	—	.10		
2003-S (proof only)	*3,362,834*	—	—	—	—		2.00
2004-P Clasped hands ...	361,440,000	—	—	—	.10		
2004-P Boat	366,720,000	—	—	—	.10		
2004-D Clasped hands ...	372,010,000	—	—	—	.10		
2004-D Boat	344,880,000	—	—	—	.10		
2004-S (proof only)							
Clasped hands	*2,992,069*	—	—	—	—		2.00
2004-S (proof only) Boat .	*2,992,069*	—	—	—	—		2.00
2005-P Bison	448,320,000	—	—	—	.10		
2005-P Ocean View	394,080,000	—	—	—	.10		

	Mintage	Fine-12	EF-40	AU-55	MS-63	MS-65	Proof-65
2005-D Bison	487,680,000		—	—	—	.10	
2005-D Ocean View	411,120,000		—	—	—	.10	
2005-S (proof only)							
Bison	*3,273,000*		—	—	—	—	2.00
2005-S (proof only)							
Ocean View	*3,273,000*		—	—	—	—	2.00
2006-P	693,120,000		—	—	—	.10	
2006-D	809,280,000		—	—	—	.10	
2006-S (proof only)	*3,054,436*		—	—	—	—	2.00
2007-P	571,680,000		—	—	—	.10	
2007-D	626,160,000		—	—	—	.10	
2007-S (proof only)	*2,563,563*		—	—	—	—	2.00
2008-P	287,760,000		—	—	—	.10	
2008-D	352,800,000		—	—	—	.10	
2008-S (proof only)	*2,145,904*		—	—	—	—	2.00
2009-P	39,840,000		—	—	—	.10	
2009-D	46,800,000		—	—	—	.10	
2009-S (proof only)	*2,172,373*		—	—	—	—	2.00
2010-P	260,640,000		—	—	—	.10	
2010-D	229,920,000		—	—	—	.10	
2010-S (proof only)			—	—	—	—	2.00
2011-P	450,000,000		—	—	—	.10	
2011-D	540,240,000		—	—	—	.10	
2011-S (proof only)			—	—	—	—	2.00
2012-P			—	—	—	.10	
2012-D			—	—	—	.10	
2012-S (proof only)			—	—	—	—	2.00
2013-P			—	—	—	.10	
2013-D			—	—	—	.10	
2013-S (proof only)			—	—	—	—	2.00
2014-P			—	—	—	.10	
2014-D			—	—	—	.10	
2014-S (proof only)			—	—	—	—	2.00

DIMES (1796–PRESENT)

Draped Bust Portrait with Small Eagle on Reverse (1796–1797)

	Mintage	Good-4	Fine-12	EF-40
1796	22,135	$3,000	$5,500	$12,000
1797 combined total.	25,261			
1797 with 16 stars.		3,400	6,000	13,500
1797 with 13 stars.		3,400	6,000	13,500

Draped Bust Portrait with Heraldic Eagle on Reverse (1798–1807)

	Mintage	Good-4	Fine-12	EF-40
1798 combined total......	27,550			
1798 regular date		$600	$1,300	$2,400
1798/7 overdate with 16 stars on reverse		700	1,200	2,700
1798/7 overdate with 13 stars on reverse		1,900	3,750	9,000
1798 with small 8	500	800	1,600	
1800	21,760	500	1,100	2,600
1801	34,640	600	1,300	5,000
1802	10,975	900	1,600	6,000
1803	33,040	600	1,150	4,000
1804	8,265	1,900	4,100	20,000
1805	120,780	370	1,200	2,900
1807	165,000	500	1,200	3,000

Capped Bust Portrait (1809–1837)

	Mintage	Good-4	Fine-12	EF-40	AU-55	MS-63
1809.................	51,065	$130	$350	$1,100	$2,100	$6,000
1811/09 overdate.......	65,180	85.00	300	1,000	1,750	6,000
1814 combined total	421,500					
1814 small date		30.00	90.00	600	1,100	5,000
1814 large date.........		25.00	40.00	500	675	2,500
1814 STATESOFAMERICA		25.00	40.00	600	725	5,000
1820 combined total	942,587					
1820 small 0		25.00	40.00	280	650	2,200
1820 large 0		25.00	45.00	270	650	2,200
1820 STATESOFAMERICA		25.00	40.00	550	875	4,500
1821 combined total	1,186,512					
1821 small date		25.00	100	300	700	3,000
1821 large date.........		25.00	32.00	275	675	2,500
1822.................	100,000	300	725	2,000	4,250	20,000
1823/2 overdate........	440,000	25.00	30.00	260	700	3,000
1824/2 overdate........	100,000	25.00	45.00	700	950	4,200
1825.................	410,000	25.00	30.00	260	625	3,000
1827.................	1,215,000	25.00	30.00	260	625	2,600
1828 combined total	125,000					
1828 large date.........		24.00	60.00	700	1,100	
1828 small date		24.00	70.00	500	800	2,800
1829 combined total	770,000					
1829 with curl-base 2 ...		3,500	9,000			
1829 small 10c		30.00	40.00	325	500	2,200
1829 large 10c		30.00	80.00	350	750	3,000
1830 combined total	510,000					
1830 regular date.......		20.00	30.00	150	410	1,500

	Mintage	Good-4	Fine-12	EF-40	AU-55	MS-63
1830/29 overdate.......		35.00	90.00	350	750	4,000
1831.................	771,350	20.00	30.00	300	400	2,000
1832.................	522,500	20.00	30.00	300	400	2,000
1833.................	485,000	20.00	30.00	300	400	2,000
1834.................	635,000	20.00	30.00	150	400	2,000
1835.................	1,410,000	20.00	30.00	300	400	2,000
1836.................	1,190,000	20.00	30.00	300	400	2,000
1837.................	359,500	20.00	30.00	300	400	2,000

Seated Liberty Portrait (1837–1891)

Without Stars on Obverse (1837–1838)

	Mintage	Good-4	Fine-12	EF-40	AU-55	MS-63	MS-65
1837	682,500	$24.00	$52.50	$425	$675	$2,000	$5,500
1838-O	406,034	90.00	175	950	1,500	6,000	20,000

With Stars on Obverse (1838–1859)

	Mintage	Good-4	Fine-12	EF-40	AU-55	MS-63	MS-65
1838 combined total	1,992,500						
1838 with regular stars ..		$15.00	$20.00	$65.00	$130	$925	$3,250
1838 with small stars		20.00	42.50	150	225	2,500	6,000
1838 with partial drapery from elbow		27.50	65.00	190	385	3,850	4,000
1839	1,053,115	15.00	20.00	65.00	130	925	2,200
1839-O	1,323,000	20.00	35.00	75.00	300	1,500	4,500
1840	981,500	20.00	35.00	72.50	150	1,000	2,000
1840-O	1,175,000	25.00	35.00	100	350	3,750	5,500

Drapery Added from Liberty's Elbow (1840–1891)

	Mintage	Good-4	Fine-12	EF-40	AU-55	MS-63	MS-65
1840	377,500	$30.00	$75.00	$350	$1,100	—	—
1841	1,622,500	10.00	20.00	60.00	150	$675	$2,800
1841-O	2,007,500	10.00	22.00	100	175	2,000	4,000
1842	1,887,500	10.00	20.00	55.00	150	675	2,500
1842-O	2,020,000	15.00	27.50	125.00	250	6,200	—
1843	1,370,000	10.00	20.00	60.00	150	675	2,800
1843-O	150,000	50.00	150	750	1,250	—	—
1844	72,500	50.00	125	1,100	2,000	—	—
1845	1,755,000	10.00	20.00	55.00	150	675	2,800
1845-O	230,000	25.00	75.00	750	1,250	—	—
1846	31,300	80.00	175	900	1,500	—	—
1847	245,000	25.00	40.00	110	275	2,500	5,000
1848	451,500	20.00	40.00	52.50	175	1,700	7,000
1849	839,000	15.00	30.00	37.50	95.00	1,900	4,500
1849-O	300,000	17.50	27.50	275	1,100	6,500	—
1850	1,931,500	15.00	25.00	42.50	150	900	4,000
1850-O	510,000	15.00	35.00	110	175	2,800	5,000
1851	1,026,500	15.00	25.00	32.50	100	1,050	2,850
1851-O	400,000	25.00	50.00	120	200	3,500	—
1852	1,535,500	15.00	20.00	32.50	90.00	900	2,850
1852-O	430,000	20.00	45.00	200	325	3,000	—
1853 without arrows	95,000	45.00	150	275	375	1,600	4,000

With Arrows Beside the Date (1853–1855)

	Mintage	Good-4	Fine-12	EF-40	AU-55	MS-63	MS-65	Proof-65
1853	12,078,010	$7.50	$15.00	$36.00	$110	$1,000	$3,200	
1853-O	1,100,000	12.00	15.00	92.50	350	1,700	7,500	
1854	4,470,000	7.50	15.00	36.00	110	1,000	2,500	$36,000
1854-O	1,770,000	9.00	15.00	38.00	120	1,300	3,000	
1855	2,075,000	7.50	15.00	36.00	110	1,300	3,500	35,000

Arrows Removed (1856–1859)

	Mintage	Good-4	Fine-12	EF-40	AU-55	MS-63	MS-65	Proof-65
1856	5,780,000	$15.00	$20.00	$27.50	$75.00	$675	$2,000	$10,000
1856-O	1,100,000	15.00	20.00	30.00	85.00	1,900	6,000	
1856-S	70,000	65.00	200	350	2,000	10,000	—	
1857	5,580,000	15.00	20.00	24.00	70.00	900	2,850	5,600
1857-O	1,540,000	15.00	20.00	28.00	80.00	1,000	3,150	
1858	1,540,000	15.00	20.00	24.00	70.00	900	2,850	4,000
1858-O	290,000	25.00	50.00	75.00	250	1,600	6,500	
1858-S	60,000	80.00	200	300	500	—	—	
1859 800	429,200	15.00	20.00	28.00	80.00	900	3,000	4,000
1859-O	480,000	20.00	25.00	30.00	85.00	900	3,100	

With Motto on Obverse (1860–1873)

	Mintage	Good-4	Fine-12	EF-40	AU-55	MS-63	MS-65	Proof-65
1860 1,000	608,000	$6.00	$12.00	$25.00	$80.00	$200	$1,600	$1,700
1860-O	40,000	400	900	2,500	8,000	—	—	
1861 1,000	1,883,000	6.00	12.00	25.00	80.00	200	1,400	1,700
1861-S	172,500	25.00	40.00	200	400	5,000	14,000	
1862 550	847,000	6.00	12.00	25.00	80.00	200	1,400	1,700
1862-S	180,750	25.00	45.00	135	900	3,600	9,500	
1863 460	14,000	75.00	240	375	1,300	2,100	5,200	1,700
1863-S	157,500	25.00	75.00	185	900	3,000	9,000	
1864 470	11,000	75.00	240	375	650	1,650	3,650	1,700
1864-S	230,000	25.00	75.00	185	900	2,000	8,000	
1865 500	10,000	75.00	240	375	650	1,900	4,700	1,700
1865-S	175,000	22.50	65.00	160	800	6,000	7,800	
1866 725	8,000	140	425	675	1,000	2,000	6,000	1,700
1866-S	135,000	20.00	70.00	175	600	3,000	5,000	
1867 625	6,000	140	425	675	2,000	3,300	9,000	1,700
1867-S	140,000	15.00	65.00	150	600	4,700	4,000	
1868 600	464,000	12.00	24.00	40.00	90.00	1,100	4,700	1,700
1868-S	260,000	12.00	70.00	150	250	1,200	3,500	
1869 600	256,000	12.00	24.00	60.00	150	1,200	3,000	1,700
1869-S	450,000	12.00	42.50	95.00	210	775	3,800	
1870 1,000	470,500	12.00	20.00	38.00	110	300	1,800	1,700
1870-S	50,000	150	220	450	1,200	3,000	4,200	
1871 960	906,750	6.00	8.00	27.50	110	600	1,300	1,700
1871-CC	20,100	1,500	2,700	8,250	—	—	—	
1871-S	320,000	14.00	30.00	130	350	500	1,600	
1872 950	2,395,500	12.00	20.00	30.00	150	800	4,250	1,700
1872-CC	35,480	250	900	6,000	—	—	—	
1872-S	190,000	30.00	90.00	240	650	2,700	4,000	
1873 closed 3 ..1,100	1,506,900	12.00	20.00	45.00	90.00	500	1,400	1,700
1873 open 3	60,000	25.00	50.00	185	650	1,500	3,800	
1873-CC	(unique)	—	—	—	—	—	550,000	

With Arrows Beside the Date (1873–1874)

	Mintage	Good-4	Fine-12	EF-40	AU-55	MS-63	MS-65	Proof-65
1873 800	2,377,700	$12.00	$50.00	$110	$250	$1,000	$4,000	$5,000
1873-CC	18,791	1,100	3,700	10,000	17,000	—	—	
1873-S	455,000	20.00	75.00	150	350	2,700	5,000	
1874 700	2,940,000	12.00	50.00	110	250	1,100	4,000	5,000
1874-CC	10,817	2,600	6,700	21,000	32,500	—	—	
1874-S	240,000	20.00	95.00	250	450	2,700	8,200	

Arrows Removed (1875–1891)

	Mintage	Good-4	Fine-12	EF-40	AU-55	MS-63	MS-65	Proof-65
1875 . . . . . *700*	10,350,000	$12.00	$15.00	$25.00	$100	$175	$1,200	$1,500
1875-CC combined total	4,645,000							
1875-CC with CC below								
wreath		12.00	15.00	75.00	100	175	2,600	
1875-CC with CC inside								
wreath		12.00	15.00	75.00	100	175	2,600	
1875-S combined total .	9,070,000							
1875-S with S below								
wreath		12.00	20.00	50.00	80.00	350	1,200	
1875-S with S inside								
wreath		12.00	20.00	50.00	80.00	350	1,200	
1876 . . . . . *1,150*	11,460,000	12.00	25.00	50.00	75.00	300	1,200	1,500
1876-CC	8,270,000	12.00	25.00	50.00	75.00	175	1,650	
1876-S	10,420,000	12.00	25.00	50.00	75.00	175	1,200	
1877 . . . . . *510*	7,310,000	12.00	25.00	50.00	75.00	175	1,200	1,500
1877-CC	7,700,000	12.00	30.00	55.00	100	175	1,650	
1877-S	2,340,000	12.00	25.00	50.00	75.00	175	1,200	
1878 . . . . . *800*	1,678,000	12.00	25.00	50.00	75.00	250	2,000	1,500
1878-CC	200,000	40.00	130	250	400	1,100	2,500	
1879 . . . . . *1,100*	14,000	140	325	475	800	1,250	2,000	
1880 . . . . . *1,355*	36,000	75.00	140	340	650	1,100	1,800	1,500
1881 . . . . . *975*	24,000	90.00	275	425	800	1,100	2,000	1,500
1882 . . . . . *1,100*	3,910,000	12.00	25.00	50.00	75.00	300	1,200	1,500
1883 . . . . . *1,039*	7,674,673	12.00	25.00	50.00	75.00	300	1,200	1,500
1884 . . . . . *875*	3,365,505	12.00	25.00	50.00	75.00	300	1,200	1,500
1884-S	564,969	12.50	25.00	70.00	110	1250	1,800	
1885 . . . . . *930*	2,532,497	12.00	25.00	50.00	75.00	300	1,200	1,500
1885-S	43,690	250	500	700	1,250	8,000	25,000	
1886 . . . . . *886*	6,376,684	12.00	25.00	50.00	75.00	300	1,200	1,500
1886-S	206,524	25.00	45.00	92.50	110	900	3,000	
1887 . . . . . *710*	11,283,229	12.00	25.00	50.00	75.00	300	1,200	1,500
1887-S	4,454,450	12.00	25.00	50.00	75.00	300	1,200	
1888 . . . . . *832*	5,495,655	12.00	25.00	50.00	75.00	300	1,200	1,500
1888-S	1,720,000	12.00	25.00	50.00	75.00	750	3,000	
1889 . . . . . *711*	7,380,000	12.00	25.00	50.00	75.00	375	1,200	1,500
1889-S	972,678	12.00	25.00	92.50	110	1,000	4,000	
1890 . . . . . *590*	9,910,951	12.00	25.00	75.00	200	300	1,200	1,500
1890-S	1,423,076	12.00	25.00	100	475	850	2,600	
1891 . . . . . *600*	15,310,000	12.00	25.00	75.00	150	450	1,200	1,500
1891-O	4,540,000	12.00	25.00	85.00	200	350	1,275	
1891-S	3,196,116	12.00	25.00	75.00	100	310	1,225	

Barber, or Liberty Head Portrait (1892–1916)

	Mintage	Good-4	Fine-12	EF-40	AU-55	MS-63	MS-65	Proof-65
1892 . . . . *1,245*	12,120,000	$8.00	$20.00	$40.00	$50.00	$205	$800	$1,500
1892-O	3,841,700	10.00	20.00	40.00	65.00	300	1,500	
1892-S	990,710	50.00	200	250	300	700	3,500	

	Mintage	Good-4	Fine-12	EF-40	AU-55	MS-63	MS-65	Proof-65
1893 combined total ...	3,340,000							
1893 regular date 792	—	8.00	20.00	40.00	55.00	210	1,200	1,500
1893/2 overdate	—	100	200	210	850	2,500	4,000	
1893-O	1,760,000	30.00	100	200	275	500	3,250	
1893-S	2,491,401	12.00	50.00	100	150	600	4,000	
1894 .....972	1,330,000	12.00	100	175	300	500	1,400	1,500
1894-S (proof only) 24	50,000	—	—	—	—	—	—	1,322,500*
1895 .....880	690,000	90.00	300	400	500	1,200	3,000	1,500
1895-O	440,000	300	1,000	1.850	3,850	8,200	16,000	
1895-S	1,120,000	30.00	100	300	375	1,100	7,500	
1896 .....762	2,000,000	8.00	50.00	100	150	250	1,650	1,500
1896-O	610,000	50.00	150	300	475	2,400	8,800	
1896-S	575,056	50.00	80.00	200	425	1,700	4,000	
1897 .....731	10,868,533	5.00	6.00	20.00	50.00	170	800	1,500
1897-O	666,000	35.00	110	250	495	1,500	5,000	
1897-S	1,342,844	8.00	30.00	75.00	175	1,100	5,000	
1898 .....735	16,320,000	5.00	6.00	20.00	50.00	205	800	1,500
1898-O	2,130,000	5.00	75.00	190	300	1,200	3,600	
1898-S	1,702,507	5.00	20.00	75.00	90.00	1,000	5,000	
1899 .....846	19,580,000	5.00	6.00	20.00	50.00	205	800	1,500
1899-O	2,650,000	5.00	50.00	150	275	1,200	5,600	
1899-S	1,867,493	4.25	20.00	40.00	125	700	3,300	
1900 .....912	17,600,000	4.25	6.00	30.00	100	205	850	1,500
1900-O	2,010,000	4.25	100	200	350	950	6,000	
1900-S	5,168,270	4.25	10.00	25.00	80.00	460	1,750	
1901 .....813	18,859,665	4.25	7.00	20.00	80.00	205	800	1,500
1901-O	5,620,000	4.25	20.00	40.00	200	1,100	3,400	
1901-S	593,022	35.00	300	450	525	2,100	4,350	
1902 .....777	21,380,000	4.25	7.00	20.00	50.00	205	800	1,500
1902-O	4,500,000	4.25	12.00	40.00	125	900	3,500	
1902-S	2,070,000	4.25	50.00	100	175	700	3,200	
1903 .....755	19,500,000	4.25	4.00	20.00	50.00	205	800	1,500
1903-O	8,180,000	4.25	6.00	40.00	85.00	475	4,000	
1903-S	613,300	25.00	300	650	750	1,800	4,100	
1904 .....670	14,600,357	4.25	7.00	20.00	50.00	205	1,800	1,500
1904-S	800,000	19.00	150	225	350	1,400	4,600	
1905 .....727	14,551,623	4.25	8.00	20.00	50.00	205	800	1,500
1905-O	3,400,000	4.25	35.00	40.00	95.00	500	3,000	
1905-S	6,855,199	4.25	7.00	25.00	70.00	365	1,000	
1906 .....675	19,957,731	4.25	6.00	20.00	50.00	205	800	1,500
1906-D	4,060,000	4.25	6.00	25.00	70.00	325	2,200	
1906-O	2,610,000	4.25	40.00	100	110	325	1,300	
1906-S	3,136,640	4.25	10.00	30.00	85.00	400	1,500	
1907 .....575	22,220,000	4.25	8.00	20.00	50.00	205	800	1,500
1907-D	4,080,000	4.25	7.00	30.00	80.00	800	4,000	
1907-O	5,058,000	4.25	13.00	25.00	70.00	375	1,500	
1907-S	3,178,470	4.25	9.00	40.00	95.00	850	2,900	
1908 .....545	10,600,000	4.25	8.00	20.00	50.00	205	800	1,500
1908-D	7,490,000	4.25	10.00	25.00	55.00	300	1,200	
1908-O	1,789,000	4.25	27.00	90.00	110	495	2,000	
1908-S	3,220,000	4.25	12.00	27.50	85.00	550	2,800	
1909 .....650	10,240,000	4.25	8.00	20.00	50.00	205	800	1,500
1909-D	954,000	4.25	50.00	125	140	1,100	3,200	
1909-O	2,287,000	4.25	12.00	27.50	85.00	500	1,350	
1909-S	1,000,000	4.25	100	175	250	1,400	2,800	
1910 .....551	11,520,000	4.25	6.00	20.00	50.00	205	800	1,500
1910-D	3,490,000	4.25	8.00	30.00	80.00	500	1,800	
1910-S	1,240,000	4.25	25.00	52.50	135	800	2,200	
1911 .....543	18,870,000	4.25	8.00	20.00	50.00	205	800	1,500
1911-D	11,209,000	4.25	8.00	20.00	50.00	205	800	
1911-S	3,520,000	4.25	12.00	25.00	80.00	325	1,100	
1912 .....700	19,350,000	4.25	8.00	20.00	50.00	205	850	1,500
1912-D	11,760,000	4.25	10.00	20.00	50.00	205	850	
1912-S	3,420,000	4.25	8.00	25.00	70.00	325	1,350	
1913 .....622	19,760,000	4.25	8.00	20.00	50.00	205	850	1,500

*Proof-66

	Mintage	Good-4	Fine-12	EF-40	AU-55	MS-63	MS-65	Proof-65
1913-S	510,000	8.00	100	200	275	700	1,300	
1914 .... *425*	17,360,230	4.25	7.00	25.00	50.00	205	800	1,800
1914-D	11,908,000	4.25	7.00	25.00	50.00	205	800	
1914-S	2,100,000	4.25	7.00	30.00	60.00	350	1,400	
1915 .... *450*	5,620,000	4.25	7.00	25.00	50.00	205	800	1,600
1915-S	960,000	4.25	7.00	60.00	110	500	1,700	
1916	18,490,000	4.25	7.00	20.00	55.00	205	850	
1916-S	5,820,000	4.25	7.00	20.00	55.00	205	850	

Winged Liberty Head, or "Mercury" Portrait
(1916–1945)

	Mintage	Good-4	Fine-12	EF-40	AU-55	MS-63	MS-65	Proof-65
1916	22,180,080	$4.00	$8.00	$10.00	$25.00	$50.00	$150	
1916-D	264,000	1,000	2,500	5,000	7,800	15,000	40,000	
1916-S	10,450,000	5.00	6.00	20.00	25.00	80.00	200	
1917	55,230,000	5.00	5.50	9.00	12.00	70.00	200	
1917-D	9,402,000	5.00	6.00	40.00	65.00	400	1,400	
1917-S	27,330,000	4.50	5.00	16.00	25.00	200	500	
1918	26,680,000	4.50	5.00	25.00	35.00	190	900	
1918-D	22,674,800	4.50	5.00	25.00	36.00	275	750	
1918-S	19,300,000	4.50	5.00	15.00	30.00	200	800	
1919	35,740,000	4.50	5.00	12.00	25.00	150	300	
1919-D	9,939,000	4.50	5.00	35.00	65.00	450	1,700	
1919-S	8,850,000	4.50	5.00	30.00	65.00	500	1,000	
1920	59,030,000	4.50	4.00	8.00	15.00	90.00	250	
1920-D	19,171,000	4.50	5.00	20.00	50.00	400	800	
1920-S	13,820,000	4.50	5.00	25.00	60.00	325	1,500	
1921	1,230,000	20.00	75.00	500	750	1,500	3,250	
1921-D	1,080,000	30.00	100	700	900	1,800	3,000	
1923	50,130,000	4.50	5.00	7.00	20.00	75.00	125	
1923-S	6,440,000	4.50	4.75	90.00	200	300	1,800	
1924	24,010,000	4.50	4.75	10.00	25.00	100	300	
1924-D	6,810,000	4.50	5.00	75.00	90.00	350	1,500	
1924-S	7,120,000	4.50	5.00	75.00	90.00	575	1,200	
1925	25,610,000	4.50	4.75	8.00	20.00	90.00	350	
1925-D	5,117,000	4.50	9.00	150	200	600	1,800	
1925-S	5,850,000	4.50	5.00	100	120	300	1,250	
1926	32,160,000	4.00	5.00	8.00	20.00	75.00	400	
1926-D	6,828,000	4.00	10.00	15.00	35.00	250	750	
1926-S	1,520,000	4.00	50.00	200	400	1,500	3,500	
1927	28,080,000	4.00	5.00	6.00	12.00	75.00	200	
1927-D	4,812,000	4.00	20.00	40.00	80.00	450	1,400	
1927-S	4,770,000	4.00	10.00	20.00	35.00	500	1,875	
1928	19,480,000	4.00	5.00	6.00	15.00	75.00	150	
1928-D	4,161,000	4.00	10.00	40.00	80.00	250	900	
1928-S	7,400,000	4.00	6.00	9.00	30.00	150	400	
1929	25,970,000	4.00	4.50	5.00	10.00	35.00	75.00	
1929-D	5,034,000	4.00	10.00	12.00	20.00	40.00	70.00	
1929-S	4,730,000	4.00	4.50	5.00	15.00	42.00	100	
1930	6,770,000	4.00	4.50	6.00	12.00	45.00	140	
1930-S	1,843,000	4.00	4.50	10.00	40.00	100	135	
1931	3,150,000	4.00	4.50	8.00	20.00	75.00	175	
1931-D	1,260,000	5.00	10.00	30.00	42.00	100	200	
1931-S	1,800,000	4.00	6.00	10.00	35.00	75.00	200	

	Mintage	Good-4	Fine-12	EF-40	AU-55	MS-63	MS-65	Proof-65
1934	24,080,000	4.00	4.50	5.00	6.00	20.00	45.00	
1934-D	6,772,000	4.00	4.50	6.00	7.50	35.00	65.00	
1935	58,830,000	4.00	4.50	5.00	4.90	20.00	28.00	
1935-D	10,477,000	4.00	4.50	4.80	4.90	35.00	65.00	
1935-S	15,840,000	4.00	4.50	4.80	4.90	30.00	60.00	
1936 ..... *4,130*	87,500,000	4.00	4.50	4.80	4.90	20.00	30.00	$800
1936-D	16,132,000	4.00	4.50	4.80	4.90	28.00	40.00	
1936-S	9,210,000	4.00	4.50	4.80	4.90	20.00	30.00	
1937 ..... *5,756*	56,860,000	4.00	4.50	4.80	4.90	18.00	25.00	225
1937-D	14,146,000	4.00	4.50	4.80	4.90	25.00	45.00	
1937-S	9,740,000	4.00	4.50	4.80	4.90	26.00	35.00	
1938 ..... *8,728*	22,190,000	4.00	4.50	4.80	4.90	20.00	28.00	180
1938-D	5,537,000	4.00	4.50	4.80	4.90	22.00	30.00	
1938-S	8,090,000	4.00	4.50	4.80	4.90	22.00	35.00	
1939 ..... *9,321*	67,740,000	4.00	4.50	4.80	4.90	20.00	25.00	200
1939-D	24,394,000	4.00	4.50	4.80	4.90	19.00	25.00	
1939-S	10,540,000	4.00	4.50	4.80	4.90	28.00	40.00	
1940 ..... *11,827*	65,350,000	4.00	4.50	4.80	4.90	15.00	25.00	125
1940-D	21,198,000	4.00	4.50	4.80	4.90	15.00	25.00	
1940-S	21,560,000	4.00	4.50	4.80	4.90	16.00	25.00	
1941 ..... *16,557*	175,090,000	4.00	4.50	4.80	4.90	12.00	25.00	120
1941-D	45,634,000	4.00	4.50	4.80	4.90	13.00	30.00	
1941-S	43,090,000	4.00	4.50	4.80	4.90	15.00	25.00	
1942 combined total ...	205,410,000							
1942 regular date	*22,329*	4.00	4.50	4.80	4.90	12.00	25.00	120
1942/1 overdate		500	700	800	1,500	3,500	20,000	
1942-D combined total .	60,740,000							
1942-D regular date		4.00	4.50	4.90	4.90	15.00	25.00	
1942/1-D overdate		500	700	1,000	1,200	3,500	17,000	
1942-S	49,300,000	4.75	4.85	4.90	4.95	16.00	25.00	
1943	191,710,000	4.75	4.85	4.90	4.95	15.00	24.00	
1943-D	71,949,000	4.75	4.85	4.90	4.95	16.00	35.00	
1943-S	60,400,000	4.75	4.85	4.90	4.95	15.00	25.00	
1944	231,410,000	4.75	4.85	4.90	4.95	15.00	25.00	
1944-D	62,224,000	4.75	4.85	4.90	4.95	15.00	25.00	
1944-S	49,490,000	4.75	4.85	4.90	4.95	15.00	25.00	
1945	159,130,000	4.75	4.85	4.90	4.95	12.00	28.00	
1945-D	40,245,000	4.75	4.85	4.90	4.95	10.00	25.00	
1945-S combined total .	41,920,000							
1945-S with regular S ...		4.75	4.85	4.90	4.95	12.00	25.00	
1945-S with microscopic S		4.75	4.85	4.90	4.95	20.00	58.00	

Roosevelt Portrait (1946–Present)

Silver Composition (1946–1964)

	Mintage	Fine-12	EF-40	AU-55	MS-60	MS-63	MS-65	Proof-65
1946	255,250,000	$3.00	$3.05	$3.10	$6.00	$7.00	$12.00	
1946-D	61,043,500	3.00	3.05	3.10	6.00	6.10	12.00	
1946-S	27,900,000	3.00	3.05	3.10	6.00	6.10	20.00	
1947	121,520,000	3.00	3.05	3.10	6.00	6.10	10.00	
1947-D	46,835,000	3.00	3.05	3.10	6.00	6.10	16.50	
1947-S	34,840,000	3.00	3.05	3.10	6.00	6.10	12.00	
1948	74,950,000	3.00	3.05	3.10	6.00	9.00	15.00	
1948-D	52,841,000	3.00	3.05	3.10	6.00	8.00	16.50	
1948-S	35,520,000	3.00	3.05	3.10	6.00	8.00	18.00	
1949	30,940,000	3.00	3.05	3.10	25.00	40.00	70.00	
1949-D	26,034,000	3.00	3.05	3.10	6.00	5.00	12.00	
1949-S	13,510,000	3.00	3.05	15.00	20.00	25.00	35.00	

	Mintage	Fine-12	EF-40	AU-55	MS-60	MS-63	MS-65	Proof-65
1950 ..... *51,386*	50,130,114	3.00	3.05	3.10	6.00	6.10	10.00	$70.00
1950-D	46,803,000	3.00	3.05	3.10	6.00	6.10	10.00	
1950-S	20,440,000	3.00	3.05	3.10	6.00	10.00	28.00	
1951 ..... *57,500*	103,880,102	3.00	3.05	3.10	6.00	6.10	9.00	65.00
1951-D	56,529,000	3.00	3.05	3.10	6.00	6.10	12.00	
1951-S	31,630,000	3.00	3.05	3.10	6.00	8.00	18.00	
1952 ..... *81,980*	99,040,093	3.85	3.90	3.95	3.97	3.00	50.00	40.00
1952-D	122,100,000	3.85	3.90	3.95	3.97	4.00	7.00	
1952-S	44,419,500	3.85	3.90	3.95	3.97	8.00	25.00	
1953 ..... *128,800*	53,490,120	3.85	3.90	3.95	3.97	4.00	10.00	15.00
1953-D	136,433,000	3.85	3.90	3.95	3.97	4.00	3.05	
1953-S	39,180,000	3.85	3.90	3.95	3.97	4.00	3.05	
1954 ..... *233,300*	114,010,203	3.85	3.90	3.95	3.97	4.00	3.05	12.00
1954-D	106,397,000	3.85	3.90	3.95	3.97	4.00	3.05	
1954-S	22,860,000	3.85	3.90	3.95	3.97	4.00	3.05	
1955 ..... *378,200*	12,450,181	3.85	3.90	3.95	3.97	4.00	3.05	9.00
1955-D	13,959,000	3.85	3.90	3.95	3.97	4.00	3.05	
1955-S	18,510,000	3.85	3.90	3.95	3.97	4.00	3.05	
1956 ..... *669,384*	108,640,000	3.85	3.90	3.95	3.97	4.00	3.05	4.00
1956-D	108,015,100	3.85	3.90	3.95	3.97	4.00	3.05	
1957 ..... *1,247,952* ...	160,160,000	3.85	3.90	3.95	3.97	4.00	3.05	3.50
1957-D	113,354,330	3.85	3.90	3.95	3.97	4.00	3.05	
1958 ..... *875,652*	31,910,000	3.85	3.90	3.95	3.97	4.00	3.05	3.50
1958-D	136,564,600	3.85	3.90	3.95	3.97	4.00	3.05	
1959 ..... *1,149,291* ...	85,780,000	3.85	3.90	3.95	3.97	4.00	3.05	3.10
1959-D	164,919,790	3.85	3.90	3.95	3.97	4.00	3.05	
1960 ..... *1,691,602* ...	70,390,000	3.85	3.90	3.95	3.97	4.00	3.05	3.10
1960-D	200,160,400	3.85	3.90	3.95	3.97	4.00	3.05	
1961 ..... *3,028,244* ...	93,730,000	3.85	3.90	3.95	3.97	4.00	3.05	3.10
1961-D	209,146,550	3.85	3.90	3.95	3.97	4.00	3.05	
1962 ..... *3,218,019* ...	72,450,000	3.85	3.90	3.95	3.97	4.00	3.05	3.10
1962-D	334,948,380	3.85	3.90	3.95	3.97	4.00	3.05	
1963 ..... *3,075,645* ...	123,650,000	3.85	3.90	3.95	3.97	4.00	3.05	3.10
1963-D	421,476,530	3.85	3.90	3.95	3.97	4.00	3.05	
1964 ..... *3,950,762* ...	929,360,000	3.85	3.90	3.95	3.97	4.00	3.05	3.10
1964-D	1,357,517,180	3.85	3.90	3.95	3.97	4.00	3.05	

Copper-Nickel Clad Composition (1965–Present)

	Mintage	EF-40	MS-65	Proof-65
1965	1,652,140,570	—	$.25	
1966	1,382,734,540	—	.25	
1967	2,244,007,320	—	.25	
1968	424,470,400	—	.25	
1968-D..................	480,748,280	—	.25	
1968-S (proof only)........	*3,041,506*	—	—	$.50
1969	145,790,000	—	.25	
1969-D..................	563,323,870	—	.25	
1969-S (proof only)........	*2,934,631*	—	—	.50
1970	345,570,000	—	.20	
1970-D..................	754,942,100	—	.20	
1970-S combined total (proof only)..................	*2,632,810*			
1970-S proof with S........		—	—	.50
1970-S proof with no mint mark..................		—	—	900
1971	162,690,000	—	.25	
1971-D..................	377,914,240	—	.25	
1971-S (proof only)........	*3,220,733*	—	—	.50
1972	431,540,000	—	.25	
1972-D..................	330,390,000	—	.25	
1972-S (proof only)........	*3,260,996*	—	—	.75
1973	315,670,000	—	.15	
1973-D..................	455,032,426	—	.15	
1973-S (proof only)........	*2,760,339*	—	—	.75
1974	470,248,000	—	.15	

	Mintage	EF-40	MS-65	Proof-65
1974-D...................	571,083,000	—	.15	
1974-S (proof only)........	2,612,568	—	—	.75
1975	585,673,900	—	.15	
1975-D...................	313,705,300	—	.15	
1975-S (proof only)........	2,845,450	—	—	.75
1976	568,760,000	—	.15	
1976-D...................	695,222,774	—	.15	
1976-S (proof only)........	4,149,730	—	—	.75
1977	796,930,000	—	.15	
1977-D...................	376,222,774	—	.15	
1977-S (proof only)........	3,251,152	—	—	.75
1978	663,980,000	—	.15	
1978-D...................	282,847,540	—	.15	
1978-S (proof only)........	3,127,781	—	—	.75
1979	315,440,000	—	.15	
1979-D...................	390,921,184	—	.15	
1979-S combined total (proof only)...................	3,677,175			
1979-S with clear S		—	—	3.00
1979-S with clogged S......		—	—	.75
1980-P...................	735,170,000	—	.15	
1980-D...................	719,354,321	—	.15	
1980-S (proof only)........	3,554,806	—	—	.65
1981-P...................	676,650,000	—	.15	
1981-D...................	712,284,143	—	.15	
1981-S (proof only)........	4,063,083	—	—	.60
1982-P combined total	519,475,000			
1982-P with P.............		—	.15	
1982-P with no mint mark ..		—	100	
1982-D...................	542,713,584	—	.15	
1982-S (proof only)........	3,857,479	—	—	.60
1983-P...................	647,025,000	—	.15	
1983-D...................	730,129,224	—	.15	
1983-S combined total (proof only)...................	3,279,126			
1983-S proof with S........		—	—	.60
1983-S proof with no mint mark		—	—	450
1984-P...................	856,669,000	—	.15	
1984-D...................	704,803,976	—	.15	
1984-S (proof only)........	3,065,110	—	—	1.00
1985-P...................	705,200,962	—	.15	
1985-D...................	587,979,970	—	.15	
1985-S (proof only)........	3,362,821	—	—	.90
1986-P...................	682,649,693	—	.15	
1986-D...................	473,326,970	—	.15	
1986-S (proof only)........	3,010,497	—	—	1.00
1987-P...................	762,709,481	—	.15	
1987-D...................	653,203,402	—	.15	
1987-S (proof only)........	3,792,233	—	—	1.00
1988-P...................	1,030,550,000	—	.15	
1988-D...................	962,385,489	—	.15	
1988-S (proof only)........	3,262,948	—	—	1.00
1989-P...................	1,298,400,000	—	.15	
1989-D...................	896,535,597	—	.15	
1989-S (proof only)........	3,215,728	—	—	1.00
1990-P...................	1,034,340,000	—	.15	
1990-D...................	839,995,824	—	.15	
1990-S (proof only)........	3,299,559	—	—	1.00
1991-P...................	927,220,000	—	.15	
1991-D...................	601,241,114	—	.15	
1991-S (proof only)........	2,867,787	—	—	1.00
1992-P...................	593,500,000	—	.15	
1992-D...................	616,273,932	—	.15	
1992-S (proof only)........	4,176,544*	—	—	1.00

*Includes 90% silver issue

	Mintage	EF-40	MS-65	Proof-65
1993-P.................	766,180,000	—	.15	
1993-D.................	750,110,166	—	.15	
1993-S (proof only)........	3,360,876*	—	—	1.00
1994-P.................	1,190,210,896	—	.15	
1994-D.................	1,304,479,006	—	.15	
1994-S (proof only)........	3,212,792*	—	—	1.00
1995-P.................	1,126,541,352	—	.15	
1995-D.................	1,275,731,352	—	.15	
1995-S (proof only)........	2,796,345*	—	—	1.00
1996-P.................	1,423,084,215	—	.15	
1996-D.................	1,401,754,215	—	.15	
1996-S (proof only)........	2,925,305*	—	—	1.00
1996-W	1,258,334	—	15.00	
1997-P.................	991,640,000	—	.15	
1997-D.................	979,810,000	—	.15	
1997-S (proof only)........	2,788,020*	—	—	1.00
1998-P.................	1,163,000,000	—	.15	
1998-D.................	1,172,300,000	—	.15	
1998-S (proof only)........	2,086,507	—	—	1.00
1998-S (silver proof)......	878,996	—	—	5.00
1999-P.................	2,164,000,000	—	.15	
1999-D.................	1,397,750,000	—	.15	
1999-S (proof only)........	2,454,319	—	—	1.00
1999-S (silver proof)......	798,780	—	—	5.00
2000-P.................	1,842,500,000	—	.15	
2000-D.................	1,818,700,000	—	.15	
2000-S (proof only)........	3,030,000	—	—	1.00
2000-S (silver proof)......	904,200	—	—	5.00
2001-P.................	1,369,590,000	—	.15	
2001-D.................	1,412,800,000	—	.15	
2001-S (proof only)........	2,294,900	—	—	1.00
2001-S (silver proof)......	891,400	—	—	5.00
2002-P.................	1,187,500,000	—	.15	
2002-D.................	1,379,500,000	—	.15	
2002-S (proof only)........	2,323,848	—	—	1.00
2002-S (silver proof)......	888,826	—	—	5.00
2003-P.................	1,086,502,555	—	.15	
2003-D.................	987,502,555	—	.15	
2003-S (proof only)........	2,243,340	—	—	1.00
2003-S (silver proof)......	1,119,494	—	—	5.00
2004-P.................	1,159,500,000	—	.15	
2004-D.................	1,328,000,000	—	.15	
2004-S (proof only)........	1,804,396	—	—	1.00
2004-S (silver proof)......	1,187,673	—	—	5.00
2005-P.................	1,412,000,000	—	.15	
2005-D.................	1,423,500,000	—	.15	
2005-S (proof only)........	2,275,000	—	—	1.00
2005-S (silver proof)......	998,000	—	—	5.00
2006-P.................	1,381,000,000	—	.15	
2006-D.................	1,447,000,000	—	.15	
2006-S (proof only)........	2,000,438	—	—	1.00
2006-S (silver proof)......	1,054,008	—	—	5.00
2007-P.................	1,047,500,000	—	.15	
2007-D.................	1,042,000,000	—	.15	
2007-S (proof only)........	1,702,116	—	—	1.00
2007-S (silver proof)......	861,447	—	—	5.00
2008-P.................	413,000,000	—	.15	
2008-D.................	637,500,000	—	.15	
2008-S (proof only)........	1,382,017	—	—	1.00
2008-S (silver proof)......	763,887	—	—	5.00
2009-P.................	96,500,000	—	.15	
2009-D.................	49,500,000	—	.15	
2009-S (proof only)........	1,477,967	—	—	1.00
2009-S (silver proof)......	694,406	—	—	5.00
2010-P.................	557,000,000	—	.15	

*Includes 90% silver issue

	Mintage	EF-40	MS-65	Proof-65
2010-D.................	562,000,000	—	.15	
2010-S (proof only)........		—	—	3.00
2010-S (silver proof).......		—	—	5.00
2011-P.................	748,000,000	—	.15	
2011-D.................	754,000,000	—	.15	
2011-S (proof only)........		—	—	3.00
2011-S (silver proof).......		—	—	5.00
2012-P.................		—	.15	
2012-D.................		—	.15	
2012-S (proof only)........		—	—	3.00
2012-S (silver proof).......		—	—	5.00
2013-P.................		—	.15	
2013-D.................		—	.15	
2013-S (proof only)........		—	—	3.00
2013-S (silver proof).......		—	—	5.00
2014-P.................		—	.15	
2014-D.................		—	.15	
2014-S (proof only)........		—	—	3.00
2014-S (silver proof).......		—	—	5.00

TWENTY-CENT PIECES (1875–1878)

	Mintage	Good-4	Fine-12	EF-40	AU-55	MS-63	MS-65	Proof-65
1875 ...*2,790*	36,910	$200	$275	$500	$800	$1,600	$6,800	$12,000
1875-CC	133,290	400	500	1,000	1,200	1,900	10,000	
1875-S	1,155,000	100	150	250	450	1,300	6,000	
1876 ...*1,150*	14,640	200	300	500	600	1,600	4,000	12,000
1876-CC (fewer than 20 known)	—	—	—	—	—	—	400,000	
1877 (proof only)	510	1,900	2,500	3,500	4,000	—	—	15,000
1878 (proof only)	600	2,000	2,300	3,000	3,800	—	—	12,000

QUARTER DOLLARS (1796–PRESENT)

Draped Bust Portrait with Small Eagle on Reverse (1796)

	Mintage	Good-4	Fine-12	EF-40
1796	6,146	$12,000	$37,000	$50,000

Draped Bust Portrait with Heraldic Eagle on Reverse (1804–1807)

	Mintage	Good-4	Fine-12	EF-40
1804	6,738	$6,000	$10,000	$30,000
1805	121,394	500	1,000	3,600
1806 combined total	206,124			
1806 regular date		500	1,000	3,600
1806/5 overdate		500	1,000	3,600
1807	220,643	500	1,000	3,600

Capped Bust Portrait (1815–1838)

Large Size (1815–1828)

	Mintage	Good-4	Fine-12	EF-40	AU-55	MS-63
1815	89,235	$65.00	$100	$900	$1,750	$5,000
1818 combined total	361,174					
1818 regular date		65.00	90.00	900	1,500	5,000
1818/5 overdate		65.00	120	1,200	1,850	5,000
1819 combined total	144,000					
1819 small 9		65.00	90.00	900	1,700	7,000
1819 large 9		65.00	90.00	900	1,700	7,000
1820 combined total	127,444					
1820 small 0		65.00	95.00	900	1,700	10,000
1820 large 0		65.00	90.00	900	1,700	10,000
1821	216,851	65.00	90.00	560	1,500	5,000
1822 combined total	64,080					
1822 regular 25c		80.00	130	850	2,400	7,500
1822 25/50c		800	1,600	10,000	16,000	—
1823/2 overdate	17,800	10,000	20,000	50,000	—	—
1824/2 overdate (mintage included with 1825) . . .		500	2,000	7,000	8,000	—
1825 combined total	174,000					
1825/2 overdate		75.00	210	1,100	3,000	—
1825/3 overdate		35.00	90.00	560	1,500	5,000
1825/4 overdate		65.00	90.00	560	1,500	5,000
1827 original (curl-base 2 in 25c)	(only a few proofs known)				—	100,000
1827 restrike (square-base 2 in 25c)	(only a few proofs known)				—	65,000
1828 combined total	100,000					
1828 regular 25c		65.00	90.00	560	1,900	6,000
1828 25/50c		100	300	1,300	5,000	—

Reduced Size (1831–1838)

	Mintage	Good-4	Fine-12	EF-40	AU-55	MS-63
1831 combined total	398,000					
1831 with small letters ..		$65.00	$100	$200	$800	$2,600
1831 with large letters ..		65.00	100	200	800	2,600
1832...................	320,000	65.00	100	200	800	3,100
1833...................	156,000	65.00	110	210	900	3,700
1834...................	286,000	65.00	100	200	950	2,700
1835...................	1,952,000	65.00	100	200	950	2,700
1836...................	472,000	65.00	100	200	950	3,700
1837...................	252,400	65.00	100	200	950	2,700
1838...................	366,000	65.00	110	210	1,000	2,700

Seated Liberty Portrait (1838–1891)

	Mintage	Good-4	Fine-12	EF-40	AU-55	MS-63	MS-65
1838	466,000	$10.00	$23.00	$300	$600	$4,600	$35,000
1839	491,146	10.00	23.00	300	600	4,600	37,500
1840-O	382,200	10.00	30.00	350	705	7,600	—

With Drapery Hanging from Elbow (1840–1891)

	Mintage	Good-4	Fine-12	EF-40	AU-55	MS-63	MS-65
1840	188,127	$30.00	$60.00	$150	$300	$3,000	$9,750
1840-O	43,000	30.00	60.00	160	475	5,000	—
1841	120,000	50.00	100	140	300	5,000	—
1841-O	452,000	30.00	60.00	135	310	4,600	7,500
1842 small date	(only a few proofs known)			—	—	—	
1842 large date	88,000	55.00	100	350	400	6,100	—
1842-O combined total ..	769,000						
1842-O small date		210	605	1,500	3,000	15,000	—
1842-O large date		30.00	50.00	70.00	300	2,800	—
1843	645,600	25.00	45.00	60.00	200	1,300	—
1843-O	968,000	25.00	50.00	150	350	3,300	—
1844	421,200	20.00	40.00	60.00	150	1,600	—
1844-O	740,000	20.00	50.00	90.00	175	4,100	—
1845	922,000	20.00	50.00	80.00	110	1,300	—
1846	510,300	20.00	50.00	85.00	130	1,600	—
1847	734,000	20.00	50.00	80.00	110	1,300	7,000
1847-O	368,000	40.00	80.00	175	260	7,800	—
1848	146,000	35.00	80.00	175	250	3,000	13,000
1849	340,000	30.00	90.00	110	200	1,900	13,750
1849-O	16,000	600	1,200	4,500	7,000	—	—
1850	190,800	50.00	90.00	175	205	2,600	—
1850-O	412,000	18.00	45.00	95.00	215	3,600	—
1851	160,000	30.00	54.00	110	205	2,600	8,500
1851-O	88,000	110	350	1,150	4,100	—	—
1852	177,060	38.00	55.00	150	200	1,600	—
1852-O	96,000	135	300	865	1,750	20,000	—
1853 without arrows or rays	44,200	140	345	440	825	5,600	—

With Arrows Beside the Date, Rays Around the Eagle (1853)

	Mintage	Good-4	Fine-12	EF-40	AU-55	MS-63	MS-65	Proof-65
1853 combined total ...	15,210,020							
1853 regular date		$10.00	$25.00	$175	$400	$3,500	$24,000	—
1853/4 overdate		50.00	110	300	900	12,500	—	—
1853-O	1,332,000	12.50	30.00	200	1,000	10,000	—	—

With Arrows Beside the Date, No Rays Around the Eagle (1854–1855)

	Mintage	Good-4	Fine-12	EF-40	AU-55	MS-63	MS-65	Proof-65
1854	12,380,000	$20.00	$50.00	$80.00	$200	$2,100	$10,000	
1854-O combined total .	1,484,000							

	Mintage	Good-4	Fine-12	EF-40	AU-55	MS-63	MS-65	Proof-65
1854-O regular date		20.00	50.00	80.00	200	3,000		
1854-O with huge O		110	180	400	1,000	4,500		
1855	2,857,000	20.00	50.00	80.00	200	2,600	10,000	
1855-O	176,000	35.00	100	300	600	—	—	
1855-S	396,400	30.00	60.00	250	600	6,100	—	

Arrows Removed, Without Motto (1856–1866)

	Mintage	Good-4	Fine-12	EF-40	AU-55	MS-63	MS-65	Proof-65
1856	7,264,000	$20.00	$50.00	$65.00	$100	$900	$5,000	$12,500
1856-O	968,000	20.00	50.00	65.00	200	2,500	10,000	
1856-S combined total .	286,000							
1856-S regular date		50.00	80.00	300	600	9,100	—	
1856-S/S	40.00	100	400	775	—	—		
1857 ..... 9,644,000 ...	20.00	45.00	60.00	110	1,000	4,600	11,000	
1857-O	1,180,000	20.00	45.00	60.00	225	3,100	—	
1857-S	82,000	35.00	125	485	750	8,200	—	
1858	7,368,000	20.00	40.00	50.00	110	900	4,000	9,500
1858-O	520,000	25.00	50.00	60.00	275	6,500	15,000	
1858-S	121,000	35.00	125	290	625	4,000	—	
1859 ..... 800	1,343,200	25.00	50.00	58.00	130	1,500	7,500	4,800
1859-O	260,000	30.00	50.00	65.00	250	6,000	15,000	
1859-S	80,000	68.00	125	390	675	4,500	—	
1860 ..... 1,000	804,400	20.00	50.00	60.00	100	1,000	4,500	5,250
1860-O	388,000	25.00	50.00	70.00	350	2,600	7,500	
1860-S	56,000	110	250	1,200	3,000	10,000	—	
1861 ..... 1,000	4,853,600	25.00	50.00	60.00	110	1,000	4,000	4,750
1861-S	96,000	50.00	275	1,500	4,000	—	—	4,800
1862 ..... 550	932,000	20.00	50.00	60.00	100	1,200	4,000	4,800
1862-S	67,000	50.00	80.00	280	550	—	—	
1863 ..... 460	191,600	35.00	40.00	100	225	1,600	4,500	4,600
1864 ..... 470	93,600	55.00	80.00	150	250	1,800	5,000	4,600
1864-S	20,000	135	250	900	1,500	—	—	
1865 ..... 500	58,800	38.00	80.00	150	250	1,500	8,000	5,000
1865-S	41,000	60.00	100	250	625	4,000	12,500	
1866	(unique)	—	—	—	250,000	—	—	

With Motto Above the Eagle (1866–1891)

	Mintage	Good-4	Fine-12	EF-40	AU-55	MS-63	MS-65	Proof-65
1866 ..... 725	16,800	$150	$450	$550	$775	$3,000	$5,800	$3,000
1866-S	28,000	140	325	560	925	6,500	—	
1867 ..... 625	20,000	100	300	400	475	1,800	—	2,400
1867-S	48,000	90.00	350	450	775	—	—	
1868 ..... 600	29,400	90.00	250	275	425	2,000	4,500	2,500
1868-S	96,000	49.00	240	425	875	8,000	—	
1869 ..... 600	16,000	150	425	450	675	3,500	—	2,550
1869-S	76,000	80.00	300	425	950	6,000	20,000	

	Mintage	Good-4	Fine-12	EF-40	AU-55	MS-63	MS-65	Proof-65
1870 ..... *1,000*	86,400	50.00	200	225	375	2,000	7,000	2,400
1870-CC	8,340	1,100	3,500	3,900	7,000	—	—	
1871 ...... *960*	118,200	30.00	100	125	350	1,200	7,500	2,300
1871-CC	10,890	740	2,500	3,700	5,100	—	—	
1871-S	30,900	200	450	600	775	5,000	12,500	
1872 ...... *950*	182,000	50.00	80.00	100	225	2,500	7,500	2,300
1872-CC	22,850	250	1,800	2,300	5,000	—	—	
1872-S	83,000	200	500	600	975	25,000	50,000	
1873 closed 3 .. *600* ...	40,000	69.00	300	400	475	2,200	—	2,500
1873 open 3	172,000	50.00	100	110	200	1,500	4,750	
1873-CC	(4 known)	—	—	—				

With Arrows Beside the Date (1873–1874)

	Mintage	Good-4	Fine-12	EF-40	AU-55	MS-63	MS-65	Proof-65
1873 ...... *540*	1,271,160	$25.00	$100	$200	$475	$2,000	$5,500	$5,000
1873-CC	12,462	1,200	3,000	5,000	9,000	—	—	
1873-S	156,000	40.00	100	200	475	3,000	—	
1874 ...... *700*	471,200	24.00	100	200	450	2,000	4,000	5,000
1874-S	392,000	32.00	150	200	460	2,000	4,000	

Arrows Removed, with Motto (1875–1891)

	Mintage	Good-4	Fine-12	EF-40	AU-55	MS-63	MS-65	Proof-65
1875 ...... *700*	4,292,800	$18.00	$40.00	$50.00	$100	$700	$2,000	$2,000
1875-CC	140,000	100	200	300	500	3,000	—	
1875-S	680,000	70.00	150	200	400	1,800	2,800	
1876 ...... *1,150*	17,816,000	20.00	36.00	50.00	100	800	2,000	2,000
1876-CC	4,944,000	18.00	38.00	50.00	100	1,300	1,600	
1876-S	8,596,000	18.00	36.00	50.00	100	800	2,200	
1877 ...... *510*	10,911,200	18.00	36.00	50.00	100	800	1,300	2,000
1877-CC	4,192,000	18.00	38.00	50.00	100	1,100	1,400	
1877-S combined total ..	18,996,000							
1877-S with regular mint mark		18.00	36.00	50.00	100	800	1,400	
1877-S with S struck over horizontal S		50.00	140	225	300	2,600	—	
1878 ...... *800*	2,260,000	18.00	30.00	50.00	100	800	2,000	2,000
1878-CC	996,000	50.00	80.00	100	135	1,300	3,500	
1878-S	125	190	300	450	3,000	—		
1879 ...... *1,100*	13,600	150	175	300	465	1,250	1,400	2,000
1880 ...... *1,355*	13,600	150	185	275	350	1,300	1,400	2,000
1881 ...... *975*	12,000	150	200	285	360	1,300	1,400	2,000
1882 ...... *1,100*	15,200	150	200	295	360	1,400	1,600	2,000
1883 ...... *1,039*	14,400	150	200	295	380	1,600	—	2,000
1884 ...... *875*	8,000	110	225	295	360	1,400	2,100	2,000
1885 ...... *930*	13,600	110	200	325	390	1,600	2,000	2,000
1886 ...... *886*	5,000	190	300	400	425	2,000	2,600	2,000
1887 ...... *710*	10,000	140	225	300	325	1,600	2,100	2,000
1888 ...... *832*	10,001	140	225	300	325	1,300	2,100	2,000
1888-S	1,216,000	10.00	30.00	50.00	100	1,300	3,000	
1889 ...... *711*	12,000	100	225	300	350	1,300	1,800	2,000
1890 ...... *590*	80,000	60.00	90.00	200	275	1,300	1,800	2,000
1891 ...... *600*	3,920,000	20.00	40.00	50.00	150	850	1,800	2,000
1891-O	68,000	100	265	475	650	7,600	—	
1891-S	2,216,000	20.00	50.00	75.00	125	750	2,000	

Barber, or Liberty Head Portrait
(1892–1916)

	Mintage	Good-4	Fine-12	EF-40	AU-55	MS-63	MS-65	Proof-65
1892 . . . . . . *1,245*	8,236,000	$7.00	$15.00	$55.00	$110	$395	$1,400	$2,200
1892-O	2,640,000	7.00	16.00	60.00	130	395	2,500	
1892-S	964,079	25.00	35.00	100	250	750	4,000	
1893 . . . . . . *792*	5,444,023	7.00	15.00	55.00	110	395	1,400	2,200
1893-O	3,396,000	8.00	18.00	60.00	130	500	2,200	
1893-S	1,454,535	10.00	22.50	90.00	250	750	6,500	
1894 . . . . . . *972*	3,432,000	7.00	15.00	55.00	110	450	1,500	2,200
1894-O	2,852,000	8.00	18.00	60.00	170	1,700	3,800	
1894-S	2,648,821	8.00	17.50	60.00	150	650	5,600	
1895 . . . . . . *880*	4,440,000	8.00	15.00	55.00	125	525	1,400	2,200
1895-O	2,816,000	8.00	18.00	70.00	210	700	2,500	
1895-S	1,764,681	8.00	25.00	70.00	210	750	4,000	
1896 . . . . . . *762*	3,874,000	8.00	15.00	55.00	110	450	2,000	2,200
1896-O	1,484,000	8.00	40.00	300	600	2,000	7,300	
1896-S	188,039	1,000	2,300	5,000	7,500	17,500	50,000	
1897 . . . . . . *731*	8,140,000	8.00	15.00	55.00	110	395	1,700	2,200
1897-O	1,414,800	8.00	50.00	300	600	1,800	5,000	
1897-S	542,229	10.00	60.00	220	600	1,800	6,500	
1898 . . . . . . *735*	11,100,000	8.00	15.00	55.00	110	395	1,500	2,200
1898-O	1,868,000	8.00	30.00	140	350	1,800	7,000	
1898-S	1,020,592	8.00	20.00	60.00	160	1,200	5,600	
1899 . . . . . . *846*	12,624,000	6.00	15.00	55.00	110	395	1,800	2,200
1899-O	2,644,000	7.00	20.00	75.00	225	725	4,950	
1899-S	708,000	12.00	20.00	70.00	175	1,200	3,500	
1900 . . . . . . *912*	10,016,000	6.00	15.00	55.00	110	395	1,800	2,200
1900-O	3,416,000	7.00	25.00	85.00	215	1,000	3,400	
1900-S	1,858,585	7.00	18.00	60.00	110	1,000	4,500	
1901 . . . . . . *813*	8,892,000	6.00	15.00	55.00	110	395	2,700	2,200
1901-O	1,612,000	15.00	50.00	260	550	2,000	5,500	
1901-S	72,664	6,000	16,000	28,000	33,000	50,000	90,000	
1902 . . . . . . *777*	12,196,967	6.00	15.00	55.00	110	395	1,400	2,200
1902-O	4,748,000	7.00	20.00	90.00	175	1,300	5,000	
1902-S	1,524,612	6.00	20.00	75.00	175	900	3,500	
1903 . . . . . . *755*	9,669,309	6.00	15.00	55.00	110	500	2,200	2,200
1903-O	3,500,000	6.00	20.00	75.00	175	1,200	5,200	
1903-S	1,036,000	15.00	25.00	85.00	225	900	2,750	
1904 . . . . . . *670*	9,588,143	6.00	15.00	55.00	110	395	2,200	2,200
1904-O	2,456,000	7.00	25.00	150	325	1,400	2,950	
1905 . . . . . . *727*	4,967,523	6.00	15.00	55.00	110	395	2,300	2,200
1905-O	1,230,000	7.00	23.00	110	250	1,100	6,100	
1905-S	1,884,000	9.00	15.00	75.00	175	1,100	3,500	
1906 . . . . . . *675*	3,655,760	6.00	15.00	55.00	110	395	1,400	2,200
1906-D	3,280,000	6.00	17.50	60.00	140	550	3,250	
1906-O	2,056,000	6.00	20.00	70.00	170	550	1,750	
1907 . . . . . . *575*	7,192,000	6.00	15.00	55.00	110	395	1,400	2,200
1907-D	2,484,000	9.00	17.50	60.00	160	750	3,250	
1907-O	4,560,000	9.00	17.50	55.00	130	650	3,000	
1907-S	1,360,000	9.00	20.00	90.00	195	1,100	3,950	
1908 . . . . . . *545*	4,232,000	6.00	40.00	55.00	110	395	1,600	2,200
1908-D	5,788,000	6.00	40.00	60.00	110	425	2,000	
1908-O	6,244,000	9.00	40.00	60.00	110	395	1,700	
1908-S	784,000	12.00	40.00	210	375	1,500	6,100	
1909 . . . . . . *650*	9,268,000	6.00	40.00	55.00	110	395	1,400	2,200
1909-D	5,114,000	12.00	40.00	60.00	150	450	1,950	
1909-O	712,000	10.00	32.50	150	325	1,100	7,500	

	Mintage	Good-4	Fine-12	EF-40	AU-55	MS-63	MS-65	Proof-65
1909-S	1,348,000	8.00	25.00	65.00	165	650	2,100	
1910 ...... *551*	2,244,000	7.00	25.00	55.00	110	395	1,400	2,200
1910-D	1,500,000	8.00	25.00	70.00	170	800	2,350	
1911 ..... *543*	3,720,000	6.00	25.00	55.00	110	395	1,400	2,200
1911-D	933,600	8.00	100	275	395	875	4,500	
1911-S	988,000	8.00	30.00	80.00	185	800	2,000	
1912 ...... *700*	4,400,000	6.00	30.00	55.00	110	395	1,400	2,200
1912-S	708,000	6.00	40.00	75.00	195	1,100	3,000	
1913 ..... *622*	484,000	6.00	100	330	525	1,100	4,500	2,200
1913-D	1,450,800	6.00	17.50	60.00	150	475	1,700	
1913-S	40,000	2,000	5,000	10,000	12,000	17,000	35,000	
1914 ...... *425*	6,244,230	5.00	15.00	55.00	110	395	1,400	2,600
1914-D	3,046,000	5.00	15.00	55.00	110	395	2,000	
1914-S	264,000	45.00	110	325	535	1,600	3,600	
1915 ...... *450*	3,480,000	5.00	15.00	55.00	110	395	1,300	2,600
1915-D	3,694,000	5.00	15.00	55.00	110	395	2,000	
1915-S	704,000	10.00	17.50	70.00	175	395	2,050	
1916	1,788,000	5.00	15.00	55.00	110	395	2,000	
1916-D	6,540,800	5.00	15.00	55.00	110	395	2,000	

Standing Liberty Portrait (1916–1930)

Liberty with Bare Breast (1916–1917)

	Mintage	Good-4	Fine-12	EF-40	AU-55	MS-63	MS-65
1916	52,000	$3,000	$9,000	$12,500	$20,000	$30,000	$35,000
1917 (Type 1)	8,740,000	30.00	50.00	57.00	115	300	1,000
1917-D (Type 1)	1,509,200	45.00	60.00	85.00	120	500	1,500
1917-S (Type 1)	1,952,000	45.00	100	125	200	1,100	2,000

Liberty Wearing Coat of Mail (1917–1930)

	Mintage	Good-4	Fine-12	EF-40	AU-55	MS-63	MS-65
1917 (Type 2)	13,880,000	$25.00	$30.00	$40.00	$60.00	$200	$700
1917-D (Type 2)	6,224,400	50.00	65.00	85.00	100	300	1,600
1917-S (Type 2)	5,552,000	50.00	60.00	70.00	90.00	250	1,400
1918	14,240,000	20.00	30.00	40.00	75.00	175	600
1918-D	7,380,000	30.00	40.00	80.00	140	280	1,500
1918-S combined total ...	11,072,000						
1918-S regular date		15.00	25.00	50.00	80.00	300	1,500
1918/17-S overdate		1,500	3,500	9,500	14,000	45,000	125,000
1919	11,324,000	25.00	50.00	75.00	90.00	200	550
1919-D	1,944,000	60.00	90.00	300	325	900	2,500
1919-S	1,836,000	60.00	90.00	350	450	1,200	3,250

	Mintage	Good-4	Fine-12	EF-40	AU-55	MS-63	MS-65
1920	27,860,000	15.00	20.00	30.00	60.00	200	550
1920-D	3,586,400	35.00	50.00	90.00	150	500	2,000
1920-S	6,380,000	18.00	20.00	50.00	80.00	600	2,500
1921	1,916,000	90.00	125	240	350	725	2,100
1923	9,716,000	15.00	25.00	35.00	60.00	200	550
1923-S	1,360,000	100	150	325	425	690	1,850
1924	10,920,000	15.00	20.00	35.00	65.00	175	550
1924-D	3,112,000	30.00	40.00	80.00	95.00	160	550
1924-S	2,860,000	16.00	20.00	75.00	185	725	2,000

Date Recessed (1925–1930)

	Mintage	Good-4	Fine-12	EF-40	AU-55	MS-63	MS-65
1925	12,280,000	$6.00	$20.00	$30.00	$50.00	$300	$550
1926	11,316,000	6.00	20.00	30.00	50.00	250	550
1926-D	1,716,000	10.00	20.00	40.00	75.00	250	550
1926-S	2,700,000	7.00	20.00	100	200	900	2,000
1927	11,912,000	6.00	20.00	30.00	50.00	185	550
1927-D	976,000	10.00	50.00	75.00	125	200	600
1927-S	396,000	20.00	300	950	3,000	8,250	14,000
1928	6,336,000	6.00	20.00	30.00	60.00	175	550
1928-D	1,627,600	10.00	20.00	35.00	75.00	185	550
1928-S	2,644,000	10.00	20.00	35.00	75.00	185	550
1929	11,140,000	10.00	20.00	35.00	75.00	185	550
1929-D	1,358,000	10.00	20.00	35.00	75.00	185	550
1929-S	1,764,000	10.00	20.00	35.00	75.00	185	550
1930	5,632,000	10.00	20.00	35.00	75.00	185	550
1930-S	1,556,000	10.00	20.00	35.00	75.00	185	550

Washington Portrait (1932–Present)

Silver Composition (1932–1964)

	Mintage	Good-4	Fine-12	EF-40	AU-55	MS-63	MS-65	Proof-65
1932	5,404,080	$5.00	$6.00	$8.00	$15.00	$70.00	$600	
1932-D	436,800	150	225	350	500	2,500	20,000	
1932-S	408,000	200	250	300	350	1,000	5,000	
1934 combined total	31,912,052							
1934 regular date		—	2.00	3.50	8.00	25.00	80.00	
1934 doubled die		20.00	50.00	100	200	1,500	7,500	
1934-D	3,527,200	5.00	6.00	9.00	40.00	440	1,800	
1935	32,484,000	—	1.75	3.00	9.00	25.00	50.00	
1935-D	5,780,000	5.00	6.00	10.00	50.00	85.00	650	
1935-S	5,660,000	5.00	5.75	6.00	20.00	50.00	300	
1936 . . . . . . 3,837	41,300,000	5.00	6.00	7.00	7.50	25.00	75.00	$1,100
1936-D	5,374,000	5.00	6.50	25.00	105	350	675	
1936-S	3,828,000	5.00	6.00	9.75	25.00	70.00	140	
1937 . . . . . . 5,542	19,696,000	5.00	5.25	5.75	12.00	25.00	70.00	450
1937-D	7,189,600	5.00	5.25	6.00	15.00	40.00	90.00	
1937-S	1,652,000	6.00	10.00	20.00	50.00	80.00	250	
1938 . . . . . . 8,045	9,472,000	5.00	10.00	12.00	30.00	50.00	150	200
1938-S	2,832,000	5.00	6.00	12.00	30.00	50.00	160	
1939 . . . . . . 8,795	33,540,000	5.00	6.00	7.00	10.00	18.00	50.00	200
1939-D	7,092,000	5.00	6.00	7.00	12.00	30.00	80.00	

	Mintage	Good-4	Fine-12	EF-40	AU-55	MS-63	MS-65	Proof-65
1939-S	2,628,000	5.00	6.00	9.00	30.00	60.00	125	
1940 ... *11,246*	35,704,000	5.00	6.00	7.00	10.00	15.00	50.00	90.00
1940-D	2,797,600	5.00	6.00	9.00	30.00	60.00	125	
1940-S	8,244,000	5.00	6.00	7.00	9.00	20.00	50.00	
1941 ...*15,287*	79,032,000	5.00	6.00	6.50	6.75	7.00	20.00	90.00
1941-D	16,714,800	5.00	5.10	5.50	6.00	15.00	35.00	
1941-S	16,080,000	5.00	5.10	5.50	6.00	17.00	75.00	
1942 ... *21,123*	102,096,000	5.00	5.10	5.50	6.00	8.00	25.00	95.00
1942-D	17,487,200	5.00	5.10	5.50	10.00	12.00	26.00	
1942-S	19,384,000	5.00	5.10	5.50	14.00	75.00	150	
1943	99,700,000	5.00	5.10	5.50	7.00	8.00	26.00	
1943-D	16,095,000	5.00	5.10	5.50	6.00	15.00	30.00	
1943-S combined total .	21,700,000							
1943-S regular strike ...		5.00	5.25	6.00	12.00	28.00	200	
1943-S with doubled obverse		190	225	500	890	1,375	8,650	
1944	104,956,000	5.00	6.00	7.00	12.00	50.00	90.00	
1944-D	14,600,800	5.00	6.00	7.00	12.00	30.00	75.00	
1944-S	12,560,000	5.00	6.00	7.00	12.00	30.00	125	
1945	74,372,000	5.00	6.00	7.00	10.00	12.00	40.00	
1945-D	12,341,600	5.00	6.00	7.00	12.00	30.00	40.00	
1945-S	17,004,001	5.00	6.00	7.00	12.00	15.00	30.00	
1946	53,436,000	5.00	6.00	7.00	12.00	15.00	50.00	
1946-D	9,072,800	5.00	6.00	7.00	12.00	25.00	45.00	
1946-S	4,204,000	5.00	6.00	7.00	12.00	20.00	40.00	
1947	22,556,000	5.00	6.00	7.00	12.00	25.00	40.00	
1947-D	15,338,400	5.00	6.00	7.00	12.00	20.00	30.00	
1947-S	5,532,000	5.00	6.00	7.00	12.00	20.00	30.00	
1948	35,196,000	5.00	6.00	7.00	12.00	20.00	30.00	
1948-D	16,766,800	5.00	6.00	7.00	12.00	20.00	30.00	
1948-S	15,960,000	5.00	6.00	7.00	12.00	20.00	40.00	
1949	9,312,000	5.00	6.00	7.00	12.00	40.00	90.00	
1949-D	10,068,400	5.00	6.00	7.00	12.00	30.00	60.00	
1950.... *51,386*	24,920,126	5.00	6.00	7.00	12.00	25.00	40.00	95.00
1950-D combined total..	21,075,600							
1950-D with regular mint mark		5.00	6.00		12.00	25.00	50.00	
1950-D/S		30.00	140	200	450	500	8,000	
1950-S combined total..	10,284,004							
1950-S with regular mint mark		5.00	5.75	6.50	7.00	14.00	75.00	
1950-S/D		30.00	60.00	250	300	500	1,500	600
1951.... *57,500*	43,448,102	5.00	5.75	6.50	7.00	14.00	40.00	50.00
1951-D	35,354,800	5.00	5.75	6.50	7.00	14.00	40.00	
1951-S	9,048,000	5.00	5.75	6.50	7.00	14.00	75.00	
1952.... *81,980*	38,780,093	5.00	5.75	6.50	7.00	14.00	40.00	45.00
1952-D	49,795,200	5.00	5.75	6.50	7.00	14.00	40.00	
1952-S	13,707,800	5.00	5.75	6.50	7.00	14.00	100	
1953.... *128,800*	18,536,120	5.00	5.75	6.50	7.00	14.00	100	40.00
1953-D	56,112,400	5.00	5.75	6.50	7.00	14.00	100	
1953-S	14,016,000	5.00	5.75	6.50	7.00	14.00	100	
1954.... *233,300*	54,412,203	5.00	5.75	6.50	7.00	14.00	40.00	18.00
1954-D	42,305,500	5.00	5.75	6.50	7.00	14.00	40.00	
1954-S	11,834,722	5.00	5.75	6.50	7.00	14.00	40.00	
1955.... *378,200*	18,180,181	5.00	5.75	6.50	7.00	14.00	40.00	15.00
1955-D	3,182,400	5.00	5.75	6.50	7.00	14.00	40.00	
1956.... *669,384*	44,144,000	5.00	5.75	6.50	7.00	14.00	20.00	8.00
1956-D	32,334,500	5.00	5.10	5.75	6.00	10.00	20.00	
1957.... *1,247,952*	46,532,000	5.00	5.10	5.75	6.00	10.00	20.00	9.50
1957-D	77,924,160	5.00	5.10	5.75	6.00	10.00	20.00	
1958.... *875,652*	6,360,000	5.00	5.10	5.75	6.00	10.00	20.00	9.50
1958-D	78,124,900	5.00	5.10	5.75	6.00	10.00	20.00	
1959.... *1,149,291*	24,384,000	5.00	5.10	5.75	6.00	10.00	20.00	9.50
1959-D	62,054,232	5.00	5.10	5.75	6.00	10.00	20.00	
1960.... *1,691,602*	29,164,000	5.00	5.10	5.75	6.00	10.00	20.00	9.50
1960-D	63,000,324	5.00	5.10	5.75	6.00	10.00	20.00	
1961.... *3,028,244*	37,036,000	5.00	5.10	5.75	6.00	10.00	20.00	9.50

	Mintage	Good-4	Fine-12	EF-40	AU-55	MS-63	MS-65	Proof-65
1961-D	88,656,928	5.00	5.10	5.75	6.00	10.00	20.00	
1962....*3,218,019*	36,156,000	5.00	5.10	5.75	6.00	10.00	20.00	9.00
1962-D	127,554,756	5.00	5.10	5.75	6.00	10.00	20.00	
1963....*3,075,645*	74,316,000	5.00	5.10	5.75	6.00	10.00	20.00	9.00
1963-D	135,288,184	5.00	5.10	5.75	6.00	10.00	20.00	
1964....*3,950,762*	560,390,585	5.00	5.10	5.75	6.00	10.00	20.00	8.75
1964-D	704,135,528	5.00	5.10	5.75	6.00	10.00	20.00	

Copper-Nickel Clad Composition (1965–Present)

	Mintage	EF-40	MS-65	Proof-65
1965	1,819,717,540	—	$.60	
1966	821,101,500	—	.60	
1967	1,524,031,848	—	.75	
1968	220,731,500	—	.60	
1968-D...................	101,534,000	—	.75	
1968-S (proof only)........	*3,041,506*	—	—	$1.20
1969	176,212,000	—	.75	
1969-D...................	114,372,000	—	.75	
1969-S (proof only)........	*2,934,631*	—	—	1.20
1970	136,420,000	—	.40	
1970-D...................	417,341,364	—	.35	
1970-S (proof only)........	*2,632,810*	—	—	1.90
1971	109,284,000	—	.45	
1971-D...................	258,634,428	—	.35	
1971-S (proof only)........	*3,220,733*	—	—	1.20
1972	215,048,000	—	.35	
1972-D...................	311,067,732	—	.35	
1972-S (proof only)........	*3,260,996*	—	—	—
1973	346,924,000	—	.35	
1973-D...................	232,977,400	—	.35	
1973-S (proof only)........	*2,760,339*	—	—	1.35
1974	801,456,000	—	.35	
1974-D...................	353,160,300	—	.35	
1974-S (proof only)........	*2,612,568*	—	—	1.50

Bicentennial Portrait (1975–1976)

	Mintage	EF-40	MS-65	Proof-65
1776–1976 copper-nickel clad	809,784,016	—	$.40	
1776–1976-D copper-nickel clad...................	860,118,839	—	.40	
1776–1976-S copper-nickel clad (proof only; includes coins from both 1975 and 1976 proof sets)	*6,968,506*	—	—	$1.60
1776–1976-S silver clad ....*3,998,621*......	4,908,319	—	1.50	2.25

Regular Design Returns (1977–Present)

	Mintage	EF-40	MS-65	Proof-65
1977	468,556,000	—	$.35	
1977-D.................	256,524,978	—	.35	
1977-S (proof only)........	*3,251,152*	—	—	$1.75
1978	521,452,000	—	.35	
1978-D.................	287,373,152	—	.35	
1978-S (proof only)........	*3,127,781*	—	—	1.80
1979	515,708,000	—	.40	
1979-D.................	489,789,780	—	.40	
1979-S combined total (proof only)	*3,677,175*			
1979-S with clear S		—	—	14.50
1979-S with clogged S......		—	—	1.65
1980-P..................	635,832,000	—	.40	

	Mintage	EF-40	MS-65	Proof-65
1980-D.	518,327,487	—	.40	
1980-S (proof only)	3,554,806	—	—	1.80
1981-P	601,716,000	—	.40	
1981-D	575,722,833	—	.40	
1981-S (proof only)	4,063,083	—	—	1.60
1982-P	500,931,000	—	3.50	
1982-D	480,042,788	—	2.25	
1982-S (proof only)	3,857,479	—	—	1.65
1983-P	673,535,000	—	4.50	
1983-D	617,806,446	—	6.00	
1983-S (proof only)	3,279,126	—	—	1.75
1984-P	676,545,000	—	.60	
1984-D	546,483,064	—	1.25	
1984-S (proof only)	3,065,110	—	—	3.00
1985-P	775,818,962	—	.90	
1985-D	519,962,888	—	2.00	
1985-S (proof only)	3,362,821	—	—	1.80
1986-P	551,199,333	—	2.50	
1986-D	504,298,660	—	2.50	
1986-S (proof only)	3,010,497	—	—	6.00
1987-P	582,499,481	—	.40	
1987-D	655,594,696	—	.40	
1987-S (proof only)	3,792,233	—	—	1.65
1988-P	562,052,000	—	.40	
1988-D	596,810,688	—	.40	
1988-S (proof only)	3,262,948	—	—	3.00
1989-P	512,868,000	—	.40	
1989-D	896,535,597	—	.40	
1989-S (proof only)	3,215,728	—	—	2.40
1990-P	613,792,000	—	.40	
1990-D	927,638,181	—	.40	
1990-S (proof only)	3,299,559	—	—	4.00
1991-P	570,968,000	—	.40	
1991-D	630,966,693	—	.40	
1991-S (proof only)	2,867,787	—	—	4.00
1992-P	384,764,000	—	.40	
1992-D	389,777,107	—	.40	
1992-S (proof only)	4,176,544*	—	—	4.00
1993-P	639,276,000	—	.40	
1993-D	645,476,128	—	.40	
1993-S (proof only)	3,360,876*	—	—	4.00
1994-P	827,010,896	—	.40	
1994-D	881,245,006	—	.40	
1994-S (proof only)	3,212,792*	—		4.00
1995-P	1,005,377,352	—	.40	
1995-D	1,104,257,352	—	.40	
1995-S (proof only)	2,796,345*	—	—	4.00
1996-P	926,494,215	—	.40	
1996-D	908,322,215	—	.40	
1996-S (proof only)	2,925,305*	—	—	4.00
1997-P	595,740,000	—	.40	
1997-D	599,680,000	—	.40	
1997-S (proof only)	2,788,020*	—	—	4.00
1998-P	960,400,000	—	.40	
1998-D	907,000,000	—	.40	
1998-S (proof only)	2,086,507	—	—	4.00
1998-S (silver proof)	878,996	—	—	10.00

*Includes 90% silver issue

50 State Quarter Dollars (1999–)

Delaware

	Mintage	EF-40	MS-65	Proof-65
1999-P	373,400,000	—	$3.00	—
1999-D	401,424,000	—	3.00	—
1999-S (copper-nickel proof)	3,624,009	—	—	$4.00
1999-S (silver proof)	798,780	—	—	10.00

Pennsylvania

1999-P	349,000,000	—	3.00	—
1999-D	358,332,000	—	3.00	—
1999-S (copper-nickel proof)	3,624,009	—	—	4.00
1999-S (silver proof)	798,780	—	—	10.00

New Jersey

1999-P	363,200,000	—	2.00	—
1999-D	299,028,000	—	3.00	—
1999-S (copper-nickel proof)	3,624,009	—	—	4.00
1999-S (silver proof)	798,780	—	—	10.00

Georgia

1999-P	451,188,000	—	2.00	—
1999-D	488,744,000	—	2.00	—
1999-S (copper-nickel proof)	3,624,009	—	—	4.00
1999-S (silver proof)	798,780	—	—	10.00

Connecticut

1999-P	688,744,000	—	1.50	—
1999-D	657,880,000	—	1.50	—
1999-S (copper-nickel proof)	3,624,009	—	—	4.00
1999-S (silver proof)	798,780	—	—	10.00

Massachusetts

2000-P	628,600,000	—	1.00	—
2000-D	535,184,000	—	1.00	—
2000-S (copper-nickel proof)	3,992,800	—	—	4.00
2000-S (silver proof)	904,200	—	—	10.00

Maryland

2000-P	678,200,000	—	1.00	—
2000-D	556,532,000	—	1.00	—
2000-S (copper-nickel proof)	3,992,800	—	—	4.00
2000-S (silver proof)	904,200	—	—	10.00

South Carolina

2000-P	742,576,000	—	1.00	—
2000-D	566,208,000	—	1.00	—
2000-S (copper-nickel proof)	3,992,800	—	—	4.00
2000-S (silver proof)	904,200	—	—	10.00

New Hampshire

2000-P	673,040,000	—	1.00	—
2000-D	495,576,000	—	1.00	—
2000-S (copper-nickel proof)	3,992,800	—	—	4.00
2000-S (silver proof)	904,200	—	—	10.00

Virginia

2000-P	943,000,000	—	1.00	—
2000-D	651,616,000	—	1.00	—
2000-S (copper-nickel proof)	3,992,800	—	—	4.00
2000-S (silver proof)	904,200	—	—	10.00

New York

2001-P	655,400,000	—	1.00	—
2001-D	619,640,000	—	1.00	—
2001-S (copper-nickel proof)	3,094,900	—	—	4.00
2001-S (silver proof)	891,400	—	—	10.00

North Carolina

	Mintage	EF-40	MS-65	Proof-65
2001-P	627,600,000	—	1.00	—
2001-D	427,876,000	—	1.00	—
2001-S (copper-nickel proof)	3,094,900	—	—	4.00
2001-S (silver proof)	891,400	—	—	10.00

Rhode Island

	Mintage	EF-40	MS-65	Proof-65
2001-P	423,000,000	—	1.00	—
2001-D	447,100,000	—	1.00	—
2001-S (copper-nickel proof)	3,094,900	—	—	4.00
2001-S (silver proof)	891,400	—	—	10.00

Vermont

	Mintage	EF-40	MS-65	Proof-65
2001-P	423,400,000	—	1.00	—
2001-D	459,404,000	—	1.00	—
2001-S (copper-nickel proof)	3,094,900	—	—	4.00
2001-S (silver proof)	891,400	—	—	10.00

Kentucky

	Mintage	EF-40	MS-65	Proof-65
2001-P	353,000,000	—	1.00	—
2001-D	370,564,000	—	1.00	—
2001-S (copper-nickel proof)	3,094,900	—	—	4.00
2001-S (silver proof)	891,400	—	—	10.00

Tennessee

	Mintage	EF-40	MS-65	Proof-65
2002-P	361,600,000	—	1.00	—
2002-D	286,468,000	—	1.00	—
2002-S (copper-nickel proof)	3,085,940	—	—	4.00
2002-S (silver proof)	888,826	—	—	10.00

Ohio

	Mintage	EF-40	MS-65	Proof-65
2002-P	217,200,000	—	1.00	—
2002-D	414,832,000	—	1.00	—
2002-S (copper-nickel proof)	3,085,940	—	—	4.00
2002-S (silver proof)	888,826	—	—	10.00

Louisiana

	Mintage	EF-40	MS-65	Proof-65
2002-P	362,000,000	—	1.00	—
2002-D	402,204,000	—	1.00	—
2002-S (copper-nickel proof)	3,085,940	—	—	4.00
2002-S (silver proof)	888,826	—	—	10.00

Indiana

	Mintage	EF-40	MS-65	Proof-65
2002-P	362,600,000	—	1.00	—
2002-D	327,200,000	—	1.00	—
2002-S (copper-nickel proof)	3,085,940	—	—	4.00
2002-S (silver proof)	888,826	—	—	10.00

Mississippi

	Mintage	EF-40	MS-65	Proof-65
2002-P	290,000,000	—	1.00	—
2002-D	289,600,000	—	1.00	—
2002-S (copper-nickel proof)	3,085,940	—	—	4.00
2002-S (silver proof)	888,826	—	—	10.00

Illinois

	Mintage	EF-40	MS-65	Proof-65
2003-P	226,802,555	—	1.00	—
2003-D	238,402,555	—	1.00	—
2003-S (copper-nickel proof)	3,479,172	—	—	4.00
2003-S (silver proof)	1,119,494	—	—	10.00

Alabama

	Mintage	EF-40	MS-65	Proof-65
2003-P	226,002,555	—	1.00	—
2003-D	233,402,555	—	1.00	—
2003-S (copper-nickel proof)	3,479,172	—	—	4.00
2003-S (silver proof)	1,119,494	—	—	10.00

Maine

	Mintage	EF-40	MS-65	Proof-65
2003-P..................	218,402,555	—	1.00	—
2003-D..................	232,402,555	—	1.00	—
2003-S (copper-nickel proof)	3,479,172	—	—	4.00
2003-S (silver proof).......	1,119,494	—	—	10.00

Missouri

	Mintage	EF-40	MS-65	Proof-65
2003-P..................	226,002,555	—	1.00	—
2003-D..................	229,202,555	—	1.00	—
2003-S (copper-nickel proof)	3,479,172	—	—	4.00
2003-S (silver proof).......	1,119,494	—	—	10.00

Arkansas

	Mintage	EF-40	MS-65	Proof-65
2003-P..................	229,002,555	—	1.00	—
2003-D..................	230,802,555	—	1.00	—
2003-S (copper-nickel proof)	3,479,172	—	—	4.00
2003-S (silver proof).......	1,119,494	—	—	10.00

Michigan

	Mintage	EF-40	MS-65	Proof-65
2004-P..................	233,800,000	—	1.00	—
2004-D..................	225,800,000	—	1.00	—
2004-S (copper-nickel proof)	2,761,163	—	—	4.00
2004-S (silver proof).......	1,787,673	—	—	10.00

Florida

	Mintage	EF-40	MS-65	Proof-65
2004-P..................	240,200,000	—	1.00	—
2004-D..................	241,600,000	—	1.00	—
2004-S (copper-nickel proof)	2,761,163	—	—	4.00
2004-S (silver proof).......	1,787,673	—	—	10.00

Texas

	Mintage	EF-40	MS-65	Proof-65
2004-P..................	278,800,000	—	1.00	—
2004-D..................	263,000,000	—	1.00	—
2004-S (copper-nickel proof)	2,761,163	—	—	4.00
2004-S (silver proof).......	1,787,673	—	—	10.00

Iowa

	Mintage	EF-40	MS-65	Proof-65
2004-P..................	213,800,000	—	1.00	—
2004-D..................	251,400,000	—	1.00	—
2004-S (copper-nickel proof)	2,761,163	—	—	4.00
2004-S (silver proof).......	1,787,673	—	—	10.00

Wisconsin

	Mintage	EF-40	MS-65	Proof-65
2004-P..................	226,400,000	—	1.00	—
2004-D..................	226,800,000	—	1.00	—
2004-S (copper-nickel proof)	2,761,163	—	—	4.00
2004-S (silver proof).......	1,787,673	—	—	10.00

California

	Mintage	EF-40	MS-65	Proof-65
2005-P..................	257,200,000	—	1.00	—
2005-D..................	263,200,000	—	1.00	—
2005-S (copper-nickel proof)	3,262,000	—	—	4.00
2005-S (silver proof).......	1,606,970	—	—	10.00

Minnesota

	Mintage	EF-40	MS-65	Proof-65
2005-P..................	239,600,000	—	1.00	—
2005-D..................	248,400,000	—	1.00	—
2005-S (copper-nickel proof)	3,262,000	—	—	4.00
2005-S (silver proof).......	1,606,970	—	—	10.00

Oregon

	Mintage	EF-40	MS-65	Proof-65
2005-P..................	316,200,000	—	1.00	—
2005-D..................	404,000,000	—	1.00	—
2005-S (copper-nickel proof)	3,262,000	—	—	4.00
2005-S (silver proof).......	1,606,970	—	—	10.00

Kansas

	Mintage	EF-40	MS-65	Proof-65
2005-P..................	263,400,000	—	1.00	—
2005-D..................	300,000,000	—	1.00	—
2005-S (copper-nickel proof)	3,262,000	—	—	4.00
2005-S (silver proof).......	1,606,970	—	—	10.00

West Virginia

2005-P..................	365,400,000	—	1.00	—
2005-D..................	356,200,000	—	1.00	—
2005-S (copper-nickel proof)	3,262,000	—	—	4.00
2005-S (silver proof).......	1,606,970	—	—	10.00

Nevada

2006-P..................	277,000,000	—	1.00	—
2006-D..................	312,800,000	—	1.00	—
2006-S (copper-nickel proof)	2,882,428	—	—	4.00
2006-S (silver proof).......	1,585,008	—	—	10.00

Nebraska

2006-P..................	318,000,000	—	1.00	—
2006-D..................	273,000,000	—	1.00	—
2006-S (copper-nickel proof)	2,882,428	—	—	4.00
2006-S (silver proof).......	1,585,008	—	—	10.00

Colorado

2006-P..................	274,800,000	—	1.00	—
2006-D..................	294,200,000	—	1.00	—
2006-S (copper-nickel proof)	2,882,428	—	—	4.00
2006-S (silver proof).......	1,585,008	—	—	10.00

North Dakota

2006-P..................	305,800,000	—	1.00	—
2006-D..................	359,000,000	—	1.00	—
2006-S (copper-nickel proof)	2,882,428	—	—	4.00
2006-S (silver proof).......	1,585,008	—	—	10.00

South Dakota

2006-P..................	245,000,000	—	1.00	—
2006-D..................	265,800,000	—	1.00	—
2006-S (copper-nickel proof)	2,882,428	—	—	4.00
2006-S (silver proof).......	1,585,008	—	—	10.00

Montana

2007-P..................	257,000,000	—	1.00	—
2007-D..................	256,240,000	—	1.00	—
2007-S (copper-nickel proof)	2,374,778	—	—	4.00
2007-S (silver proof).......	1,299,878	—	—	10.00

Washington

2007-P..................	265,200,000	—	1.00	—
2007-D..................	280,000,000	—	1.00	—
2007-S (copper-nickel proof)	2,374,778	—	—	4.00
2007-S (silver proof).......	1,299,878	—	—	10.00

Idaho

2007-P..................	294,600,000	—	1.00	—
2007-D..................	286,800,000	—	1.00	—
2007-S (copper-nickel proof)	2,374,778	—	—	4.00
2007-S (silver proof).......	1,299,878	—	—	10.00

Wyoming

2007-P..................	243,600,000	—	1.00	—
2007-D..................	320,800,000	—	1.00	—
2007-S (copper-nickel proof)	2,374,778	—	—	4.00
2007-S (silver proof).......	1,299,878	—	—	10.00

Utah

	Mintage	EF-40	MS-65	Proof-65
2007-P.................	255,000,000	—	1.00	—
2007-D.................	253,200,000	—	1.00	—
2007-S (copper-nickel proof)	2,374,778	—	—	4.00
2007-S (silver proof).......	1,299,878	—	—	10.00

Oklahoma

2008-P.................	222,000,000	—	1.00	—
2008-D.................	194,600,000	—	1.00	—
2008-S (copper-nickel proof)	2,045,508	—	—	4.00
2008-S (silver proof).......	1,187,835	—	—	10.00

New Mexico

2008-P.................	244,200,000	—	1.00	—
2008-D.................	244,400,000	—	1.00	—
2008-S (copper-nickel proof)	2,045,508	—	—	4.00
2008-S (silver proof).......	1,187,835	—	—	10.00

Arizona

2008-P.................	244,600,000	—	1.00	—
2008-D.................	265,000,000	—	1.00	—
2008-S (copper-nickel proof)	2,045,508	—	—	4.00
2008-S (silver proof).......	1,187,835	—	—	10.00

Alaska

2008-P.................	251,800,000	—	1.00	—
2008-D.................	254,000,000	—	1.00	—
2008-S (copper-nickel proof)	2,045,508	—	—	4.00
2008-S (silver proof).......	1,187,835	—	—	10.00

Hawaii

2008-P.................	254,000,000	—	1.00	—
2008-D.................	263,600,000	—	1.00	—
2008-S (copper-nickel proof)	2,045,508	—	—	4.00
2008-S (silver proof).......	1,187,835	—	—	10.00

District of Columbia

2009-P.................	83,600,000	—	1.00	—
2009-D.................	88,800,000	—	1.00	—
2009-S (copper-nickel proof)	2,113,390	—	—	4.00
2009-S (silver proof).......	993,584	—	—	10.00

Puerto Rico

2009-P.................	53,200,000	—	1.00	—
2009-D.................	86,000,000	—	1.00	—
2009-S (copper-nickel proof)	2,113,390	—	—	4.00
2009-S (silver proof).......	993,584	—	—	10.00

Guam

2009-P.................	45,000,000	—	1.00	—
2009-D.................	42,600,000	—	1.00	—
2009-S (copper-nickel proof)	2,113,390	—	—	4.00
2009-S (silver proof).......	993,584	—	—	10.00

American Samoa

2009-P.................	42,600,000	—	1.00	—
2009-D.................	39,600,000	—	1.00	—
2009-S (copper-nickel proof)	2,113,390	—	—	4.00
2009-S (silver proof).......	993,584	—	—	10.00

United States Virgin Islands

2009-P.................	41,000,000	—	1.00	—
2009-D.................	41,000,000	—	1.00	—
2009-S (copper-nickel proof)	2,113,390	—	—	4.00
2009-S (silver proof).......	993,584	—	—	10.00

Northern Mariana Islands

	Mintage	EF-40	MS-65	Proof-65
2009-P.................	35,200,000	—	1.00	—
2009-D.................	37,600,000	—	1.00	—
2009-S (copper-nickel proof)	2,113,390	—	—	4.00
2009-S (silver proof).......	993,584	—	—	10.00

Hot Springs National Park

2010-P.................	29,000,000	—	1.00	—
2010-D.................	30,600,000	—	1.00	—
2010-S (copper-nickel proof)	—	—	—	4.00
2010-S (silver proof).......	—	—	—	10.00

Yellowstone National Park

2010-P.................	33,600,000	—	1.00	—
2010-D.................	34,800,000	—	1.00	—
2010-S (copper-nickel proof)	—	—	—	4.00
2010-S (silver proof).......	—	—	—	10.00

Yosemite National Park

2010-P.................	35,200,000	—	1.00	—
2010-D.................	34,800,000	—	1.00	—
2010-S (copper-nickel proof)	—	—	—	4.00
2010-S (silver proof).......	—	—	—	10.00

Grand Canyon National Park

2010-P.................	34,800,000	—	1.00	—
2010-D.................	35,400,000	—	1.00	—
2010-S (copper-nickel proof)	—	—	—	4.00
2010-S (silver proof).......	—	—	—	10.00

Mount Hood National Forest

2010-P.................	34,400,000	—	1.00	—
2010-D.................	34,400,000	—	1.00	—
2010-S (copper-nickel proof)	—	—	—	4.00
2010-S (silver proof).......	—	—	—	10.00

Gettysburg National Military Park

2011-P.................	30,400,000	—	1.00	—
2011-D.................	30,800,000	—	1.00	—
2011-S (copper-nickel proof)	—	—	—	4.00
2011-S (silver proof).......	—	—	—	10.00

Glacier National Park

2011-P.................	30,400,000	—	1.00	—
2011-D.................	31,200,000	—	1.00	—
2011-S (copper-nickel proof)	—	—	—	4.00
2011-S (silver proof).......	—	—	—	10.00

Olympic National Park

2011-P.................	30,400,000	—	1.00	—
2011-D.................	30,600,000	—	1.00	—
2011-S (copper-nickel proof)	—	—	—	4.00
2011-S (silver proof).......	—	—	—	7.00

Vicksburg National Military Park

2011-P.................	30,800,000	—	1.00	—
2011-D.................	33,400,000	—	1.00	—
2011-S (copper-nickel proof)	—	—	—	4.00
2011-S (silver proof).......	—	—	—	7.00

Chickasaw National Recreation Area

2011-P.................	73,800,000	—	1.00	—
2011-D.................	69,400,000	—	1.00	—
2011-S (copper-nickel proof)	—	—	—	4.00
2011-S (silver proof).......	—	—	—	7.00

El Yunque National Forest

	Mintage	EF-40	MS-65	Proof-65
2012-P...................	—	—	1.00	—
2012-D...................	—	—	1.00	—
2012-S (proof only)........	—	—	—	4.00
2012-S (silver proof).......	—	—	—	9.00

Chaco Culture National Historical Park

2012-P...................	—	—	1.00	—
2012-D...................	—	—	1.00	—
2012-S (proof only)........	—	—	—	4.00
2012-S (silver proof).......	—	—	—	9.00

Acadia National Park

2012-P...................	—	—	1.00	—
2012-D...................	—	—	1.00	—
2012-S (proof only)........	—	—	—	4.00
2012-S (silver proof).......	—	—	—	9.00

Hawai'i Volcanoes National Park

2012-P...................	—	—	1.00	—
2012-D...................	—	—	1.00	—
2012-S (proof only)........	—	—	—	4.00
2012-S (silver proof).......	—	—	—	9.00

Denali National Park and Preserve

2012-P...................	—	—	1.00	—
2012-D...................	—	—	1.00	—
2012-S (proof only)........	—	—	—	4.00
2012-S (silver proof).......	—	—	—	9.00

White Mountain National Forest

2013-P...................	—	—	1.00	—
2013-D...................	—	—	1.00	—
2013-S (proof only)........	—	—	—	4.00
2013-S (silver proof).......	—	—	—	8.00

Perry's Victory and International Peace Memorial

2013-P...................	—	—	1.00	—
2013-D...................	—	—	1.00	—
2013-S (proof only)........	—	—	—	4.00
2013-S (silver proof).......	—	—	—	8.00

Great Basin National Park

2013-P...................	—	—	1.00	—
2013-D...................	—	—	1.00	—
2013-S (proof only)........	—	—	—	4.00
2013-S (silver proof).......	—	—	—	8.00

Fort McHenry National Monument and Historic Shrine

2013-P...................	—	—	1.00	—
2013-D...................	—	—	1.00	—
2013-S (proof only)........	—	—	—	4.00
2013-S (silver proof).......	—	—	—	8.00

Mount Rushmore National Memorial

2013-P...................	—	—	1.00	—
2013-D...................	—	—	1.00	—
2013-S (proof only)........	—	—	—	4.00
2013-S (silver proof).......	—	—	—	9.00

Great Smoky Mountains National Park

2014-P...................	—	—	1.00	—
2014-D...................	—	—	1.00	—
2014-S (proof only)........	—	—	—	4.00
2014-S (silver proof).......	—	—	—	9.00

Shenandoah National Park

	Mintage	EF-40	MS-65	Proof-65
2014-P...................	—	—	1.00	—
2014-D...................	—	—	1.00	—
2014-S (proof only)........	—	—	—	4.00
2014-S (silver proof).......	—	—	—	9.00

Arches National Park

	Mintage	EF-40	MS-65	Proof-65
2014-P...................	—	—	1.00	—
2014-D...................	—	—	1.00	—
2014-S (proof only)........	—	—	—	4.00
2014-S (silver proof).......	—	—	—	9.00

Great Sand Dunes National Park

	Mintage	EF-40	MS-65	Proof-65
2014-P...................	—	—	1.00	—
2014-D...................	—	—	1.00	—
2014-S (proof only)........	—	—	—	4.00
2014-S (silver proof).......	—	—	—	9.00

Everglades National Park

	Mintage	EF-40	MS-65	Proof-65
2014-P...................	—	—	1.00	—
2014-D...................	—	—	1.00	—
2014-S (proof only)........	—	—	—	4.00
2014-S (silver proof).......	—	—	—	9.00

HALF DOLLARS (1794–PRESENT)

Flowing Hair Portrait (1794–1795)

	Mintage	Good-4	Fine-12	EF-40
1794	23,464	$6,000	$18,000	$40,000
1795 combined total.......	299,680			
1795 with 2 leaves under each wing.............		1,200	5,000	12,500
1795 with 3 leaves under each wing.............		2,000	7,500	20,000

Draped Bust Portrait with Small Eagle on Reverse (1796–1797)

	Mintage	Good-4	Fine-12	EF-40
1796 combined total.......	934			
1796 with 15 stars.........		$30,000	$60,000	$90,000
1796 with 16 stars.........		32,000	60,000	100,000
1797	2,984	30,000	50,000	100,000

Draped Bust Portrait with Heraldic Eagle on Reverse (1801–1807)

	Mintage	Good-4	Fine-12	EF-40
1801	30,289	$900	$2,000	$10,000
1802	29,890	900	2,000	10,000
1803 combined total.......	188,234			
1803 with small 3		900	1,000	3,000
1803 with large 3..........		900	1,000	2,000
1805 combined total.......	211,722			
1805 with regular date		200	275	2,000
1805/4 overdate		200	400	1,900
1806 combined total.......	839,576			
1806/5 overdate		225	350	1,600
1806 with horizontal 0 in date		150	450	1,800
1806 with knob-top 6 and no stem through eagle's claw	(4 known)	20,000	40,000	90,000
1806, all others		200	300	1,100
1807	301,076	225	275	1,100

Capped Bust Portrait, Lettered Edge (1807–1836)

	Mintage	Good-4	Fine-12	EF-40	AU-55	MS-63
1807 combined total	750,500					
1807 with small stars . . .		$200	$250	$1,000	$5,000	$12,500
1807 with large stars		200	225	975	4,750	11,750
1807 with 50c. over 20c. .		100	200	1,000	2,100	10,000
1808 combined total	1,368,600					
1808 regular date		75.00	100	210	1,000	4,000
1808/7 overdate		75.00	125	285	900	6,500
1809	1,405,810	75.00	100	200	900	4,000
1810	1,276,276	75.00	110	175	550	3,700
1811 combined total	1,203,644					
1811 with small 8		75.00	110	150	375	1,900
1811 with large 8		75.00	110	175	425	2,000
1811/10 overdate		75.00	250	280	600	7,200
1812 combined total	1,628,059					
1812 regular date		75.00	110	150	450	2,500
1812/11 with small 8		75.00	200	300	1,000	6,000
1812/11 with large 8		1,700	4,000	12,000	—	—
1813 combined total	1,241,903					
1813 regular date		75.00	100	150	450	3,000
1813 with 50c. over UNI .		75.00	125	250	1,100	7,000
1814 combined total	1,039,075					
1814 regular date		75.00	100	175	600	3,500
1814/3 overdate		75.00	125	340	850	—
1815/2 overdate	47,150	1,500	3,500	6,000	12,000	30,000
1817 combined total	1,215,567					
1817 regular date		75.00	100	150	450	3,000
1817/3 overdate		75.00	400	510	2,600	—
1817/4 overdate		50,000	150,000	250,000	—	—
1818 combined total	1,960,322					
1818 regular date		75.00	100	125	400	2,200
1818/7 overdate		75.00	95.00	180	550	—
1819 combined total	2,208,000					
1819 regular date		75.00	100	125	375	2,900
1819/8 overdate		75.00	110	140	450	2,200
1820	751,122	75.00	100	210	600	4,200
1821	1,305,797	75.00	100	125	375	2,300
1822 combined total	1,559,573					
1822 regular date		75.00	100	125	375	2,200
1822/1 overdate		90.00	175	275	900	3,000
1823 combined total	1,694,200					
1823 regular date		75.00	100	120	375	2,000
1823 with broken 3		100	160	300	800	2,500
1824 combined total	3,504,954					
1824 regular date		75.00	100	200	350	1,600
1824/1 overdate		75.00	100	250	450	2,300
1824/4 overdate		75.00	100	250	1,400	2,300
1825	2,943,166	75.00	100	200	300	1,700
1826	4,004,180	75.00	100	200	300	1,650
1827 combined total	5,493,400					
1827 with square-base 2 .		75.00	100	120	400	1,650
1827 with curl-base 2 . . .		75.00	100	120	400	1,650
1827/6 overdate		75.00	100	120	400	2,500
1828 combined total	3,075,200					
1828 with small 8s		75.00	100	120	400	1,600

	Mintage	Good-4	Fine-12	EF-40	AU-55	MS-63
1828 with large 8s		75.00	100	120	400	1,600
1828, all others		75.00	100	120	400	1,600
1829 combined total	3,712,156					
1829 regular date.		75.00	100	120	400	1,650
1829/7 overdate.		75.00	100	120	400	3,200
1830 combined total	4,764,800					
1830 with small O		75.00	100	120	400	1,600
1830 with large O.		75.00	100	120	400	1,600
1831.	5,873,660	75.00	100	120	400	1,600
1832 combined total	4,797,000					
1832 with regular letters on reverse		75.00	100	120	400	1,600
1832 with large letters . .		75.00	100	120	400	1,600
1833.	5,206,000	75.00	100	120	400	1,600
1834.	6,412,004	75.00	100	120	400	1,550
1835.	5,352,006	75.00	100	120	400	1,600
1836 combined total	6,545,000					
1836 with regular 50c. . . .		75.00	100	120	425	1,750
1836 with 50c. over 00c. .		90.00	100	300	1,500	4,150

Capped Bust Portrait, Reeded Edge (1836–1839)

"50 CENTS" on Reverse (1836–1837)

	Mintage	Good-4	Fine-12	EF-40	AU-55	MS-65
1836.	5,000	$700	$975	$2,650	$4,600	$40,000
1837.	3,629,820	30.00	50.00	150	350	18,750

"HALF DOL." on Reverse (1838–1839)

	Mintage	Good-4	Fine-12	EF-40	AU-55	MS-65
1838.	3,546,000	$50.00	$80.00	$200	$300	$21,700
1838-O (proof only).	20	—	—	—	—	800,000*
1839.	1,392,976	50.00	90.00	200	300	30,700
1839-O.	178,976	200	300	575	—	35,500

*Proof-64

Seated Liberty Portrait (1839–1891)

	Mintage	Good-4	Fine-12	EF-40	AU-55	MS-63	MS-65
1839 combined total	1,972,400						
1839 with no drapery hanging from elbow . . .		$40.00	$100	$675	$1,200	$19,000	$192,500
1839 with drapery from elbow		25.00	45.00	100	250	2,600	—
1840 with small letters . .	1,435,008	30.00	45.00	100	300	1,000	—
1840 with medium letters (struck at New Orleans without mint mark) . . .		125	240	350	790	4,600	—
1840-O	855,100	25.00	45.00	125	250	2,600	—
1841	310,000	30.00	75.00	210	325	3,100	—
1841-O	401,000	20.00	35.00	110	200	3,100	—
1842 combined total	2,012,764						
1842 small date		25.00	75.00	120	190	1,100	—
1842 medium date		20.00	45.00	110	250	1,000	—
1842-O combined total . .	754,000						
1842-O small date		600	900	1,150	3,800	6,000	—
1842-O large date		25.00	35.00	110	240	—	—
1843	3,844,000	22.00	35.00	75.00	150	1,300	—
1843-O	2,268,000	22.00	35.00	80.00	175	2,150	—
1844	1,766,000	22.00	35.00	75.00	160	1,300	—

	Mintage	Good-4	Fine-12	EF-40	AU-55	MS-63	MS-65
1844-O combined total ..	2,005,000						
1844-O regular date		22.00	32.00	75.00	140	2,700	—
1844-O with double date .			800	2,400	4,000		
1845	589,000	30.00	55.00	175	300	4,200	—
1845-O combined total ..	2,094,000						
1845-O with drapery		20.00	35.00	75.00	180	2,100	
1845-O with no drapery .		30.00	65.00	175	350	5,000	—
1846 combined total	2,210,000						
1846 small date		20.00	35.00	85.00	150	1,700	—
1846 tall date		20.00	35.00	125	200	2,000	—
1846/horizontal 6 overdate		150	225	400	1,000	—	
1846-O combined total ..	2,304,000						
1846-O medium date		25.00	35.00	100	300	2,700	—
1846-O tall date		150	300	750	1,500	13,000	—
1847 combined total	1,156,000						
1847 regular date		20.00	35.00	80.00	150	1,300	—
1847/6 overdate		2,000	3,000	7,600	9,000	36,000	—
1847-O	2,584,000	20.00	35.00	80.00	150	2,600	—
1848	580,000	30.00	65.00	200	450	2,100	—
1848-O	3,180,000	20.00	35.00	75.00	225	2,600	—
1849	1,252,000	25.00	50.00	150	300	2,600	—
1849-O	2,310,000	25.00	35.00	100	225	2,600	—
1850	227,000	175	300	550	800	5,600	—
1850-O	2,456,000	25.00	35.00	100	225	1,700	9,500
1851	200,750	190	300	450	525	3,150	—
1851-O	402,000	25.00	50.00	140	200	1,600	9,500
1852	77,130	250	400	625	700	2,950	—
1852-O	144,000	40.00	140	300	600	10,000	25,750
1853-O without arrows or rays (3 known)	400,000	—	—	—	—	—	

With Arrows Beside the Date, Rays Around the Eagle (1853)

	Mintage	Good-4	Fine-12	EF-40	AU-55	MS-63	MS-65	Proof-65
1853	3,532,708	$20.00	$40.00	$200	$600	$4,100	$21,000	—
1853-O	1,328,000	25.00	50.00	250	650	5,000	—	—

With Arrows Beside the Date, No Rays Around the Eagle (1854–1855)

	Mintage	Good-4	Fine-12	EF-40	AU-55	MS-63	MS-65	Proof-65
1854	2,982,000	$20.00	$40.00	$125	$250	$2,100	$8,700	—
1854-O	1,328,000	20.00	40.00	125	250	2,100	8,250	
1855 combined total ...	759,500							
1855 regular date		25.00	40.00	110	250	2,250	9,250	
1855/4 overdate		60.00	160	350	500	—	—	—
1855-O	3,688,000	20.00	35.00	120	240	1,600	7,500	
1855-S	129,950	390	600	2,500	11,000	—	—	

Arrows Removed (1856–1866)

	Mintage	Good-4	Fine-12	EF-40	AU-55	MS-63	MS-65	Proof-65
1856	938,000	$20.00	$35.00	$80.00	$150	$1,100	$6,800	—
1856-O	2,658,000	20.00	35.00	80.00	150	1,100	—	
1856-S	211,000	45.00	85.00	325	600	—	—	

	Mintage	Good-4	Fine-12	EF-40	AU-55	MS-63	MS-65	Proof-65
1857	1,988,000	20.00	40.00	80.00	140	1,100	6,700	$14,500
1857-O	818,000	20.00	40.00	75.00	160	3,600	—	
1857-S	158,000	45.00	110	350	450	—		
1858	4,226,000	20.00	40.00	80.00	150	1,200	6,000	12,500
1858-O	7,294,000	20.00	40.00	80.00	160	1,450	—	
1858-S	476,000	20.00	45.00	200	350	4,000	—	
1859 ....*800*	747,200	30.00	55.00	85.00	170	1,100	5,000	5,250
1859-O	2,834,000	20.00	40.00	80.00	150	1,100	5,000	
1859-S	566,000	20.00	50.00	150	275	3,000		
1860 ....*1,000*	302,700	20.00	40.00	75.00	300	1,500	6,200	5,250
1860-O	1,290,000	18.00	35.00	80.00	150	1,025	5,700	
1860-S	472,000	20.00	40.00	85.00	165	3,150		
1861 ....*1,000*	2,887,400	18.00	35.00	85.00	145	925	5,600	5,250
1861-O	2,532,633	18.00	35.00	85.00	145	1,600	6,700	
1861-S	939,500	19.00	40.00	90.00	165	3,700	10,000	
1862 ....*550*	253,000	30.00	50.00	140	250	1,200	6,700	5,250
1862-S	1,352,000	18.00	35.00	80.00	150	2,600	—	
1863 ....*460*	503,200	20.00	40.00	90.00	200	1,000	6,000	5,300
1863-S	916,000	18.00	35.00	80.00	150	2,000	—	
1864 ....*470*	379,100	21.00	45.00	150	200	1,000	6,000	5,400
1864-S	658,000	20.00	30.00	80.00	150	3,000	—	
1865 ....*500*	511,400	20.00	50.00	150	225	1,400	5,700	5,250
1865-S	675,000	15.00	35.00	80.00	175	3,200	—	
1866	(unique)	—	—	—	—	—	215,000	
1866-S	60,000	200	350	1,000	1,500	2,000	11,000	

With Motto Above the Eagle (1866–1891)

	Mintage	Good-4	Fine-12	EF-40	AU-55	MS-63	MS-65	Proof-65
1866 ....*725*	744,900	$20.00	$45.00	$100	$190	$1,600	$6,000	$4,000
1866-S	994,000	20.00	35.00	75.00	150	2,700	—	
1867 ....*625*	449,300	20.00	55.00	140	250	1,500	6,700	4,200
1867-S	1,196,000	20.00	35.00	75.00	135	3,000	—	
1868 ....*600*	417,600	35.00	70.00	175	225	1,100	—	4,000
1868-S	1,160,000	20.00	40.00	125	200	3,000	—	
1869 ....*600*	795,300	25.00	42.00	130	175	1,300	3,600	4,000
1869-S	656,000	18.00	35.00	150	190	3,700	—	
1870 ....*1,000*	633,900	20.00	35.00	140	175	1,300	—	4,000
1870-CC	54,617	475	1,175	4,000	6,250	—	—	
1870-S	1,004,000	18.00	40.00	90.00	225	3,000	—	
1871 ....*960*	1,203,600	20.00	35.00	80.00	140	1,100	5,000	4,000
1871-CC	153,950	140	210	750	1,250	—	—	
1871-S	2,178,000	16.00	35.00	80.00	190	1,800	4,600	
1872 ....*950*	880,600	16.00	35.00	80.00	190	1,800	4,000	4,000
1872-CC	257,000	50.00	135	340	900	—	—	
1872-S	580,000	30.00	60.00	165	375	3,600	—	
1873 closed 3 ..*600*...	587,000	25.00	65.00	125	200	1,300	4,000	4,000
1873 open 3	214,200	2,250	3,500	6,000	7,800	—	—	
1873-CC	122,500	110	225	650	1,900	—	—	

With Arrows Beside the Date (1873–1874)

	Mintage	Good-4	Fine-12	EF-40	AU-55	MS-63	MS-65	Proof-65
1873 ....540	1,815,150	$20.00	$35.00	$200	$475	$2,600	$25,000	$12,500
1873-CC	214,560	110	250	1,000	5,000	—	—	
1873-S	228,000	40.00	100	400	675	—	—	
1874 ....700	2,359,600	20.00	30.00	175	450	2,000	25,000	11,750
1874-CC	59,000	210	525	1,650	3,000	—	—	
1874-S	394,000	32.00	60.00	375	500	5,250	—	

Arrows Removed (1875–1891), with Motto

	Mintage	Good-4	Fine-12	EF-40	AU-55	MS-63	MS-65	Proof-65
1875 ....700	6,026,800	$20.00	$35.00	$75.00	$150	$800	$4,500	$4,300
1875-CC	1,008,000	21.00	50.00	125	225	1,600	—	
1875-S	3,200,000	20.00	45.00	100	125	800	4,500	
1876 ....1,150	8,418,000	20.00	35.00	75.00	150	800	4,500	4,300
1876-CC	1,956,000	20.00	38.00	90.00	190	2,000	6,000	
1876-S	4,528,000	20.00	35.00	75.00	175	1,100	5,100	
1877 ....510	8,304,000	20.00	35.00	80.00	175	1,100	4,700	4,800
1877-CC	1,420,000	22.00	45.00	110	190	1,550	4,700	
1877-S	5,356,000	20.00	35.00	100	130	850	4,700	4,500
1878 ....800	1,377,600	22.00	45.00	110	135	1,300	4,900	6,000
1878-CC	62,000	275	360	1,250	3,300	20,000	—	
1878-S	12,000	6,500	7,000	12,000	18,500	80,000	—	
1879 ....1,100	4,800	200	300	400	480	1,100	4,500	4,300
1880 ....1,355	8,400	200	250	300	380	1,100	4,600	4,300
1881 ....975	10,000	190	240	300	380	1,300	5,600	4,300
1882 ....1,100	4,400	200	340	375	410	1,300	5,100	4,300
1883 ....1,039	8,000	190	300	350	400	1,300	5,150	4,300
1884 ....875	4,400	210	360	425	485	1,300	4,500	4,300
1885 ....930	5,200	200	240	325	410	1,500	4,500	4,300
1886 ....886	5,000	210	310	360	490	1,500	4,500	4,300
1887 ....710	5,000	225	400	500	575	1,700	4,500	4,300
1888 ....832	12,001	190	250	300	400	1,200	4,500	4,300
1889 ....711	12,000	190	250	325	360	1,200	4,500	4,300
1890 ....590	12,000	200	225	335	400	1,200	4,500	4,300
1891 ....600	200,000	60.00	100	135	245	900	4,500	4,300

Barber, or Liberty Head Portrait (1892–1915)

	Mintage	Good-4	Fine-12	EF-40	AU-55	MS-63	MS-65	Proof-65
1892 .... 1,245	934,000	$12.50	$35.00	$170	$275	$750	$2,900	$4,000
1892-O	390,000	70.00	150	390	475	1,150	5,500	
1892-S	1,029,028	95.00	165	375	550	2,000	5,000	
1893 .... 792	1,826,000	10.00	35.00	150	300	1,100	3,250	4,000
1893-O	1,389,000	15.00	45.00	250	325	1,150	8,500	
1893-S	740,000	50.00	110	325	450	1,800	20,000	
1894 .... 972	1,148,000	10.00	45.00	170	295	925	3,750	4,000
1894-O	2,138,000	9.00	43.00	240	325	1,100	6,000	
1894-S	4,048,690	9.00	40.00	185	300	925	11,000	
1895 .... 880	1,834,338	8.00	35.00	170	285	950	2,800	4,000
1895-O	1,766,000	8.00	40.00	210	325	1,100	6,000	
1895-S	1,108,086	15.00	50.00	235	325	1,500	6,800	
1896 .... 762	950,000	15.00	35.00	175	275	900	4,500	4,000
1896-O	924,000	20.00	70.00	325	600	3,200	11,000	
1896-S	1,140,948	50.00	90.00	340	525	2,700	12,000	
1897 .... 731	2,480,000	20.00	25.00	110	275	900	3,700	4,000
1897-O	632,000	40.00	225	725	950	3,000	6,500	
1897-S	933,900	70.00	225	600	900	3,200	7,500	
1898 .... 735	2,956,000	20.00	25.00	110	275	1,000	3,500	4,000
1898-O	874,000	20.00	55.00	285	425	2,600	7,000	
1898-S	2,358,550	20.00	30.00	190	325	2,400	8,250	
1899 .... 846	5,538,000	20.00	25.00	110	275	900	3,400	4,000
1899-O	1,724,000	20.00	40.00	210	310	1,250	5,300	
1899-S	1,686,411	20.00	35.00	175	300	1,250	5,750	
1900 .... 912	4,762,000	20.00	25.00	110	275	900	3,700	4,000
1900-O	2,744,000	20.00	35.00	225	325	3,000	11,000	
1900-S	2,560,322	20.00	30.00	175	300	2,000	7,000	
1901 .... 813	4,268,000	20.00	25.00	110	275	900	3,700	4,000
1901-O	1,124,000	20.00	40.00	250	425	3,000	14,000	
1901-S	847,044	20.00	80.00	500	825	4,000	14,000	
1902 .... 777	4,922,000	20.00	25.00	110	275	900	3,700	4,000
1902-O	2,526,000	20.00	35.00	170	325	2,000	8,000	
1902-S	1,460,670	20.00	40.00	180	350	1,400	7,000	
1903 .... 755	2,278,000	20.00	28.00	135	275	1,400	7,000	4,000
1903-O	2,100,000	20.00	35.00	170	325	1,500	8,000	
1903-S	1,920,772	20.00	35.00	200	330	1,600	6,500	
1904 .... 670	2,992,000	20.00	25.00	110	275	1,200	4,000	4,000
1904-O	1,117,000	20.00	45.00	275	450	2,500	7,500	
1904-S	553,038	20.00	75.00	450	750	4,000	15,500	
1905 .... 727	662,000	20.00	40.00	175	350	1,300	4,950	4,000
1905-O	505,000	20.00	25.00	200	350	1,700	5,000	
1905-S	2,494,000	20.00	35.00	175	325	2,000	6,500	
1906 .... 675	2,638,000	20.00	25.00	110	275	900	3,700	4,000
1906-D	4,028,000	20.00	25.00	135	275	900	3,950	
1906-O	2,446,000	20.00	30.00	150	280	950	5,500	
1906-S	1,740,154	20.00	35.00	175	325	1,000	4,500	
1907 .... 575	2,598,000	20.00	25.00	110	275	900	3,700	4,000
1907-D	3,856,000	20.00	25.00	110	275	900	3,700	
1907-O	3,946,600	20.00	25.00	110	275	900	4,000	
1907-S	1,250,000	20.00	35.00	250	350	3,000	10,000	
1908 .... 545	1,354,000	20.00	25.00	110	275	900	3,750	4,000
1908-D	3,280,000	20.00	25.00	110	275	900	3,700	
1908-O	5,360,000	20.00	25.00	110	275	900	3,700	

	Mintage	Good-4	Fine-12	EF-40	AU-55	MS-63	MS-65	Proof-65
1908-S	1,644,828	20.00	35.00	175	300	2,200	6,500	
1909 ....650	2,368,000	20.00	25.00	110	275	900	3,700	4,000
1909-O	925,400	20.00	35.00	250	425	1,600	6,000	
1909-S	1,764,000	20.00	25.00	165	300	1,000	3,950	
1910 ....551	418,000	20.00	50.00	250	350	950	4,250	4,000
1910-S	1,948,000	20.00	26.00	160	290	1,200	4,500	
1911 ....543	1,406,000	20.00	25.00	110	275	900	3,700	4,000
1911-D	695,080	20.00	30.00	150	300	900	3,700	
1911-S	1,272,000	20.00	30.00	150	300	1,300	6,000	
1912 ....700	1,550,000	20.00	25.00	130	300	900	3,700	4,000
1912-D	2,300,800	20.00	25.00	120	275	900	3,700	
1912-S	1,370,000	20.00	27.50	150	290	1,000	5,000	
1913 ....627	188,000	20.00	75.00	300	625	1,250	3,500	4,000
1913-D	534,800	20.00	35.00	170	300	900	5,000	
1913-S	604,000	20.00	35.00	170	350	1,100	4,700	
1914 ....380	124,230	20.00	150	425	700	1,500	8,000	4,000
1914-S	992,000	20.00	30.00	170	350	1,100	4,000	
1915 ....450	138,000	20.00	80.00	325	650	1,700	5,500	4,000
1915-D	1,170,400	20.00	25.00	110	275	900	3,700	
1915-S	1,604,000	20.00	25.00	110	275	900	3,700	

Walking Liberty Portrait (1916–1947)

	Mintage	Good-4	Fine-12	EF-40	AU-55	MS-63	MS-65	Proof-65
1916	608,080	$50.00	$100	$200	$300	$500	$2,100	
1916-D	1,014,400	50.00	75.00	200	300	700	2,450	
1916-S	508,000	100	300	900	1,300	2,100	7,700	
1917	12,292,000	20.00	22.00	30.00	60.00	250	1,300	
1917-D with D on obverse	765,400	20.00	28.00	110	270	1,300	8,000	
1917-D with D on reverse	1,940,000	20.00	22.00	115	350	2,700	30,000	
1917-S with S on obverse	952,000	20.00	30.00	430	600	7,800	36,500	
1917-S with S on reverse	5,554,000	20.00	22.00	40.00	140	2,100	19,000	
1918	6,634,000	20.00	30.00	100	420	1,300	5,600	
1918-D	3,853,040	20.00	30.00	120	350	3,000	25,000	
1918-S	10,282,000	20.00	25.00	50.00	140	1,050	18,000	
1919	962,000	20.00	28.00	300	625	3,700	9,000	
1919-D	1,165,000	20.00	29.00	370	1,100	21,000	118,500	
1919-S	1,552,000	20.00	24.00	500	1,000	7,700	19,000	
1920	6,372,000	20.00	22.00	50.00	115	800	6,000	
1920-D	1,551,000	20.00	24.00	275	625	4,700	16,000	
1920-S	4,624,000	20.00	22.00	140	400	3,200	37,000	
1921	246,000	40.00	170	1,200	1,200	9,000	18,000	
1921-D	208,000	60.00	200	1,700	1,700	13,000	24,500	
1921-S	548,000	20.00	65.00	3,400	4,600	31,000	120,000	
1923-S	2,178,000	20.00	22.00	170	625	4,100	19,000	
1927-S	2,392,000	20.00	22.00	65.00	375	2,100	13,000	
1928-S	1,940,000	20.00	22.00	85.00	325	3,100	13,000	
1929-D	1,001,200	20.00	22.00	55.00	165	900	4,100	
1929-S	1,902,000	20.00	22.00	50.00	135	1,100	4,100	
1933-S	1,786,000	20.00	22.00	45.00	225	1,500	4,100	
1934	6,964,000	20.00	22.00	22.25	26.00	250	600	
1934-D	2,361,400	20.00	22.00	22.25	58.00	300	1,300	
1934-S	3,652,000	20.00	22.00	22.25	125	1,100	5,600	

	Mintage	Good-4	Fine-12	EF-40	AU-55	MS-63	MS-65	Proof-65
1935	9,162,000	20.00	22.00	22.25	23.00	100	600	
1935-D	3,003,800	20.00	22.00	22.25	55.00	350	2,600	
1935-S	3,854,000	20.00	22.00	22.25	75.00	620	3,100	
1936 3,901	12,614,000	20.00	22.00	22.25	24.00	50.00	200	$6,000
1936-D	4,252,400	20.00	22.00	22.25	46.00	90.00	400	
1936-S	3,884,000	20.00	22.00	22.25	52.00	130	925	
1937 5,728	9,522,000	20.00	22.00	22.25	22.50	45.00	225	1,500
1937-D	1,676,000	20.00	22.00	22.25	72.50	150	900	
1937-S	2,090,000	20.00	22.00	22.25	58.00	130	850	
1938 8,152	4,110,000	20.00	22.00	22.25	33.00	70.00	300	1,200
1938-D	491,600	100	150	200	300	600	1,800	
1939 8,808	6,812,000	20.00	22.00	22.25	40.00	40.00	120	1,000
1939-D	4,267,800	20.00	22.00	22.25	23.00	40.00	120	
1939-S	2,552,000	20.00	22.00	22.25	25.00	95.00	200	
1940 11,279	9,156,000	20.00	22.00	22.25	25.00	30.00	200	975
1940-S	4,550,000	20.00	22.00	22.25	24.00	32.50	475	
1941 15,412	24,192,000	20.00	22.00	22.25	25.00	30.00	200	975
1941-D	11,248,400	20.00	22.00	22.25	25.00	35.00	275	
1941-S	8,098,000	20.00	22.00	22.25	43.00	85.00	1,500	
1942 21,120	47,818,000	20.00	22.00	22.25	25.00	35.00	175	775
1942-D combined total	10,973,800							
1942-D regular mint mark		20.00	22.00	22.00	24.00	50.00	400	
1942-D/S		25.00	45.00	325	800	1,850	5,500	
1942-S	12,708,000	20.00	22.00	22.25	25.00	40.00	1,000	
1943	53,190,000	20.00	22.00	22.25	25.00	35.00	250	
1943-D	11,346,000	20.00	22.00	22.25	24.00	45.00	400	
1943-S	13,450,000	20.00	22.00	22.25	25.00	40.00	550	
1944	28,206,000	20.00	22.00	22.25	25.00	30.00	200	
1944-D	9,769,000	20.00	22.00	22.25	20.00	35.00	150	
1944-S	8,904,000	20.00	22.00	22.25	24.00	35.00	1,000	
1945	31,502,000	20.00	22.00	22.25	25.00	35.00	200	
1945-D	9,966,800	20.00	21.00	22.00	22.50	35.00	190	
1945-S	10,156,000	20.00	21.00	22.00	24.00	35.00	275	
1946	12,118,000	20.00	21.00	22.00	18.00	35.00	300	
1946-D	2,151,000	20.00	21.00	22.00	29.00	35.00	175	
1946-S	3,724,000	20.00	21.00	22.00	23.00	35.00	200	
1947	4,094,000	20.00	21.00	22.00	24.00	35.00	300	
1947-D	3,900,600	20.00	21.00	22.00	23.00	35.00	200	

Franklin Portrait (1948–1963)

	Mintage	Fine-12	EF-40	AU-55	MS-60	MS-63	MS-65	Proof-65
1948	3,006,814	$19.00	$20.00	$21.00	$27.00	$30.00	$55.00	
1948-D	4,028,600	19.00	20.00	21.00	27.00	30.00	150	
1949	5,614,000	19.00	20.00	21.00	27.00	35.00	120	
1949-D	4,120,600	19.00	20.00	21.00	27.00	33.00	1,200	
1949-S	3,744,000	19.00	20.00	21.00	27.00	50.00	150	
1950 51,386	7,742,123	19.00	20.00	21.00	27.00	40.00	100	$430
1950-D	8,031,600	19.00	20.00	21.00	27.00	32.00	450	
1951 7,500	16,802,102	19.00	20.00	21.00	27.00	32.00	55.00	300
1951-D	9,475,200	19.00	20.00	21.00	27.00	32.00	250	
1951-S	13,696,000	19.00	20.00	21.00	27.00	32.00	110	
1952 81,980	21,192,093	19.00	20.00	21.00	27.00	32.00	100	150

	Mintage	Fine-12	EF-40	AU-55	MS-60	MS-63	MS-65	Proof-65
1952-D	25,395,600	19.00	20.00	21.00	27.00	32.00	165	
1952-S	5,526,000	19.00	20.00	21.00	27.00	32.00	80.00	
1953 .... 128,800	2,668,120	19.00	20.00	21.00	27.00	32.00	190	150
1953-D	20,900,400	19.00	20.00	21.00	27.00	32.00	200	
1953-S	4,148,000	19.00	20.00	21.00	27.00	32.00	75.00	
1954 .... 233,300	13,188,203	19.00	20.00	21.00	27.00	32.00	80.00	70.00
1954-D	25,445,580	19.00	20.00	21.00	27.00	32.00	110	
1954-S	4,993,400	19.00	20.00	21.00	27.00	32.00	50.00	
1955 .... 378,200	2,498,181	19.00	20.00	21.00	27.00	32.00	45.00	60.00
1956 .... 669,384	4,032,000	19.00	20.00	21.00	27.00	32.00	50.00	22.00
1957 .... 1,247,952 ...	5,114,000	19.00	20.00	21.00	27.00	32.00	50.00	20.00
1957-D	19,966,850	19.00	22.00	25.00	27.00	32.00	50.00	
1958 .... 875,652	4,042,000	19.00	20.00	20.50	20.60	20.85	50.00	20.00
1958-D	23,962,412	19.00	20.00	20.50	20.60	20.85	50.00	
1959 .... 1,149,291 ...	6,200,000	19.00	20.00	20.50	20.60	20.85	135	20.00
1959-D	13,053,750	19.00	20.00	20.50	20.60	20.85	175	
1960 .... 1,691,602 ...	6,024,000	19.00	20.00	20.50	20.60	20.85	150	20.00
1960-D	18,215,812	19.00	20.00	20.50	20.60	20.85	530	
1961 .... 3,028,244 ...	8,290,000	19.00	20.00	20.50	20.60	20.85	150	22.00
1961-D	20,276,442	19.00	20.00	20.50	20.60	20.85	370	
1962 .... 3,218,019 ...	9,714,000	19.00	20.00	20.50	20.60	20.85	145	20.00
1962-D	35,473,281	19.00	20.00	20.50	20.60	20.85	280	
1963 .... 3,075,645 ...	22,164,000	19.00	20.00	20.50	20.60	20.85	70.00	20.00
1963-D	67,069,292	19.00	20.00	20.50	20.60	20.85	70.00	

Kennedy Portrait (1964–Present)

Silver Composition (1964)

	Mintage	EF-40	MS-65	Proof-65
1964 .... 3,950,762	273,304,004	$20.00	$22.00	$10.00
1964-D.................	156,205,446	20.00	22.00	

Silver Clad Composition (1965–1970)

	Mintage	EF-40	MS-65	Proof-65
1965	65,879,366	$8.00	$15.00	
1966	108,984,932	8.00	10.00	
1967	295,046,978	8.00	14.00	
1968-D..................	246,951,930	8.00	10.00	
1968-S (proof only)........	3,041,506	—	—	$5.00
1969-D..................	129,881,800	8.00	8.00	
1969-S (proof only)........	2,934,631	—	—	5.00
1970-D..................	2,150,000	10.00	36.00	
1970-S (proof only)........	2,632,810	—	—	6.00

Copper-Nickel Clad Composition (1971–Present)

	Mintage	MS-65	Proof-65
1971	155,164,000	$3.50	
1971-D..................	302,097,424	2.00	
1971-S (proof only)........	3,220,733	—	$3.00
1972	153,180,000	3.00	

	Mintage	MS-65	Proof-65
1972-D..................	141,890,000	3.00	
1972-S (proof only)........	*3,260,996*	—	3.00
1973	64,964,000	3.00	
1973-D..................	83,171,400	3.00	
1973-S (proof only)........	*2,760,339*	—	3.00
1974	201,596,000	1.75	
1974-D..................	79,066,300	.75	
1974-S (proof only)........	*2,612,568*	—	2.00

Bicentennial Portrait (1975–1976)

	Mintage	MS-65	Proof-65
1776–1976 copper-nickel clad	234,308,000	$.75	
1776–1976-D copper-nickel clad	287,565,248	.75	
1776–1976-S copper-nickel clad (proof only; includes coins from both 1975 and 1976 proof sets)............	*6,995,180*	—	$2.00
1776–1976-S silver clad ......*3,998,621*....	4,908,319	15.00	40.00

Regular Design Returns (1977–Present)

	Mintage	MS-65	Proof-65
1977	43,598,000	$.75	
1977-D..................	31,449,106	1.00	
1977-S (proof only)........	*3,251,152*	—	$2.00
1978	14,350,000	1.00	
1978-D..................	13,765,799	1.25	
1978-S (proof only)........	*3,127,781*	—	2.25
1979	68,312,000	.75	
1979-D..................	15,815,422	1.00	
1979-S combined total (proof only)	*3,677,175*		
1979-S with clear S		—	18.00
1979-S with clogged S......		—	2.00
1980-P..................	44,134,000	.75	
1980-D..................	33,456,449	.75	
1980-S (proof only)........	*3,554,806*	—	2.00
1981-P..................	29,544,000	.75	
1981-D..................	27,839,533	.75	
1981-S (proof only)........	*4,063,083*	—	2.00
1982-P..................	10,819,000	.75	
1982-D..................	13,140,102	.75	
1982-S (proof only)........	*3,857,479*	—	2.25
1983-P..................	34,139,000	.75	
1983-D..................	32,472,244	1.00	
1983-S (proof only)........	*3,279,126*	—	2.50
1984-P..................	26,029,000	1.25	
1984-D..................	26,262,158	.75	
1984-S (proof only)........	*3,065,110*	—	4.00
1985-P..................	18,706,962	1.25	
1985-D..................	19,814,034	1.25	
1985-S (proof only)........	*3,362,821*	—	2.50
1986-P..................	13,107,633	.75	
1986-D..................	15,336,145	1.00	
1986-S (proof only)........	*3,010,497*	—	6.50
1987-P..................	2,890,758	1.50	
1987-D..................	2,890,758	1.50	
1987-S (proof only)........	*3,792,233*	—	2.50
1988-P..................	13,626,000	.75	
1988-D..................	12,000,096	.75	
1988-S (proof only)........	*3,262,948*	—	3.75
1989-P..................	24,542,000	.75	
1989-D..................	23,000,216	.75	
1989-S (proof only)........	*3,215,728*	—	3.25
1990-P..................	22,278,000	.75	

	Mintage	MS-65	Proof-65
1990-D	20,096,242	.75	
1990-S (proof only)	3,299,559	—	5.25
1991-P	14,874,000	.75	
1991-D	15,054,678	.75	
1991-S (proof only)	2,867,787	—	8.00
1992-P	17,628,000	.75	
1992-D	17,000,106	.75	
1992-S (proof only)	4,176,544*	—	15.00
1993-P	15,510,000	.75	
1993-D	15,000,006	.75	
1993-S (proof only)	3,360,876*	—	16.00
1994-P	24,928,896	.75	
1994-D	25,039,006	.75	
1994-S (proof only)	3,212,792*	—	15.00
1995-P	27,537,352	.75	
1995-D	27,329,352	.75	
1995-S (proof only)	2,799,213*	—	25.00
1996-P	25,896,215	.75	
1996-D	26,198,215	.75	
1996-S (proof only)	2,925,305*	—	10.00
1997-P	20,882,000	.75	
1997-D	40,758,000	.75	
1997-S (proof only)	2,788,020	—	12.00
1998-P	15,646,000	.75	
1998-D	15,064,000	.75	
1998-S (proof only)	2,086,507	—	8.00
1998-P matte finish silver . . .	64,141	100	
1998-S (silver proof)	878,996	—	30.00
1999-P	8,900,000	.75	
1999-D	10,682,000	.75	
1999-S (proof only)	2,454,319	—	8.00
1999-S (silver proof)	798,780	—	30.00
2000-P	22,600,000	.75	
2000-D	19,466,000	.75	
2000-S (proof only)	3,030,000	—	8.00
2000-S (silver proof)	904,200	—	30.00
2001-P	21,200,000	.75	
2001-D	19,504,000	.75	
2001-S (proof only)	2,294,900	—	8.00
2001-S (silver proof)	891,400	—	30.00
2002-P	3,100,000	.75	
2002-D	2,500,000	.75	
2002-S (proof only)	2,321,848	—	8.00
2002-S (silver proof)	888,826	—	30.00
2003-P	3,502,555	.75	
2003-D	3,502,555	.75	
2003-S (proof only)	2,243,340	—	8.00
2003-S (silver proof)	1,119,494	—	30.00
2004-P	2,900,000	.75	
2004-D	2,900,000	.75	
2004-S (proof only)	1,804,396	—	8.00
2004-S (silver proof)	1,187,673	—	30.00
2005-P	3,800,000	.75	
2005-D	3,500,000	.75	
2005-S (proof only)	2,275,000	—	8.00
2005-S (silver proof)	998,000	—	30.00
2006-P	2,400,000	.75	
2006-D	2,000,000	.75	
2006-S (proof only)	2,000,428	—	8.00
2006-S (silver proof)	1,054,008	—	30.00
2007-P	4,100,000	.75	
2007-D	4,100,000	.75	
2007-S (proof only)	1,702,116	—	8.00
2007-S (silver proof)	1,299,878	—	30.00
2008-P	1,700,000	.75	
2008-D	1,700,000	.75	

*Includes 90% silver issue

	Mintage	MS-65	Proof-65
2008-S (proof only)	*1,382,017*		8.00
2008-S (silver proof)	*763,887*		30.00
2009-P	1,900,000	.75	
2009-D	1,900,000	.75	
2009-S (proof only)	1,477,967		8.00
2009-S (silver proof)	694,406		30.00
2010-P	1,800,000	.75	
2010-D	1,700,000	.75	
2010-S (proof only)			8.00
2010-S (silver proof)			30.00
2011-P	1,750,000	.75	
2011-D	1,700,000	.75	
2011-S (proof only)			8.00
2011-S (silver proof)			30.00
2012-P		.75	
2012-D		.75	
2012-S (proof only)			8.00
2012-S (silver proof)			30.00
2013-P		.75	
2013-D		.75	
2013-S (proof only)			8.00
2013-S (silver proof)			30.00
2014-P		.75	
2014-D		.75	
2014-S (proof only)			8.00
2014-S (silver proof)			30.00

SILVER DOLLARS (1794–1935)

Flowing Hair Portrait (1794–1795)

	Mintage	Good-4	Fine-12	EF-40
1794	1,758	$90,000	$125,000	$190,000
1795 combined total.......	160,295			
1795 with 2 leaves under each wing........		2,500	5,000	14,500
1795 with 3 leaves under each wing........		2,500	5,000	14,000

Draped Bust Portrait with Small Eagle on Reverse (1795–1798)

	Mintage	Good-4	Fine-12	EF-40
1795	42,738	$1,200	$2,700	$8,750
1796 combined total.	72,920			
1796 with small date and small letters		1,800	4,000	10,000
1796 with small date and large letters		1,800	5,000	10,000
1796 with large date and small letters		1,800	4,000	12,000
1797 combined total.	7,776			
1797 with 9 stars left, 7 right and small letters . . .		1,800	4,250	18,500
1797 with 9 stars left, 7 right and large letters. . . .		1,800	4,250	10,000
1797 with 10 stars left, 6 right		1,700	4,250	10,000
1798 combined total.	327,536			
1798 with 13 stars.		1,500	4,250	12,000
1798 with 15 stars.		2,200	4,000	13,500

Draped Bust Portrait with Heraldic Eagle on Reverse (1798–1804)

	Mintage	Good-4	Fine-12	EF-40	Proof
1798 (mintage included above).		$800	$1,600	$3,500	
1799 combined total	423,515				
1799 regular date.		800	1,300	4,100	
1799 with 8 stars left, 5 right.		900	1,300	4,100	
1799/8 overdate.		900	1,500	4,600	
1800.	220,920	900	1,500	4,100	
1801.	54,454	900	1,600	4,500	
1802 combined total	41,650				
1802 regular date.		900	1,400	4,500	
1802/1 overdate.		900	1,500	4,500	
1803 combined total	85,634				
1803 with small 3.		900	1,300	4,500	

	Mintage	Good-4	Fine-12	EF-40	Proof
1803 with large 3	325	1,000	1,600		
1804 original.	(8 proofs)	—	—	—	$6,000,000
1804 restrike	(7 proofs)	—	—	—	2,500,000*

*Proof-64

(NOTE: All silver dollars dated 1804 were actually minted decades later, and all are extremely rare. The so-called "original" specimens were struck in the 1830s as presentation pieces intended as gifts for monarchs in the Far and Middle East. The restrikes were produced in 1859 to fill demand from collectors who wanted examples of this great rarity. All 15 known examples are accounted for, and all bring enormous premiums whenever they're offered for sale. In 1999, one of the eight known original examples changed hands for $4,140,000 at a major auction.)

Gobrecht Dollars (1836–1839)

	Mintage	Fine-12	EF-40	AU-55	MS-65	Proof-65
1836 pattern*	(unknown)					$85,000
1836 circulation strike with 416 grains of silver . . .	1,000	$8,000	$15,000	$22,000	$35,000	$75,000
1836 circulation strike with 412½ grains of silver .	600	8,000	15,000	22,000	48,000	75,000
1838 pattern	(unknown)	22,500	34,000	40,000	60,000	100,000
1839 circulation strike . .	300	17,500	27,000	32,000	45,000	100,000

*The 1836 pattern has C. Gobrecht F. just above the date and below the figure of Liberty. Dollars dated 1838 and 1839 are known only as restrikes from the late 1850s.

Seated Liberty Portrait (1840–1873)

	Mintage	Good-4	Fine-12	EF-40	AU-55	MS-63	MS-65	Proof-65
1840	61,005	$250	$350	$500	$1,200	$21,000	—	—
1841	173,000	250	350	500	1,000	4,600	48,000	—
1842	184,618	250	350	500	1,000	5,100	25,000	—
1843	165,100	250	350	500	1,000	6,100	25,000	—
1844	20,000	250	350	500	1,800	8,200	75,000	—
1845	24,500	250	350	500	2,500	36,000	—	—
1846	110,600	260	300	550	1,000	6,200	32,500	—

	Mintage	Good-4	Fine-12	EF-40	AU-55	MS-63	MS-65	Proof-65
1846-O	59,000	260	300	600	1,500	23,000	60,000	—
1847	140,750	260	300	400	1,000	5,000	30,000	—
1848	15,000	260	300	800	2,500	11,000	50,000	—
1849	62,600	260	300	350	900	5,200	40,000	—
1850	7,500	260	600	900	2,500	17,000	—	—
1850-O	40,000	260	350	1,200	5,000	31,000	—	—
1851 original	1,300	15,000	23,000	28,000	36,000	45,000	85,000	—
1851 restrike	(unknown)	—	—	—	—	—	—	—
1852 original	1,100	15,000	23,000	23,000	36,000	45,000	75,000	—
1852 restrike	(unknown)	—	—	—	—	—	—	—
1853	46,118	260	300	600	1,800	7,100	35,000	—
1854	33,140	650	1,600	3,500	5,500	11,000	35,000	—
1855	26,000	600	1,600	3,500	5,500	28,000	—	—
1856	63,500	260	500	1,200	3,000	8,100	—	—
1857	94,000	260	500	1,200	2,000	5,600	35,000	—
1858 (proof only)	(about 300)	—	—	—	—	—	—	$35,000
1859 800	255,700	—	—	—	—	6,100	30,000	20,000
1859-O	360,000	260	400	650	800	5,000	30,000	—
1859-S	20,000	300	400	2,000	5,000	52,000	75,000	—
1860 1,330	217,600	275	375	675	800	5,000	30,000	20,000
1860-O	515,000	95.00	300	375	800	5,000	20,000	—
1861 1,000	77,500	325	800	1,100	2,200	5,700	25,000	17,500
1862 550	11,540	350	800	1,100	2,000	6,700	40,000	20,000
1863 460	27,200	260	500	650	1,000	5,200	30,000	15,000
1864 470	30,700	260	500	600	1,100	6,200	25,000	12,500
1865 500	46,500	260	500	550	1,000	5,000	20,000	15,000
1866 with no motto above the eagle	(2 known)	—	—	—	—	—	—	1,500,000*

*Proof-63

With Motto Above the Eagle (1866–1873)

	Mintage	Good-4	Fine-12	EF-40	AU-55	MS-63	MS-65	Proof-65
1866 725	48,900	$225	$400	$550	$1,200	$4,800	$48,000	$20,000
1867 625	46,900	225	400	600	1,200	4,800	48,000	20,000
1868 600	162,100	225	400	550	1,200	4,800	49,500	20,000
1869 600	423,700	225	400	550	1,200	4,800	48,000	20,000
1870 1,000	415,000	225	400	550	1,200	4,800	48,000	20,000
1870-CC	12,462	225	475	1,100	2,350	50,000	100,000	
1870-S	(about 10)	—	—	850,000	900,000	—	—	
1871 960	1,073,800	225	400	550	1,200	4,800	27,500	20,000
1871-CC	1,376	2,000	3,300	8,500	15,000	100,000	200,000	
1872 950	1,105,500	225	400	550	1,200	4,800	50,000	20,000
1872-CC	3,150	900	1,400	3,800	6,000	35,000	60,000	
1872-S	9,000	225	410	900	1,500	25,000	50,000	
1873 600	293,000	225	400	550	1,200	4,800	48,500	22,000
1873-CC	2,300	2,250	4,750	12,500	17,500	150,000	250,000	
1873-S	700	(no examples known to exist)						

Morgan, or Liberty Head Portrait (1878–1921)

(NOTE: Values shown for MS-65 examples apply only to coins that have been certified in that grade by the Professional Coin Grading Service or the Numismatic Guaranty Corporation of America.)

	Mintage	Fine-12	EF-40	AU-55	MS-63	MS-65	Proof-65
1878 with 8 tail feathers....*500*......	749,500	$38.00	$50.00	$100	$200	$1,200	$11,500
1878 with 7 tail feathers, combined total.*50*....	9,759,300						
1878 with 7 tail feathers, reverse of 1878.......		30.00	48.00	55.00	100	1,500	14,000
1878 with 7 tail feathers, reverse of 1879.......		30.00	40.00	70.00	225	3,300	
1878 with 7 tail feathers over 8		30.00	48.00	100	400	3,600	
1878-CC..............	2,212,000	150	175	225	300	2,100	
1878-S	9,774,000	30.00	40.00	50.00	100	300	
1879 ..... *1,100*........	14,806,000	30.00	35.00	40.00	60.00	1,100	9,000
1879-CC combined total..	756,000						
1879-CC with regular mint mark		250	800	1,900	6,000	25,500	
1879-CC with muddled mint mark		225	775	1,800	6,000	50,000	
1879-O................	2,887,000	30.00	40.00	50.00	215	3,000	
1879-S combined total ...	9,110,000						
1879-S with reverse of 1878		30.00	40.00	48.00	350	9,500	
1879-S with reverse of 1879		30.00	35.00	45.00	52.00	185	
1880 ..... *1,355*	12,600,000	30.00	35.00	45.00	60.00	675	9,000
1880-CC..............	591,000	175	350	425	550	1,300	
1880-O...............	5,305,000	30.00	35.00	38.00	600	25,000	
1880-S	8,900,000	30.00	35.00	40.00	60.00	185	
1881 ..... *975*	9,163,000	30.00	35.00	40.00	60.00	875	9,000
1881-CC..............	296,000	500	600	650	650	900	
1881-O...............	5,708,000	30.00	35.00	40.00	60.00	2,000	
1881-S	12,760,000	30.00	35.00	40.00	60.00	185	
1882 ..... *1,100*	11,100,000	30.00	35.00	40.00	60.00	400	9,000
1882-CC..............	1,133,000	40.00	145	155	300	500	
1882-O...............	6,090,000	30.00	35.00	40.00	60.00	1,300	
1882-S	9,250,000	30.00	35.00	40.00	60.00	185	
1883 ..... *1,039*	12,290,000	30.00	35.00	40.00	60.00	180	9,000
1883-CC..............	1,204,000	40.00	145	155	250	550	
1883-O...............	8,725,000	30.00	35.00	40.00	60.00	185	
1883-S	6,250,000	30.00	50.00	400	3,500	30,000	
1884 ..... *875*........	14,070,000	30.00	35.00	40.00	60.00	300	9,000
1884-CC..............	1,136,000	145	155	170	200	500	
1884-O...............	9,730,000	30.00	35.00	40.00	60.00	185	
1884-S	3,200,000	30.00	35.00	1,200	30,000	225,000	
1885 ..... *930*.........	17,786,837	30.00	35.00	40.00	60.00	185	9,000
1885-CC..............	228,000	575	695	750	900	1,250	
1885-O...............	9,185,000	30.00	35.00	40.00	60.00	185	
1885-S	1,497,000	30.00	50.00	100	225	2,300	
1886 ..... *886*.........	19,963,000	30.00	35.00	40.00	60.00	185	9,000

	Mintage	Fine-12	EF-40	AU-55	MS-63	MS-65	Proof-65
1886-O	10,710,000	30.00	35.00	150	3,800	200,000	
1886-S	750,000	30.00	45.00	75.00	285	3,600	
1887 combined total *710*	20,290,000						9,000
1887 with regular date ...		30.00	35.00	40.00	100	185	
1887/6 overdate		30.00	75.00	300	3,000	5,000	
1887-O combined total ..	11,550,000						
1887-O with regular date .		30.00	35.00	40.00	160	3,350	
1887/6-O overdate		30.00	100	300	2,750	32,000	
1887-S	1,771,000	30.00	35.00	40.00	210	4,000	
1888 ...... *832*	19,183,000	30.00	35.00	40.00	60.00	200	9,000
1888-O	12,150,000	30.00	35.00	40.00	55.00	350	
1888-S	657,000	30.00	35.00	50.00	280	3,500	
1889 ...... *811*	21,726,000	30.00	35.00	40.00	60.00	300	9,000
1889-CC	350,000	1,000	3,000	9,000	40,000	350,000	
1889-O	11,875,000	30.00	35.00	45.00	210	5,500	
1889-S	700,000	30.00	35.00	100	200	1,800	
1890 ...... *590*	16,802,000	30.00	35.00	45.00	60.00	2,500	9,000
1890-CC	2,309,041	40.00	50.00	200	900	6,000	
1890-O	10,701,000	30.00	35.00	45.00	80.00	1,800	
1890-S	8,230,373	30.00	35.00	45.00	80.00	900	
1891 ...... *650*	8,693,556	30.00	35.00	45.00	130	6,500	9,000
1891-CC	1,618,000	135	175	300	675	6,000	
1891-O	7,954,529	30.00	35.00	50.00	425	8,000	
1891-S	5,296,000	30.00	35.00	40.00	200	1,200	
1892 ...... *1,245*	1,036,000	35.00	40.00	60.00	500	3,500	9,000
1892-CC	1,352,000	200	600	900	2,000	10,000	
1892-O	2,744,000	30.00	40.00	60.00	300	6,000	
1892-S	1,200,000	130	500	5,000	70,000	300,000	
1893 ...... *792*	389,000	250	300	400	1300	6,000	9,000
1893-CC	677,000	400	2,000	2,500	6,000	50,000	
1893-O	300,000	300	800	1000	7,000	200,000	
1893-S	100,000	5,000	9,000	35,000	200,000	700,000	
1894 ...... *972*	110,000	1,500	2,250	3,000	6,000	45,000	9,000
1894-O	1,723,000	30.00	50.00	140	4,000	50,000	
1894-S	1,260,000	100	200	500	2,000	6,000	
1895 ...... *880*	12,000*	30,000	35,000	40,000	55,000		95,000
1895-O	450,000	400	800	2000	50,000	200,000	
1895-S	400,000	500	1200	2300	6,000	20,000	
1896 ...... *762*	9,976,000	30.00	35.00	60.00	100	300	9,000
1896-O	4,900,000	30.00	40.00	350	6,000	175,000	
1896-S	5,000,000	50.00	95.00	295	2,000	15,000	
1897 ...... *731*	2,822,000	30.00	35.00	40.00	65.00	275	9,000
1897-O	4,004,000	30.00	35.00	200	20,000	60,000	
1897-S	5,825,000	30.00	35.00	80.00	200	600	
1898 ...... *725*	5,884,000	30.00	35.00	40.00	65.00	225	9,000
1898-O	4,440,000	30.00	35.00	45.00	60.00	185	
1898-S	4,102,000	30.00	35.00	55.00	400	2,000	
1899 ...... *846*	330,846	48.00	85.00	70.00	200	500	9,000
1899-O	12,290,000	30.00	35.00	40.00	52.00	185	
1899-S	2,562,000	30.00	50.00	100	400	2,200	
1900 ...... *912*	8,830,000	30.00	35.00	45.00	65.00	200	9,000
1900-O combined total ..	12,590,000						
1900-O with regular mint mark		35.00	40.00	60.00	200		
1900-O/CC		35.00	300	1,000	4,000		
1900-S	3,540,000	30.00	75.00	200	400	1,400	
1901 ...... *813*	6,962,000	35.00	90.00	800	20,000	300,000	10,000
1901-O	13,320,000	30.00	35.00	50.00	160	200	
1901-S	2,284,000	35.00	75.00	100	600	3,700	
1902 ...... *777*	7,994,000	30.00	35.00	40.00	65.00	400	9,000
1902-O	8,636,000	30.00	35.00	45.00	75.00	200	
1902-S	1,530,000	35.00	85.00	125	310	3,000	
1903 ...... *755*	4,652,000	30.00	35.00	40.00	65.00	225	9,000
1903-O	4,450,000	350	400	450	550	750	

*Only proofs are known to exist for 1895 silver dollars from the Philadelphia Mint.

	Mintage	Fine-12	EF-40	AU-55	MS-63	MS-65	Proof-65
1903-S	1,241,000	150	500	2,300	6,500	10,000	
1904 ...... *650*	2,788,000	30.00	35.00	45.00	300	4,000	9,000
1904-O	3,720,000	30.00	35.00	40.00	60.00	185	
1904-S	2,304,000	40.00	200	600	5,000	9,000	
1921	44,690,000	30.00	35.00	40.00	60.00	185	
1921-D	20,345,000	30.00	35.00	40.00	60.00	275	
1921-S	21,695,000	30.00	35.00	40.00	60.00	1,600	

Peace Portrait (1921–1935)

	Mintage	Fine-12	EF-40	AU-55	MS-63	MS-65	Proof-65
1921	1,006,473	$60.00	$75.00	$90.00	$300	$2,600	
1922	51,737,000	30.00	32.00	35.00	50.00	175	
1922-D	15,063,000	30.00	32.00	35.00	50.00	575	
1922-S	17,475,000	30.00	32.00	35.00	70.00	2,600	
1923	30,800,000	30.00	32.00	35.00	50.00	175	
1923-D	6,811,000	30.00	32.00	35.00	125	1,700	
1923-S	19,020,000	30.00	32.00	35.00	80.00	9,000	
1924	11,811,000	30.00	32.00	35.00	40.00	175	
1924-S	1,728,000	30.00	32.00	100	400	12,500	
1925	10,198,000	30.00	32.00	45.00	75.00	175	
1925-S	1,610,000	30.00	32.00	40.00	170	27,500	
1926	1,939,000	30.00	32.00	35.00	43.00	350	
1926-D	2,348,700	30.00	32.00	35.00	125	600	
1926-S	6,980,000	30.00	32.00	35.00	80.00	750	
1927	848,000	30.00	32.00	40.00	130	4,000	
1927-D	1,268,900	30.00	32.00	75.00	375	5,000	
1927-S	866,000	30.00	32.00	60.00	250	12,500	
1928	360,649	300	350	400	500	4,000	
1928-S	1,632,000	30.00	40.00	50.00	500	25,000	
1934	954,057	30.00	40.00	50.00	300	1,650	
1934-D	1,569,500	30.00	32.00	45.00	190	1,500	
1934-S	1,011,000	30.00	150	450	3,000	9,000	
1935	1,576,000	30.00	40.00	50.00	125	900	
1935-S	1,964,000	30.00	39.00	100	600	1,700	

TRADE DOLLARS (1873–1885)

	Mintage	Fine-12	EF-40	AU-55	MS-63	MS-65	Proof-65
1873 ...... *865*	396,635	$190	$250	$500	$3,000	$16,000	$12,000
1873-CC	124,500	190	450	750	25,000	125,000	

	Mintage	Fine-12	EF-40	AU-55	MS-63	MS-65	Proof-65
1873-S	703,000	190	250	500	3,100	14,000	
1874 ...... *700*	987,100	190	250	500	2,500	13,000	12,000
1874-CC	1,373,200	190	250	500	4,000	20,000	
1874-S	2,549,000	90.00	250	500	2,500	12,500	
1875 ...... *700*	218,200	275	550	850	2,500	12,500	11,500
1875-CC	1,573,700	85.00	250	500	2,500	16,000	
1875-S combined total ...	4,487,000						
1875-S with regular mint							
mark		190	250	500	2,500	8,000	
1875-S/CC		600	1,700	2,200	6,500	40,000	
1876 ...... *1,150*	455,000	190	250	500	2,500	8,000	11,500
1876-CC	509,000	190	600	1,200	25,000	100,000	
1876-S	5,227,000	90.00	250	500	2,500	8,000	
1877 ...... *510*	3,039,200	90.00	250	500	2,500	12,000	11,500
1877-CC	534,000	190	350	600	10,000	60,000	
1877-S	9,519,000	190	250	500	2,500	8,000	
1878 (proof only)	*900*	—	—	—	—	—	13,000
1878-CC	97,000	500	1,400	2,750	21,000	60,000	
1878-S	4,162,000	190	250	500	2,500	8,000	
1879 (proof only)	*1,541*	—	—	—	—	—	10,500
1880 (proof only)	*1,987*	—	—	—	—	—	10,500
1881 (proof only)	*960*	—	—	—	—	—	10,500
1882 (proof only)	*1,097*	—	—	—	—	—	10,500
1883 (proof only)	*979*	—	—	—	—	—	10,500
1884 (proof only)	*10*	—	—	—	—	—	750,000
1885 (proof only)	*5*	—	—	—	—	—	2,750,000

CLAD DOLLARS (1971–1981)

Eisenhower Portrait (1971–1978)

	Mintage	MS-65	Proof-65
1971 copper-nickel clad	47,799,000	$175	
1971-D copper-nickel clad	68,587,424	25.00	
1971-S silver clad *4,265,234*	6,868,530	25.00	$25.00
1972 copper-nickel clad	75,890,000	240	
1972-D copper-nickel clad	92,548,511	35.00	
1972-S silver clad *1,811,631*	2,193,056	25.00	25.00
1973 copper-nickel clad	2,000,056	75.00	
1973-D copper-nickel clad	2,000,000	45.00	
1973-S copper-nickel clad (proof only) ...	*2,760,339*	—	12.00
1973-S silver clad *1,013,646*	1,883,140	25.00	25.00
1974 copper-nickel clad	27,366,000	50.00	
1974-D copper-nickel clad	45,517,000	25.00	
1974-S copper-nickel clad (proof only) ...	*2,612,568*	—	12.00
1974-S silver clad *1,306,579*	1,900,156	25.00	25.00

Bicentennial Portrait (1975–1976)

	Mintage	MS-65	Proof-65
1776–1976 copper-nickel clad with thick lettering on reverse	4,019,000	$120	
1776–1976 copper-nickel clad with thin lettering	113,318,000	60.00	

	Mintage	MS-65	Proof-65
1776–1976-D copper-nickel clad with thick lettering	21,048,710	40.00	
1776–1976-D copper-nickel clad with thin lettering	82,179,564	20.00	
1776–1976-S copper-nickel clad (proof only; includes coins from both 1975 and 1976 proof sets)	*6,995,180*		$12.00
1776–1976-S silver clad ... *3,998,621*	4,908,319	12.00	25.00

Regular Design Returns (1977–1978)

	Mintage	MS-65	Proof-65
1977 copper-nickel clad	12,596,000	$45.00	
1977-D copper-nickel clad	32,983,006	40.00	
1977-S copper-nickel clad (proof only) ...	*3,251,152*	—	$12.00
1978 copper-nickel clad	25,702,000	45.00	
1978-D copper-nickel clad	33,012,890	50.00	
1978-S copper-nickel clad (proof only) ...	*3,127,781*	—	12.00

Susan B. Anthony Portrait (1979–1999)

	Mintage	MS-65	Proof-65
1979-P	360,222,000	$2.00	
1979-D	288,015,744	2.00	
1979-S combined total *3,677,175*	109,576,000		
1979-S with clear S		2.00	$70.00
1979-S with clogged S		2.00	5.00
1980-P	27,610,000	2.00	
1980-D	41,628,708	2.00	
1980-S *3,554,806*	20,422,000	2.00	5.00
1981-P	3,000,000	3.00	
1981-D	3,250,000	3.00	
1981-S combined total *4,063,083*	3,492,000		
1981-S with clear S		3.00	65.00
1981-S with clogged S		3.00	7.00
1999-P	25,592,000	1.50	
1999-D	11,776,000	1.50	
1999-S (proof only)	*555,276*	—	15.00

Sacagawea Dollars (2000–Present)

	Mintage	MS-65	Proof-65
2000-P	767,140,000	$2.50	
2000-D	518,916,000	2.50	
2000-S (proof only)	*3,030,000*	—	$10.00
2001-P	62,468,000	1.50	
2001-D	70,939,500	1.50	
2001-S (proof only)	*3,186,300*	—	10.00
2002-P	3,865,310	1.50	
2002-D	3,732,000	1.50	
2002-S (proof only)	*3,210,674*	—	7.00
2003-P	4,082,555	1.50	

	Mintage	MS-65	Proof-65
2003-D	4,082,555	1.50	
2003-S (proof only)	*3,362,834*	—	7.00
2004-P	2,660,000	1.50	
2004-D	2,660,000	1.50	
2004-S (proof only)	*2,992,069*	—	7.00
2005-P	2,520,000	1.50	
2005-D	2,520,000	1.50	
2005-S (proof only)	*3,273,000*	—	7.00
2006-P	4,900,000	1.50	
2006-D	2,800,000	1.50	
2006-S (proof only)	*3,054,436*	—	7.00
2007-P	3,640,000	1.50	
2007-D	5,740,000	1.50	
2007-S (proof only)	*2,563,563*	—	7.00
2008-P	9,800,000	1.50	
2008-D	14,840,000	1.50	
2008-S (proof only)	*2,145,904*	—	7.00
2009-P	37,380,000	1.50	
2009-D	33,880,000	1.50	
2009-S (proof only)	*2,172,373*	—	7.00
2010-P	32,060,000	1.50	
2010-D	48,720,000	1.50	
2010-S (proof only)		—	7.00
2011-P	29,400,000	1.50	
2011-D	48,160,000	1.50	
2011-S (proof only)		—	7.00
2012-P		1.50	
2012-D		1.50	
2012-S (proof only)		—	7.00
2013-P		1.50	
2013-D		1.50	
2013-S (proof only)		—	7.00
2014-P		1.50	
2014-D		1.50	
2014-S (proof only)		—	7.00

PRESIDENTIAL DOLLAR COINS

George Washington

	Mintage	MS-65	Proof-65
2007-P	176,680,000	1.50	
2007-D	163,680,000	1.50	
2007-S (proof only)	*3,849,535*		6.00

John Adams

	Mintage	MS-65	Proof-65
2007-P	112,420,000	1.50	
2007-D	112,140,000	1.50	
2007-S (proof only)	*3,849,535*		6.00

Thomas Jefferson

	Mintage	MS-65	Proof-65
2007-P	100,800,000	1.50	1.50
2007-D	102,810,000	1.50	
2007-S (proof only)	*3,849,535*		6.00

James Madison

	Mintage	MS-65	Proof-65
2007-P	84,560,000	1.50	
2007-D	87,780,000	1.50	
2007-S (proof only)	*3,849,535*		6.00

James Monroe

	Mintage	MS-65	Proof-65
2008-P	64,260,000	1.50	
2008-D	60,230,000	1.50	
2008-S (proof only)	2,982,634		7.00

John Quincy Adams

2008-P	57,540,000	1.50	
2008-D	57,720,000	1.50	
2008-S (proof only)	2,982,634		7.00

Andrew Jackson

2008-P	61,180,000	1.50	
2008-D	61,070,000	1.50	
2008-S (proof only)	2,982,634		7.00

Martin Van Buren

2008-P	51,520,000	1.50	
2008-D	50,960,000	1.50	
2008-S (proof only)	2,982,634		7.00

William Henry Harrison

2009-P	43,260,000	1.50	
2009-D	55,160,000	1.50	
2009-S (proof only)	2,800,298		7.00

John Tyler

2009-P	43,540,000	1.50	
2009-D	43,540,000	1.50	
2009-S (proof only)	2,800,298		7.00

James K. Polk

2009-P	46,620,000	1.50	
2009-D	41,720,000	1.50	
2009-S (proof only)	2,800,298		7.00

Zachary Taylor

2009-P	41,580,000	1.50	
2009-D	36,680,000	1.50	
2009-S (proof only)	2,800,298		7.00

Millard Fillmore

2010-P	37,520,000	1.50	
2010-D	36,960,000	1.50	
2010-S (proof only)			7.00

Franklin Pierce

2010-P	38,220,000	1.50	
2010-D	38,360,000	1.50	
2010-S (proof only)			7.00

James Buchanan

2010-P	36,820,000	1.50	
2010-D	36,540,000	1.50	
2010-S (proof only)			7.00

Abraham Lincoln

	Mintage	MS-65	Proof-65
2010-P	49,000,000	1.50	
2010-D	48,020,000	1.50	
2010-S (proof only)			7.00

Andrew Johnson

2011-P	35,560,000	1.50	
2011-D	37,100,000	1.50	
2011-S (proof only)			7.00

Ulysses S. Grant

2011-P	38,080,000	1.50	
2011-D	37,940,000	1.50	
2011-S (proof only)			7.00

Rutherford B. Hayes

2011-P	37,660,000	1.50	
2011-D	36,820,000	1.50	
2011-S (proof only)			7.00

James A. Garfield

2011-P	37,100,000	1.50	
2011-D	37,100,000	1.50	
2011-S (proof only)			7.00

Chester A. Arthur

2012-P		1.50	
2012-D		1.50	
2012-S (proof only)			7.00

Grover Cleveland (1st Term)

2012-P		1.50	
2012-D		1.50	
2012-S (proof only)			7.00

Benjamin Harrison

2012-P		1.50	
2012-D		1.50	
2012-S (proof only)			7.00

Grover Cleveland (2nd Term)

2012-P		1.50	
2012-D		1.50	
2012-S (proof only)			7.00

William McKinley

2013-P		1.50	
2013-D		1.50	
2013-S (proof only)			7.00

Theodore Roosevelt

2013-P		1.50	
2013-D		1.50	
2013-S (proof only)			7.00

William H. Taft

2013-P		1.50	
2013-D		1.50	
2013-S (proof only)			7.00

Woodrow Wilson

	Mintage	MS-65	Proof-65
2013-P		1.50	
2013-D		1.50	
2013-S (proof only)			7.00

Warren G. Harding

	Mintage	MS-65	Proof-65
2014-P		1.50	
2014-D		1.50	
2014-S (proof only)			7.00

Calvin Coolidge

	Mintage	MS-65	Proof-65
2014-P		1.50	
2014-D		1.50	
2014-S (proof only)			7.00

Herbert Hoover

	Mintage	MS-65	Proof-65
2014-P		1.50	
2014-D		1.50	
2014-S (proof only)			7.00

Franklin D. Roosevelt

	Mintage	MS-65	Proof-65
2014-P		1.50	
2014-D		1.50	
2014-S (proof only)			7.00

GOLD DOLLARS (1849–1889)
Liberty Head Portrait (1849–1854)

	Mintage	Fine-12	EF-40	AU-50	MS-65	Proof-65
1849 combined total	688,567					
1849 with open wreath ..		$175	$250	$350	$6,500	
1849 with closed wreath.		175	250	300	6,000	
1849-C combined total ..	11,634					
1849-C with open wreath		150,000	300,000	—	1,000,000*	
1849-C with closed wreath		800	1,400	2,400	—	
1849-D	21,588	900	1,700	2,400	—	
1849-O...............	215,000	175	300	400	13,500	
1850.................	481,953	150	250	300	6,750	
1850-C...............	6,966	1,000	1,600	3,000	—	
1850-D...............	8,382	1,250	1,600	3,000	—	
1850-O...............	14,000	250	475	775	25,000	
1851.................	3,317,671	175	250	300	6,100	
1851-C...............	41,267	1,000	1,600	2,000	30,000	
1851-D...............	9,882	1,250	1,800	2,200	—	
1851-O...............	290,000	175	250	300	11,000	
1852.................	2,045,351	175	250	300	5,500	
1852-C...............	9,434	1,000	1,600	1,750	35,000	
1852-D...............	6,360	1,250	1,600	2,300	—	
1852-O...............	140,000	175	250	375	—	
1853.................	4,076,051	175	250	300	5,500	
1853-C...............	11,515	1,000	1,600	2,200	—	
1853-D...............	6,583	1,250	1,600	2,600	—	
1853-O...............	290,000	175	250	350	11,000	
1854.................	855,502	170	250	300	5,500	
1854-D...............	2,935	1,250	2,200	6,000	—	
1854-S	14,632	300	450	725	24,000	

*MS-63

Indian Head Portrait with Small Head (1854–1856)

	Mintage	Fine-12	EF-40	AU-50	MS-65	Proof-65
1854.................	783,943	$200	$450	$550	$40,000	—
1855.................	758,269	200	450	550	40,000	$300,000
1855-C...............	9,803	850	3,800	12,000	—	
1855-D...............	1,811	3,500	9,000	23,000	—	
1855-O...............	55,000	330	750	1,600	—	
1856-S	24,600	440	1,350	2,500	—	

Indian Head Portrait with Large Head (1856–1889)

	Mintage	Fine-12	EF-40	AU-50	MS-65	Proof-65
1856 combined total	1,762,936					
1856 with upright 5		$150	$260	$285	$7,500	
1856 with slanted 5		150	260	300	3,000	$50,000
1856-D	1,460	2,500	6,000	6,700	—	
1857	774,789	150	260	300	4,000	35,000
1857-C	13,280	800	1,600	3,000	—	
1857-D	3,533	900	1,800	4,000	—	
1857-S	10,000	250	700	1,150	—	
1858	117,995	150	300	320	5,100	28,500
1858-D	3,477	900	1,800	3,000	—	70,000
1858-S	10,000	275	525	1,575	—	
1859 ...... 80	168,164	150	300	320	2,800	17,000
1859-C	5,235	750	2,000	3,200	—	
1859-D	4,952	1,000	1,550	2,800	—	
1859-S	15,000	240	500	1,300	—	
1860 ...... 154	36,514	150	300	295	6,500	15,000
1860-D	1,566	2,000	4,200	6,500	—	
1860-S	13,000	300	475	700	26,000	
1861 ...... 349	527,150	150	300	320	2,800	13,000
1861-D	(unknown)	5,500	21,000	33,000	180,000	
1862 ...... 35	1,361,355	150	300	320	2,800	14,500
1863 ...... 50	6,200	390	1000	2,500	22,000	—
1864 ...... 50	5,900	275	500	750	8,000	19,000
1865 ...... 25	3,700	275	650	750	9,000	17,000
1866 ...... 30	7,100	275	500	675	5,200	17,000
1867 ...... 50	5,200	300	550	600	5,500	17,000
1868 ...... 25	10,500	250	400	500	5,500	17,000
1869 ...... 25	5,900	300	500	700	5,500	17,000
1870 ...... 35	6,300	250	400	500	5,500	17,000
1870-S	3,000	300	750	1,400	25,000	
1871 ...... 30	3,900	275	400	500	4,600	18,000
1872 ...... 30	3,500	250	350	500	5,600	18,000
1873 closed 3 ... 25	1,800	300	700	1,000	17,000	35,000
1873 open 3	123,300	150	300	300	2,600	
1874 ...... 20	198,800	150	300	300	2,600	20,000
1875 ...... 20	400	1,600	3,500	5,300	25,000	36,500
1876 ...... 45	3,200	220	375	450	4,200	15,000
1877 ...... 20	3,900	200	350	450	4,200	20,000
1878 ...... 20	3,000	200	350	470	3,000	17,000
1879 ...... 30	3,000	150	300	375	2,600	15,000

	Mintage	Fine-12	EF-40	AU-50	MS-65	Proof-65
1880 ...... *36*	1,600	150	300	300	2,600	15,000
1881 ...... *87*	7,620	150	300	300	2,600	13,000
1882 ...... *125*	5,000	150	300	300	2,600	10,000
1883 ...... *207*	10,800	150	300	300	2,600	10,000
1884 ...... *1,006*	5,230	150	300	300	2,600	10,000
1885 ...... *1,105*	11,156	150	300	300	2,600	10,000
1886 ...... *1,016*	5,000	150	300	300	2,600	10,000
1887 ...... *1,043*	7,500	150	300	300	2,600	10,000
1888 ...... *1,079*	15,501	150	300	300	2,600	10,000
1889 ...... *1,779*	28,950	100	300	300	2,600	10,000

QUARTER EAGLES, OR $2.50 GOLD PIECES (1796–1929)
Capped Bust Portrait Facing Right (1796–1807)

	Mintage	Fine-12	EF-40	MS-60
1796 with no stars	963	$60,000	$85,000	$275,000
1796 with stars	432	42,000	78,500	250,000
1797	427	18,000	42,500	140,000
1798	1,094	7,500	17,000	75,000
1802/1 overdate	3,035	6,000	17,500	37,000
1804 combined total.......	3,327			
1804 with 13 stars........		45,000	90,000	400,000
1804 with 14 stars........		5,000	15,500	40,000
1805	1,781	5,500	16,500	38,000
1806/4 overdate	1,136	6,000	16,500	38,000
1806/5 overdate	480	9,000	20,000	100,000
1807	6,812	5,500	16,000	38,000

Capped Bust Portrait Facing Left (1808)

	Mintage	Fine-12	EF-40	MS-60
1808	2,710	$30,000	$57,000	$185,000

Capped Head Portrait (1821–1834)

	Mintage	Fine-12	EF-40	AU-50	MS-60	MS-63
1821	6,448	$7,000	$12,000	$15,500	$35,000	$65,000
1824/1 overdate	2,600	7,000	12,000	15,500	35,000	65,000
1825	4,434	7,000	12,000	15,500	35,000	66,000
1826/5	760	9,000	15,000	20,000	50,000	125,000
1827	2,800	9,000	12,000	15,500	35,000	65,000

Size Reduced (1829–1834)

	Mintage	Fine-12	EF-40	AU-50	MS-60	MS-63
1829	3,403	$6,500	$10,000	$12,500	$23,000	$37,000
1830	4,540	6,500	10,000	12,500	23,000	37,000
1831	4,520	6,500	10,000	12,500	23,000	37,000
1832	4,400	6,500	10,000	12,500	23,000	37,000
1833	4,160	6,500	10,000	12,500	23,000	37,000
1834 (E PLURIBUS UNUM on reverse)	4,000	12,500	20,000	32,500	60,000	120,000

Classic Head Portrait (1834–1839)

	Mintage	Fine-12	EF-40	AU-50	MS-60	MS-63
1834 (no motto on reverse)	112,234	$300	$800	$1,500	$3,800	$12,000
1835	131,402	300	800	1,500	4,100	11,750
1836	547,986	300	800	1,500	3,800	12,000
1837	45,080	675	1,300	2,300	6,000	18,000
1838	47,030	300	1,000	1,600	4,300	12,500
1838-C	7,880	900	3,500	9,000	30,000	60,000
1839	27,021	800	1,500	3,000	8,000	22,500
1839-C	18,140	975	3,400	5,500	28,000	55,000
1839-D	13,674	975	4,700	9,250	35,000	52,000
1839-O	17,781	400	1,500	3,300	11,000	31,000

Coronet Portrait (1840–1907)

	Mintage	EF-40	AU-50	MS-60	MS-63	Proof-65
1840	18,859	$900	$2,500	$6,500	$14,000	
1840-C	12,822	2,100	4,000	13,000	30,000	
1840-D	3,532	8,000	12,500	35,000	150,000	
1840-O	33,580	800	1,800	10,000	25,000	
1841 (proof only)	*(very rare)*	100,000	125,000	—	—	$325,000
1841-C	10,281	2,200	3,400	16,000	40,000	
1841-D	4,164	4,500	9,000	25,000	55,000	
1842	2,823	3,000	7,000	23,000	50,000	
1842-C	6,729	3,200	7,000	25,000	50,000	
1842-D	4,643	4,250	11,000	40,000	70,000	
1842-O	19,800	1,200	2,400	12,000	35,000	
1843	100,546	450	800	2,800	6,500	
1843-C small date	2,988	5,300	9,000	30,000	70,000	
1843-C large date	23,076	1,800	3,000	8,000	24,000	
1843-D	36,209	2,100	3,000	8,000	29,000	
1843-O small date	288,002	375	475	2,000	7,000	
1843-O large date	76,000	600	1,800	7,000	24,000	
1844	6,784	950	2,200	7,600	22,000	175,000
1844-C	11,622	2,600	6,000	20,000	40,000	

	Mintage	EF-40	AU-50	MS-60	MS-63	Proof-65
1844-D	17,332	2,400	3,000	7,500	25,000	
1845	91,051	400	500	1,300	5,500	175,000
1845-D	19,460	2,400	3,000	11,500	40,000	
1845-O	4,000	2,400	9,000	22,000	50,000	
1846	21,598	600	1,000	6,000	27,500	
1846-C	4,808	3,000	7,000	20,000	42,500	
1846-D	19,303	2,400	3,000	10,000	30,000	
1846-O	62,000	450	1,100	6,000	20,000	
1847	29,814	400	900	4,000	9,500	
1847-C	23,226	2,200	3,000	7,000	17,000	
1847-D	15,784	2,400	3,000	9,500	24,000	
1847-O	124,000	400	1,000	4,000	19,000	
1848	7,497	900	2,300	6,500	17,000	
1848 with CAL. above eagle	1,389	45,000	52,000	80,000	110,000	
1848-C	16,788	2,200	3,300	12,000	36,000	
1848-D	13,771	2,400	3,300	10,000	30,000	
1849	23,294	500	900	2,800	7,500	
1849-C	10,200	2,400	5,000	20,000	58,500	
1849-D	10,945	2,200	3,500	15,000	42,000	
1850	252,923	375	400	1,100	4,250	
1850-C	9,148	2,200	3,600	14,000	38,500	
1850-D	12,148	2,300	3,300	15,000	50,000	
1850-O	84,000	500	1,200	4,800	14,250	
1851	1,372,748	350	375	450	1,400	
1851-C	14,923	2,200	4,000	12,750	32,500	
1851-D	11,264	2,400	3,900	12,500	33,000	
1851-O	148,000	350	900	5,000	14,000	
1852	1,159,681	350	375	450	1,400	
1852-C	9,772	2,200	4,000	15,500	38,500	
1852-D	4,078	3,000	7,000	18,000	52,000	
1852-O	140,000	375	1,000	5,000	13,000	
1853	1,404,668	350	375	450	1,400	
1853-D	3,178	3,400	5,000	17,500	50,000	
1854	596,258	350	375	450	1,450	
1854-C	7,295	2,500	4,600	14,000	40,000	
1854-D	1,760	7,000	13,000	28,000	70,000	
1854-O	153,000	350	500	1,500	9,000	
1854-S	246	300,000	425,000	—	—	
1855	235,480	350	375	450	1,600	
1855-C	3,677	3,400	6,000	21,000	50,000	
1855-D	1,123	8,000	15,000	48,000	80,000	
1856	384,240	350	375	450	1,400	110,000
1856-C	7,913	2,700	4,600	15,000	33,000	
1856-D	874	13,500	33,000	80,000	125,000	
1856-O	21,100	725	1,300	8,000	30,000	
1856-S	72,120	400	900	5,000	13,000	
1857	214,130	350	395	450	1,500	110,000
1857-D	2,364	3,000	4,000	13,500	30,000	
1857-O	34,000	400	1,100	4,500	14,000	
1857-S	69,200	450	1,000	5,500	15,000	
1858	47,377	350	400	1,400	3,600	100,000
1858-C	9,056	2,200	3,300	11,000	28,000	
1859 . . . . . . *80*	39,364	350	500	1,400	3,300	80,000
1859-D	2,244	3,200	5,000	20,000	70,000	
1859-S	15,200	1,000	2,500	6,000	19,000	
1860 . . . . . . *112*	22,563	350	500	1,200	2,900	43,000
1860-C	7,469	2,400	4,000	22,000	40,000	
1860-S	35,600	700	1,300	4,000	15,000	
1861 . . . . . . *90*	1,283,788	350	375	800	1,500	43,000
1861-S	24,000	1,000	3,000	8,500	19,000	
1862 combined total	98,543					
1862 regular date . . *35* . .		600	1,300	5,000	13,000	40,000
1862/1 overdate		2,000	3,500	8,000	32,000	
1862-S	8,000	2,500	4,500	18,000	34,000	
1863 (proof only)	*30*	—	—	—	—	120,000
1863-S	10,800	1,500	3,500	15,000	30,000	
1864 . . . . . . *50*	2,824	12,000	25,000	45,000	65,000	35,000

	Mintage	EF-40	AU-50	MS-60	MS-63	Proof-65
1865 . . . . *25*	1,520	8,400	19,000	38,000	70,000	45,000
1865-S	23,376	700	1,400	4,500	11,000	
1866 . . . . . . *30*	3,080	3,500	6,000	13,000	30,000	35,000
1866-S	38,960	700	1,600	7,000	20,000	
1867 . . . . . . *50*	3,200	700	1,400	5,000	9,500	35,000
1867-S	28,000	650	1,600	4,500	13,500	
1868 . . . . . . *25*	3,600	500	700	2,000	8,000	38,000
1868-S	34,000	400	1,100	4,000	12,000	
1869 . . . . . . *25*	4,320	450	800	3,000	9,500	35,000
1869-S	29,500	500	925	4,000	9,500	
1870 . . . . . . *35*	4,520	450	850	4,000	9,500	35,000
1870-S	16,000	400	900	5,000	16,000	
1871 . . . . . . *30*	5,320	400	700	2,600	5,000	35,000
1871-S	22,000	400	600	2,500	5,000	
1872 . . . . . . *30*	3,000	750	1,200	5,000	15,000	35,000
1872-S	18,000	500	1,000	4,800	12,000	
1873 closed 3 . . . . . *25* . .	55,200	375	390	600	1,400	35,000
1873 open 3	122,800	350	390	450	1,100	
1873-S	27,000	450	1,000	3,000	8,000	
1874 . . . . . . *20*	3,920	450	700	2,500	7,500	45,000
1875 . . . . *20*	400	5,500	13,000	25,000	40,000	55,000
1875-S	11,600	350	800	4,000	8,500	
1876 . . . . . . *45*	4,176	700	1,100	3,300	6,750	29,000
1876-S	5,000	600	1,100	3,000	9,000	
1877 . . . . . . *20*	1,632	800	1,100	3,000	8,750	30,000
1877-S	35,400	350	400	700	2,600	
1878 . . . . . . *20*	286,240	350	390	450	1,100	32,000
1878-S	178,000	350	390	500	1,900	
1879 . . . . . . *30*	88,960	350	390	475	1,200	30,000
1879-S	43,500	390	500	2,200	5,500	
1880 . . . . . . *36*	2,960	390	700	1,400	3,800	27,000
1881 . . . . . . *51*	640	3,000	5,000	11,000	24,000	26,000
1882 . . . . . . *67*	4,000	390	400	820	3,100	23,000
1883 . . . . . . *82*	1,920	400	950	2,700	6,700	23,000
1884 . . . . . . *73*	1,950	400	700	1,600	3,200	23,000
1885 . . . . . . *87*	800	1,800	2,600	5,000	8,000	23,000
1886 . . . . . . *88*	4,000	390	400	1,200	3,000	23,000
1887 . . . . . . *122*	6,160	390	400	800	3,000	24,000
1888 . . . . . . *97*	16,001	360	400	450	1,000	23,000
1889 . . . . . . *48*	17,600	350	390	450	1,000	24,000
1890 . . . . . . *93*	8,720	350	390	450	1,600	21,000
1891 . . . . . . *80*	10,960	350	390	450	1,300	20,000
1892 . . . . . . *105*	2,440	350	390	800	2,575	21,000
1893 . . . . . . *106*	30,000	350	390	450	1,000	20,000
1894 . . . . . . *122*	4,000	350	390	800	1,800	20,000
1895 . . . . . . *119*	6,000	350	390	500	1,300	19,000
1896 . . . . . . *132*	19,070	350	390	450	900	19,000
1897 . . . . . . *136*	29,768	350	390	450	900	19,000
1898 . . . . . . *165*	24,000	350	390	450	900	19,000
1899 . . . . . . *150*	27,200	350	390	450	900	19,000
1900 . . . . . . *205*	67,000	350	390	450	850	19,000
1901 . . . . . . *223*	91,100	350	390	450	850	19,000
1902 . . . . . . *193*	133,540	350	390	450	850	19,000
1903 . . . . . . *197*	201,060	350	390	450	850	19,000
1904 . . . . . . *170*	160,790	350	390	450	850	19,000
1905 . . . . . . *144*	217,800	350	390	450	850	19,000
1906 . . . . . . *160*	176,330	350	390	450	850	19,000
1907 . . . . . . *154*	336,294	350	390	450	850	19,000

Indian Head Portrait (1908–1929)

	Mintage	AU-50	MS-60	MS-63	MS-65	Proof-65
1908 . . . . . *236*	564,821	$350	$420	$1,300	$4,250	$28,000
1909 . . . . . *139*	441,760	350	420	2,100	8,000	42,000
1910 . . . . . *682*	492,000	350	420	1,900	8,000	35,000
1911 . . . . . *191*	704,000	350	420	1,300	9,000	28,000
1911-D	55,680	4,800	10,000	25,000	85,000	
1912 . . . . . *197*	616,000	350	420	2,100	15,000	28,000
1913 . . . . . *165*	722,000	350	420	1,300	8,500	29,000
1914 . . . . . *117*	240,000	350	650	6,250	44,000	30,000
1914-D	448,000	350	425	2,100	45,000	
1915 . . . . . *100*	606,000	350	425	1,300	8,000	35,000
1925-D	578,000	350	425	1,100	3,000	
1926	446,000	350	425	1,100	3,000	
1927	388,000	350	425	1,100	3,000	
1928	416,000	350	425	1,100	3,000	
1929	532,000	350	425	1,100	7,000	

$3 GOLD PIECES (1854–1889)

	Mintage	Fine-12	EF-40	AU-50	MS-60	MS-63	Proof-65
1854	138,618	$650	$1,300	$2,000	$2,800	$7,700	$200,000
1854-D	1,120	7,500	20,000	40,000	85,000	—	
1854-O	24,000	800	2,500	6,000	30,000		
1855	50,555	700	1,300	2,000	3,750	10,500	160,000
1855-S	6,600	900	3,000	8,000	28,000	—	
1856	26,010	800	1,300	2,000	3,800	10,500	140,000
1856-S	34,500	800	1,700	3,200	14,000	—	
1857	20,891	800	1,300	1,800	3,500	14,000	110,000
1857-S	14,250	800	3,000	6,000	23,000	—	
1858	2,133	750	2,100	4,000	12,000	28,000	100,000
1859 . . . . . *80*	15,558	700	1,600	2,200	3,800	11,000	60,000
1860 . . . . . *119*	7,036	700	1,600	2,200	4,000	12,000	60,000
1860-S	4,408	700	3,000	9,000	26,000	65,000	
1861 . . . . . *113*	5,959	700	2,500	5,000	8,500	14,000	60,000
1862 . . . . . *35*	5,750	700	2,500	5,000	8,500	14,000	60,000
1863 . . . . . *39*	5,000	700	2,500	5,000	8,500	14,000	60,000
1864 . . . . . *50*	2,630	700	2,500	5,000	8,500	14,000	60,000
1865 . . . . . *25*	1,140	1,300	3,100	8,000	13,000	28,000	65,000
1866 . . . . . *30*	4,000	700	1,500	4,000	4,500	14,000	60,000
1867 . . . . . *50*	2,600	700	1,500	4,000	4,500	14,000	60,000
1868 . . . . . *25*	4,850	700	1,500	4,000	4,500	14,000	60,000
1869 . . . . . *25*	2,500	700	1,500	4,500	4,500	16,000	60,000
1870 . . . . . *35*	3,500	700	1,600	4,500	4,000	16,000	60,000
1870-S	(1 known)	—	5,500,000	—	—		
1871 . . . . . *30*	1,300	700	1,600	4,200	4,500	14,000	60,000
1872 . . . . . *30*	2,000	700	1,600	4,000	4,400	14,000	60,000
1873 closed 3	(unknown)	2,800	6,000	15,000	30,000	60,000	
1873 open 3 (proof only) .	25	—	—	—	—	—	80,000

	Mintage	Fine-12	EF-40	AU-50	MS-60	MS-63	Proof-65
1874 . . . . . . *20*	41,800	700	1,200	1,400	2,800	6,750	70,000
1875 (proof only)	*20*	—	—	—	—	—	250,000
1876 (proof only)	*45*	—	—	26,000	—	—	100,000
1877 . . . . . . *20*	1,468	1,000	3,500	10,000	26,000	46,000	65,000
1878 . . . . . . *20*	82,304	700	1,200	1,400	2,800	6,750	65,000
1879 . . . . . . *30*	3,000	700	1,400	2,000	3,200	10,000	50,000
1880 . . . . . . *36*	1,000	700	2,200	4,500	5,000	12,000	40,000
1881 . . . . . . *54*	500	1,200	3,500	7,500	13,000	19,000	37,000
1882 . . . . . . *76*	1,500	700	1,600	2,500	4,200	12,000	37,000
1883 . . . . . . *89*	900	700	1,800	3,200	4,500	12,000	36,000
1884 . . . . . . *106*	1,000	950	1,900	3,200	4,500	12,000	36,000
1885 . . . . . . *109*	801	950	1,900	4,100	5,000	14,000	36,000
1886 . . . . . . *142*	1,000	950	2,200	3,500	5,000	16,000	33,000
1887 . . . . . . *160*	6,000	700	1,400	2,500	3,600	10,000	33,000
1888 . . . . . . *291*	5,000	700	1,400	2,500	3,600	8,500	33,000
1889 . . . . . . *129*	2,300	700	1,400	2,500	3,600	10,000	33,000

$4 GOLD PIECES, OR "STELLAS" (1879–1880)

	Mintage	Proof-60	Proof-63	Proof-65
1879 with flowing hair (proof only)	*425*	$125,000	$165,000	$240,000
1879 with coiled hair (proof only)	*10*	190,000	350,000	625,000
1880 with flowing hair (proof only)	*15*	160,000	230,000	425,000
1880 with coiled hair (proof only)	*10*	400,000	575,000	1,300,000

HALF EAGLES, OR $5 GOLD PIECES (1795–1929)

Capped Bust Portrait Facing Right with Small Eagle on Reverse (1795–1798)

	Mintage	Fine-12	EF-40	MS-60
1795	8,707	$21,000	$33,000	$85,000
1796/5 overdate	6,196	21,000	38,500	110,000
1797 combined total.	3,609			
1797 with 15 stars.		22,000	55,000	225,000
1797 with 16 stars.		22,000	45,000	190,000
1798	(7 known)	100,000	400,000	900,000

Capped Bust Portrait Facing Right with Heraldic Eagle on Reverse (1795–1807)

	Mintage	Fine-12	EF-40	MS-60
1795 (mintage included in 1798).................		$12,000	$35,000	$110,000
1797/5 overdate (mintage included in 1798)		15,000	35,000	180,000
1797 with 16 stars (mintage included in 1798)	(1 known)	—	—	—
1798 combined total.......	24,867			
1798 with small 8	5,000	10,000	40,000	
1798 with large 8 and 13 stars		4,500	9,000	30,000
1798 with large 8 and 14 stars		4,500	9,000	100,000
1799	7,451	4,500	8,500	29,000
1800	37,628	4,000	8,000	17,000
1802/1 overdate	53,176	4,000	8,000	17,000
1803/2 overdate	33,506	4,000	8,000	17,000
1804 combined total.......	30,475			
1804 with small 8		4,000	8,000	17,000
1804 with small 8 over large 8		4,000	8,000	19,000
1805	33,183	4,000	8,000	17,000
1806 with pointed 6	9,676	4,000	8,000	19,000
1806 with round-top 6	54,417	4,000	8,000	17,000
1807	32,488	4,000	8,000	17,000

Capped Draped Bust Portrait Facing Left (1807–1812)

	Mintage	Fine-12	EF-40	MS-60
1807	51,605	$3,000	$5,000	$14,000
1808 combined total.......	55,578			
1808 regular date		3,000	5,000	14,000
1808/7 overdate		3,000	6,000	20,000
1809/8 overdate		3,000	5,000	14,000
1810 combined total.......	100,287			
1810 small date with small 5		13,000	45,000	140,000
1810 small date with tall 5..		3,000	5,000	14,000
1810 large date with small 5		16,000	50,000	150,000
1810 large date with large 5.		3,000	5,000	14,000
1811	99,581	3,000	5,000	14,000
1812	58,087	3,000	5,000	14,000

Capped Head Portrait (1813–1829)

	Mintage	Fine-12	EF-40	AU-55	MS-60	MS-63
1813................	95,428	$3,000	$6,000	$9,000	$12,000	$24,000
1814/3 overdate........	15,454	5,000	8,000	12,500	18,000	35,000
1815................	635	38,250	160,000	250,000	280,000	400,000
1818 combined total....	48,588					
1818 regular strike.....		5,000	11,000	16,000	20,000	43,000
1818 with 5D over 50....		6,000	11,000	17,000	24,000	60,000
1819 combined total....	51,723					
1819 regular strike......		11,000	50,000	60,000	75,000	100,000
1819 with 5D over 50....		9,000	34,000	45,000	75,000	100,000
1820................	263,806	5,000	10,000	12,500	20,000	36,000
1821................	34,641	12,000	40,000	65,000	100,000	175,000
1822 (3 known)........	17,796	—	—	—	—	7,500,000
1823................	14,485	5,000	9,000	13,000	20,000	44,000
1824................	17,340	6,000	24,000	28,000	39,000	70,000
1825 combined total....	29,060					
1825/1...............		6,000	20,000	25,000	41,000	75,000
1825/4...............	(2 known)	—	—	—	—	600,000
1826................	18,069	6,000	16,000	20,000	30,000	75,000
1827................	24,913	6,000	25,000	27,000	35,000	80,000
1828 combined total....	28,029					
1828 regular date.......		10,000	30,000	40,000	80,000	120,000
1828/7 overdate........		16,000	60,000	80,000	140,000	250,000
1829 large date........	57,442	20,000	60,000	80,000	125,000	220,000

Size Reduced (1829–1834)

	Mintage	Fine-12	EF-40	AU-50	MS-60	MS-63
1829 small date (mintage included with large date)		$36,000	$95,000	$115,000	$150,000	$230,000
1830................	126,351	15,000	42,000	50,000	65,000	95,000
1831................	140,594	15,000	42,000	50,000	65,000	95,000
1832 combined total....	157,487					
1832 with 12 stars......	(6 known)	58,000	100,000	125,000	—	—
1832 with 13 stars......		15,000	42,000	50,000	65,000	95,000
1833 with large date....	193,630	15,000	42,000	50,000	65,000	95,000
1834 combined total....	50,141					
1834 with plain 4.......		15,000	42,000	50,000	65,000	95,000
1834 with crosslet 4		15,000	42,000	50,000	75,000	110,000

Classic Head Portrait (1834–1838)

	Mintage	Fine-12	EF-40	AU-50	MS-60	MS-63
1834 combined total....	657,460					
1834 with plain 4		$500	$800	$1,700	$4,200	$12,000

	Mintage	Fine-12	EF-40	AU-50	MS-60	MS-63
1834 with crosslet 4		1,100	3,600	8,000	28,000	60,000
1835.................	371,534	500	800	1,700	4,500	13,000
1836.................	553,147	500	800	1,700	4,500	12,000
1837.................	207,121	500	900	2,100	4,500	19,000
1838.................	286,588	500	900	2,000	4,500	14,000
1838-C	17,179	1,500	6,000	14,000	38,000	100,000
1838-D	20,583	1,400	5,000	11,000	26,000	60,000

Coronet Portrait (1839–1908)

No Motto over Eagle (1839–1866)

	Mintage	EF-40	AU-50	MS-60	MS-63	Proof-65
1839.................	118,143	$550	$1,100	$3,500	$25,000	
1839-C	17,205	3,300	6,500	20,000	60,000	
1839-D	18,939	4,500	7,000	25,000	—	
1840.................	137,382	550	1,400	3,400	10,000	
1840-C	18,992	3,000	6,500	25,000	60,000	
1840-D	22,896	3,500	6,000	15,000	45,000	
1840-O	40,120	900	1,800	9,250	40,000	
1841.................	15,833	1,000	1,800	5,000	10,000	
1841-C	21,467	2,000	3,000	16,000	42,000	
1841-D	29,392	2,200	3,500	13,000	30,000	
1841-O	50	(unknown in any collection)				
1842 combined total	27,578					
1842 with small letters ..		975	3,000	12,500	23,500	
1842 with large letters ..		1,800	3,000	11,000	23,000	
1842-C combined total ..	27,432					
1842-C small date		20,000	40,000	100,000	275,000	
1842-C large date.......		2,200	3,000	17,000	40,000	
1842-D combined total ..	59,608					
1842-D small date		2,200	3,100	15,000	40,000	
1842-D large date.......		6,000	14,000	45,000	125,000	
1842-O	16,400	3,200	10,000	25,000	42,500	
1843.................	611,205	550	575	2,000	11,500	
1843-C	44,277	1,800	4,000	11,000	33,500	
1843-D	98,452	2,000	3,000	11,000	24,000	
1843-O with small letters	19,075	1,400	2,500	18,000	45,000	
1843-O with large letters.	82,000	1,100	2,000	12,000	27,500	
1844.................	340,330	550	575	2,000	9,000	
1844-C	23,631	2,900	6,200	20,000	42,000	
1844-D	88,982	2,300	3,000	12,000	27,500	
1844-O	364,600	550	600	4,000	15,000	
1845.................	417,099	550	575	2,000	9,000	
1845-D	90,629	2,200	3,000	11,000	25,000	
1845-O	41,000	700	2,800	11,000	25,000	
1846.................	395,942	550	575	2,500	14,000	
1846-C	12,995	2,200	7,000	20,000	70,000	
1846-D	80,294	2,200	3,000	12,000	22,500	
1846-O	58,000	900	3,000	10,000	25,000	
1847.................	915,981	550	575	2,000	7,250	
1847-C	84,151	2,000	3,000	13,000	28,500	
1847-D	64,405	2,200	3,000	10,000	18,000	
1847-O	12,000	7,000	10,000	25,000	45,000	
1848.................	260,775	550	575	2,000	12,000	
1848-C	64,472	2,000	3,000	19,000	44,000	

	Mintage	EF-40	AU-50	MS-60	MS-63	Proof-65
1848-D...............	47,465	2,200	3,100	14,000	28,000	
1849.................	133,070	550	750	3,000	15,000	
1849-C...............	64,823	2,000	3,000	11,500	27,500	
1849-D...............	39,036	2,200	3,000	14,000	35,000	
1850.................	64,491	600	1,000	4,000	17,000	
1850-C...............	63,591	2,000	2,700	12,000	20,000	
1850-D...............	43,984	2,200	4,000	29,000	90,000	
1851.................	377,505	550	575	2,600	10,000	
1851-C...............	49,176	2,000	3,400	14,000	47,500	
1851-D...............	62,710	2,200	3,000	15,000	26,000	
1851-O...............	41,000	1,400	4,000	13,000	22,000	
1852.................	573,901	550	575	2,000	7,000	
1852-C...............	72,574	2,100	3,000	7,000	25,000	
1852-D...............	91,584	2,200	3,000	11,000	28,000	
1853.................	305,770	550	575	2,000	9,000	
1853-C...............	65,571	2,000	3,000	8,000	28,000	
1853-D...............	89,678	2,200	3,000	8,500	22,500	
1854.................	160,675	550	600	2,200	9,000	
1854-C...............	39,283	2,100	3,500	13,000	40,000	
1854-D...............	56,413	2,200	2,800	9,000	30,000	
1854-O...............	46,000	575	1,300	8,000	25,000	
1854-S...............	268	200,000	300,000	—	—	
1855.................	117,098	550	575	2,000	9,000	—
1855-C...............	39,788	1,900	3,000	15,000	45,000	
1855-D...............	22,432	2,300	3,000	16,000	45,000	
1855-O...............	11,100	2,400	4,000	20,000	50,000	
1855-S...............	61,000	1,100	2,500	17,000	45,000	
1856.................	197,990	550	575	2,000	10,000	—
1856-C...............	28,457	2,300	3,200	21,000	40,000	
1856-D...............	19,786	2,400	3,500	12,000	40,000	
1856-O...............	10,000	1,200	5,000	15,500	45,000	
1856-S...............	105,100	700	1,300	6,500	30,000	
1857.................	98,188	550	575	2,000	8,000	220,000
1857-C...............	31,360	2,000	2,600	9,000	30,000	
1857-D...............	17,046	2,200	3,200	13,000	40,000	
1857-O...............	13,000	1,500	4,600	17,000	52,000	
1857-S...............	87,000	600	1,250	9,000	20,000	
1858.................	15,136	575	700	3,300	11,000	250,000
1858-C...............	38,856	2,200	3,000	11,000	35,000	
1858-D...............	15,362	2,300	2,900	13,000	40,000	
1858-S...............	18,600	2,000	5,000	30,000	85,000	
1859......*80*.........	16,734	575	800	6,500	16,000	125,000
1859-C...............	31,847	2,300	3,500	15,000	45,000	—
1859-D...............	10,366	2,300	2,800	13,000	40,000	
1859-S...............	13,220	3,300	5,000	28,000	50,000	
1860......*62*.........	19,763	600	1,000	4,500	16,000	110,000
1860-C...............	14,813	2,100	3,500	13,000	24,000	
1860-D...............	14,635	2,400	3,300	14,000	45,000	—
1860-S...............	21,200	1,800	5,500	25,000	60,000	
1861......*66*.........	688,084	550	575	2,000	7,000	115,000
1861-C...............	6,879	4,000	8,000	25,000	95,000	
1861-D...............	1,597	14,000	28,000	65,000	240,000	
1861-S...............	18,000	4,000	7,000	32,500	95,000	
1862......*35*.........	4,430	1,800	3,300	20,000	45,000	110,000
1862-S...............	9,500	5,000	10,000	55,000	120,000	
1863......*30*.........	2,442	3,400	6,000	25,000	85,000	110,000
1863-S...............	17,000	3,500	10,000	35,000	90,000	
1864......*50*.........	4,170	1,700	4,000	15,000	50,000	110,000
1864-S...............	3,888	15,000	30,000	60,000	120,000	
1865......*25*.........	1,270	4,500	9,000	22,000	55,000	110,000
1865-S...............	27,612	2,200	5,000	16,000	29,000	
1866-S...............	9,000	4,000	12,500	35,000	85,000	

Motto over Eagle (1866–1908)

	Mintage	EF-40	AU-50	MS-60	MS-63	Proof-65
1866 . . . . . . *30*	6,700	$1,500	$3,500	$14,000	$55,000	$70,000
1866-S	34,920	2,500	8,000	25,000	65,000	
1867 . . . . . . *50*	6,870	1,500	3,500	11,000	45,000	70,000
1867-S	29,000	2,500	8,000	30,000	45,000	
1868 . . . . . . *25*	5,700	1,000	3,300	11,000	40,000	70,000
1868-S	52,000	1,500	3,500	16,000	45,000	
1869 . . . . . . *25*	1,760	2,000	4,100	16,000	35,000	70,000
1869-S	31,000	1,700	4,000	24,000	55,000	
1870 . . . . . . *35*	4,000	1,950	2,700	17,000	50,000	70,000
1870-CC	7,675	20,000	32,000	100,000	140,000	
1870-S	17,000	2,800	7,000	25,000	65,000	
1871 . . . . . . *30*	3,200	1,600	3,200	10,000	45,000	70,000
1871-CC	20,770	3,500	12,000	60,000	100,000	
1871-S	25,000	950	3,200	12,000	45,000	
1872 . . . . . . *30*	1,660	1,900	3,000	13,500	20,000	70,000
1872-CC	16,980	5,000	17,000	60,000	—	—
1872-S	36,400	800	3,500	14,000	—	
1873 combined total	112,480					
1873 closed 3 . . . . . . *25* .		550	600	1,200	6,500	70,000
1873 open 3	122,800	550	600	1,000	4,000	
1873-CC	7,416	12,000	25,000	60,000	—	
1873-S	31,000	1,500	3,000	20,000	—	
1874 . . . . . . *20*	3,488	1,600	2,500	12,000	25,000	65,000
1874-CC	21,198	2,100	11,000	36,000	—	
1874-S	16,000	2,500	4,000	19,500	—	
1875 . . . . . . *20*	200	60,000	90,000	240,000	—	160,000
1875-CC	11,828	3,700	10,500	50,000	125,000	
1875-S	9,000	2,400	5,000	16,000	30,000	
1876 . . . . . . *45*	1,432	2,500	5,000	14,000	24,000	55,000
1876-CC	6,887	4,200	13,000	46,000	70,000	
1876-S	4,000	3,100	10,000	27,000	—	
1877 . . . . . . *20*	1,132	2,900	4,200	11,400	28,000	70,000
1877-CC	8,680	3,000	10,000	45,000	—	
1877-S	26,700	700	1,700	9,000	22,000	
1878 . . . . . . *20*	131,720	550	575	525	2,100	70,000
1878-CC	9,054	6,800	18,000	80,000	—	
1878-S	144,700	550	575	800	4,350	
1879 . . . . . . *30*	301,920	550	575	525	2,200	60,000
1879-CC	17,281	1,500	3,000	20,000	—	
1879-S	426,200	550	575	800	3,250	
1880 . . . . . . *36*	3,166,400	550	575	500	1,100	50,000
1880-CC	51,017	800	1,300	12,000	45,000	
1880-S	1,348,900	550	575	500	1,100	
1881 combined total	5,708,760					
1881 regular date . . . *42* .		550	575	500	1,000	45,000
1881/0 overdate		600	1,500	1,700	4,500	
1881-CC	13,886	1,600	6,000	24,000	58,000	
1881-S	969,000	550	575	500	1,000	
1882 . . . . . . *48*	2,514,520	550	575	500	1,100	45,000
1882-CC	82,817	600	1,200	11,000	40,000	
1882-S	969,000	550	575	500	1,100	
1883 . . . . . . *61*	233,400	550	575	500	1,300	45,000
1883-CC	12,958	1,100	4,000	18,000	35,000	
1883-S	83,200	550	575	995	3,000	
1884 . . . . . . *48*	191,030	550	575	650	2,200	40,000
1884-CC	16,402	1,000	3,500	21,000	40,000	
1884-S	177,000	550	575	550	1,700	
1885 . . . . . . *66*	601,440	550	575	500	1,100	40,000
1885-S	1,211,500	550	575	500	1,000	
1886 . . . . . . *72*	388,360	550	575	625	1,100	40,000
1886-S	3,268,000	550	575	625	1,000	
1887 (proof only)	87	—	—	—	—	150,000
1887-S	1,912,000	550	575	625	1,100	
1888 . . . . . . *95*	18,201	550	575	650	1,800	38,000
1888-S	293,900	550	575	1,200	3,500	

	Mintage	EF-40	AU-50	MS-60	MS-63	Proof-65
1889 . . . . . . 45	7,520	550	600	1,100	2,800	38,000
1890 . . . . . . 88	4,240	575	600	2,300	5,800	35,000
1890-CC	53,800	600	750	1,600	8,000	
1891 . . . . . . 53	61,360	550	575	625	2,000	35,000
1891-CC	208,000	625	800	1,500	4,000	
1892 . . . . . . 92	753,480	550	575	625	1,100	35,000
1892-CC	82,968	625	800	1,900	7,000	
1892-O	10,000	900	1,400	3,300	12,000	
1892-S	298,400	550	575	675	3,000	
1893 . . . . . . 77	1,528,120	550	575	625	1,000	35,000
1893-CC	60,000	675	850	1,600	7,000	
1893-O	110,000	550	600	1,000	6,750	
1893-S	224,000	550	575	625	1,100	
1894 . . . . . . 75	957,880	550	575	625	1,000	35,000
1894-O	16,600	550	600	1,200	7,000	
1894-S	55,900	550	700	3,000	10,000	
1895 . . . . . . 81	1,345,855	550	575	625	1,100	35,000
1895-S	112,000	550	575	3,000	6,000	
1896 . . . . . . 103	58,960	550	575	625	1,000	33,000
1896-S	155,400	550	575	1,200	6,200	
1897 . . . . . . 83	867,800	550	575	625	1,100	33,000
1897-S	354,000	550	575	625	5,000	
1898 . . . . . . 75	633,420	550	575	625	1,100	33,000
1898-S	1,397,400	550	575	625	1,200	
1899 . . . . . . 99	1,710,630	550	575	625	1,000	33,000
1899-S	1,545,000	550	575	625	1,200	
1900 . . . . . . 230	1,405,500	550	575	625	1,000	33,000
1900-S	329,000	550	575	625	1,200	
1901 . . . . . . 140	615,900	550	575	625	1,000	33,000
1901-S combined total . .	3,648,000					
1901-S regular date		550	575	625	1,000	
1901/0-S overdate		550	575	625	1,200	
1902 . . . . . . 162	172,400	550	575	625	1,000	33,000
1902-S	939,000	550	575	625	1,000	
1903 . . . . . . 154	226,870	550	575	625	1,100	33,000
1903-S	1,855,000	550	575	625	1,000	
1904 . . . . . . 136	392,000	550	575	625	1,000	33,000
1904-S	97,000	550	575	750	3,850	
1905 . . . . . . 108	302,200	550	575	625	1,000	33,000
1905-S	880,700	550	575	625	2,100	
1906 . . . . . . 85	348,735	550	575	625	1,000	33,000
1906-D	320,000	550	575	625	1,000	
1906-S	598,000	550	575	625	1,100	
1907 . . . . . . 92	626,100	550	575	625	1,000	33,000
1907-D	888,000	550	575	625	1,000	
1908	421,874	550	575	625	1,000	

Indian Head Portrait (1908–1929)

	Mintage	EF-40	AU-50	MS-60	MS-63	Proof-65
1908 . . . . . . 167	577,845	$550	$450	$625	$2,400	$42,000
1908-D	148,000	550	450	625	3,400	
1908-S	82,000	550	500	1,500	9,000	
1909 . . . . . . 78	627,060	550	450	625	2,500	46,000
1909-D	3,423,560	550	450	625	2,400	

	Mintage	EF-40	AU-50	MS-60	MS-63	Proof-65
1909-O................	34,200	4,800	8,200	35,000	85,000	
1909-S................	297,200	550	475	1,500	15,000	
1910 ...... *250*	604,000	550	450	625	2,500	45,000
1910-D................	193,600	550	450	625	3,900	
1910-S................	770,200	550	475	1,200	9,500	
1911 ...... *139*	915,000	550	450	625	3,400	42,000
1911-D................	72,500	850	1,300	7,000	52,000	
1911-S................	1,416,000	550	450	800	6,700	
1912 ...... *144*	790,000	550	450	625	2,400	42,000
1912-S................	392,000	550	475	1,700	17,000	
1913 ...... *99*	915,901	550	450	625	2,400	42,000
1913-S................	408,000	550	475	1,700	16,000	
1914 ...... *125*	247,000	550	450	625	2,700	42,000
1914-D................	247,000	550	450	625	3,100	
1914-S................	263,000	550	500	1,600	15,000	
1915 ...... *75*	588,000	550	450	625	2,400	45,000
1915-S................	164,000	550	525	2,300	20,000	
1916-S................	240,000	550	500	900	8,500	
1929................	662,000	14,000	18,000	26,000	48,000	

EAGLES, OR $10 GOLD PIECES
(1795–1933)

Capped Bust Portrait Facing Right with Small Eagle on Reverse (1795–1797)

	Mintage	VF-20	EF-40	MS-60
1795 combined total............	5,583			
1795 with 9 leaves below eagle ...		$50,000	$75,000	$275,000
1795 with 13 leaves below eagle ..		33,000	48,000	110,000
1796.........................	4,146	36,000	50,000	130,000
1797.........................	3,615	42,000	70,000	210,000

Capped Bust Portrait Facing Right with Heraldic Eagle on Reverse (1797–1804)

	Mintage	VF-20	EF-40	MS-60
1797..........................	10,940	$14,000	$22,000	$60,000
1798/7 overdate with 9 stars left, 4 right	900	18,000	35,000	135,000
1798/7 overdate with 7 stars left, 6 right	842	42,000	70,000	250,000
1799..........................	37,449	11,000	18,000	37,000
1800..........................	5,999	11,000	18,000	40,000
1801..........................	44,344	11,000	18,000	37,000
1803..........................	15,017	11,000	18,000	40,000
1804..........................	3,757	24,000	33,000	100,000

Coronet Portrait (1838–1907)

No Motto over Eagle (1838–1866)

	Mintage	VF-20	EF-40	AU-50	MS-60	MS-63	Proof-65
1838	7,200	$3,000	$6,500	$15,000	$40,000	$90,000	
1839 with large letters ...	25,801	1,300	2,500	6,000	29,000	80,000	

Modified Portrait of Liberty, Smaller Letters (1839–1866)

	Mintage	VF-20	EF-40	AU-50	MS-60	MS-65	Proof-65
1839 with small letters ..	12,447	$1,500	$3,700	$8,000	$34,000	—	
1840	47,338	1,000	1,050	1,500	9,000	—	
1841	63,131	1,000	1,050	1,200	8,000	$85,000	
1841-O	2,500	3,000	6,000	16,000	37,000	—	
1842 small date	18,623	1,000	1,050	1,200	16,000	85,000	
1842 large date	62,884	1,000	1,050	1,200	16,000		
1842-O	27,400	1,000	1,050	3,000	20,000	—	
1843	75,462	1,000	1,050	1,600	19,000	—	
1843-O	175,162	1,000	1,050	1,300	12,500	—	
1844	6,361	1,200	3,000	6,000	17,000	—	
1844-O	118,700	1,000	1,200	1,800	15,000	—	
1845	26,153	1,000	1,050	2,100	18,000	—	
1845-O	47,500	1,000	1,050	2,800	16,000	—	
1846	20,095	1,000	1,200	6,000	24,000	—	
1846-O	81,780	1,000	1,200	3,500	16,000	—	
1847	862,258	1,000	1,050	1,200	4,000	75,000	

	Mintage	VF-20	EF-40	AU-50	MS-60	MS-65	Proof-65
1847-O	571,500	1,000	1,050	1,250	6,000	85,000	
1848	145,484	1,000	1,050	1,250	5,500	70,000	
1848-O	35,850	1,000	1,200	4,000	17,000	—	
1849	653,618	1,000	1,050	1,200	4,000	60,000	
1849-O	23,900	1,000	2,400	5,500	29,000	—	
1850 combined total	291,451						
1850 small date		1,000	1,050	2,000	10,000	—	
1850 large date		1,000	1,050	1,250	4,500	60,000	
1850-O	57,500	1,000	1,050	3,200	19,000	125,000	
1851	176,328	1,000	1,050	1,200	5,000	100,000	
1851-O	263,000	1,000	1,050	1,200	7,000	—	
1852	263,106	1,000	1,050	1,200	5,500	100,000	
1852-O	18,000	1,000	1,200	3,600	28,000	—	
1853 combined total	201,253						
1853 regular date		1,000	1,050	1,200	4,400	80,000	
1853/2 overdate		1,000	1,200	2,000	15,000	—	
1853-O	51,000	1,000	1,050	1,250	14,000	—	
1854	54,250	1,000	1,050	1,200	6,500	—	
1854-O combined total	52,500						
1854-O small date		1,000	1,050	2,000	11,000	—	
1854-O large date		1,000	1,200	2,500	13,000	—	
1854-S	123,826	1,000	1,050	1,400	11,000	—	
1855	121,701	1,000	1,050	1,200	5,000	—	
1855-O	18,000	1,000	1,800	6,000	28,000	—	
1855-S	9,000	1,800	3,000	7,500	34,000	—	
1856	60,490	1,000	1,050	1,200	4,000	75,000	—
1856-O	14,500	1,050	1,600	4,200	18,000	—	
1856-S	68,000	1,050	1,200	1,300	10,000	—	
1857	16,666	1,050	1,200	2,000	14,000	—	—
1857-O	5,500	1,100	2,000	5,000	29,000	—	
1857-S	26,000	1,050	1,250	2,500	12,000	—	
1858	2,521	5,500	7,000	12,000	40,000	—	—
1858-O	20,000	1,050	1,200	1,800	10,000	—	
1858-S		1,600	3,000	5,000	33,000	150,000	—
1859 .....*80*	16,013	1,050	1,200	1,300	11,000	—	220,000
1859-O	2,300	4,500	9,500	23,000	47,500	—	
1859-S	7,000	2,800	5,500	14,000	45,000	—	
1860 .....*50*	15,055	1,050	1,200	1,300	9,000	—	210,000
1860-O	11,100	1,050	1,700	3,500	14,000	—	
1860-S	5,000	2,800	5,500	16,000	42,000	—	
1861 .....*69*	113,164	1,050	1,200	1,300	5,400	80,000	210,000
1861-S	15,500	1,500	3,400	6,500	34,000	—	
1862 .....*35*	10,960	1,050	1,200	2,600	12,000	—	210,000
1862-S	12,500	1,800	3,500	6,000	40,000	—	
1863 .....*30*	1,218	4,500	10,000	19,000	57,500	—	200,000
1863-S	10,000	1,500	4,000	10,000	28,000	—	
1864 .....*50*	3,530	1,800	3,950	9,000	18,000	—	200,000
1864-S	2,500	6,000	16,000	32,000	57,500	—	
1865 .....*25*	3,980	1,900	4,200	7,000	35,000	—	200,000
1865-S combined total	16,700						
1865-S regular date		3,500	10,000	21,000	45,000	—	
1865-S with 865 over inverted 186		3,600	8,000	15,000	50,000	—	
1866-S	8,500	2,500	4,500	13,000	45,000	—	

Motto over Eagle (1866–1907)

	Mintage	VF-20	EF-40	AU-50	MS-60	MS-63	Proof-65
1866 . . . . . . 30	3,750	$1,050	$2,000	$5,000	$24,000	—	$98,000
1866-S	11,500	1,700	4,000	8,500	25,000	—	
1867 . . . . . . 50	3,090	1,700	2,500	6,000	28,000	—	85,000
1867-S	9,000	2,300	7,000	9,500	42,500	—	
1868 . . . . . . 5	10,630	1,050	1,100	1,800	19,000	—	80,000
1868-S	13,500	1,500	3,000	4,400	28,000	—	
1869 . . . . . . 25	1,830	1,500	3,000	5,000	35,000	$65,000	80,000
1869-S	6,430	1,500	3,000	6,000	26,000	—	
1870 . . . . . . 35	3,990	1,050	1,200	2,500	21,000	—	85,000
1870-CC	5,908	18,000	30,000	55,000	—	—	
1870-S	8,000	1,200	3,000	6,500	37,000	—	
1871 . . . . . . 30	1,790	1,500	3,100	5,000	20,000	—	85,000
1871-CC	8,085	2,700	5,500	17,000	67,000	—	
1871-S	16,500	1,300	1,800	5,500	30,000	—	
1872 . . . . . . 30	1,620	2,700	4,000	9,500	16,000	—	85,000
1872-CC	4,680	3,000	10,000	25,000	70,000	—	
1872-S	17,300	1,050	1,200	2,100	21,000	—	
1873 . . . . . . 25	800	4,300	10,000	17,000	50,000	—	85,000
1873-CC	4,543	4,300	11,000	30,000	—	—	
1873-S	12,000	1,150	2,000	4,200	27,000	—	
1874 . . . . . . 20	53,140	1,050	1,200	1,300	2,000	8,000	85,000
1874-CC	16,767	950	3,000	9,000	55,000	—	
1874-S	10,000	1,300	3,000	5,800	50,000	—	
1875 . . . . . . 20	100	50,000	85,000	130,000	—	—	200,000
1875-CC	7,715	4,100	8,500	20,000	72,000	—	
1876 . . . . . . 45	687	3,000	6,700	19,000	67,000	—	75,000
1876-CC	4,696	3,500	7,000	20,000	67,000	—	
1876-S	5,000	1,300	2,000	6,000	42,000	—	
1877 . . . . . . 20	797	2,500	5,200	8,500	35,000	60,000	75,000
1877-CC	3,332	3,000	6,000	14,000	52,000	—	
1877-S	17,000	1,050	1,200	2,100	30,000	—	
1878 . . . . . . 20	73,780	1,050	1,200	1,300	1,350	6,700	75,000
1878-CC	3,244	3,600	9,500	20,000	53,000	—	
1878-S	26,100	1,050	1,200	1,900	18,000	—	
1879 . . . . . . 30	384,740	1,050	1,200	1,300	1,350	4,750	65,000
1879-CC	1,762	5,700	14,000	25,000	72,000	—	
1879-O	1,500	2,000	4,500	11,000	40,000	—	
1879-S	224,000	1,050	1,200	1,300	1,300	8,000	
1880 . . . . . . 36	1,644,840	1,050	1,200	1,300	1,350	4,200	65,000
1880-CC	11,190	1,050	1,200	1,800	14,000	—	
1880-O	9,200	1,050	1,200	1,700	8,500	—	
1880-S	506,250	1,050	1,200	1,300	1,350	5,300	
1881 . . . . . . 40	3,877,220	1,050	1,200	1,300	1,350	1,700	60,000
1881-CC	24,015	1,050	1,200	1,300	6,500	22,000	
1881-O	8,350	1,050	1,200	1,300	7,300	—	
1881-S	970,000	1,050	1,200	1,300	1,350	5,500	
1882 . . . . . . 40	2,324,440	1,050	1,200	1,300	1,350	1,500	60,000
1882-CC	6,764	1,050	1,400	3,500	24,000	45,000	
1882-O	10,820	1,050	1,200	1,300	6,500	19,500	
1882-S	132,000	1,050	1,200	1,250	1,300	5,000	
1883 . . . . . . 40	208,700	1,050	1,200	1,250	1,300	3,200	50,000
1883-CC	12,000	1,100	1,300	2,200	14,000	40,000	
1883-O	800	4,000	12,000	30,000	85,000	—	
1883-S	38,000	1,050	1,200	1,250	1,500	11,000	
1884 . . . . . . 45	76,860	1,050	1,200	1,250	1,300	4,700	

	Mintage	VF-20	EF-40	AU-50	MS-60	MS-63	Proof-65
1884-CC	9,925	1,100	1,400	2,600	13,000	45,000	
1884-S	124,250	1,050	1,200	1,250	1,300	6,700	
1885 ....65	253,462	1,050	1,200	1,250	1,300	4,700	50,000
1885-S	228,000	1,050	1,200	1,250	1,300	3,000	
1886 ......60	236,100	1,050	1,200	1,250	1,300	4,000	50,000
1886-S	826,000	1,050	1,200	1,250	1,300	1,800	
1887 ......80	53,600	1,050	1,200	1,250	1,300	5,500	50,000
1887-S	817,000	1,050	1,200	1,250	1,300	3,000	
1888 ....75	132,921	1,050	1,200	1,250	1,300	6,500	48,000
1888-O	21,335	1,050	1,200	1,250	1,300	5,500	
1888-S	648,700	1,050	1,200	1,250	1,300	3,200	
1889 ......45	4,440	1,050	1,300	1,350	2,700	7,500	50,000
1889-S	425,400	1,050	1,200	1,250	1,300	1,800	
1890 ......63	57,980	1,050	1,200	1,250	1,300	6,000	45,000
1890-CC	17,500	1,100	1,300	1.350	2,000	14,000	
1891 ......48	91,820	1,050	1,200	1,250	1,300	4,400	45,000
1891-CC	103,732	1,150	1,300	1,350	1,700	6,500	
1892 ....72	797,480	1,050	1,200	1,250	1,300	1,700	45,000
1892-CC	40,000	1,050	1,300	1,350	3,500	11,000	
1892-O	28,688	1,050	1,200	1,250	1,300	6,800	
1892-S	115,500	1,050	1,200	1,250	1,300	4,000	
1893 ......55	1,840,840	1,050	1,200	1,250	1,300	1,500	45,000
1893-CC	14,000	800	1,200	1,600	7,200	23,000	
1893-O	17,000	1,050	1,200	1,250	1,300	5,500	
1893-S	141,350	1,050	1,200	1,250	1,300	4,700	
1894 ......43	2,470,735	1,050	1,200	1,250	1,300	1,500	45,000
1894-O	107,500	1,050	1,200	1,250	1,350	5,500	
1894-S	25,000	1,050	1,200	1,250	3,600	13,500	
1895 ......56	567,770	1,050	1,200	1,250	1,300	1,500	45,000
1895-O	98,000	1,050	1,200	1,250	1,300	5,800	
1895-S	49,000	1,050	1,200	1,250	2,700	10,000	
1896 ......78	76,270	1,050	1,200	1,250	1,300	2,500	45,000
1896-S	123,750	1,050	1,200	1,250	2,500	12,000	
1897 ......69	1,000,090	1,050	1,200	1,250	1,300	1,500	45,000
1897-O	42,500	1,050	1,200	1,250	1,300	5,400	
1897-S	234,750	1,050	1,200	1,250	1,300	5,400	
1898 ......67	812,130	1,050	1,200	1,250	1,300	1,500	45,000
1898-S	473,600	1,050	1,200	1,250	1,300	4,400	
1899 ......86	1,262,219	1,050	1,200	1,250	1,300	1,500	45,000
1899-O	37,047	1,050	1,200	1,250	1,300	6,500	
1899-S	841,000	1,050	1,200	1,250	1,300	3,500	
1900 ......120	293,840	1,050	1,200	1,250	1,300	1,500	45,000
1900-S	81,000	1,050	1,200	1,250	1,300	6,600	
1901 ......85	1,718,740	1,050	1,200	1,250	1,300	1,500	45,000
1901-O	72,041	1,050	1,200	1,250	1,300	3,400	
1901-S	2,812,750	1,050	1,200	1,250	1,300	1,500	
1902 ......113	82,400	1,050	1,200	1,250	1,300	3,000	45,000
1902-S	469,500	1,050	1,200	1,250	1,300	1,600	
1903 ......96	125,830	1,050	1,200	1,250	1,300	2,300	45,000
1903-O	112,771	1,050	1,200	1,250	1,300	3,000	
1903-S	538,000	1,050	1,200	1,250	1,300	1,800	
1904 ......108	161,930	1,050	1,200	1,250	1,300	2,400	45,000
1904-O	108,950	1,050	1,200	1,250	1,300	3,500	
1905 ......86	200,992	1,050	1,200	1,250	1,300	1,500	45,000
1905-S	369,250	1,050	1,200	1,250	1,300	6,000	
1906 ......77	165,420	1,050	1,200	1,250	1,300	2,200	45,000
1906-D	981,000	1,050	1,200	1,250	1,300	1,500	
1906-O	86,895	1,050	1,200	1,250	1,300	5,000	
1906-S	457,000	1,050	1,200	1,250	1,300	4,600	
1907 ......74	1,203,899	1,050	1,200	1,250	1,300	1,500	45,000
1907-D	1,030,000	1,050	1,200	1,250	1,300	2,400	
1907-S	210,500	1,050	1,200	1,250	1,300	5,500	

Indian Head Portrait (1907–1933)

	Mintage	VF-20	EF-40	AU-50	MS-60	MS-63	MS-65
1907 with wire rim and periods before and after E PLURIBUS UNUM ...	500	$14,000	$20,000	$22,000	$31,000	$55,000	$85,000
1907 with rounded rim and periods	42	30,000	40,000	50,000	72,000	135,000	315,000
1907 with no periods	239,406	1,050	1,200	1,250	1,300	4,200	
1908 without IN GOD WE TRUST	33,500	1,050	1,200	1,250	1,300	5,500	
1908-D without motto ...	210,000	1,050	1,200	1,250	1,300	8,500	

Motto Added to Reverse (1908–1933)

	Mintage	EF-40	AU-50	MS-60	MS-63	Proof-65
1908 ...... 116	341,370	$1,050	$1,200	$1,250	$3,000	$60,000
1908-D	836,500	1,050	1,200	1,250	8,000	
1908-S	59,850	1,050	1,200	3,200	13,000	
1909 ...... 74	184,789	1,050	1,200	1,250	4,500	66,000
1909-D	121,540	1,050	1,200	1,250	7,000	
1909-S	292,350	1,050	1,200	1,250	8,000	
1910 ...... 204	318,500	1,050	1,200	1,250	2,000	70,000
1910-D	2,356,640	1,050	1,200	1,250	2,000	
1910-S	811,000	1,050	1,200	1,250	11,000	
1911 ...... 95	505,500	1,050	1,200	1,250	2,000	60,000
1911-D	30,100	1,300	1,800	9,000	34,000	
1911-S	51,000	1,050	1,200	1,700	13,000	
1912 ...... 83	405,000	1,050	1,200	1,250	2,000	60,000
1912-S	300,000	1,050	1,200	1,500	9,500	
1913 ...... 71	442,000	1,050	1,200	1,250	2,000	60,000
1913-S	66,000	1,050	1,200	4,600	31,000	
1914 ...... 50	151,000	1,050	1,200	1,250	2,700	60,000
1914-D	343,500	1,050	1,200	1,250	2,700	
1914-S	208,000	1,050	1,200	1,500	9,500	
1915 ...... 75	351,000	1,050	1,200	1,250	2,500	64,000
1915-S	59,000	1,050	1,200	3,300	19,000	
1916-S	138,500	1,050	1,200	1,500	7,500	
1920-S	126,500	17,500	22,000	44,000	95,000	
1926	1,014,000	1,050	875	900	1,500	
1930-S	96,000	12,000	16,000	25,000	50,000	
1932	4,463,000	1,050	1,200	1,250	1,500	
1933	312,500	120,000	150,000	200,000	270,000	

DOUBLE EAGLES, OR $20 GOLD PIECES (1849–1933)

Coronet Portrait (1849–1907)

No Motto over Eagle (1849–1866)

	Mintage	VF-20	EF-40	AU-50	MS-60	MS-63	Proof-63
1849	1	(part of the U.S. Mint Collection)					$15,000,000
1850	1,170,261	$2,200	$2,400	$3,000	$9,000	$50,000	
1850-O	141,000	2,300	4,000	10,000	50,000	125,000	
1851	2,087,155	2,200	2,300	2,500	3,500	23,000	
1851-O	315,000	2,300	3,000	5,000	21,000	70,000	
1852	2,053,026	2,200	2,300	2,500	4,200	19,000	
1852-O	190,000	2,300	2,600	4,000	22,000	60,000	
1853 combined total	1,261,326						
1853 regular date		2,200	2,300	2,500	5,000	25,000	
1853/2 overdate		2,300	2,400	4,000	30,000	—	
1853-O	71,000	2,300	2,500	6,000	30,000	60,000	
1854	757,899	2,300	2,300	2,500	8,500	25,000	
1854-O	3,250	100,000	200,000	400,000	700,000	—	
1854-S	141,468	2,200	2,300	4,000	12,500	18,000	
1855	364,666	2,200	2,300	2,500	8,000	60,000	
1855-O	8,000	5,000	10,000	30,000	100,000		
1855-S	879,675	2,200	2,300	2,500	6,800	18,000	
1856	329,878	2,200	2,300	2,500	8,500	30,000	
1856-O	2,250	110,000	200,000	400,000	700,000	1,000,000	
1856-S	1,189,750	2,200	2,300	2,500	6,000	15,000	
1857	439,375	2,200	2,300	2,500	3,500	25,000	
1857-O	30,000	2,200	3,000	6,000	40,000	100,000	
1857-S	970,500	2,200	2,300	2,600	6,500	10,000	
1858	211,714	2,200	2,300	2,500	4,500	40,000	
1858-O	35,250	2,300	3,000	6,000	40,000	125,000	
1858-S	846,710	2,200	2,300	2,500	8,000	35,000	
1859 80	43,517	2,400	2,500	4,500	30,000	60,000	100,000
1859-O	9,100	4,500	18,000	30,000	100,000	225,000	
1859-S	636,445	2,200	2,300	2,500	5,500	33,000	
1860 59	577,611	2,200	2,300	2,500	5,000	20,000	90,000
1860-O	6,600	4,500	15,000	28,000	120,000	375,000	
1860-S	544,950	2,200	2,300	2,500	8,000	20,000	
1861 combined total	2,976,387						
1861 with regular reverse 66	550	2,200	2,300	2,600	4,500	14,000	90,000
1861 with Paquet reverse (tall letters)		—	—	—	—	3,000,000*	
1861-O	17,741	4,500	17,000	36,000	100,000	200,000	
1861-S with regular reverse	748,750	2,200	2,300	2,500	11,000	35,000	
1861-S with Paquet reverse (tall letters)	19,250	22,000	60,000	100,000	235,000	—	
1862 35	92,098	2,200	2,300	6,500	17,000	35,000	90,000
1862-S	854,173	2,200	2,300	2,500	11,000	35,000	
1863 30	142,760	2,200	2,300	4,000	20,000	35,000	90,000
1863-S	966,570	2,200	2,300	2,500	7,000	31,000	
1864 50	204,235	2,200	2,300	2,600	12,000	38,000	90,000
1864-S	793,660	2,200	2,300	2,500	8,000	40,000	

*MS-67 specimen

	Mintage	VF-20	EF-40	AU-50	MS-60	MS-63	Proof-63
1865 ..... 25	351,175	2,200	2,300	2,500	6,000	25,000	
1865-S	1,042,500	2,200	2,300	2,500	6,000	10,000	
1866-S	120,000	3,500	12,000	35,000	150,000	—	

Motto over Eagle (1866–1876)

	Mintage	VF-20	EF-40	AU-50	MS-60	MS-63	Proof-65
1866 ..... 30	698,745	$2,200	$2,300	$2,500	$9,000	$32,000	$250,000
1866-S	722,250	2,200	2,300	2,600	18,000	50,000	
1867 ..... 50	251,015	2,200	2,300	2,500	3,500	20,000	250,000
1867-S	920,750	2,200	2,300	2,500	17,000	50,000	
1868 ..... 25	98,575	2,200	2,300	2,600	15,000	45,000	250,000
1868-S	837,500	2,200	2,300	2,500	13,000	40,000	
1869 ..... 25	175,130	2,200	2,300	2,500	8,300	25,000	250,000
1869-S	686,750	2,200	2,300	2,500	7,000	42,000	
1870 ..... 35	155,150	2,200	2,300	2,800	9,000	48,000	250,000
1870-CC	3,789	215,000	310,000	425,000	—	—	
1870-S	982,000	2,200	2,300	2,500	6,000	35,000	
1871 ..... 30	80,120	2,200	2,300	2,400	6,000	25,000	250,000
1871-CC	17,387	9,000	22,000	40,000	90,000	225,000	
1871-S	928,000	2,200	2,300	2,500	4,750	25,000	
1872 ..... 30	251,850	2,200	2,300	2,500	4,200	30,000	250,000
1872-CC	26,900	3,000	5,000	10,000	42,000	—	
1872-S	780,000	2,200	2,300	2,500	3,500	25,000	
1873 combined total	1,709,800						
1873 closed 3 ..... 25 ..		2,200	2,300	2,500	3,500	24,000	250,000
1873 open 3		2,200	2,300	2,500	2,600	12,000	
1873-CC	22,410	3,000	5,000	12,000	46,000	125,000	
1873-S	1,040,600	2,200	2,300	2,500	2,600	25,000	
1874 ..... 20	366,780	2,200	2,300	2,500	2,600	21,000	250,000
1874-CC	115,085	2,400	2,500	3,400	15,000	—	
1874-S	1,214,000	2,200	2,300	2,500	2,700	25,000	
1875 ..... 20	295,720	2,200	2,300	2,500	1,950	15,000	300,000
1875-CC	111,151	2,400	2,500	2,500	5,000	30,000	
1875-S	1,230,000	2,200	2,300	2,500	2,600	20,000	
1876 ..... 45	583,860	2,200	2,300	2,500	2,600	15,000	250,000
1876-CC	138,441	2,200	2,500	2,800	9,000	40,000	
1876-S	1,597,000	2,200	2,300	2,500	2,600	15,000	

TWENTY DOLLARS Spelled Out (1877–1907)

	Mintage	VF-20	EF-40	AU-50	MS-60	MS-63	Proof-65
1877 ..... 20	397,650	$2,200	$2,300	$2,400	$2,500	$19,000	$125,000
1877-CC	42,565	2,200	2,400	3,600	20,000	—	
1877-S	1,735,000	2,200	2,300	2,400	2,500	21,000	
1878 ..... 20	543,625	2,200	2,300	2,400	2,500	16,000	125,000
1878-CC	13,180	2,400	4,000	7,000	28,000	—	
1878-S	1,739,000	2,200	2,300	2,400	2,500	23,000	
1879 ..... 30	207,600	2,200	2,300	2,400	2,500	18,000	125,000
1879-CC	10,708	2,400	5,000	9,500	35,000	—	
1879-O	2,325	10,000	20,000	40,000	85,000	150,000	
1879-S	1,223,800	2,200	2,300	2,400	2,500	47,000	
1880 ..... 36	51,420	2,200	2,300	2,400	6,000	26,000	125,000

	Mintage	VF-20	EF-40	AU-50	MS-60	MS-63	Proof-65
1880-S	836,000	2,200	2,300	2,400	2,500	20,000	
1881 ...... *61*	2,199	12,500	23,000	33,000	70,000	100,000	130,000
1881-S	727,000	2,200	2,300	2,400	2,500	24,000	
1882 ...... *59*	571	11,000	40,000	100,000	150,000	200,000	130,000
1882-CC	39,140	2,300	2,500	2,800	10,750	60,000	
1882-S	1,125,000	2,200	2,300	2,100	2,500	20,000	
1883 (proof only)	92	—	—	—	—	—	250,000
1883-CC	59,962	2,300	2,300	2,600	8,000	25,000	
1883-S	1,189,000	2,200	2,300	2,500	2,500	11,000	
1884 (proof only)	71	—	—	—	—	—	250,000
1884-CC	81,139	2,300	2,500	2,500	6,500	24,000	
1884-S	916,000	2,200	2,300	2,400	2,500	7,000	
1885 ...... *77*	751	8,000	13,000	20,000	66,000	100,000	120,000
1885-CC	9,450	2,800	4,000	8,000	24,000	—	
1885-S	683,500	2,200	2,300	2,400	2,500	7,000	
1886 ...... *106*	1,000	12,000	18,000	35,000	80,000	100,000	120,000
1887 (proof only)	121	—	—	—	—	—	140,000
1887-S	283,000	2,200	2,300	2,400	2,500	20,000	
1888 ...... *105*	226,161	2,200	2,300	2,400	2,500	11,000	110,000
1888-S	859,600	2,200	2,300	2,400	2,500	5,600	
1889 ...... *45*	44,070	2,200	2,300	2,400	2,500	16,000	120,000
1889-CC	30,945	2,300	2,500	3,000	8,000	28,000	
1889-S	774,700	2,200	2,300	2,400	2,500	7,000	
1890 ...... *55*	75,940	2,200	2,300	2,400	2,500	12,500	120,000
1890-CC	91,209	2,300	1,900	2,400	5,000	32,000	
1890-S	802,750	2,200	2,300	2,400	2,500	8,000	
1891 ...... *52*	1,390	8,000	14,000	22,000	60,000	100,000	120,000
1891-CC	5,000	5,000	10,000	12,000	26,500	—	
1891-S	1,288,125	2,200	2,300	2,400	2,300	4,800	
1892 ...... *93*	4,430	2,500	4,000	6,500	12,000	30,000	110,000
1892-CC	27,265	2,300	2,500	3,000	8,500	35,000	
1892-S	930,150	2,200	2,300	2,400	2,500	4,000	
1893 ...... *59*	344,280	2,200	2,300	2,400	2,500	3,100	120,000
1893-CC	18,402	2,300	2,500	3,000	8,500	30,000	
1893-S	996,175	2,200	2,300	2,400	2,500	4,500	
1894 ...... *50*	1,368,940	2,200	2,300	2,400	2,500	3,000	105,000
1894-S	1,048,550	2,200	2,300	2,400	2,500	3,100	
1895 ...... *51*	1,114,605	2,200	2,300	2,400	2,500	2,700	105,000
1895-S	1,143,500	2,200	2,300	2,400	2,500	2,800	
1896 ...... *128*	792,535	2,200	2,300	2,400	2,500	2,700	105,000
1896-S	1,403,925	2,200	2,300	2,400	2,500	3,000	
1897 ...... *86*	1,383,175	2,200	2,300	2,400	2,500	2,600	105,000
1897-S	1,470,250	2,200	2,300	2,400	2,500	2,700	
1898 ...... *75*	170,395	2,200	2,300	2,400	2,500	5,000	100,000
1898-S	2,575,175	2,200	2,300	2,400	2,500	2,700	
1899 ...... *84*	1,669,300	2,200	2,300	2,400	2,500	2,600	100,000
1899-S	2,010,300	2,200	2,300	2,350	2,400	3,000	
1900 ...... *124*	1,874,460	2,200	2,300	2,350	2,400	2,500	100,000
1900-S	2,459,500	2,200	2,300	2,350	2,400	3,300	
1901 ...... *96*	111,430	2,200	2,300	2,350	2,400	2,500	100,000
1901-S	1,596,000	2,200	2,300	2,350	2,400	5,000	
1902 ...... *114*	31,140	2,200	2,300	2,350	2,400	14,000	100,000
1902-S	1,753,625	2,200	2,300	2,350	2,400	4,200	
1903 ...... *158*	287,270	2,200	2,300	2,350	2,400	2,500	100,000
1903-S	954,000	2,200	2,300	2,350	2,400	3,000	
1904 ...... *98*	6,256,699	2,200	2,300	2,350	2,400	2,400	100,000
1904-S	5,134,175	2,200	2,300	2,350	2,400	2,500	
1905 ...... *92*	58,919	2,200	2,300	2,350	2,400	17,000	100,000
1905-S	1,813,000	2,200	2,300	2,350	2,400	5,000	
1906 ...... *94*	69,596	2,200	2,300	2,350	2,400	9,000	100,000
1906-D	620,250	2,200	2,300	2,350	2,400	4,200	
1906-S	2,065,750	2,200	2,300	2,350	2,400	3,200	
1907 ...... *78*	1,451,786	2,200	2,300	2,350	2,400	2,600	100,000
1907-D	842,250	2,200	2,300	2,350	2,400	3,300	
1907-S	2,165,800	2,200	2,300	2,350	2,400	3,200	

Saint-Gaudens Portrait of Liberty (1907–1933)

	Mintage	AU-50	MS-60	MS-63	MS-64	MS-65	Proof-65
1907 ultra high relief, plain edge	(1 known)	—	—	—	—	—	$2,500,000
1907 ultra high relief, lettered edge (proof only)	24	—	—	—	—	—	2,200,000
1907 high relief with Roman-numeral date MCMVII, combined total	11,250						
1907 high relief with wire rim		$13,000	$16,000	$30,000	$38,000	$55,000	
1907 high relief with flat rim		13,000	16,000	30,000	38,000	55,000	
1907 with Arabic numerals	361,667	2,200	2,300	2,500	2,800	5,000	
1908 without IN GOD WE TRUST	4,271,551	2,200	2,300	2,500	2,600	2,700	
1908-D without motto ...	663,750	2,200	2,300	2,600	3,000	12,000	

Motto Added to Reverse (1908–1933)

	Mintage	AU-50	MS-60	MS-63	MS-64	MS-65	Proof-65
1908 ...... *101*	156,258	$2,200	$2,300	$2,500	$5,200	$27,000	$75,000
1908-D	349,500	2,200	2,300	2,500	3,000	7,200	
1908-S	22,000	5,500	12,000	25,000	32,000	60,000	
1909 combined total	161,282						
1909 regular date *74* ...		2,200	2,300	3,200	10,000	50,000	77,000
1909/8 overdate		2,200	2,400	6,000	16,500	55,000	
1909-D	52,500	2,200	3,000	10,000	16,500	60,000	
1909-S	2,774,925	2,200	2,300	2,500	2,500	7,500	
1910 ...... *167*	482,000	2,200	2,300	2,500	2,800	9,500	75,000
1910-D	429,000	2,200	2,300	2,500	2,500	3,700	
1910-S	2,128,250	2,200	2,300	2,500	3,000	13,000	
1911 ...... *100*	197,250	2,200	2,300	3,000	6,000	22,000	75,000
1911-D	846,500	2,200	2,300	2,500	2,500	3,200	
1911-S	775,750	2,200	2,300	2,500	2,700	6,700	
1912 ... *74*	149,750	2,200	2,300	3,000	8,000	34,000	75,000
1913 ...... *58*	168,780	2,200	2,300	3,500	10,000	55,000	75,000
1913-D	393,500	2,200	2,300	2,500	2,800	8,000	
1913-S	34,000	2,200	2,400	5,000	8,100	38,000	
1914 ... *70*	95,250	2,200	2,300	4,000	7,500	28,000	75,000
1914-D	453,000	2,200	2,300	2,500	2,500	3,700	
1914-S	1,498,000	2,200	2,300	2,500	2,500	3,000	
1915 ...... *50*	152,000	2,200	2,300	2,900	7,000	30,000	77,000
1915-S	567,500	2,200	2,300	2,500	2,500	3,000	
1916-S	796,000	2,200	2,300	2,500	2,500	3,600	

	Mintage	AU-50	MS-60	MS-63	MS-64	MS-65	Proof-65
1920	228,250	2,200	2,300	2,500	6,000	100,000	
1920-S	558,000	30,000	55,000	110,000	210,000	350,000	
1921	528,500	60,000	120,000	280,000	450,000	800,000	
1922	1,375,500	2,200	2,300	2,500	2,600	8,000	
1922-S	2,658,000	2,200	2,500	5,600	12,000	65,000	
1923	566,000	2,200	2,300	2,500	2,600	7,700	
1923-D	1,702,250	2,200	2,300	2,500	2,600	2,700	
1924	4,323,500	2,200	2,300	2,500	2,600	2,700	
1924-D	3,049,500	2,200	4,200	12,000	20,000	120,000	
1924-S	2,927,500	2,200	4,200	13,000	25,000	160,000	
1925	2,831,750	2,200	2,300	2,500	2,600	2,300	
1925-D	2,938,500	2,500	4,200	12,000	23,000	145,000	
1925-S	3,776,500	3,800	10,000	18,000	55,000	190,000	
1926	816,750	2,200	2,300	2,500	2,600	2,300	
1926-D	481,000	19,000	28,000	40,000	85,000	200,000	
1926-S	2,041,500	2,200	3,000	5,500	11,000	32,000	
1927	2,946,750	2,200	2,300	2,500	2,600	2,700	
1927-D	180,000	350,000	450,000	1,300,000	1,500,000	1,800,000	
1927-S	3,107,000	12,000	28,000	60,000	85,000	150,000	
1928	8,816,000	2,200	2,300	2,500	2,600	2,700	
1929	1,779,750	14,000	20,000	40,000	50,000	100,000	
1930-S	74,000	45,000	70,000	120,000	160,000	225,000	
1931	2,938,250	20,000	38,000	70,000	90,000	125,000	
1931-D	106,500	22,000	42,000	90,000	100,000	135,000	
1932	1,101,750	18,000	28,000	70,000	90,000	120,000	
1933	445,500					7,590,020	

COMMEMORATIVE COINS
(1892–PRESENT)

Traditional Commemoratives (1892–1954)

	Number Minted	Number Melted	EF-40	MS-63	MS-65	Proof-63
COLUMBIAN EXPOSITION HALF DOLLARS						
1892 ...... *104*	949,896	None	$16.00	$85.00	$800	$7,500
1893 ...... *3 reported* ..	4,052,104	2,501,700	16.00	80.00	900	15,000
ISABELLA QUARTER DOLLAR						
1893 ...... *20*	39,120	15,809	$475	$1,200	$3,200	$10,000
LAFAYETTE SILVER DOLLAR						

	Number Minted	Number Melted	EF-40	MS-63	MS-65	Proof-63
1900 ...... *1 known*	50,025	14,000	$600	$2,000	$11,000	$100,000
LOUISIANA PURCHASE EXPOSITION GOLD DOLLARS						
Combined total	250,058	215,250				
1903 Jefferson ... *100* ..			$750	$1,200	$4,000	$12,500
1903 McKinley ... *100* ..			750	1,200	4,000	12,500
LEWIS AND CLARK EXPOSITION GOLD DOLLARS						
1904 ...... *about 7*	25,021	15,003	$1,000	$2,500	$12,000	$75,000
1905 ...... *about 4*	35,037	25,000	1,200	3,000	19,000	80,000

	Number Minted	Number Melted	EF-40	MS-63	MS-65	Proof-63
PANAMA-PACIFIC EXPOSITION HALF DOLLAR						
1915-S .. *2 reported*	60,028	32,896	$145	$625	$3,000	$35,000
PANAMA-PACIFIC EXPOSITION GOLD DOLLAR						
1915-S .. *1 reported*	25,033	10,034	$275	$500	$3,000	$75,000

PANAMA-PACIFIC EXPOSITION QUARTER EAGLE ($2.50 GOLD PIECE)

	Number Minted	Number Melted	EF-40	MS-63	MS-65	Proof-63
1915-S .. *1 reported*	10,016	3,268	$1,050	$2,600	$5,300	$100,000

PANAMA-PACIFIC EXPOSITION $50 GOLD PIECES

	Number Minted	Number Melted	EF-40	MS-63	MS-65	Proof-63
1915-S round	1,510	1,027	$52,500	$90,000	$175,000	
1915-S octagonal	1,509	864	52,500	85,000	140,000	
McKINLEY MEMORIAL GOLD DOLLARS						
1916 .... *at least 6*	20,020	10,049	$800	$900	$3,000	$30,000
1917 .... *at least 5*	10,009	14	800	1,200	4,000	30,000
ILLINOIS CENTENNIAL HALF DOLLAR						
1918 .... *at least 2*	100,056	None	$60.00	$85.00	$450	$30,000
MAINE CENTENNIAL HALF DOLLAR						
1920 .... *1 known*	50,027	None	$60.00	$145	$550	$35,000
PILGRIM TERCENTENARY HALF DOLLARS						
1920 .... *2 reported*	200,110	48,000	$45.00	$70.00	$350	$30,000
1921 .... *1 reported*	100,052	80,000	85.00	125	475	35,000
ALABAMA CENTENNIAL HALF DOLLARS						
1921 with 2 X 2 .. *1*	6,005	None	$130	$600	$2,500	$50,000
1921 without 2 X 2	64,038	5,000	65.00	450	2,550	
MISSOURI CENTENNIAL HALF DOLLARS						
1921 with 2 X 4 .. *1*	4,999	None	$240	$700	$5,500	$85,000
1921 without 2 X 4	45,028	29,600	160	600	5,600	
GRANT MEMORIAL HALF DOLLARS						
1922 with star ... *4 reported*	5,002	750	$410	$2,000	$7,500	$50,000
1922 without star *4 reported*	95,051	27,650	60.00	165	1000	50,000
GRANT MEMORIAL GOLD DOLLARS						
1922 with star	5,016	None	$950	$2,000	$4,000	
1922 without star	5,000	None	925	2,000	4,000	
MONROE DOCTRINE CENTENNIAL HALF DOLLAR						
1923-S .. *2 reported*	274,075	None	$31.00	$105	$2,700	$50,000
HUGUENOT-WALLOON TERCENTENARY HALF DOLLAR						
1924 .... *1 reported*	142,079	None	$60.00	$90.00	$500	$35,000

	Number Minted	Number Melted	EF-40	MS-63	MS-65	Proof-63
CALIFORNIA DIAMOND JUBILEE HALF DOLLAR						
1925-S .. *1 reported*	150,199	63,606	$80.00	$220	$1,200	$50,000
FORT VANCOUVER CENTENNIAL HALF DOLLAR						
1925 .... *3 reported*	50,025	35,034	$180	$400	$1,500	$30,000
LEXINGTON-CONCORD SESQUICENTENNIAL HALF DOLLAR						
1925 .... *1 reported*	162,098	86	$60.00	$90.00	$700	$35,000
STONE MOUNTAIN HALF DOLLAR						
1925 .... *1 reported*	2,314,708	1,000,000	$35.00	$45.00	$185	$30,000
OREGON TRAIL MEMORIAL HALF DOLLARS						
1926 .... *2 known*	48,028	75	$75.00	$120	$185	$35,000
1926-S	100,055	17,000	75.00	120	185	
1928	50,028	44,000	135	160	300	
1933-D	5,250	242	225	280	375	
1934-D	7,006	None	115	185	275	
1936	10,006	None	105	135	195	
1936-S	5,006	None	120	175	260	
1937-D	12,008	None	90.00	185	220	
1938	6,006	None	190	220	240	
1938-D	6,005	None	190	220	240	
1938-S	6,006	None	145	200	240	
1939	3,004	None	300	450	650	
1939-D	3,004	None	300	450	650	
1939-S	3,005	None	300	450	650	
SESQUICENTENNIAL OF AMERICAN INDEPENDENCE HALF DOLLAR						
1926 .... *4 reported*	1,000,524	859,408	$60.00	$165	$4,250	$50,000
SESQUICENTENNIAL OF AMERICAN INDEPENDENCE QUARTER EAGLE ($2.50 GOLD PIECE)						
1926 .... *2 reported*	200,224	154,207	$500	$900	$3,500	$100,000
VERMONT SESQUICENTENNIAL HALF DOLLAR						
1927 ... *1 reported*	40,033	11,892	$110	$180	$675	$30,000
HAWAIIAN SESQUICENTENNIAL HALF DOLLAR						
1928 .... *50*	9,958	None	$775	$1,600	$4,000	$18,000
DANIEL BOONE BICENTENNIAL HALF DOLLARS						
1934	10,007	None	$75.00	$85.00	$145	
1935 plain	10,010	None	75.00	80.00	140	
1935-D plain	5,005	None	75.00	80.00	140	
1935-S plain	5,005	None	75.00	100	140	
1935 with small 1934 on reverse	10,008	None	75.00	90.00	140	
1935-D with small 1934 on reverse	2,003	None	275	300	775	
1935-S with small 1934 on reverse	2,004	None	275	300	775	
1936	12,012	None	75.00	80.00	140	
1936-D	5,005	None	75.00	80.00	140	
1936-S	5,006	None	75.00	80.00	140	
1937 .... *1 known proof* .	15,009	9,810	75.00	80.00	140	$25,000
1937-D .. *1 known proof* .	7,505	5,000	180	275	350	25,000
1937-S .. *1 known proof* .	5,005	2,500	180	275	350	25,000
1938	5,005	2,905	225	300	475	
1938-D	5,005	2,905	225	300	475	
1938-S	5,006	2,906	225	300	475	
MARYLAND TERCENTENARY HALF DOLLAR						
1934 .... *3 known*	25,012	None	$105	$130	$275	$30,000
TEXAS INDEPENDENCE CENTENNIAL HALF DOLLARS						
1934	205,113	143,650	$70.00	$90.00	$160	
1935	10,008	12	70.00	90.00	160	
1935-D	10,007	None	70.00	90.00	160	
1935-S	10,008	None	70.00	90.00	160	

	Number Minted	Number Melted	EF-40	MS-63	MS-65	Proof-63
1936	10,008	1,097	70.00	90.00	160	
1936-D	10,007	968	70.00	90.00	160	
1936-S	10,008	943	70.00	90.00	160	
1937	8,005	1,434	80.00	100	210	
1937-D	8,006	1,401	80.00	100	210	
1937-S	8,007	1,370	80.00	100	210	
1938	5,005	1,225	150	280	350	
1938-D	5,005	1,230	150	280	350	
1938-S	5,006	1,192	150	280	350	

ARKANSAS CENTENNIAL HALF DOLLARS

	Number Minted	Number Melted	EF-40	MS-63	MS-65	Proof-63
1935 .... *1 reported*	13,011	None	$65.00	$80.00	$260	$30,000
1935-D	5,505	None	65.00	85.00	260	
1935-S	5,506	None	65.00	85.00	260	
1936	10,010	350	65.00	80.00	260	
1936-D	10,010	350	65.00	80.00	260	
1936-S	10,012	350	65.00	80.00	260	
1937	5,505	None	70.00	90.00	230	
1937-D	5,505	None	70.00	95.00	230	
1937-S	5,506	None	70.00	95.00	300	
1938 .... *1 known proof* .	6,006	2,850	90.00	140	750	15,000
1938-D .. *1 known proof* .	6,005	2,850	90.00	140	750	15,000
1938-S .. *1 known proof* .	6,006	2,850	90.00	140	750	15,000
1939	2,104	None	100	225	900	
1939-D	2,104	None	100	225	900	
1939-S	2,105	None	100	225	900	

CONNECTICUT TERCENTENARY HALF DOLLAR

	Number Minted	Number Melted	EF-40	MS-63	MS-65	Proof-63
1935 .... *about 6*	25,012	None	$160	$190	$400	$45,000

HUDSON, N.Y., SESQUICENTENNIAL HALF DOLLAR

1935 .... *2 reported*	10,006	None	$380	$450	$1,500	$45,000

OLD SPANISH TRAIL HALF DOLLAR

1935 .... *2 reported*	10,006	None	$625	$725	$925	$45,000

SAN DIEGO/CALIFORNIA-PACIFIC EXPOSITION HALF DOLLARS

1935-S .. *2 reported*	250,130	180,000	$45.00	$65.00	$85.00	$20,000
1936-D	180,092	150,000	60.00	75.00	105	

ALBANY, N.Y., CHARTER HALF DOLLAR

1936	25,013	7,342	$190	$215	$300	

BRIDGEPORT, CONN., CENTENNIAL HALF DOLLAR

1936	25,015	None	$90.00	$100	$200	

CINCINNATI MUSIC CENTER HALF DOLLARS

1936	5,005	None	$195	$350	$665	
1936-D	5,005	None	195	325	665	
1936-S	5,006	None	195	475	750	

CLEVELAND CENTENNIAL/GREAT LAKES EXPOSITION HALF DOLLAR

1936	50,030	None	$50.00	$60.00	$220	

COLUMBIA, S.C., SESQUICENTENNIAL HALF DOLLARS

1936	9,007	None	$150	$180	$200	
1936-D	8,009	None	150	180	200	
1936-S	8,007	None	150	180	220	

	Number Minted	Number Melted	EF-40	MS-63	MS-65	Proof-63
DELAWARE TERCENTENARY HALF DOLLAR						
1936	25,015	4,022	$140	$180	$325	
ELGIN, ILL., CENTENNIAL HALF DOLLAR						
1936	25,014	5,000	$170	$195	$220	
GETTYSBURG BATTLE HALF DOLLAR						
1936	50,028	23,100	$210	$240	$475	
LONG ISLAND TERCENTENARY HALF DOLLAR						
1936	100,053	18,227	$50.00	$60.00	$300	
LYNCHBURG, VA., SESQUICENTENNIAL HALF DOLLAR						
1936	20,013	None	$130	$160	$220	
NORFOLK, VA., TERCENTENARY HALF DOLLAR						
1936	25,013	8,077	$250	$300	$450	
PROVIDENCE, R.I., TERCENTENARY HALF DOLLARS						
1936	20,013	None	$60.00	$75.00	$200	
1936-D	15,010	None	60.00	80.00	200	
1936-S	15,011	None	60.00	80.00	200	
ROBINSON-ARKANSAS CENTENNIAL HALF DOLLAR						
1936	25,256	None	$65.00	$85.00	$190	
SAN FRANCISCO–OAKLAND BAY BRIDGE HALF DOLLAR						
1936-S	100,055	28,631	$70.00	$150	$225	
WISCONSIN TERRITORIAL CENTENNIAL HALF DOLLAR						
1936	25,015	None	$140	$160	$200	
YORK COUNTY, MAINE, TERCENTENARY HALF DOLLAR						
1936	25,015	None	$135	$140	$190	
ANTIETAM BATTLE HALF DOLLAR						
1937	50,028	32,000	$335	$385	$675	
ROANOKE ISLAND, N.C., HALF DOLLAR						
1937	49,080	21,000	$165	$185	$225	
NEW ROCHELLE, N.Y., HALF DOLLAR						
1938 .... *about 10*	25,003	9,749	$225	$285	$300	$30,000
IOWA STATEHOOD CENTENNIAL HALF DOLLAR						
1946	100,057	None	$55.00	$67.00	$95.00	

BOOKER T. WASHINGTON HALF DOLLARS

1946	1,000,546	Unknown	$15.00	$40.00	$50.00
1946-D	200,113	Unknown	15.00	40.00	50.00
1946-S	500,279	Unknown	15.00	40.00	50.00
1947	100,017	Unknown	15.00	50.00	80.00
1947-D	100,017	Unknown	15.00	50.00	140
1947-S	100,017	Unknown	15.00	50.00	80.00
1948	20,005	12,000	15.00	50.00	60.00
1948-D	20,005	12,000	15.00	50.00	60.00
1948-S	20,005	12,000	15.00	50.00	60.00
1949	12,004	6,000	20.00	60.00	100.00

	Number Minted	Number Melted	EF-40	MS-63	MS-65	Proof-63
1949-D	12,004	6,000	20.00	60.00	100.00	
1949-S	12,004	6,000	20.00	60.00	100.00	
1950	12,004	6,000	18.00	50.00	100.00	
1950-D	12,004	6,000	18.00	50.00	100.00	
1950-S	512,091	Unknown	15.00	50.00	100.00	
1951	510,082	Unknown	15.00	50.00	100.00	
1951-D	12,004	5,000	15.00	50.00	100.00	
1951-S	12,004	5,000	15.00	50.00	100.00	

GEORGE WASHINGTON CARVER/BOOKER T. WASHINGTON HALF DOLLARS

1951	110,018*	Unknown	$15.00	$55.00	$175	
1951-D	10,004*	Unknown	15.00	65.00	150	
1951-S	10,004*	Unknown	15.00	65.00	150	
1952	2,006,292*	Unknown	15.00	25.00	50.00	
1952-D	8,006*	Unknown	15.00	60.00	140	
1952-S	8,006*	Unknown	15.00	60.00	140	
1953	8,003*	Unknown	15.00	60.00	140	
1953-D	8,003*	Unknown	15.00	60.00	140	
1953-S	108,020*	Unknown	15.00	60.00	100	
1954	12,006*	Unknown	15.00	60.00	125	
1954-D	12,006*	Unknown	15.00	60.00	125	
1954-S	122,024*	Unknown	15.00	30.00	75.00	

*These are net mintages, after melting. The quantities actually minted and melted are unknown.

Modern Commemoratives (1982–Present)

(NOTE: For commemorative coins issued since 1982, the U.S. Mint has not disclosed the number actually minted and the number melted. The figures shown here are net mintages furnished by the Mint. The George Washington and Bill of Rights half dollars are of traditional 90-percent-silver composition. All other half dollars in the modern commemorative series are of copper-nickel-clad composition, with no precious-metal content.)

	Net Mintage	MS-65	Proof-67
GEORGE WASHINGTON HALF DOLLAR			
1982-D uncirculated	2,210,458	$20.00	
1982-S proof	4,894,044	—	$20.00
LOS ANGELES OLYMPIC SILVER DOLLARS			
1983-P uncirculated	294,543	$30.00	
1983-D uncirculated	174,014	30.00	
1983-S uncirculated	174,014	30.00	
1983-S proof	1,577,025	—	$30.00
1984-P uncirculated	217,954	30.00	
1984-D uncirculated	116,675	30.00	
1984-S uncirculated	116,675	30.00	
1984-S proof	1,801,210	—	30.00
LOS ANGELES OLYMPIC EAGLES ($10 GOLD PIECES)			
1984-P proof	33,309	—	$1,100
1984-D proof	34,533	—	1,100
1984-S proof	48,551	—	1,100
1984-W uncirculated	75,886	$1,100	
1984-W proof	381,085	—	1,100
STATUE OF LIBERTY HALF DOLLARS			
1986-D uncirculated	928,008	$15.00	
1986-S proof	6,925,627	—	$15.00

	Net Mintage	MS-65	Proof-67
STATUE OF LIBERTY SILVER DOLLARS			
1986-P uncirculated	723,635	$30.00	
1986-S proof	*6,414,638*	—	$30.00
STATUE OF LIBERTY HALF EAGLES ($5 GOLD PIECES)			
1986-W uncirculated	95,248	$600	
1986-W proof	*404,013*	—	$600
CONSTITUTION BICENTENNIAL SILVER DOLLARS			
1987-P uncirculated	451,629	$30.00	
1987-S proof	*2,747,116*	—	$30.00
CONSTITUTION BICENTENNIAL HALF EAGLES ($5 GOLD PIECES)			
1987-W uncirculated	214,225	$600	
1987-W proof	*651,659*	—	$600
1988 OLYMPIC SILVER DOLLARS			
1988-D uncirculated	191,368	$30.00	
1988-S proof	*1,359,366*	—	$30.00
1988 OLYMPIC HALF EAGLES ($5 GOLD PIECES)			
1988-W uncirculated	62,913	$600	
1988-W proof	*281,465*	—	$600
CONGRESS BICENTENNIAL HALF DOLLARS			
1989-D uncirculated	163,753	$15.00	
1989-S proof	*767,897*	—	$15.00
CONGRESS BICENTENNIAL SILVER DOLLARS			
1989-D uncirculated	135,203	$35.00	
1989-S proof	*762,198*	—	$35.00
CONGRESS BICENTENNIAL HALF EAGLES ($5 GOLD PIECES)			
1989-W uncirculated	46,899	$600	
1989-W proof	*164,690*	—	$600
EISENHOWER CENTENNIAL SILVER DOLLARS			
1990-W uncirculated	239,777	$35.00	
1990-P proof	*1,137,805*	—	$35.00
KOREAN WAR MEMORIAL SILVER DOLLARS			
1991-D uncirculated	213,049	$35.00	
1991-P proof	*618,488*	—	$35.00
MOUNT RUSHMORE 50TH ANNIVERSARY HALF DOLLARS			
1991-D uncirculated	172,754	$17.00	
1991-S proof	*753,257*	—	$17.00
MOUNT RUSHMORE 50TH ANNIVERSARY SILVER DOLLARS			
1991-P uncirculated	133,139	$35.00	
1991-S proof	*738,419*	—	$35.00
MOUNT RUSHMORE 50TH ANNIVERSARY HALF EAGLES ($5 GOLD PIECES)			
1991-W uncirculated	31,959	$600	
1991-W proof	*111,991*	—	$600
UNITED SERVICE ORGANIZATIONS (USO) SILVER DOLLARS			
1991-D uncirculated	124,958	$35.00	
1991-S proof	*321,275*	—	$35.00
1992 OLYMPIC HALF DOLLARS			
1992-P uncirculated	161,607	$17.00	
1992-S proof	*519,645*	—	$17.00
1992 OLYMPIC SILVER DOLLARS			
1992-D uncirculated	187,552	$35.00	
1992-S proof	*504,505*	—	$35.00
1992 OLYMPIC HALF EAGLES ($5 GOLD PIECES)			
1992-W uncirculated	27,732	$600	
1992-W proof	*77,313*	—	$600

	Net Mintage	MS-65	Proof-67
1992 WHITE HOUSE SILVER DOLLARS			
1992-D uncirculated	123,803	$35.00	
1992-W proof	375,851	—	$35.00
1992 COLUMBUS QUINCENTENARY HALF DOLLARS			
1992-D uncirculated	135,702	$17.00	
1992-S proof	390,154	—	$17.00
1992 COLUMBUS QUINCENTENARY SILVER DOLLARS			
1992-D uncirculated	106,949	$35.00	
1992-P proof	385,241	—	$35.00
1992 COLUMBUS QUINCENTENARY HALF EAGLES ($5 GOLD PIECES)			
1992-W uncirculated	24,329	$350	
1992-W proof	79,730	—	$350
1993 BILL OF RIGHTS HALF DOLLARS (SILVER)			
1993-W uncirculated	194,420	$17.00	
1993-S proof	585,821	—	$17.00
1993 BILL OF RIGHTS SILVER DOLLARS			
1993-D uncirculated	98,571	$35.00	
1993-S proof	534,007	—	$35.00
1993 BILL OF RIGHTS HALF EAGLES ($5 GOLD PIECES)			
1993-W uncirculated	23,455	$350	
1993-W proof	78,840	—	$350
1993 WORLD WAR II HALF DOLLARS			
1993-P uncirculated	197,072	$17.00	
1993-P proof	317,396	—	$17.00
1993 WORLD WAR II SILVER DOLLARS			
1993-D uncirculated	107,240	$35.00	
1993-W proof	342,041	—	$35.00
1993 WORLD WAR II HALF EAGLES ($5 GOLD PIECES)			
1993-W uncirculated	23,672	$600	
1993-W proof	67,026	—	$600
1994 WORLD CUP SOCCER HALF DOLLARS			
1994-D uncirculated	168,208	$17.00	
1994-P proof	609,354	—	$17.00
1994 WORLD CUP SOCCER SILVER DOLLARS			
1994-D uncirculated	81,524	$35.00	
1994-S proof	577,090	—	$35.00
1994 WORLD CUP HALF EAGLES ($5 GOLD PIECES)			
1994-W uncirculated	22,447	$600	
1994-W proof	89,614	—	$600
1994 THOMAS JEFFERSON 250TH ANNIVERSARY SILVER DOLLARS			
1994-P uncirculated	600,000	$80.00	
1994-S proof	600,000	—	$75.00
1994 PRISONER OF WAR SILVER DOLLARS			
1994-W uncirculated	54,894	$45.00	
1994-P proof	224,350	—	$35.00
1994 VIETNAM VETERANS MEMORIAL SILVER DOLLARS			
1994-W uncirculated	57,291	$80.00	
1994-P proof	227,573	—	$75.00
1994 WOMEN IN MILITARY SERVICE FOR AMERICA SILVER DOLLARS			
1994-W uncirculated	53,571	$35.00	
1994-P proof	222,852	—	$35.00
1994 U.S. CAPITOL SILVER DOLLARS			
1994-D uncirculated	68,332	$35.00	
1994-S proof	279,579	—	$35.00

	Net Mintage	MS-65	Proof-67
1995 CIVIL WAR BATTLEFIELD HALF DOLLARS			
1995-S uncirculated	119,303	$60.00	
1995-S proof	*328,398*	—	$60.00
1995 CIVIL WAR BATTLEFIELD SILVER DOLLARS			
1995-P uncirculated	45,604	$35.00	
1995-S proof	*328,569*	—	$35.00
1995 CIVIL WAR BATTLEFIELD HALF EAGLES ($5 GOLD PIECES)			
1995-W uncirculated	12,660	$500	
1995-W proof	*55,010*	—	$500
1995 OLYMPIC BASKETBALL HALF DOLLARS			
1995-S uncirculated	171,001	$17.00	
1995-S proof	*169,655*	—	$17.00
1995 OLYMPIC GYMNAST SILVER DOLLARS			
1995-D uncirculated	42,497	$70.00	
1995-P proof	*182,676*	—	$35.00
1995 OLYMPIC BLIND RUNNER SILVER DOLLARS			
1995-D uncirculated	28,649	$80.00	
1995-P proof	*138,337*	—	$35.00
1995 OLYMPIC TORCH RUNNER GOLD HALF EAGLES ($5 GOLD PIECES)			
1995-W uncirculated	14,675	$600	
1995-W proof	*57,442*	—	$600
1995 SPECIAL OLYMPIC WORLD GAMES SILVER DOLLARS (PORTRAIT OF EUNICE KENNEDY SHRIVER)			
1995-W uncirculated	89,298	$35.00	
1995-P proof	*352,449*	—	$35.00
1995 OLYMPIC BASEBALL HALF DOLLARS			
1995-S uncirculated	164,605	$35.00	
1995-S proof	*118,087*	—	$35.00
1995 OLYMPIC TRACK AND FIELD SILVER DOLLARS			
1995-D uncirculated	24,796	$52.00	
1995-P proof	*136,935*	—	$35.00
1995 OLYMPIC CYCLING SILVER DOLLARS			
1995-D uncirculated	19,662	$80.00	
1995-P proof	*118,795*	—	$35.00
1995 OLYMPIC STADIUM GOLD HALF EAGLES ($5 GOLD PIECES)			
1995-W uncirculated	10,579	$600	
1995-W proof	*43,124*	—	$600
1996 NATIONAL COMMUNITY SERVICE SILVER DOLLARS			
1996-S uncirculated	23,468	$250	
1996-S proof	*100,787*	—	$35.00
1996 OLYMPIC SWIMMING HALF DOLLARS			
1996-S uncirculated	49,533	$50.00	
1996-S proof	*114,315*	—	$18.00
1996 OLYMPIC SOCCER HALF DOLLARS			
1996-S uncirculated	52,836	$35.00	
1996-S proof	*122,412*	—	$60.00
1996 OLYMPIC TENNIS SILVER DOLLARS			
1996-D uncirculated	15,983	$250	
1996-P proof	*92,016*	—	$45.00
1996 OLYMPIC WHEELCHAIR ATHLETE SILVER DOLLARS			
1996-D uncirculated	14,497	$250	
1996-P proof	*84,280*	—	$40.00
1996 OLYMPIC ROWING SILVER DOLLARS			
1996-D uncirculated	16,258	$250	
1996-P proof	*151,890*	—	$35.00

	Net Mintage	MS-65	Proof-67
1996 OLYMPIC HIGH JUMP SILVER DOLLARS			
1996-D uncirculated	15,697	$160	
1996-P proof	124,502	—	$35.00
1996 OLYMPIC FLAG BEARER GOLD HALF EAGLES ($5 GOLD PIECES)			
1996-W uncirculated	9,174	$600	
1996-W proof	32,886	—	$600
1996 OLYMPIC CAULDRON GOLD HALF EAGLES ($5 GOLD PIECES)			
1996-W uncirculated	9,210	$600	
1996-W proof	38,555	—	$600
1996 SMITHSONIAN SESQUICENTENNIAL SILVER DOLLARS			
1996-D uncirculated	30,593	$125	
1996-P proof	126,616	—	$50
1996 SMITHSONIAN SESQUICENTENNIAL GOLD HALF EAGLES ($5 GOLD PIECES)			
1996-W uncirculated	8,948	$900	
1996-W proof	21,840	—	$600
1997 U.S. BOTANIC GARDEN SILVER DOLLARS			
1997-P uncirculated	57,272	$38.00	—
1997-P proof	264,528	—	$40.00
1997 FRANKLIN D. ROOSEVELT HALF EAGLES ($5 GOLD PIECES)			
1997-W uncirculated	11,805	$600	
1997-W proof	29,233	—	$600
1997 JACKIE ROBINSON SILVER DOLLARS			
1997-S uncirculated	27,170	$90.00	—
1997-W proof	98,297	—	$100
1997 JACKIE ROBINSON HALF EAGLES ($5 GOLD PIECES)			
1997-W uncirculated	4,594	$4,000	—
1997-W proof	21,760	—	$700
1997 NATIONAL LAW ENFORCEMENT SILVER DOLLARS			
1997-P uncirculated	28,575	$150	—
1997-P proof	110,428	—	$100
1998 BLACK REVOLUTIONARY WAR PATRIOTS SILVER DOLLARS			
1998-S uncirculated	37,210	$125	—
1998-S proof	75,070	—	$100
1998 ROBERT F. KENNEDY COMMEMORATIVE SILVER DOLLARS			
1998-S uncirculated	106,422	$35.00	—
1998-S proof	99,020	—	$35.00
1999 GEORGE WASHINGTON HALF EAGLES ($5 GOLD PIECES)			
1999-W uncirculated	22,508	$600	—
1999-W proof	41,688	—	$600
1999 DOLLEY MADISON SILVER DOLLARS			
1999-P uncirculated	89,203	$40.00	—
1999-P proof	224,495	—	$42.00
1999 YELLOWSTONE SILVER DOLLARS			
1999-P uncirculated	73,886	$40.00	—
1999-P proof	171,010	—	$40.00
2000 LIBRARY OF CONGRESS EAGLE ($10 BIMETALLIC: GOLD AND PLATINUM)			
2000 uncirculated	6,683	$6,500	—
2000 proof	27,167	—	$2,200
2000 LIBRARY OF CONGRESS SILVER DOLLARS			
2000 uncirculated	52,771	$35.00	—
2000 proof	196,900	—	$40.00
2001 LEIF ERICSON SILVER DOLLARS			
2001 uncirculated	28,100	$35.00	—
2001 proof	144,800	—	$43.00

	Net Mintage	MS-65	Proof-67
2001 CAPITOL VISITOR CENTER HALF DOLLARS			
2001 uncirculated	99,157	$18.00	—
2001 proof	*77,962*	—	$18.00
2001 CAPITOL VISITOR CENTER SILVER DOLLARS			
2001 uncirculated	35,380	$40.00	—
2001 proof	*143,793*	—	$50.00
2001 CAPITOL VISITOR CENTER HALF EAGLES ($5 GOLD PIECES)			
2001 uncirculated	6,761	$1,500	—
2001 proof	*27,652*	—	$650
2001 AMERICAN BUFFALO SILVER DOLLARS			
2001 uncirculated	227,131	$150	—
2001 proof	*272,869*	—	$160
2002 WEST POINT SILVER DOLLARS			
2002 uncirculated	103,201	$40.00	—
2002 proof	*288,293*	—	$50.00
2002 OLYMPIC SILVER DOLLARS			
2002 uncirculated	40,257	$40.00	—
2002 proof	*166,864*	—	$50.00
2002 OLYMPIC GOLD HALF EAGLES ($5 GOLD PIECES)			
2002 uncirculated	10,585	$700	—
2002 proof	*32,877*	—	$700
2003 FIRST FLIGHT EAGLES ($10 GOLD PIECES)			
2003 uncirculated	10,009	$900	—
2003 proof	*21,676*	—	$900
2003 FIRST FLIGHT SILVER DOLLARS			
2003 uncirculated	53,533	$38.00	—
2003 proof	*190,240*	—	$42.00
2003 FIRST FLIGHT HALF DOLLARS			
2003 uncirculated	57,122	$35.00	—
2003 proof	*109,710*	—	$35.00
2004 THOMAS EDISON SILVER DOLLARS			
2004 uncirculated	92,150	$38.00	—
2004 proof	*211,055*	—	$42.00
2004 LEWIS & CLARK SILVER DOLLARS			
2004 uncirculated	142,015	$40.00	—
2004 proof	*351,989*	—	$42.00
2005 JOHN MARSHALL SILVER DOLLARS			
2005 uncirculated	67,087	$40.00	—
2005 proof	*141,933*	—	$42.00
2005 UNITED STATES MARINE CORPS 230TH ANNIVERSARY SILVER DOLLARS			
2005 uncirculated	179,856	$60.00	—
2005 proof	*419,000*	—	$70.00
2006 BENJAMIN FRANKLIN BIRTH TRICENTENNIAL SILVER DOLLARS "SCIENTIST"			
2006 uncirculated	108,000	$70.00	—
2006 proof	*142,000*	—	$72.00
2006 BENJAMIN FRANKLIN BIRTH TRICENTENNIAL SILVER DOLLARS "FOUNDING FATHER"			
2006 uncirculated	58,000	$70.00	—
2006 proof	*142,000*	—	$72.00
2006 SAN FRANCISCO OLD MINT SILVER DOLLARS			
2006 uncirculated	67,100	$35.00	
2006 proof	*210,870*		$35.00
2006 SAN FRANCISCO OLD MINT HALF EAGLES ($5 GOLD PIECES)			
2006 uncirculated	17,500	$600	
2006 proof	*44,174*		$600

	Net Mintage	MS-65	Proof-67
2007 JAMESTOWN 400TH ANNIVERSARY SILVER DOLLARS			
2007 uncirculated	81,034	$35.00	
2007 proof	*260,363*		$35.00
2007 JAMESTOWN 400TH ANNIVERSARY HALF EAGLES ($5 GOLD PIECES)			
2007 uncirculated	16,623	$600	
2007 proof	*74,146*		$600
2007 LITTLE ROCK CENTRAL HIGH SCHOOL SILVER DOLLARS			
2007 uncirculated	66,359	$35.00	
2007 proof	*125,370*		$35.00
2008 BALD EAGLE HALF EAGLES ($5 GOLD PIECES)			
2008 uncirculated	15,133	$600	
2008 proof	*60,022*		$600
2008 BALD EAGLE SILVER DOLLARS			
2008 uncirculated	118,237	$35.00	
2008 proof	*296,942*		$35.00
2008 BALD EAGLE HALF DOLLARS			
2008 uncirculated	120,887	$18.00	
2008 proof	*211,293*		$18.00
2009 ABRAHAM LINCOLN SILVER DOLLARS			
2009 uncirculated	175,000	$50.00	
2009 proof	*325,000*		$50.00
2009 LOUIS BRAILLE SILVER DOLLARS			
2009 uncirculated	82,639	$35.00	
2009 proof	*135,235*		$35.00
2010 BOY SCOUTS SILVER DOLLARS			
2010 uncirculated	105,000	$35.00	
2010 proof	*245,000*		$35.00
2010 DISABLED AMERICAN VETERANS SILVER DOLLARS			
2010 uncirculated	77,859	$35.00	
2010 proof	*189,881*		$35.00
2011 U.S. ARMY HALF EAGLES ($5 GOLD PIECES)			
2011 uncirculated	8,062	$600	
2011 proof	*17,173*		$650
2011 U.S. ARMY SILVER DOLLARS			
2011 uncirculated	43,517	$35.00	
2011 proof	*119,829*		$38.00
2011 U.S. ARMY HALF DOLLARS			
2011 uncirculated	39,461	$18.00	
2011 proof	*68,349*		$20.00
2011 MEDAL OF HONOR HALF EAGLES ($5 GOLD PIECES)			
2011 uncirculated	8,251	$600	
2011 proof	*18,012*		$650
2011 MEDAL OF HONOR SILVER DOLLARS			
2011 uncirculated	44,769	$35.00	
2011 proof	*112,850*		$38.00
2012 STAR-SPANGLED BANNER HALF EAGLES ($5 GOLD PIECES)			
2012 uncirculated		$600	
2012 proof			$650
2012 STAR-SPANGLED BANNER SILVER DOLLARS			
2012 uncirculated		$35.00	
2012 proof			$35.00
2012 NATIONAL INFANTRY MUSEUM & SOLDIER CENTER HALF EAGLES ($5 GOLD PIECES)			
2012 uncirculated		$600	
2012 proof			$650
2012 NATIONAL INFANTRY MUSEUM & SOLDIER CENTER SILVER DOLLARS			
2012 uncirculated		$35.00	
2012 proof			$35.00

AMERICAN EAGLE BULLION COINS
(1986–PRESENT)
$10 Platinum (⅒ Ounce)

(NOTE: Bullion-sensitive coins priced in this book were based on spot metal prices of gold at $1,600 to $1,730 per ounce, silver at $25 to $35 per ounce, and platinum at $1,500 to $1,600 per ounce. These metal prices are extremely volatile and are outdated on publication. Consequently, transactions should be consummated only after consumers confirm the current respective metals price.)

	Mintage	MS-67	Proof-67
1997 uncirculated	70,250	$200	
1997-W proof	37,260	—	$220
1998 uncirculated	66,000	200	
1998-W proof	19,919	—	220
1999 uncirculated	40,000	200	
1999-W proof	19,123	—	220
2000 uncirculated	28,000	200	
2000-W proof	15,600	—	220
2001 uncirculated	52,017	200	
2001-W proof	12,193	—	220
2002 uncirculated	23,005	200	
2002-W proof	12,392	—	220
2003 uncirculated	22,007	200	
2003-W proof	9,218	—	220
2004 uncirculated	15,010	200	
2004-W proof	7,202	—	550
2005 uncirculated	14,013	200	
2005-W proof	8,000	—	220
2006 uncirculated	11,001	200	
2006-W proof	10,356	—	280
2006-W uncirculated/burnished	3,080	430	
2007 uncirculated	13,003	200	
2007-W proof	7,906	—	220
2007-W uncirculated/burnished	3,080	300	
2008 uncirculated	17,000	200	
2008-W proof	5,650	—	550
2008-W uncirculated/burnished	4,623	300	

$25 Platinum (¼ Ounce)

	Mintage	MS-67	Proof-67
1997 uncirculated	27,100	$500	
1997-W proof	18,726	—	$550
1998 uncirculated	47,800	500	
1998-W proof	14,919	—	550
1999 uncirculated	31,800	500	
1999-W proof	13,514	—	550
2000 uncirculated	19,400	500	
2000-W proof	11,900	—	550
2001 uncirculated	21,815	500	
2001-W proof	8,858	—	550
2002 uncirculated	27,405	500	
2002-W proof	9,299	—	550
2003 uncirculated	25,207	500	
2003-W proof	6,811	—	550
2004 uncirculated	18,010	500	
2004-W proof	5,226	—	1,200
2005 uncirculated	12,013	600	
2005-W proof	6,424	—	625
2006 uncirculated	12,001	500	
2006-W proof	7,946	—	550
2006-W uncirculated/burnished	2,700	610	
2007 uncirculated	8,402	500	
2007-W proof	5,824		550
2007-W uncirculated/burnished	1,204	600	
2008 uncirculated	22,800	500	

	Mintage	MS-67	Proof-67
2008-W proof	*3,891*		900
2008-W uncirculated/burnished	3,894	700	

$50 Platinum (½ Ounce)

	Mintage	MS-67	Proof-67
1997 uncirculated	20,500	$1,000	
1997-W proof	*15,515*	—	$1,100
1998 uncirculated	37,200	1,000	
1998-W proof	*13,919*	—	1,100
1999 uncirculated	28,200	1,000	
1999-W proof	*11,098*	—	1,100
2000 uncirculated	18,800	1,000	
2000-W proof	*11,000*	—	1,100
2001 uncirculated	12,815	1,000	
2001-W proof	*8,268*	—	1,100
2002 uncirculated	24,005	1,000	
2002-W proof	*8,810*	—	1,100
2003 uncirculated	17,409	1,000	
2003-W proof	*6,944*	—	1,100
2004 uncirculated	13,236	1,000	
2004-W proof	*5,095*	—	1,900
2005 uncirculated	9,013	1,000	
2005-W proof	*5,720*	—	1,300
2006 uncirculated	9,602	1,000	
2006-W proof	*7,846*	—	1,100
2006-W uncirculated/burnished	2,650	1,300	
2007 uncirculated	7,001	1,000	
2007-W proof	*5,845*	—	1,100
2007-W reverse proof*			
2007-W uncirculated/burnished	1,149	1,500	
2008 uncirculated	14,000	1,000	
2008-W proof	*3,654*	—	1,700
2008-W uncirculated/burnished	11,156	1,500	

*A reverse proof has brilliant devices and matte surfaces for the fields.

$100 Platinum (1 Ounce)

	Mintage	MS-67	Proof-67
1997 uncirculated	56,000	$2,000	
1997-W proof	*21,000*	—	$2,350
1998 uncirculated	138,500	2,000	
1998-W proof	*14,203*	—	2,350
1999 uncirculated	45,000	2,000	
1999-W proof	*12,351*	—	2,350
2000 uncirculated	10,000	2,000	
2000-W proof	*12,400*	—	2,350
2001 uncirculated	14,070	2,000	
2001-W proof	*8,990*	—	2,350
2002 uncirculated	11,502	2,000	
2002-W proof	*9,946*	—	2,350
2003 uncirculated	8,007	2,000	
2003-W proof	*8,136*	—	2,350
2004 uncirculated	7,009	2,000	
2004-W proof	*6,074*	—	2,800
2005 uncirculated	6,310	2,000	
2005-W proof	*6,700*	—	2,600
2006 uncirculated	6,000	2,000	
2006-W proof	*9,320*	—	2,350
2006-W uncirculated/burnished	3,100	2,325	
2007 uncirculated	7,202	2,000	
2007-W proof	*9,268*	—	2,350
2007-W uncirculated/burnished	1,691	2,325	
2008 uncirculated	21,800	2,000	

	Mintage	MS-67	Proof-67
2008-W proof	*5,030*	—	2,900
2008-W uncirculated/burnished	4,063	2,325	
2009-W proof	*8,000*	—	2,950
2010-W proof	*10,000*	—	2,350
2011-W proof		—	2,350
2012-W proof		—	2,350
2013-W proof		—	2,350

(NOTE: Bullion-sensitive coins priced in this book were based on spot metal prices of gold at $1,600 to $1,730 per ounce, silver at $25 to $35 per ounce, and platinum at $1,500 to $1,600 per ounce. These metal prices are extremely volatile and are outdated on publication. Consequently, transactions should be consummated only after consumers confirm the current respective metals price.)

$5 Gold (¹⁄₁₀ Ounce)

	Mintage	MS-67	Proof-67
1986 (MCMLXXXVI) uncirculated	912,609	$210	
1987 (MCMLXXXVII) uncirculated	580,266	210	
1988 (MCMLXXXVIII) uncirculated	159,500	275	
1988-P (MCMLXXXVIII) proof	*143,881*	—	$275
1989 (MCMLXXXIX) uncirculated	264,790	210	
1989-P (MCMLXXXIX) proof	*84,647*	—	275
1990 (MCMXC) uncirculated	210,210	210	
1990-P (MCMXC) proof	*99,349*	—	275
1991 (MCMXCI) uncirculated	165,200	220	
1991-P (MCMXCI) proof	*70,334*	—	275
1992 uncirculated	209,300	210	
1992-P proof	*64,874*	—	275
1993 uncirculated	210,709	210	
1993-P proof	*58,649*	—	275
1994 uncirculated	206,380	210	
1994-W proof	*62,794*	—	275
1995 uncirculated	223,025	210	
1995-W proof	*62,731*	—	275
1996 uncirculated	425,000	210	
1996-W proof	*55,964*	—	275
1997 uncirculated	528,515	210	
1997-W proof	*35,164*	—	275
1998 uncirculated	1,445,000	210	
1998-W proof	*39,706*	—	275
1999 uncirculated	2,700,000	210	
1999-W proof	*48,426*	—	275
2000 uncirculated	245,000	210	
2000-W proof	*50,000*	—	275
2001 uncirculated	269,147	210	
2001-W proof	*37,547*	—	275
2002 uncirculated	230,027	210	
2002-W proof	*40,803*	—	275
2003 uncirculated	245,029	210	
2003-W proof	*40,634*	—	275
2004 uncirculated	250,016	210	
2004-W proof	*35,487*	—	275
2005 uncirculated	300,043	210	
2005-W proof	*48,455*	—	275
2006 uncirculated	285,006	210	
2006-W proof	*49,016*	—	275
2006-W uncirculated/burnished	21,000	230	
2007 uncirculated	190,010	210	
2007-W proof	*61,741*	—	275
2007-W uncirculated/burnished	24,293	230	
2008 uncirculated	305,000	210	
2008-W proof	*29,155*	—	275
2008-W uncirculated/burnished	13,376	300	

	Mintage	MS-67	Proof-67
2009 uncirculated	270,000	210	
2010 uncirculated	380,000	210	
2010-W proof	*55,000*	210	275
2011 uncirculated		210	
2011-W proof		—	275
2012 uncirculated		210	
2012-W proof		—	275
2013 uncirculated		210	
2013-W proof		—	275

$10 Gold (¼ Ounce)

	Mintage	MS-67	Proof-67
1986 (MCMLXXXVI) uncirculated	726,031	$525	
1987 (MCMLXXXVII) uncirculated	269,255	525	
1988 (MCMLXXXVIII) uncirculated	49,000	525	
1988-P (MCMLXXXVIII) proof	*98,028*	—	$675
1989 (MCMLXXXIX) uncirculated	81,789	525	
1989-P (MCMLXXXIX) proof	*54,170*	—	675
1990 (MCMXC) uncirculated	41,000	525	
1990-P (MCMXC) proof	*62,674*	—	675
1991 (MCMXCI) uncirculated	36,100	525	
1991-P (MCMXCI) proof	*50,839*	—	675
1992 uncirculated	59,546	525	
1992-P proof	*46,269*	—	675
1993 uncirculated	71,864	525	
1993-P proof	*46,464*	—	675
1994 uncirculated	72,650	525	
1994-W proof	*48,128*	—	675
1995 uncirculated	83,752	525	
1995-W proof	*47,553*	—	675
1996 uncirculated	68,000	525	
1996-W proof	*37,320*	—	675
1997 uncirculated	108,805	525	
1997-W proof	*29,984*	—	675
1998 uncirculated	342,000	525	
1998-W proof	*29,731*	—	675
1999 uncirculated	560,000	525	
1999-W proof	*34,416*	—	675
2000 uncirculated	64,000	525	
2000-W proof	*36,000*	—	675
2001 uncirculated	71,280	525	
2001-W proof	*25,630*	—	675
2002 uncirculated	62,027	525	
2002-W proof	*29,268*	—	675
2003 uncirculated	74,029	525	
2003-W proof	*31,000*	—	675
2004 uncirculated	72,014	525	
2004-W proof	*29,127*	—	675
2005 uncirculated	72,015	525	
2005-W proof	*34,637*	—	675
2006 uncirculated	60,004	525	
2006-W proof	*37,764*	—	675
2006-W uncirculated/burnished	15,500	950	
2007 uncirculated	34,004	525	
2007-W proof	*48,680*	—	675
2007-W uncirculated/burnished	14,633	950	
2008 uncirculated	70,000	525	
2008-W proof	*28,301*	—	675
2008-W uncirculated/burnished	9,200	1,700	
2009 uncirculated	110,000	525	
2010 uncirculated	58,000	525	
2010-W proof	*45,000*	525	
2011 uncirculated		525	
2011-W proof		525	
2012 uncirculated		525	
2012-W proof		—	675

	Mintage	MS-67	Proof-67
2013 uncirculated		525	
2013-W proof		—	675

First Spouse $10 Gold Coins (½ Ounce)

	Mintage	MS-67	Proof-67
Martha Washington			
2007-W uncirculated	20,000	$1,100	
2007-W proof	20,000	—	$1,100
Abigail Adams			
2007-W uncirculated	20,000	1,100	
2007-W proof	20,000	—	1,100
Jefferson Liberty Head			
2007-W uncirculated	20,000	1,100	
2007-W proof	20,000	—	1,100
Dolley Madison			
2007-W uncirculated	12,541	1,100	
2007-W proof	18,355	—	1,100
Elizabeth Monroe			
2008-W uncirculated	4,519	1,100	
2008-W proof	7,933	—	1,100
Louisa Adams			
2008-W uncirculated	4,223	1,100	
2008-W proof	7,454	—	1,100
Jackson Liberty Head			
2008-W uncirculated	4,754	1,100	
2008-W proof	7,806	—	1,100
Van Buren Seated Liberty			
2008-W uncirculated	4,334	1,100	
2008-W proof	7,515	—	1,100
Anna Harrison			
2009-W uncirculated	3,537	1,100	
2009-W proof	6,250	—	1,100
Letitia Tyler			
2009-W uncirculated	3,152	1,100	
2009-W proof	5,163	—	1,100
Julia Tyler			
2009-W uncirculated	2,861	1,100	
2009-W proof	4,830	—	1,100
Sarah Polk			
2009-W uncirculated	3,501	1,100	
2009-W proof	5,157	—	1,100
Margaret Taylor			
2009-W uncirculated	3,430	1,100	
2009-W proof	4,787	—	1,100
Abigail Fillmore			
2010-W uncirculated	3,489	1,100	
2010-W proof	6,140	—	1,100
Jane Pierce			
2010-W uncirculated	3,333	1,100	
2010-W proof	4,843	—	1,100
James Buchanan's Liberty			
2010-W uncirculated	5,348	1,100	
2010-W proof	7,304	—	1,100
Mary Lincoln			
2010-W uncirculated	3,760	1,100	
2010-W proof	6,904	—	1,100
Eliza Johnson			
2011-W uncirculated		1,150	
2011-W proof		—	1,150
Julia Grant			
2011-W uncirculated		1,150	
2011-W proof		—	1,150
Lucy Hayes			
2011-W uncirculated		1,150	
2011-W proof		—	1,150
Lucretia Garfield			

	Mintage	MS-67	Proof-67
2011-W uncirculated		1,150	
2011-W proof		—	1,150
Chester A. Arthur's Liberty			
2012–W uncirculated		1,100	
2012–W proof			1,100
Grover Cleveland's Liberty (1st Term)			
2012–W uncirculated		1,100	
2012–W proof			1,100
Caroline Harrison			
2012–W uncirculated		1,100	
2012–W proof			1,100
Frances Cleveland			
2012–W uncirculated		1,100	
2012–W proof			1,100
Ida McKinley			
2013–W uncirculated		1,100	
2013–W proof			1,100
Edith Roosevelt			
2013–W uncirculated		1,100	
2013–W proof			1,100
Helen Taft			
2013–W uncirculated		1,100	
2013–W proof			1,100
Ellen Wilson			
2013–W uncirculated		1,100	
2013–W proof			1,100
Edith Wilson			
2013–W uncirculated		1,100	
2013–W proof			1,100
Florence Harding			
2014–W uncirculated		1,100	
2014–W proof			1,100
Grace Coolidge			
2014–W uncirculated		1,100	
2014–W proof			1,100
Lou Hoover			
2014–W uncirculated		1,100	
2014–W proof			1,100
Eleanor Roosevelt			
2014–W uncirculated		1,100	
2014–W proof			1,100

$25 Gold (½ Ounce)

	Mintage	MS-67	Proof-67
1986 (MCMLXXXVI) uncirculated	599,566	$1,200	
1987 (MCMLXXXVII) uncirculated	131,255	1,000	
1987-P (MCMLXXXVII) proof	*143,398*	—	$1,200
1988 (MCMLXXXVIII) uncirculated	45,000	1,850	
1988-P (MCMLXXXVIII) proof	*76,528*	—	1,200
1989 (MCMLXXXIX) uncirculated	44,829	1,950	
1989-P (MCMLXXXIX) proof	*44,798*	—	1,200
1990 (MCMXC) uncirculated	31,000	2,400	
1990-P (MCMXC) proof	*51,636*	—	1,200
1991 (MCMXCI) uncirculated	24,100	3,200	
1991-P (MCMXCI) proof	*53,125*	—	1,200
1992-P uncirculated	54,404	1,600	
1992-P proof	*40,976*	—	1,200
1993 uncirculated	73,324	1,300	
1993-P proof	*43,819*	—	1,200
1994 uncirculated	62,400	1,300	
1994-W proof	*44,595*	—	1,200
1995 uncirculated	53,474	1,700	
1995-W proof	*45,487*	—	1,200
1996 uncirculated	42,000	1,700	
1996-W proof	*34,375*	—	1,200

	Mintage	MS-67	Proof-67
1997 uncirculated	79,605	1,300	
1997-W proof	26,801	—	1,200
1998 uncirculated	182,000	1,300	
1998-W proof	25,550	—	1,200
1999 uncirculated	244,000	1,000	
1999-W proof	30,452	—	1,200
2000 uncirculated	60,000	1,000	
2000-W proof	32,000	—	1,200
2001 uncirculated	48,047	1,500	
2001-W proof	23,261	—	1,200
2002 uncirculated	70,027	1,000	
2002-W proof	26,603	—	1,200
2003 uncirculated	79,029	1,000	
2003-W proof	29,000	—	1,200
2004 uncirculated	98,040	1,000	
2004-W proof	27,731	—	1,200
2005 uncirculated	80,023	1,000	
2005-W proof	33,598	—	1,200
2006 uncirculated	66,005	1,000	
2006-W proof	36,097	—	1,200
2006-W uncirculated/burnished	15,500	2,100	
2007 uncirculated	47,002	1,300	
2007-W proof	45,398	—	1,200
2007-W uncirculated/burnished	13,358	2,200	
2008 uncirculated	61,000	1,000	
2008-W proof	27,864	—	1,200
2008-W uncirculated/burnished	16,126	1,900	
2009 uncirculated	110,000	1,000	
2010 uncirculated	40,000	1,000	
2010-W proof	45,000	—	1,200
2011 uncirculated		1,000	
2011-W proof		—	1,200
2012 uncirculated		1,000	
2012-W proof		—	1,200
2013 uncirculated		1,000	
2013-W proof		—	1,200

$50 Gold (1 Ounce)

	Mintage	MS-67	Proof-67
1986 (MCMLXXXVI) uncirculated	1,362,650	$2,000	
1986-W (MCMLXXXVI) proof	446,290	—	$2,400
1987 (MCMLXXXVII) uncirculated	1,045,500	2,000	
1987-W (MCMLXXXVII) proof	147,498	—	2,400
1988 (MCMLXXXVIII) uncirculated	465,000	2,000	
1988-W (MCMLXXXVIII) proof	87,133	—	2,400
1989 (MCMLXXXIX) uncirculated	415,790	2,000	
1989-W (MCMLXXXIX) proof	54,570	—	2,400
1990 (MCMXC) uncirculated	373,210	2,000	
1990-W (MCMXC) proof	62,401	—	2,400
1991 (MCMXCI) uncirculated	243,100	2,000	
1991-W (MCMXCI) proof	50,411	—	2,400
1992 uncirculated	275,000	2,000	
1992-W proof	44,826	—	2,400
1993 uncirculated	480,192	2,000	
1993-W proof	34,369	—	2,400
1994 uncirculated	221,663	2,000	
1994-W proof	46,741	—	2,400
1995 uncirculated	200,636	2,000	
1995-W proof	46,524	—	2,400
1996 uncirculated	194,500	2,000	
1996-W proof	35,680	—	2,400
1997 uncirculated	664,508	2,000	
1997-W proof	32,803	—	2,400
1998 uncirculated	1,518,500	2,000	
1998-W proof	26,047	—	2,400

	Mintage	MS-67	Proof-67
1999 uncirculated	1,491,000	2,000	
1999-W proof	*31,446*	—	2,400
2000 uncirculated	94,000	2,000	
2000-W proof	*33,000*	—	2,400
2001 uncirculated	143,605	2,000	
2001-W proof	*24,580*	—	2,400
2002 uncirculated	222,029	2,000	
2002-W proof	*27,603*	—	2,400
2003 uncirculated	416,032	2,000	
2003-W proof	*29,000*	—	2,400
2004 uncirculated	417,019	2,000	
2004-W proof	*28,731*	—	2,400
2005 uncirculated	356,555	2,000	
2005-W proof	*34,695*	—	2,400
2006 uncirculated	237,510	2,000	
2006-W proof	*48,747*	—	2,400
2006-W reverse proof*	*10,000*		3,000
2006-W uncirculated/burnished	45,839	2,200	
2007 uncirculated	140,016	2,100	
2007-W proof	*53,618*	—	2,400
2007-W uncirculated/burnished	24,902	2,200	
2008 uncirculated	710,000	2,000	
2008-W proof	*29,399*	—	2,400
2008-W uncirculated/burnished	12,387	2,300	
2009 uncirculated	1,493,000	2,200	
2010 uncirculated	988,500	2,200	
2010-W proof	*60,000*	—	2,400
2011 uncirculated		2,200	
2011-W proof		—	2,400
2012 uncirculated		1,900	
2012-W proof		—	2,300
2013 uncirculated		1,900	
2013-W proof			2,300

*A reverse proof has brilliant devices and matte surfaces for the fields.

American Buffalo $5 One-Tenth Ounce .9999 Gold Coins

	Mintage	MS-67	Proof-67
2008–W uncirculated	17,429	$650	
2008–W proof	*18,864*	—	$750

American Buffalo $10 One-Quarter Ounce .9999 Gold Coins

	Mintage	MS-67	Proof-67
2008–W uncirculated	9,949	$1,700	
2008–W proof	*13,125*	—	$2,000

American Buffalo $25 One-Half Ounce .9999 Gold Coins

	Mintage	MS-67	Proof-67
2008–W uncirculated	16,908	$1,900	
2008–W proof	*12,169*	—	$2,000

American Buffalo $50 One-Ounce .9999 Gold Coins

	Mintage	MS-67	Proof-67
2006 uncirculated	337,012	$2,000	
2006-W proof	*252,000*	—	$2,000
2007 uncirculated	136,503	2,000	
2007-W proof	*58,998*	—	2,000
2008 uncirculated	9,064	2,000	
2008-W proof	*18,863*	—	4,800
2009 uncirculated	200,000	2,000	
2009-W proof	*49,388*	—	2,000
2010 uncirculated	209,000	2,000	
2010-W proof	*49,374*	—	2,000
2011 uncirculated		2,000	
2011-W proof		—	2,000
2012 uncirculated		2,000	
2012-W proof		—	2,000
2013 uncirculated		2,000	
2013-W proof		—	2,000

MMIX Ultra High Relief $20 Gold Coin

	Mintage	MS-67	Proof-67
MMIX (2009) uncirculated	115,178		$2,800

Proof Platinum Coin Sets

	Mintage	MS-67	Proof-67
1997 (all four platinum coins)			$4,450
1998 (all four platinum coins)			4,450
1999 (all four platinum coins)			4,450
2000 (all four platinum coins)			4,450
2001 (all four platinum coins)			4,450
2002 (all four platinum coins)			4,450
2003 (all four platinum coins)			4,450
2004 (all four platinum coins)			6,525
2005 (all four platinum coins)			5,000
2006 (all four platinum coins)			4,450
2007 (all four platinum coins)			4,450
2008 (all four platinum coins)			6,000
2008 (three-coin set containing platinum, gold, and silver one-ounce Eagles)			5,600

Proof Gold Coin Sets

	Mintage	MS-67	Proof-67
1987 ($50 and $25 coins only)			$3,600
1988 ($50 and $25 coins only)			3,600
1989 (all four coins)			4,440
1990 (all four coins)			4,440
1992 (all four coins)			4,440
1993 (all four coins)			4,440
1994 (all four coins)			4,440
1995 (all four coins)			4,440
1995 (10th anniversary five-coin set, including silver Eagle)			8,000
1996 (all four gold coins)			4,440
1997 (all four coins)			4,440

	Mintage	MS-67	Proof-67
1998 (all four coins)			4,440
1999 (all four coins)			4,440
2000 (all four coins)			4,440
2001 (all four coins)			4,440
2002 (all four coins)			4,440
2003 (all four coins)			4,440
2004 (all four coins)			4,440
2005 (all four coins)			4,440
2006 (all four coins)			4,440
2007 (all four coins)			4,440
2008 (all four coins)			4,440
2010 (all four coins)			4,440
2011 (all four coins)			4,440
2012 (all four coins)			4,440
2013 (all four coins)			4,440

(NOTE: Bullion-sensitive coins priced in this book were based on spot metal prices of gold at $1,600 to $1,730 per ounce, silver at $25 to $35 per ounce, and platinum at $1,500 to $1,600 per ounce. These metal prices are extremely volatile and are outdated on publication. Consequently, transactions should be consummated only after consumers confirm the current respective metals price.)

$1 Silver (1 Ounce)

	Mintage	MS-67	Proof-67
1986 uncirculated	5,393,005	$35.00	
1986-S proof	1,446,778	—	$70.00
1987 uncirculated	11,442,335	35.00	
1987-S proof	904,732	—	70.00
1988 uncirculated	5,004,500	35.00	
1988-S proof	557,370	—	70.00
1989 uncirculated	5,203,327	35.00	
1989-S proof	617,694	—	70.00
1990 uncirculated	5,840,210	35.00	
1990-S proof	695,510	—	70.00
1991 uncirculated	7,191,066	35.00	
1991-S proof	511,924	—	70.00
1992 uncirculated	5,540,068	35.00	
1992-S proof	498,543	—	70.00
1993 uncirculated	6,763,762	35.00	
1993-P proof	403,625	—	90.00
1994 uncirculated	4,227,319	50.00	
1994-P proof	355,531	—	85.00
1995 uncirculated	4,672,051	150.00	
1995-P proof	408,293	—	80.00
1995-W proof	30,110	—	3,000
1996 uncirculated	3,466,000	125.00	
1996-P proof	465,629	—	75.00
1997 uncirculated	4,295,004	90.00	
1997-P proof	434,682	—	70.00
1998 uncirculated	4,270,000	50.00	
1998-P proof	452,319	—	70.00
1999 uncirculated	8,883,000	37.00	
1999-P proof	549,769	—	70.00
2000 uncirculated	9,133,000	37.00	
2000-P proof	600,000	—	70.00
2001 uncirculated	9,001,711	39.00	
2001-W proof	746,154	—	70.00
2002 uncirculated	10,539,026	35.00	
2002-W proof	646,901	—	70.00
2003 uncirculated	8,495,008	35.00	
2003-W proof	750,000	—	70.00
2004 uncirculated	8,882,754	35.00	

	Mintage	MS-67	Proof-67
2004-W proof	*813,477*	—	70.00
2005 uncirculated	8,891,025	35.00	
2005-W proof	*823,000*	—	70.00
2006 uncirculated	10,676,522	35.00	
2006-P reverse proof*	*250,000*	—	230
2006-W proof	*1,098,000*	—	70.00
2006-W uncirculated/burnished	470,000	110.00	
2007 uncirculated	9,028,036	35.00	
2007-W proof	*821,759*	—	70.00
2007-W uncirculated/burnished	563,771	35.00	
2008 uncirculated	20,583,000	35.00	
2008-W proof	*713,353*	—	70.00
2008-W uncirculated/burnished	444,558	35.00	
2009 uncirculated	30,459,000	20.00	
2010 uncirculated	29,110,500	20.00	
2010–W proof	*860,000*		250.00
2011 uncirculated		45.00	
2011–W proof			95.00
2011–S uncirculated	(100,000)	300.00	
2011–W uncirculated	(100,000)	70.00	
2011–P reverse proof..................	*(100,000)*		350.00
2011 set of all five coins**	100,000	1,000.00	
2012 uncirculated		45.00	
2012–W proof			95.00
2013 uncirculated		45.00	
2013–W proof			95.00

*A reverse proof has brilliant devices and matte surfaces for the fields.

**Special five-piece set issued for the 25th anniversary of the silver eagle. Figures in parentheses indicate pieces included in the special set.

Silver Quarter Dollars (Five Ounces)

	Mintage	MS-67	Proof-67
Hot Springs National Park			
2010 bullion	33,000	$200	
2010 collector	27,000	200	
Yellowstone National Park			
2010 bullion	33,000	200	
2010 collector	27,000	200	
Yosemite National Park			
2010 bullion	33,000	200	
2010 collector	27,000	200	
Grand Canyon National Park			
2010 bullion	33,000	200	
2010 collector	26,019	200	
Mount Hood National Forest			
2010 bullion	33,000	200	
2010 collector		200	
Gettysburg National Military Park			
2011 bullion		200	
2011 collector		200	
Glacier National Park			
2011 bullion		200	
2011 collector		200	
Olympic National Park			
2011 bullion		200	
2011 collector		200	
Vicksburg National Military Park			
2011 bullion		200	
2011 collector		200	
Chickasaw National Recreation Area			
2011 bullion		200	
2011 collector		200	
El Yunque National Forest			
2012 bullion		200	

	Mintage	MS-67	Proof-67
2012 collector		200	
Chaco Culture National Historical Park			
2012 bullion		200	
2012 collector		200	
Acadia National Park			
2012 bullion		200	
2012 collector		200	
Hawai'i Volcanoes National Park			
2012 bullion		200	
2012 collector		200	
Denali National Park and Preserve			
2012 bullion		200	
2012 collector		200	
White Mountain National Forest			
2013 bullion		200	
2013 collector		200	
Perry's Victory and International Peace Memorial			
2013 bullion		200	
2013 collector		200	
Great Basin National Park			
2013 bullion		200	
2013 collector		200	
Fort McHenry National Monument and Historic Shrine			
2013 bullion		200	
2013 collector		200	
Mount Rushmore National Memorial			
2013 bullion		200	
2013 collector		200	
Great Smoky Mountains National Park			
2014 bullion		200	
2014 collector		200	
Shenandoah National Park			
2014 bullion		200	
2014 collector		200	
Arches National Park			
2014 bullion		200	
2014 collector		200	
Great Sand Dunes National Park			
2014 bullion		200	
2014 collector		200	
Everglades National Park			
2014 bullion		200	
2014 collector		200	

MODERN PROOF SETS (1950–PRESENT)

(NOTE: Since 1955, the United States Mint has packaged its annual proof sets in sealed holders. Proof sets made up of coins that have been removed from those holders and then reassembled may be worth substantially less than the prices listed here.)

	Number Sold	Issue Price	Market Value
1950	51,386	$2.10	$725
1951	57,500	2.10	700
1952	81,980	2.10	300
1953	128,800	2.10	250
2000-S silver set	904,200	31.95	80.00
2001-S (full set)	2,294,900	19.95	70.00
2001-S (partial set, quarter dollars only) .	800,000	13.95	50.00
2001-S silver set	891,400	31.95	120
2002-S (full set)	2,321,848	19.95	30.00
2002-S (partial set, quarter dollars only) .	764,092	13.95	22.00
2002-S silver set	888,826	31.95	75.00
2003-S (full set)	2,243,340	19.95	20.00
2003-S (partial set, quarter dollars only) .	1,235,832	13.95	12.00

	Number Sold	Issue Price	Market Value
2003-S silver set	1,119,494	31.95	65.00
2004-S (full set)	1,804,396	22.95	30.00
2004-S (partial set, quarter dollars only) .	956,767	15.95	20.00
2004-S silver set	1,187,673	31.95	65.00
2004-S (silver set, quarter dollars only) ..	600,000	23.95	45.00
2005-S (full set)	2,275,000	22.95	14.00
2005-S (partial set, quarter dollars only) .	987,000	15.95	12.00
2005-S silver set	998,000	37.95	65.00
2005-S (silver set, quarter dollars only) ..	608,970	23.95	45.00
2006-S (full set)	2,000,428	22.95	30.00
2006-S (partial set, quarter dollars only) .	882,000	15.95	20.00
2006-S silver set	1,054,008	37.95	65.00
2006-S (silver set, quarter dollars only) ..	531,000	23.95	45.00
2007-S (full set)	1,702,116	—	45.00
2007-S (partial set, quarter dollars only) .	672,662	—	20.00
2007-S silver set	861,447	—	75.00
2007-S (silver set, quarter dollars only) ..	438,431	—	50.00
2007-S (partial set, Presidential dollars only)	1,285,972	—	20.00
2008-S (full set)	1,382,017	—	80.00
2008-S (partial set, quarter dollars only) .	663,491	—	60.00
2008-S silver set	763,887	—	90.00
2008-S (silver set, quarter dollars only) ..	423,948	—	53.00
2008-S (partial set, Presidential dollars only)	836,730	—	8.00
2009-S (full set)	1,477,967	—	30.00
2009-S (partial set, quarter dollars only) .	635,423	—	20.00
2009-S silver set	694,406	—	68.00
2009-S (silver set, quarter dollars only) ..	299,178	—	45.00
2009-S (partial set, Presidential dollars only)	627,925	—	20.00
2010-S (full set)	—	—	30.00
2010-S (partial set, quarter dollars only) .	—	—	20.00
2010-S (silver set)	—	—	68.00
2010-S (silver set, quarter dollars only) ..	—	—	45.00
2010-S (partial set, Presidential dollars only)	—	—	17.00
2011-S (full set)	—	—	90.00
2011-S (partial set, quarter dollars only) .	—	—	15.00
2011-S (silver set)	—	—	68.00
2011-S (silver set, quarter dollars only) ..	—	—	45.00
2011-S (partial set, Presidential dollars only)	—	—	20.00
2012–S (full set)	—	—	90.00
2012–S (partial set, quarter dollars only) .	—	—	15.00
2012–S silver set	—	—	68.00
2012–S (silver set, quarter dollars only) .	—	—	45.00
2012–S (partial set, presidential dollars only)	—	—	20.00
2013–S (full set)	—	—	
2013–S (partial set, quarter dollars only) .	—	—	
2013–S silver set	—	—	
2013–S (silver set, quarter dollars only) .	—	—	
2013–S (partial set, presidential dollars only)	—	—	
2014–S (full set)	—	—	
2014–S (partial set, quarter dollars only) .	—	—	
2014–S silver set	—	—	
2014–S (silver set, quarter dollars only) .	—	—	
2014–S (partial set, presidential dollars only)	—	—	

SPECIAL MINT SETS (1965–1967)

	Number Sold	Issue Price	Market Value
1965	2,360,000	$4.00	$8.00
1966	2,261,583	4.00	8.00
1967	1,863,344	4.00	13.00

TYPE COINS

Many collectors acquire U.S. coins by "type." This means they purchase just one specimen of a certain kind of coin—one Lincoln cent, for example, to represent the entire series of Lincoln cents. Because they are buying just one coin, they usually acquire a piece that is exceptionally attractive, one in a very high grade or level of preservation. But, to avoid paying a prohibitive premium, they select a date for which the mintage is fairly high—a so-called "common-date" coin. Coins acquired in this fashion are known as "type coins," and many buyers and sellers track the value of U.S. coins as a whole by following the performance of these "type coins."

The following chart is updated annually by Sal Germano. It provides a convenient look at U.S. type coins and their values. In using it, you will note such terms as "Liberty" and "Indian Head." These refer to elements of the coins' designs. For assistance in identifying these coins, refer to the illustrations accompanying the price listings earlier in this chapter.

United States Coins by Type

	MS-60	MS-63	MS-65
HALF CENT (brown)	$170	$350	$1,000
LARGE CENT (brown)	$160	$225	$900
FLYING EAGLE CENT	$325	$600	$3,500
INDIAN CENT (brown)	$30	$40	$90
TWO-CENT PIECE (brown)	$90	$150	$450
THREE-CENT NICKEL	$100	$150	$650
THREE-CENT SILVER	$150	$275	$900
SHIELD NICKEL	$130	$175	$650
"V" OR LIBERTY NICKEL (NO CENTS)	$35	$50	$300
"BUFFALO" NICKEL	$20	$25	$50
CAPPED BUST HALF DIME	$350	$850	$3,600
LIBERTY SEATED HALF DIME	$115	$225	$950
CAPPED BUST DIME (REDUCED)	$850	$2,000	$8,000
LIBERTY SEATED DIME	$130	$200	$1,000
BARBER DIME	$110	$150	$650
"MERCURY" DIME	$7	$12	$25
TWENTY-CENT PIECE	$550	$1,200	$6,000
CAPPED BUST QUARTER (SMALL)	$1,100	$5,000	$24,000
LIBERTY SEATED QUARTER	$235	$475	$2,000

	MS-60	MS-63	MS-65
BARBER QUARTER	$175	$300	$1,400
LIBERTY STANDING QUARTER	$100	$200	$550
CAPPED BUST HALF	$1,000	$2,300	$11,000
LIBERTY SEATED HALF	$350	$800	$4,500
BARBER HALF	$450	$900	$3,700
LIBERTY WALKING HALF	$30	$60	$170
LIBERTY SEATED DOLLAR (NO MOTTO)	$2,000	$4,750	$50,000
MORGAN DOLLAR	$30	$50	$185
PEACE DOLLAR	$20	$40	$160
ONE DOLLAR GOLD PIECE (TYPE 3)	$400	$1,000	$2,600
$2.50 LIBERTY GOLD	$450	$1,000	$2,300
$2.50 INDIAN GOLD	$450	$1,100	$4,200
$3 GOLD	$2,400	$7,000	$20,000
$5 LIBERTY GOLD	$500	$1,100	$4,000
$5 INDIAN GOLD	$550	$2,300	$20,000
$10 LIBERTY GOLD	$850	$1,500	$6,000
$10 INDIAN GOLD	$900	$1,500	$5,700
$20 LIBERTY GOLD	$1,600	$2,400	$4,800
$20 ST.-GAUDENS GOLD	$1,600	$1,700	$2,400

CHAPTER 5

MARKETPLACE PSYCHOLOGY

To buy and sell coins advantageously you need to understand what makes the market tick.

People who buy and sell coins are really no different from buyers and sellers in most other fields. They base their decisions on a number of different factors, both practical and emotional—and marketplace psychology plays an important part in determining what they buy or sell, and when they buy or sell it.

I've developed a three-step system to help you understand the psychology of the coin market—three easy steps by which you can determine how hot (or how cold) the coin investment environment may be at a given time by using the thermometer of market psychology.

These three basic steps are as follows:

- First, identify the prevailing psychological trend.

- Second, learn how *you* can benefit.

- Third, determine the proper way to buy and sell in this environment, taking into consideration the types of people you're dealing with and how much *more* than the price-guide price—or how much *less*—you'll have to pay when buying, or have to take when selling.

First, let's consider the question of psychological trends.

In the coin market as in many other markets, including the stock market, herd mentality governs most people's behavior. People feel very uncomfortable doing something alone.

People have a tendency to do things which are socially acceptable, and society encourages conformity. We can see this in the way young people are educated, not only in America but throughout the world. Conformity is encouraged: Those who are conformists are rewarded; those who are risk-takers are punished. Consequently, the vast majority of people do things to conform. They do things so they won't be viewed as outcasts.

This has quite a bit to do with psychological trends in the coin market. When the market has achieved a good deal of momentum and prices are higher than they've ever been before, this tendency to conform gives people a false sense of security. It makes them feel comfortable, and they continue to buy when, in actuality, they may very well be buying at the absolute height of the market.

Conversely, this predisposition to conformity makes people reluctant to buy when the market is weak. Since few other people are buying, they don't want to be nonconformist. Yet this may be the best time of all to buy. With the market at the bottom, there's very little "downside risk," as money experts like to call it—very little likelihood of losing money. In fact, there may be great "upside potential"—a strong possibility that prices will go up. But because of their reluctance to stand out from the crowd, many people won't take the plunge at such a time—even though the water may be perfect for investment.

Many of the world's greatest capitalists have been nonconformists—people who had no compunctions about deviating from the norm. These people have achieved remarkable success by disregarding the herd and following their own intuition—doing what their training and experience told them to do. They really haven't cared what was socially acceptable—or, for that matter, what they may have learned at some of our great institutions of learning. Keep in mind that even some of our finest business schools instill an overriding sense of conformity in their students. Thus, when they enter the marketplace, many graduates of these institutions—with all their knowledge and savvy—still find it difficult to buy when things seem bleak and others are sitting on the sidelines, even though their technical training would tell them to do otherwise.

In measuring the temperature of the marketplace, and thereby learning how to take full advantage of the thermometer of market psychology, you need to understand the distinction between a *bear* market and a *bull* market.

Whether in coins or any other field, a bear market is a period when people are selling things off—when the outlook seems grim and there isn't much hope on the horizon. In a bear market, you often see prices go down on a regular basis.

A bull market is just the opposite. People are extraordinarily enthusiastic—often falling all over each other in their headlong rush to buy coins.

In between a bull market and a bear market is a compromise situation called a *business-as-usual market*.

To simplify comparisons, let's calibrate our thermometer of market psychology from 1 to 10, with 1 being the coldest point and 10 being the hottest. (If you'd be more comfortable using some other type of scale, you're free to do so.)

On a 1 to 10 scale, it's prudent to sell when the marketplace reaches a heat level of 8 or above, and it's prudent to buy at levels no higher than 6 or 7.

Let's say the market is gathering momentum; the increases have begun and the psychological level has moved up from 5 to 6. What you should do at this point is compare the current price of a given coin to its "book value"—how it has performed in the past—and try to determine where a reasonable person might expect it to go in the future. If the current price doesn't seem exaggerated by these standards, you can feel reasonably confident buying it, even at levels 6 or 7, with the goal of taking some short-term profits as it moves up from there toward 10.

Not too long ago, this type of thinking would have been looked upon as heresy. The conventional wisdom was to buy coins and hold them as long-term investments. The buy-and-hold philosophy isn't nearly as popular today. Experience has shown that it has some serious shortcomings, especially in regard to commoditized coins—those which change hands routinely on a sight-unseen basis like stocks and bonds. (We'll discuss these coins in greater detail in a later chapter.)

As part of your assessment of the market's overall temperature, you need to determine what's hot and what's not—what's the hottest area of the marketplace and what's the coldest.

You can trace the recent performance of various kinds of coins by following the price charts in major periodicals that cater to buyers and sellers in this field. Coins that are hot are probably showing phenomenal increases in these charts, possibly reflected by plus signs. Coins that are cold may have dropped in value sharply and may have minus signs. Keep in mind that very few coin advisory services recommend when to *sell* coins. Their emphasis is on *buying*. Thus, it is difficult to know when to sell unless you monitor market levels yourself.

In determining what's hot and what's not, you won't find every decision cut and dried. Sometimes, certain coins are just lukewarm. Other times, given items may remain out of favor for extended lengths of time, and thus may stay at the bottom, rather than moving up in a cyclical way. With this in mind, it's not a good idea to assume that just because something is cold, it's bound to turn warmer sometime soon.

ROTATIONAL LEADERSHIP

Another factor you have to keep in mind in assessing the coin market's psychology is the issue of *rotational leadership*. This sounds like a complicated concept, but its meaning is really quite simple: In a rip-roaring bull market, different coins often take turns increasing in value.

One week, commemorative coins may jump in price. Another week, silver dollars may go up. The next week, the big winner may be Liberty Seated quarters or Barber half dollars. Some coins may level off while others are taking a turn. Thus, in a sense, the baton is passed around so that different kinds of coins lead the advances.

Rotational leadership also can occur in a marketplace retreat. In a declining marketplace, you might see silver dollars decreasing in value one week, type coins (representative coins of a particular series which are not rare dates of that series) might be the biggest losers the next week, and yet another series—commemoratives, perhaps—might then take a hit the week after that.

Rotational leadership should be taken into account when assessing the strength or weakness of any particular area of the market. Before deciding just how bullish or bearish Morgan silver dollars are, for example, you also need to look at other major areas of the market. Check your price guides to see how commemoratives or Walking Liberty half dollars are doing; while you're at it, take a look at type coins. The market is a mosaic, and every piece has bearing on every other one.

BENEFITING FROM MARKET PSYCHOLOGY

Now that you understand the thermometer of market psychology, you can learn very quickly and easily how to benefit from its use. This brings us to the second of our three basic steps in understanding and using marketplace psychology.

Before going any farther, it's worth recalling an old expression often heard on Wall Street, but equally true with rare coins: "Bulls make money, bears make money, but pigs lose out." Keep in mind, too, that there's a name for people who always buy low and sell high. They're called liars. Suffice it to say that one of the primary ways to benefit from market psychology is not to be a pig—not to try to squeeze every last dime out of every deal.

Let's say you've bought a coin at level 6 or level 7 on our market-cycle scale of 1 to 10. As the market then climbs closer to the top, you'll start to notice shudders—chinks in the market's armor, if you will. But, while there may be some small disappointments, the feeling will persist that there's no place to go but up. It's sort of like a boxing match where one of the boxers absorbs a couple of whacks but stays on his feet and seems to be going strong. Then comes the knockout punch—a 10-count for the boxer but a knockdown for the coin market all the way from 10 back to 1.

You have to be on your guard. A hot market is persuasive; it mesmerizes you and lures you in. The time to sell that coin you bought at level 6 is really level 7 or level 8; if you wait for level 10, you'll probably end up owning it back at level 1.

Contrary to what you may have been told, the coin market is not a standard financial market. It's a supplement to traditional modes of investment. And, at the time of this writing, it's a totally unregulated marketplace, in no way subject to the jurisdiction of either the Securities and Exchange Commission (SEC) or the Commodity Futures Trading Commission (CFTC). The only government activity now taking place in this industry is the limited involvement of the Federal Trade Commission (FTC), which has charged a number of coin dealers with false, deceptive, and misleading practices in trade and in commerce. These dealers have signed consent decrees with the commission and this has served to clean up the industry.

Because of the absence of government controls, the coin market may react differently from standard financial markets. Thus, when the coin market shudders, prices may continue to escalate—go right through the stop sign, so to speak. In large part, that's because there isn't a federal "policeman" sitting behind a billboard at the corner. This is expected to change shortly.

Under the circumstances, you have to be able to recognize the stop signs and police your own buy-and-sell activities. Otherwise, you may end up being one of the victims when the market crashes.

For one thing, you should watch for signs of rotational leadership. If you see several different areas of the market experiencing declines in value in a relatively short period, the market may be sending you a signal: It may be saying the boom-and-bust theory is absolutely true and that bulls and bears make money while pigs—those who are too greedy—just make bacon and ham.

ACTUAL BUYING AND SELLING

The third and final step in understanding and using market psychology involves the actual buying and selling of coins.

For all practical purposes, you'll have to deal with a dealer in buying coins. Rare coins are viewed as a credence good. In other words, you—as a non-dealer—are not expected to be able to tell the difference between a coin grading Mint State-64 and its counterpart grading Mint State-65. The burden is on the dealer or, in a sense, on the grading service whose product you are buying.

Leading coin-grading services have somewhat solved the grading problem for you. You don't have to know how to grade coins; you don't have to be able to tell the difference between a 65 and a 56. As I explained earlier, these expert services have achieved outstanding records for accuracy and consistency, and you can rely on their judgments. Nevertheless, still use your common sense. If a coin looks ugly to you, don't buy it.

What you *do* need to know about is pricing.

You can work out commissions with your dealer. But you should be aware that many dealers have earned commissions of 75 percent—or even 100 percent—and yet haven't been viewed as overcharging their clients. Substantial legal precedent exists on this point: The Federal Trade Commission, for example, has allowed some coin merchants to charge upwards of 90 percent as a commission or markup.

You're entitled to ask your dealer how much of a markup he's charging—and you should. And you should make every effort to limit this premium, especially when you're buying certified coins. Because of their liquidity, these normally carry much more modest markups than "raw" coins—those that haven't been certified.

In a very hot market, or even just a moderately hot market (one that might rate a 7 on the 1 to 10 scale), you'll probably have to pay a premium over the values published in the price guides.

Let's say prices are increasing at frequent intervals and let's say you're purchasing a Liberty Seated quarter whose wholesale price-guide value (the typical cost to a dealer) is $5,000. In order for a dealer to buy that coin in a rising market, chances are he'll have to pay $5,500 or $5,800. Newsletter writer Maurice Rosen calls this the "market premium factor." Obviously, the dealer will then have to charge *you* more, as well.

In a business-as-usual market (5 on the 1 to 10 thermometer) or a cold market (1, 2, 3, or 4), you can buy coins very close to the levels in the wholesale price guides. In fact, in such markets, dealers sometimes get nominal discounts off the wholesale prices. These discounts are not tremendous; they might amount to 3 to 5 percent. Still, they represent savings that the dealer can then pass along. In a rip-roaring bull market, by contrast, a dealer might have to pay 10 percent more than the level in current price guides.

This is really an anticipatory factor. It's based on what the market is expected to do in the very near future. If the market is in the 7 position, for example, you may have to pay $6,500 for that Liberty Seated quarter that shows up on the wholesale price list at $5,000. That's because with prices trending higher, short-term profits can be made, and these are being anticipated each time the coin changes hands.

Does this mean your dealer is pocketing a profit of $1,500? Not necessarily. In fact, there's an excellent chance that he's making a good deal less—say, $500 or so.

There you have it: the way to understand the psychological makeup of the rare-coin marketplace and use the thermometer to your advantage.

The coin market, like the weather, can be changeable. At times, it can be as hot as the Sahara and at other times as cold as a barren tundra. But if you equip yourself with the tools in this chapter, you'll find that you can prosper in any kind of weather from 1 to 10.

REGISTRY SETS

Statehood Washington quarters are far from the only modern coins that dealers and collectors are seeking in very high grades. Lincoln cents, Jefferson nickels, Roosevelt dimes, Franklin half dollars—these and other late-date coins also have become the objects of a nationwide search for the very best pieces available. This quest gained new impetus in 1997, when the Professional Coin Grading Service introduced its Set Registry™ program, and really took off in 2001, when PCGS expanded this program to the Internet. The concept of the "registry" program is simplicity itself: Collectors who own coins certified by PCGS form those coins into sets, then "register" these sets with the grading service by entering their serial numbers on the company's Web site. At that point, PCGS uses special software to assign a rating to each set, based upon the rarity of the coins—not just in absolute terms but also in the grades at which they were certified. A particular modern coin may have a relatively high mintage and thus may not be rare in absolute terms, but may have had only one example, or just a few examples, certified as perfect (Proof- or Mint State-70) or virtually so (Proof- or Mint State-69). As registry sets grew in popularity, collectors began pursuing such coins in an effort to obtain higher ratings for their sets—since the sets are listed sequentially on the Web site, from the highest rating down, and the top-rated sets in various categories are singled out for special recognition. This competition boosted demand to white-hot levels in certain series, such as Lincoln cents—and since the supply of pristine, high-grade coins is surprisingly small for certain dates in these series, prices went through the roof. In some cases, in fact, they went all the way to the Moon. Coins that normally sell for just a few dollars in average mint condition—say, Mint State-63—were bringing thousands of dollars in ultra-high grades, and many collectors were shaking their heads in amazement.

CHAPTER 6

HOW YOU CAN MAKE
BIG PROFITS FROM
SMALL COINS

Many coins rise in value, but often there's great disparity in how much—and how fast—they go up.

You can reap big profits by acquiring the coins with the greatest potential, and in this chapter I show you how to spot these coins quickly and easily. I've put together the ultimate list of secret insider tips—tips available nowhere else in the world—revealing how coin dealers operate and what happens behind the scenes in the marketplace.

Before we go behind the scenes on the sellers' end, let's first take a look at the principal *buyers* of coins and get a better idea how people in general play this money game—how they go about parlaying their small change into big net gains.

For the purposes of our discussion, there are four major groups of people who seek to acquire coins and then put them together—to a greater or lesser extent—systematically: (1) accumulators, (2) collectors, (3) collector/investors, and (4) investors.

Accumulators get their coins out of circulation—from pocket change, at the bank, or possibly in their travels to other countries. The unifying thread is that accumulators don't buy coins; they obtain them for face value.

Collectors, too, look for interesting coins in pocket change. But unlike accumulators, they also *buy* coins—and however they obtain them, they derive great pride and pleasure from assembling their acquisitions into sets. Some collectors purchase coins with million-dollar price tags; others buy coins costing only 50 cents. Whatever the outlay in money or time, true collectors savor the thrill of the hunt. They get much of their satisfaction from *finding* a worthwhile coin—whether that coin is an 1804 silver dollar costing a million dollars or a 1968 Lincoln cent worth only 5 or 10 cents, and whether they find it in pocket change or in a dealer's showcase.

The final two groups of coin buyers we'll consider are collector/investors and investors. These people's interest centers on coins of the highest grade (or level of preservation) and greatest rarity, and in almost every case they acquire them through purchase, rather than discovery. The coin investor looks upon his holdings not so much as a collection, but rather as a portfolio. Nonetheless, the prudent investor acquires and assembles coins systematically. And to maximize his return, he diversifies his holdings, just as he would do with stocks or bonds.

The greatest share of profits has gone to knowledgeable buyers who are either collectors or collector/investors who have studied coins first and who have bought coins based upon their own judgment. A lot of people think that if they send money to an investment advisor in the rare coin field they will make money, but historically this has not been the case.

ACCUMULATORS

Although the accumulator tends to be involved with lower-grade and lower-valued coins than either the collector or the investor, there are still many ways that this type of person can—and does—put together coins in an organized manner.

It's possible, for example, to assemble a complete set of Lincoln Memorial cents by date—or even date and mint mark—from coins found routinely in pocket change. The earlier Lincoln cents with the "wheat-ears" design on the reverse have largely disappeared from circulation, but a good cross-section of Lincoln Memorial cents can still be found, going all the way back to 1959, the year they were introduced. Not being as deeply committed to the hobby as the collector, the typical accumulator probably would be satisfied to acquire just one Lincoln Memorial cent of every date, from 1959 to the present, without going on to consider mint marks, as well.

Jefferson nickels would be another good series for the accumulator. These coins have been issued continuously since 1938 without a significant change in design, and many early dates turn up quite routinely in pocket change. Again, the accumulator would probably be content to save just one coin from every year, rather than seeking one coin from every date and mint. That would greatly improve the odds of being able to find a complete set in circulation. The toughest pieces to locate would probably be the "war nickels" minted from 1942 to 1945. Nickel was urgently needed for war-related purposes during those years, so five-cent pieces were made from a substitute alloy—and silver was used in that alloy. Most of these coins have been pulled out of circulation because their silver content gives them premium value. However, they do show up from time to time.

Yet another goal for the accumulator would be to assemble sets of "clad" Roosevelt dimes and Washington quarters—those produced since 1965, without any silver content. As with war nickels, the earlier dimes and quarters have been saved because their silver makes them worth more as metal than as money. No similar reason exists for saving the later coins, so with a little searching these can be found for every date. It might take time; it might be necessary to go to the bank, obtain some rolls and look through them. But all these coins can be found, at least by date.

Frequently, people accumulate the coins of other nations when they take international trips. They bring these coins home, put them in little envelopes or perhaps a special album, and treat them as mementos of their travels.

Sometimes coin accumulations end up being very much like collections. An accumulator would verge on becoming a collector, for example, if she started saving coins with similar themes—coins depicting animals, for example, or coins portraying ships, or possibly coins that were issued by a number of different countries for Olympic Games.

People who collect very expensive coins believe that the value of individual coins is enhanced by assembling them into sets—that the whole, so to speak, is worth more than the sum of its parts. The truth of this has been demonstrated on numerous occasions when exceptional collections have been offered for sale: Their completeness has resulted in substantially higher premiums. There's no reason why this shouldn't apply, as well, to casual accumulations. And whatever the dollars-and-cents value of such an accumulation, there's no doubt at all that the more time and effort someone invests in coins, the more emotional reward he will gain.

COLLECTORS

Collectors place heavy emphasis on completeness—much more so than accumulators do. While accumulators might be satisfied with a date set of Lincoln Memorial cents, for example, collectors would be more inclined to put together a set with not only every date but also every mint-mark variety. And they might very well extend the set back to the start of the whole Lincoln series in 1909. Such a set would require more time and effort, not to mention more expense, but true collectors have this dedication.

Often, collectors assemble sets of coins according to die varieties. Dies are pieces of steel that impart the design to a coin. You might think of them as cookie cutters. Or picture a rubber stamp and a piece of paper: The stamp corresponds to the die and the piece of paper represents the planchet—the metal blank struck by the die. Different sets of dies may vary somewhat in certain details; perhaps the date is slanted on some or the mint mark is slightly larger. The coins that result can then be differentiated, and collected, according to these varieties. Many collectors put together sets by date, mint mark, *and* die variety.

One of the great attractions of coin collecting is the diversity it provides. Coin collectors can—and do—pursue their hobby in almost innumerable ways. Some collect coins by metal, seeking to acquire a representative example of each coin struck in a specific type of metal, such as silver or gold. Others specialize in particular denominations (silver dollars, for instance) or series (Lincoln cents, perhaps) or time period (such as the twentieth century). And, as noted earlier, collecting coins by themes is another very popular approach—and this offers limitless possibilities. The theme can be broad and general, such as animals, ships, or monarchs. Or it can be quite narrow: I know of several collectors who specialize in coins that depict men or women wearing glasses.

More and more collectors have turned in recent years from date-and-mint collecting to a broader kind of approach in which they collect by *type*. In fact, this may be the single most popular method of collecting coins today. A person who collects by type seeks to obtain a single representative example of each different type of coin—one Lincoln cent, for instance, to represent the whole Lincoln series.

To a great extent, the growing popularity of type collecting reflects the fact that coins have risen in value so spectacularly. Purchasing one example for every date and mint can be prohibitively expensive at current market levels, especially in very high grades, so many collectors content themselves with just one coin from each of the different series.

Since they are acquiring only one coin to represent an entire series, most type collectors want that coin to be a particularly nice one. Thus, they seek the highest-grade piece they can find and can afford. Typically, this will be a common-date coin—since such a coin, of course, would be far more affordable than one of the scarcer and more expensive "keys" in the same high level of preservation. A "key" is a low-mintage, high-value coin. Obtaining one of these is a key to completing the series to which it belongs—hence the name.

Collectors with a great deal of patience and perseverance attempt to assemble "matched" sets of coins. These are sets in which all the coins are exactly the same—or very nearly so—not only in grade but also in appearance. If one coin is toned a certain way, all are toned that way. If one is brilliant and lustrous, so are all the others. It takes time, effort, money, and sometimes a little luck to put together a perfectly matched set, but the final result can be a breathtaking achievement—one that will be a source of enormous satisfaction and potentially significant profit.

COLLECTOR/INVESTORS AND INVESTORS

Collector/investors and investors both are impelled by the profit motive: Making money from coins is important to both these groups. But while the investor looks upon coins as commodities, the collector/investor values them as well for their beauty and historical significance.

The coins with the best track records as money-makers are those with the lowest mintages and those in the highest levels of preservation—in other words, those with the greatest rarity and quality. If profit potential is paramount in *your* scheme of things, you ought to be seeking coins that exist in the fewest numbers or that have the fewest flaws—those which haven't passed from hand to hand and betray few nicks and scratches. If you enjoy a challenge and have a well-padded wallet, you might go after coins with *both* these attributes—those which are both rare *and* well preserved.

Investors tend to favor high-grade examples of common-date coins. These coins are said to be "generic," because even though their dates and mint marks may be different, they resemble each other closely in appearance and value. Generic coins exist in significant numbers, even in high grades such as Mint State-65.

To a far greater extent than the investor, the collector/investor is interested in completeness. She shares the collector's impulse to start and finish a set. The collector/investor is a healthy, vibrant breed—one that we're seeing more and more today as the coin business grows into a thriving, bustling multibillion-dollar marketplace.

A lot of coin investors, and even collector/investors, have made mistakes in the past by failing to diversify their holdings. Simply stated, they've put all their eggs in one basket, and all too often the basket has had a hole in it. Perhaps they've heard of a friend or neighbor who made a real killing—a 50-percent profit—on 1881-S Morgan silver dollars, so they've taken all their money and bought up a quantity of 1881-S Morgan dollars graded Mint State-65. But it may have been their misfortune to buy at the top of the cycle, and instead of *making* money, the coins may have decreased in value.

My advice to collector/investors and investors is very simple: Acquire coins by type. For someone with only limited knowledge of coins, this is an excellent way to gain familiarity with the different kinds of coins that are available. It also has the advantage of building in protection against a market decline that hits one kind of coin especially hard. Take the case I just cited, where Morgan dollars suffered a cyclical decline. Chances are that rare-date gold pieces, early type coins, and a number of other coins may not have experienced the same kind of setback, and may have even held their own or gone up. A portfolio containing *all* these different coins would be much more likely to weather any storm and stay on an even keel.

When you collect or invest in coins by type, you're basically getting one representative example of each major kind of U.S. coin that was struck for people to spend. This can be extremely educational—and never underestimate the importance of education in helping you manage an investment. It also can deepen your aesthetic appreciation for U.S. coinage and stimulate your interest in pursuing one or more areas in greater depth—including certain areas you may not have thought about before, if you were aware of them at all.

SECRET TIPS TO HELP YOU MAKE MONEY

Whether you're a collector, an investor, an accumulator, or a combination of some of these, you can profit greatly from inside knowledge. With this in mind, I'm going to share some tips with you—some secret tips—and offer some valuable insights on how coin dealers operate. I've gleaned this information from years as a market insider and, to the best of my knowledge, it isn't available anywhere else except in this book.

The following information doesn't apply to every single dealer, but it does apply to *some*—even *many*. It's up to you to determine which dealers it applies to and which it doesn't apply to—and that's really a matter of using your common sense.

Dealers have an uneven knowledge of coins. Many dealers are specialists in certain areas, and their in-depth knowledge is limited to the one or two certain areas in which they specialize. If they deal in silver dollars and you bring them some Buffalo nickels for an appraisal, they're really not going to know the Buffalo nickel series that well. They might have a working knowledge, but not an intimate one. As a result, these dealers often have a tendency to overprice material in areas outside their specialties—areas about which they don't have special knowledge. They're afraid a more knowledgeable buyer may take advantage of them.

This should make you wary of buying coins from these dealers outside their specialties. At the same time, however, it also can present some exceptional opportunities. If you look closely at *all* the coins in these dealers' stock, you frequently can find a scarce die variety—or even one of the valuable varieties described in Chapter Two of this book. Invariably, you will find it among the coins outside the dealer's specialty. And when you do, you can "rip" it—get it at a price considerably cheaper than what you might have to pay a specialist. In fact, you might be able to turn right around and sell it to a specialist at a profit. This is what's known in the trade as "cherry-picking" a dealer's inventory.

A good way to learn about coins, and develop the ability to cherry-pick, is to go to public auctions, where many rare coins of all different kinds are sold in a single place in a concentrated period of time. Make notes before each auction as to which coins you feel are valuable and which you believe to be special varieties. Then see what kind of prices these coins bring at the auction, when knowledgeable professionals are bidding on them. If your selections attract unusually spirited bidding and strong prices, you've probably picked some real cherries.

Dealers can't always grade coins consistently. Many dealers are not all that astute at grading coins. They're excellent businesspeople and fine entrepreneurs; they're honest, well-meaning, hard-working people. But many smaller dealers just aren't all that proficient at grading coins.

Don't take it for granted that a dealer *is* proficient at grading unless he happens to be a market insider—a dealer who is employed by one of the leading grading services, for example, or possibly even a dealer who *owns* a grading service.

Again, this creates tremendous opportunities for *you*, assuming that you're willing to take the time and effort to gain and sharpen that edge. You can acquire a good basic knowledge of grading within six months by reading up on the subject, then attending public auctions and examining as many coins as possible. At that point, you might very well be able to spot instances where dealers have graded coins too conservatively. That would enable you to pick up some real bargains. A note of caution: This is sophisticated stuff, and I would recommend that you not risk any sizable sum of money unless and until you're ab-solutely sure of your ability. And, above all, don't pretend to be an expert unless you really are.

Dealers don't heed their own advice during market cycles. Although they may know better, many dealers tend to get caught up in the ebb and flow of cur-rent market activity. Dealers may know in principle that if certain kinds of coins—let's say Morgan dollars—are increasing in value at a frenzied pace, they're probably at or near the top of their market cycle. If they went by the book, they would stand back and say to themselves: "Wait a minute, these coins have increased 100 percent in three weeks. This increase is just too great; it's a speculative frenzy; I don't think it's going to last. What's going to happen when all these people decide to sell their coins and take some profits?"

But dealers are only human, and that makes them prone to common human frailties such as greed. Consequently, some will get greedy and continue to buy these coins for their inventory, even though their better judgment tells them the market cycle is already at the top. And this can be very profitable for *you*. Even at the top of a cycle, many dealers will still let you realize your profit and sell your coins back to them because they think the market's going to go even higher. Conversely, at the bottom of a cycle, you'll have the opportunity in many cases—not all the time, but many times—to buy coins at bargain-basement levels. At the bottom, many dealers fall prey to yet another basic human emotion: despair. They become pessimistic and fail to see the light at the end of the tunnel. The herd mentality infects dealers just as it does any other group, so often they'll give you a chance to buy coins inexpensively at the bottom of a cycle.

Thus, in a surprising number of cases, you can sell at the top, because a num-ber of dealers will continue to buy at the top. And you also can buy at the bot-tom, because so many dealers don't follow their own advice and buy coins when everyone else is selling.

Dealers borrow money for their coin activities and are caught short if the market falls quickly and without notice. It isn't unusual for the coin market to fall very quickly and without any notice. In fact, that's the way it usually *does* fall. When it does, dealers are often caught short financially. What we notice is that af-ter the market retreats, dealers are temporarily unable to buy any more coins. But this doesn't mean that your coins are now worthless, or worth a great deal less than they were before. It's just an indication of temporary market illiquidity.

Let's say a dealer is willing to pay you $100 for a certain coin on a Friday afternoon—then, on Monday morning, he doesn't want to buy it at *any* price, or offers you only $5. This kind of drop is simply too dramatic, and you should flatly refuse to sell the coin. Use your common sense: Hold out until the cash-flow position of that particular dealer—or perhaps of dealers in general—turns around. My experience has been that if you wait a week or so, the cash flow will improve and you'll be able to sell your coin for a much better price. It may be substantially less than the $100 you were offered on Friday afternoon, but it certainly will be substantially more than the $5 Monday morning offer.

Dealers are your No. 1 source of inside information. One good way to anticipate what may be due to increase in value is to check the price guides and see which coins *haven't* gone up in value for a while. Chances are, some of these coins have been at the bottom of their cycle and now may be ready to move up. And an excellent way to confirm your hunch would be to call a number of different dealers and ask them if they have these coins in stock and whether you can purchase them at the going price. If they *don't* have the coins, or won't let them go at the current market price, you can be pretty sure the supplies are thin—and that would reinforce the likelihood of higher prices soon.

Don't tip your hand, or start speculation, by calling a hundred dealers and asking for one or two particular coins. A better approach would be to ask about a number of different coins—ten or twenty, perhaps—and somewhere in that list include the one or two coins in which you're really interested. If you call a hundred dealers and few of them can provide the coins you want at the going price, that's a sure sign that the coins are ripe for a price increase.

Another tipoff would be if you learned that a certain major dealer has been buying specific coins in significant quantities. Let's say you discover that a mail-order dealer with substantial resources has become an aggressive buyer of high-grade Buffalo nickels. You could logically conclude that this dealer was preparing for a big promotional push on Buffalo nickels. That, of course, would stimulate interest—and heightened interest translates into higher prices. By acting quickly and purchasing high-grade Buffalo nickels yourself *before* the dealer's advertising started to appear, you could put yourself in a position to capitalize on the flurry of new activity. In a sense, you could ride the dealer's coattails.

Prices tend to move quickly during a promotional blitz, rising sharply while the push is on and then falling just as sharply once the campaign is over. Thus, you should view this as a short-term situation. Strike while the iron is hot, then take your profits and celebrate.

Dealers don't use magnifying glasses. Everyone should use a magnifying glass in examining coins—but, quite surprisingly, many dealers don't use a glass all the time. As a result, they sometimes overlook imperfections. This is to your advantage when selling coins to these dealers, but may be to your detriment when you buy. I recommend that you use a 5- or 10-power glass when you look at a coin. And be sure that the magnification and lighting conditions are consistent every time. If possible, coins should be viewed under a pinpoint light source such as a tensor lamp or a halogen lamp. Halogen lamps are becoming increasingly popular in examining proof coins. They enable the viewer to spot small hairline scratches quite readily on these coins.

Dealers are small entrepreneurs with families to support and a need for regular income. A dealer is entitled to a reasonable profit on the coins you buy from him; after all, he's in business to make money. However, I don't recommend that you buy into monthly programs where you give a dealer a set amount of money—say, $100 or $200—every single month to buy you coins. In certain months, there just won't be any great buys available.

Monthly programs are especially inadvisable as a method of acquiring pricier coins. If you're talking about investing 25 or 50 thousand dollars a month, you're far better off to establish a relationship with a dealer and have him call you if a suitable coin becomes available. Otherwise, you're putting too much pressure on the dealer, forcing him to get you something extraordinary when it just might not be available in the marketplace.

Dealers would be happy to take your money each month, in every kind of market, because they have families to support and they need a steady income. But that wouldn't always be best from *your* standpoint.

Dealers have a vested interest in buying coins. If you go to some dealers with a coin worth $1,000 and ask "Hey, what's this worth?" you might be told: "I'll give you $50." Needless to say, these dealers would be all too happy to buy such a coin for $50 and then turn around and sell it at a huge profit. That's why I recommend that you get your coins independently certified—a process I discuss at length in Chapter Seven.

Dealers sometimes handle coins improperly, even leaving fingerprints on the coins. When showing your dealer valuable coins—or *any* coins, for that matter, you should pay close attention and ask him politely not to touch the coins on the obverse or reverse. All too often, some dealers handle coins carelessly, sometimes even dropping them. Don't take for granted that just because someone buys and sells coins for a living, he'll treat your coins with care and pick them up only by the edges. He may *know* the right way to handle coins, but he may not always practice it, especially with regard to someone else's coins.

With certified coins, this really isn't a problem. These coins have been encapsulated in sonically sealed, tamper-resistant holders that protect them from such mishandling. What's more, the grading services will not encapsulate a coin if it has any visible residue on its surface which might cause it to deteriorate at a later date. If a certified coin does deteriorate after being encapsulated, the grading service that certified that coin will buy it back.

Dealers who buy coins in quantity often withdraw their public offers to buy these coins just before major conventions. A number of dealers post "bids" to buy coins that they haven't even seen. They place these bids on computer trading networks that are known as "sight-unseen" systems. If you're selling coins through a sight-unseen system, always check to see if any major coin conventions are taking place or are imminent. You can do this by looking in *Coin World* or *Numismatic News*, the two leading weekly coin newspapers; both publish detailed coin show schedules. Dealers often withdraw or lower their bids before a major convention, since they don't want to be locked in at a high level—with an obligation to buy at that level—if the market suddenly plunges at the convention.

The coin market is a thin marketplace; at any given time, there may be no more than half a dozen dealers with bids posted on the sight-unseen trading network for certain rare coin types. If all of them withdraw or lower their bids for those coins at the same time—and this does happen—the sight-unseen bids will be substantially lower.

As a rule, dealers attend conventions from Thursday through Saturday. With that in mind, don't sell your coins on a Friday afternoon if you know there's a major convention taking place. You might get much better prices by waiting till Monday morning, when the dealers return from the show and reinstate their normal sight-unseen bids.

Dealers sell rejects, or "off" coins, to other dealers at prices below the wholesale level. I recommend that you establish a working relationship with one or more dealers and ask them about the deals they may have available. Most dealers have certain coins they're willing to sell at discounted prices, but often they prefer to sell these coins to other dealers. By making your interest known, you can sometimes gain access to such deals.

For instance, a dealer may have a certain coin that's been in his stock for six months, and he may just be tired of seeing it. He may say to himself: "You know, it's not that great a coin. I paid $500 for it, but I'd be willing to sell it to another dealer for $300 just to get rid of it. It's not the nicest coin I've ever seen, so I don't want to sell it to a retail client." If you were able to buy this coin for $300, you might be able to turn around and sell it to somebody else for $350 or $400, so it might be a very good deal for you. You might even find it attractive and decide to keep it yourself. Beauty, after all, is often in the eye of the beholder.

By establishing a good relationship with a dealer, you can put yourself in a position to purchase cut-rate coins even before they're offered to other dealers. Remember, you *pay* for the special coins; you pay top dollar for exceptional coins that the dealer *wants* his retail clients to have. So why not cut yourself in on bargain coins when those become available?

Dealers absolutely obey the law and file IRS reports on you if you buy coins for cash. The law requires coin and bullion dealers to file a report with the Internal Revenue Service any time you—or your agent or representative—pay more than $10,000 in cash for coin purchases during a given calendar year. And whether they tell you about them or not, the dealers absolutely do file these reports. Never buy coins for cash; always pay by check.

LEGAL ADVICE

When I need legal advice about a numismatic matter, I often turn to Armen R. Vartian, an attorney in Manhattan Beach, California, who specializes in art and collectibles issues. Vartian is Legal Counsel to the Professional Numismatists Guild (PNG), former General Counsel to the American Numismatic Association (ANA), and represents many leading coin dealers and auction houses in the country, as well as individual collectors and investors.

Based on my discussions with Vartian, here are a few suggestions on what to consider when doing business with a coin dealer.

• How did you learn about the dealer? Some dealers advertise in numismatic publications, where they know that potential customers already know something about coins and are able to compare prices and get information about what they are buying. Others make "cold calls" and discourage potential customers from getting information elsewhere. A dealer who expects to sell to knowledgeable collectors is more likely to be fair than one who counts on his or her customers being totally ignorant about coins.

• What do you know about the dealer? Both honest and dishonest dealers can sound good on the telephone, but if a dealer's principles are well known and have been in the coin business for a long time, it probably means they have many satisfied customers and will treat you fairly too. Find out what professional organizations the dealer belongs to, what references they will give, and how long they have been in business.

• Will the dealer back up what he or she says about the coins? There are two aspects to this. First, be sure that all representations and warranties about a coin's description, authenticity, grade, rarity, and provenance are in writing and unambiguous. There is nothing wrong with demanding that the dealer put these important facts in clear terms on the invoice before the sale is consummated. Think twice about doing business with someone who tells you things to induce you to buy but refuses to spell them out for you on paper. Second, make sure the dealer has the financial wherewithal to honor the guarantees he or she makes. Some dealers offer buyback guarantees or promise to provide liquidity by making two-way markets in what they sell. If you are in doubt about their financial strength, ask them for financial statements.

• Do you understand fully the risks of buying coins, including the markups being charged by the dealer? Like any other collectible item, the value of coins depends upon activity in a broad but volatile marketplace. In order to make a living, dealers must buy at wholesale prices in that marketplace, and sell at a retail markup. When customers sell their coins, they do not recoup the markups unless the market has risen in the meantime. Some dealers are very straightforward about their markups, and explain that collectors and investors would take a significant loss if they sold coins the day after purchasing them. Others are far less so, misleading their customers about their true markups. And the most unscrupulous imply that coins are sold at no markup at all, or even below their wholesale value. These types of representations should be treated with some skepticism.

• Does the dealer offer a return privilege? Coins can rise or fall in value quickly after purchase, and it is not always in a dealer's interest to take them back for a full refund if a customer changes his or her mind. However, all else being equal, it is safer for a novice coin buyer to do business with a dealer who does offer such a guarantee.

- What remedy would you have if you were dissatisfied with the dealer's performance? Apart from a return privilege, look to see whether the dealer is a member of PNG, which binds members to a Code of Ethics and provides low-cost mandatory binding arbitration between member dealers and their customers. Not all reputable coin dealers are PNG members, but many will agree to arbitrate customer disputes through the local office of the American Arbitration Association or Better Business Bureau.

- Are you getting physical delivery of the coins? Vartian does not advise ever buying coins without receiving actual delivery. Obviously, this means that buyers must be prepared to incur the costs of storing and insuring their coins. However, leaving coins with a dealer limits the buyer's control over their location and treatment, and may expose the coins to claims by the dealer's creditors.

- Have you read the fine print on the dealer's invoice? Most major dealers place customer disclosures somewhere on their invoices or on a separate page transmitted with the coins. Often these disclosures are accompanied by disclaimers of liability for subjective opinions which later turn out to be untrue or for changes in industrywide grading standards. Some buyers see statements to the effect that past performance is no guarantee of future value, and others find limitations on where or for how long they may bring suit against the dealer. It is perfectly legitimate for dealers to put the terms and conditions of sale in writing on the invoice or in related documents, but be mindful of the fact that such terms and conditions are binding even if they are in fine print and appear for the first time along with the coins themselves. If you have any objections to a term or condition, contact the dealer immediately and work it out.

Above all else, Vartian emphasizes the importance of the old adage "If it sounds too good to be true, it probably isn't true." Common sense and a little homework go a long way toward avoiding ever needing the services of an attorney to protect your rights.

SUMMING UP

Unlike any other investment field, the rare coin market produces only winners. This isn't to say that coins don't go down in value; certainly, coins go down— sometimes they decrease quickly and by a big percentage. But coins are so beautiful that even if some of your coins fail to appreciate monetarily, you still come out ahead because you get *aesthetic* appreciation.

Of course, you would prefer to gain *both* types of appreciation, and that's where *The Insider's Guide to U.S. Coin Values* comes in. By following the guidelines and using the secret tips I've given you in this chapter, you'll have a big head start in picking coins with the potential to realize tremendous gains.

CHAPTER 7

HOW TO CASH IN
THOSE BIG PROFITS

Congratulations! You've looked in the cookie jar, searched the attic, checked your pocket change—and now you're ready to go to the cash window and celebrate. You've found some coins that are valuable, other coins that are extremely valuable, and still other coins that may even be super-rarities.

Maybe you've discovered a circulated 1932 double eagle ($20 gold piece) worth $5,000. Or possibly you've come up with a circulated 1797 Draped Bust half dollar with 15 stars on the front, which is worth a tidy $18,500. These coins are easy enough to sell; dealers all over the nation want to buy them. I'll provide you with details later in this chapter on how to sell them.

But suppose you've really struck it rich. Suppose, for instance, you've found a circulated 1870-S three-dollar gold piece worth half a million dollars. It's easy enough to sell this coin, too. But it's not quite so simple to obtain the full value for a coin in this rarefied price range. You may have dealers across the country beating a path to your door and wanting to buy it for $300,000. You may even find a couple of dealers willing to buy it for $400,000. But if you want to sell it for its full value, you may have to wait a little while—or even longer—in order to maximize what you can sell it for.

Generally, the higher the price you ask for your 1870-S three-dollar gold piece, or any other extremely valuable coin, the longer you'll have to wait for a buyer. But this is not unique to rare coins. It's much like what you would encounter, for example, if you tried to sell your house.

A friend of mine owned a house in New Jersey, where the real estate market was depressed at the time. He decided to move with his family to a different part of the state, and he foolishly bought a house there without first making sure to sell his first house. He was confident he could sell it with no problem at all if he simply lowered the price somewhat.

Surprise! Many months elapsed without a single offer on the old house, leaving my friend in a major cash-flow bind since he needed the proceeds from that house to help finance the new one.

Big-ticket coins are sometimes very much like real estate. If you own a coin for which you paid $100,000, selling it may not be as quick and easy a deal as you might think. You can't simply take it to any of a thousand willing dealers, all of whom have $100,000 in cash on hand and are pleading with you to let them buy that coin.

Selling your extremely valuable coins is similar to selling your house. You might be able to sell that coin, or that piece of real estate, almost instantaneously; maybe you'll simply get lucky. In most cases, though, especially in instances where the coin is worth a whole lot of money, the process of selling is a much longer one and one which requires some planning and some good, quick-witted common sense on your part.

A few years ago, a rare and beautiful U.S. gold coin was sold for more than $1.5 million. The coin is an "ultra-high-relief" 1907 double eagle, or $20 gold piece, designed by renowned sculptor Augustus Saint-Gaudens. This coin was graded Mint State-68 on the 1 through 70 scale by the Numismatic Guaranty Corporation.

This probably was not an instantaneous sale; this was not a spur-of-the-moment transaction where a coin dealer had the coin in his hip pocket and said to himself, "You know, I think I might want to sell this coin because I need the money." This wasn't a situation where he just went out and walked up to someone who said, "I'll give you a million-and-a-half for it," and then the coin dealer said "okay" and the buyer took $1.5 million out of his back pocket and put the money on the table.

Transactions such as this involve detailed negotiations—frequently extended ones. They're planned far ahead of time and the people selling these coins give careful consideration to psychological factors in the marketplace.

Financial service professionals regard stocks as being "continuously liquid." At any given time, you can take a share of stock and sell it for the price that's published in the newspaper or the current trading price of that stock—and for every share you sell, you'll receive a uniform price. At any given time, that stock is salable.

To a certain extent, some coins which are not great rarities enjoy this same advantage. We often see $1,000 coins and $500 coins and $100 coins which, for all practical purposes, are continuously liquid. But when we start talking about large groups of these coins, or coins which have fancy price tags, these coins lack continuity of liquidity. These coins are not always readily salable at any given time.

Let's say a dealer has three boxes of coins and he takes them to a show, figuring he can sell them under current market conditions for $2 million. But when he gets to the show, where many other dealers have a chance to examine the coins, the best offer he gets is only $1 million. Chances are that dealer wouldn't sell those coins. He would wait until the next show, figuring he would get a better offer. He might have to wait a month to find the right buyer, the person willing to pay $2 million—or close to $2 million—for those coins, but the difference in price would make the wait worthwhile.

In this case and other cases like it, the "right buyer" is the person who:

- *Needs the coin*—a dealer who needs it to sell to a collector; a collector who needs it to complete a collection; a collector-investor who needs it for a type set.

- *Appreciates the coin*—someone who appreciates its cultural, artistic, or historical significance; someone who appreciates its rarity; someone who appreciates its high grade; someone who likes the design of this kind of coin; someone who finds the toning unusually attractive.

- *Has the money to pay for the coin*—someone who can pay for it within a reasonable time.

If someone is buying a coin for a million dollars, he can't be expected to pay for it tomorrow. And if he is able to pay for it tomorrow, he, in turn, will expect the seller to extend advantageous terms. If he can pay for it within a month or two, that's fine. When I speak of someone who can pay for the coin, I don't necessarily mean a dealer with the money in his hip pocket. It could instead be a dealer who knows a private collector who wants that particular coin, or a dealer who can secure the proper financing. This ability, coupled with his own financial resources, would enable him to give you the best possible price for the coin you're selling.

Unless all three of these factors are involved, there won't be any sale.

This is really no different from what you would encounter in trying to sell a house. Unless you were lucky enough to find the right buyer—someone who needed your house, appreciated your house, and had the money to buy it—you wouldn't be able to swap your "For Sale" sign for one reading "Sold."

THE MONEY SUPPLY

The coin market's money supply is governed by four basic factors: cash flow, debt payments, bank collateral, and market fluctuations.

Cash flow is the two-way pattern of payments: money received by a dealer and money spent. If a dealer sells a coin for $1,000 but doesn't get paid by his client for thirty days—even though the dealer had to pay for the coin right away—that dealer may very well have a cash-flow problem. This type of negative cash flow, multiplied by a number of different deals, could have a significant impact on that coin dealer's ability to pay a strong price for your coins at any given time.

Just about everyone has *debt payments*, and coin dealers are certainly no exception. Dealers who maintain coin shops often have heavy debts, including mortgage payments and installment-loan payments on expensive computer equipment. These debts can sometimes limit their ability to wheel and deal freely in buying and selling coins.

Many dealers also are repaying loans for which they have used coins as *bank collateral*. When the market goes down, many dealers in a sense "hock" some of their coins in order to obtain needed cash. In the late 1980s a dealer might have taken $500,000 worth of coins to the SafraBank of California, or some other institution offering such a service, and been able to obtain a loan for 50 percent—or sometimes as much as 70 percent—of the coins' value, based on the current sight-unseen prices on the computerized trading network. Some banks still offer such loans.

Dealers have to make payments on such loans—and if coin prices go down further, they have to come up with more coins (or other assets) to keep the value of their collateral at 50 or 70 percent of their loan balance. Otherwise, they have to repay the money. Thus, a declining market can place a particular strain on dealers using coins as collateral—and, in the process, magnify the weakness of the money supply in the marketplace as a whole.

Market fluctuations can never be predicted with pinpoint accuracy, but they certainly play a role in determining how much—or how little—money will be available. Dealers' profits are maximized in a rising market, and that in turn gives them more money to spend on buying coins.

SALES OPTIONS

There are three primary methods by which you can sell your coins: direct sale, electronic trading networks, and public auctions.

Direct sale is a highly personalized, specialized area which won't be covered in great detail in this book because it involves such subjectivity—such interpersonal chemistry between the seller and buyer. I don't recommend the direct sale approach because in many cases, the person buying the coins has a vested interest in the outcome of the transaction.

The buyer might say your coins are worth nothing when, in fact, they're really worth thousands—or even millions—of dollars. That's why third-party certification is so important. If you have coins and you don't know what they're worth, you should get them independently certified before you attempt to sell them.

WARNING: One state-of-the-art rip-off involves buyers of gold who set up shop in hotels and motels and take out ads offering to buy your gold coins and jewelry for top dollar. In many cases, it's the hotel coin buyers with their fancy digital scales making those top dollars, as they underpay for items brought to them. I worked with CBS-TV's *Inside Edition* and explored these practices on the air and was shocked at how low some of the offers were. Veteran coin dealer Mike Fuljenz has turned investigating this practice into an almost full-time pursuit. So shop around, and don't take the first offer.

Electronic Trading The principal network through which you can sell your coins electronically is the Certified Coin Exchange (CCE). You'll have to get your coins certified beforehand by one of the two leading coin-grading services.

The Certified Coin Exchange accepts coins certified by either the Professional Coin Grading Service (PCGS) or the Numismatic Guaranty Corporation of America (NGC).

To use this trading option, you'll need to have a dealer submit your coins to NGC or PCGS. Both firms will be happy to provide you with a free list of member dealers. You'll find these dealers extremely helpful. Once your coins are certified, the dealer you select will help you again in determining the current sight-unseen bids. Just ask him to show you the computer screen or a printout of the current high bids. Chances are, the dealer will charge a commission of 10 or 15 percent to handle the sale for you. And that is certainly fair and reasonable.

The electronic exchanges will be of greatest use to you in selling coins that are fungible—high-grade examples of common-date coins that resemble each other in appearance and value and thus are interchangeable. These coins are said to be commoditized, and they lend themselves readily to sight-unseen trading, especially when they trade for less than $250 apiece.

As I explained earlier, these coins are continuously liquid for all practical purposes—unless you have several million dollars' worth that you want to dump at one time. The coin market has a number of small entrepreneurs, and if you try to sell several million dollars' worth of anything, it's not going to be as easy as selling a smaller quantity with a lower market value. You could certainly do it; a transaction in the millions could certainly be consummated. But it probably would take a lot more time and effort.

Auction Sales Auction sales offer some highly significant advantages to you as a seller, and I happen to like this particular option very much. These sales bring many prospective buyers together in one place, and that can produce competitive bidding that will drive up the prices you receive.

In a conventional auction, your coins are showcased in a beautiful catalog, where they are described very attractively—and possibly pictured, as well. This helps produce a sort of mystique, a sense that the auction coins are special. And that, in turn, enhances the prices they realize.

Conventional auctions do have a downside, however. First and foremost is the fact that substantial time will pass between when you consign the coins and when you receive your money. Typically, it takes about two to three months for coins to come under the gavel after they're submitted to an auction company for sale in the conventional manner. Then, after the auction, another thirty to forty-five days will pass before you receive your money.

Clearly, the time lag involves a serious risk. Let's say you consign some coins to an auction house in January and they don't come up for sale until March. If the coin market experienced a cyclical decline and your coins went down in value 10 or 20 percent from January to March, you would receive a lower return. And this kind of cyclical decline isn't uncommon. There are ways to protect your coins from selling at auction for unacceptably low prices, and I'll discuss these shortly. However, there's no way to force bidders to pay January prices in March when the March prices are lower, and you should keep this in mind when deciding whether to sell your coins at auction.

The growing volatility in the marketplace has increased the possibility that coins could go down in value after being consigned for public auction. This has given rise to a quick and easy new method of selling coins at auction. One company calls this method the "express auction." Another calls it the "bullet auction." Whatever the name, it's a method that greatly reduces the delay of the conventional auction route.

Suppose you have a coin whose value has risen 200 percent since you acquired it and you want to cash out and take your profit. At the same time, however, you want to be sure of getting the highest price, and you feel the best way to do that is to sell the coin at auction. By consigning the coin to a company that conducts express—or bullet—auctions, you can benefit from the competitive bidding atmosphere of a public auction without enduring the worrisome lag time often inherent in old-style auction sales. There's a good chance your coin can be sold at one of the new, quicker auctions within a few weeks. And the payment will be quicker, too. Companies conducting express auctions require faster payment from successful bidders, and they in turn then pay their consignors almost at once.

This type of auction is becoming an extremely viable alternative. And besides saving you time, it can also save you money. That's because express or bullet auctions tend to be "no-frills" sales, creating substantial savings which then can be passed along. The catalogs for these auctions can't be as elaborate, for example, because of the limited time; they can't make lavish use of full-color illustrations as conventional auction catalogs often do. Because of such economies, the commission you'll have to pay is likely to be significantly lower than at a traditional auction house.

Market secret: If you decide to sell your coins by means of an express or bullet auction, consign them only to a company that also conducts the more elaborate, more traditional kind. These full-service companies have built up large mailing lists and enjoy the patronage of many thousands of clients to whom they can send catalogs for their sales, including the quicker auctions. If a "fly-by-night" firm were to set up one of these quickie auctions, you wouldn't get good results in many cases.

HOW TO PROTECT YOURSELF WHEN YOU SELL A COIN AT AUCTION

There are three potential risks in buying and selling coins.

Probably first and foremost is the *buy risk*—the risk that what you get will be less than what you paid for. As long as you limit your purchases to coins that have been certified, the buy risk will be greatly minimized or even eliminated.

Then there is the *market risk*—the risk that if you buy a coin, instead of going up by 300 percent it might go down a couple of percentage points.

Finally, you have the *sell risk*—the risk that when you dispose of your coins, the payment you receive will be less than what they're worth. To use an extreme example, you might have coins worth $100,000 and some unscrupulous dealer might offer you only $50. If you were naive enough to sell them for $50, the dealer would then go out and sell those coins for their true value and reap the enormous dividend that rightfully should have been yours.

Selling your less expensive coins at auction isn't like selling real estate by the same sales route. Houses and other pieces of real estate often change hands at auction for substantially less than their normal market value—what they would bring if their owners had time to sit tight and wait for the right buyer, the buyer with the combination of ingredients I outlined earlier in this chapter. Desirable coins tend to bring strong prices when sold at auction; there's great competition for these coins.

Sometimes, an auction company will agree to take raw coins—coins that have not been certified—and describe them optimistically in its catalog. This would make these coins appear to be in a higher grade than they actually are. In a sense, this is not unlike what a used car dealer does when he takes a car that's a lemon, represents it to be a cream puff, and sells it on someone's behalf to an unsuspecting consumer. An auction company might be willing to do this on your behalf—so before consigning your coins for sale in the company's auction, you should first ask what grade it intends to assign to each coin.

If the auction company doesn't want to grade your coins in accordance with your wishes, I recommend that you have them independently certified before consigning them. This would establish their actual grade beyond any reasonable doubt. They might not then be graded optimistically in the catalog, but they also wouldn't be given too low a grade. Be sure to have your coins certified only by leading grading services.

Any time you sell your coins, you should seek to take advantage of market trends; in other words, you should try to anticipate upward movements and time your auction consignments so the coins' sale coincides closely with a cycle's high. This, of course, is easier said than done, and even the experts guess wrong now and then.

To protect yourself against the possibility that you may be guessing wrong, and that the market may actually decline before your coins come up for sale, you should work out an arrangement with the auction house beforehand to assign a "reserve" value to each of your coins. If the bidding fails to reach this level, you will then get to keep the coins. You may have to pay a commission on the reserve price, but at least your coins won't be sold for less than they're worth.

The traditional, or three-month, auction route is best suited to coins that are real rarities. These coins need the exposure they receive in fancy catalogs and extensive promotional buildups. Elaborate trappings aren't really "frills" when it comes to great rarities, since it takes this kind of approach to attract the right kind of buyer for such coins.

If you have commodity-type coins such as common-date Morgan dollars graded Mint State-65, you can place these in bullet sales or sell them through the electronic exchanges.

If you have coins that fall somewhere in between, such as beautiful Mint State-65 or Proof-65 Liberty Seated quarters that are worth perhaps $2,000 each, you certainly could consign them to a bullet sale. But these coins should not be sold over the electronic exchanges. Each of these coins has an idiosyncratic quality of toning, of appearance, and the electronic exchanges tend to minimize, rather than maximize, special qualities. These exchanges emphasize the *similarities* that certain coins possess, not their *differences*—and beautiful toning can be a very positive difference that makes a coin more valuable than the norm.

Competition is healthy for sellers; when selling your coins, you want as many buyers as possible competing to purchase them. At an auction, the competition is already built in: The gallery will be filled with people who are vying for your coins. But if for some reason you don't want to sell a coin at auction, you still can stimulate strong competition for that coin—and get the highest price possible— by showing it to twelve or fifteen different dealers and having each one give you a sealed bid. This isn't nearly as effective as the public auction route, but it's better than going to just one dealer and being at his mercy.

Selling your coins can be a pleasurable and profitable experience. Just remember that some coins can be sold more readily than others, and all coins can be sold more readily at certain times than at other times. You can sell a million-dollar coin instantaneously, but you may get only $800,000 for that coin.

With super-rarities, if you want to maximize the amount of money you get, you may have to wait a little while. With coins valued at $10,000—and even $20,000 or $30,000—you can get full value almost immediately.

CHAPTER 8

SCOTT TRAVERS'
SECRET TOP TWELVE

Coins that have great potential to rise in value sharply, but aren't yet performing at close to their potential, are said to be *sleepers*.

Sleepers can be found among certified coins—coins that have been examined, graded, and encapsulated by one of the leading grading services. They also can be found among "raw" coins—coins that haven't yet been certified and encased (or "slabbed") in sonically sealed, hard plastic holders.

Some sleepers have greater potential than others. In this chapter, I reveal a secret list of twelve coins, or types of coins, which are among the biggest sleepers of all—the very best buys—in the current marketplace.

If you have money to spend on rare coins, these are potential purchases that merit your serious consideration, since all are excellent values.

You may not have to buy some of these coins; it's certainly possible to find any or all of them in an old collection or accumulation that may be sitting right now in a drawer or cigar box in your home.

Recently, I performed an appraisal for people who had come into possession of just such a group of rare coins. The people who owned these coins thought they had little or no value—but when I examined them, I found they included a number of rare and valuable pieces, among them low-mintage proofs. At my suggestion, the owners got some of them certified; the coins came back from the grading service with grades as high as Proof-65, making them worth premiums ranging as high as tens of thousands of dollars per coin.

If you do find some of the coins on my secret list—in the cookie jar, in the attic, or in an old collection you received as an inheritance—hold on to them. Because of their great potential, all these coins could rise in value dramatically in the long run, or even in a much shorter term. Think twice before selling them; they could bring you much more substantial returns later on.

If you don't find any of these twelve sleepers but are thinking of investing in coins, these would be excellent items to buy. I've chosen a cross-section of coins with current retail prices ranging from modest amounts to six-figure sums, so you'll find something here for just about every budget.

In buying them, as in selling them, certification is highly advisable. "Slabbed" coins—those that have been certified—enjoy broad popularity and great liquidity in today's coin market, and by limiting your transactions to certified coins you will greatly enhance the security of your investment.

Here, then, is my special twelve-coin list:

1. **The certified business strike United States "generic" gold coin.**
    As I have said many times in my public pronouncements, when precious metals increase, so do rare coins—and as go the metals, so goes the rare coin market.

    We are seeing feverish interest in the metals as this book is being revised in February 2012. Gold is over $1,700 an ounce. And the interest in gold coins that goes with this is exceptional.

    Saint-Gaudens double eagles ($20 gold pieces) graded Mint State-65 cost several thousand dollars apiece in 1988 and sell today for about $2,300. With the possibility of gold reaching for the moon, it's not inconceivable that they could jump to $3,000 or $3,500. In February 2012, you could buy nice Saint-Gaudens double eagles graded MS-65 by the Professional Coin Grading Service (PCGS) or the Numismatic Guaranty Corporation of America (NGC) for $2,300 or so, with hand-selected premium-quality coins trading for just a little bit more. There is a supply of these coins, but not an oversupply. They're available, but strong new demand could push their price substantially higher. They're beautiful coins, and each contains nearly an ounce of gold. With these, as with all my recommendations, I strongly urge you to buy only coins that have been certified.

    Gold coins are in demand because of what newsletter editor Maurice Rosen calls the economic justification for owning it—and those with bigger budgets might do well to consider buying more valuable examples.

    With the kind of activity we're seeing now in gold and the possibility that the yellow metal may rise to $5,000 or more an ounce, $10 Libs (with-motto Liberty eagles or $10 gold pieces) graded MS-63 appear to be very attractive coins. I like the ones from 1866 to 1907, with the motto IN GOD

WE TRUST above the eagle. In MS-63, a with-motto $10 Lib is a $1,400 coin today. The $10 Lib is a relatively large coin and is fairly scarce in this condition, both of which heighten its appeal. It was much higher-priced some years ago.

Indian $10s graded MS-63 are fabulous coins too, and people really love them. They're large gold coins with an exquisite design by Augustus Saint-Gaudens whose beauty rivals that of his magnificent double eagle. There's a wide variance of quality with these coins. You might find an MS-63 with lots of minor nicks and scratches on the obverse, and under a glass it might look like an MS-62 or even an MS-61—but at a glance, to the unaided eye, it might appear to be an MS-64 or even marginally an MS-65. Exercise great care in selecting these coins, and be aware of the variance in quality, especially regarding scratches on the obverse. These coins can be acquired at $1,750 each in February 2012.

Warning: Values of these gold coins can be extremely volatile. Learn the idiosyncratic qualities of the generic gold coin market, and consult a competent coin dealer and financial professional before jumping in. Economic conditions could actually push the price of gold downward, and that would make the performance of these coins less than golden.

2. **Scarce-date Morgan silver dollars priced from $300 to $1,000.**
There are many options in this price range. The 1881 dollar from the Philadelphia Mint is a $650 coin in MS-65. An 1879 P-mint is about $900 in that grade. You can buy all but the scarcest coins from the Carson City Mint and go down the list and find many great coins from a few hundred dollars and up.

These coins have the potential to rise in value by 50 percent. The momentum is there. Morgan dollars have always been popular with collectors and investors alike, and demand for them as collectibles is getting a powerful boost from the strong silver bullion market (over $30 an ounce as of February 2012). This may well continue, since silver, like gold, has been trending sharply higher.

In buying these coins, carefully examine Miss Liberty's cheek, which is a grade-sensitive area. Make sure it's free from nicks, flaws, scratches and other blemishes. Take the coin and tilt it under a pinpoint light source, and make sure it reflects light in a circular pattern. A truly original coin has light dancing on its surfaces. Morgan dollars are beautiful to look at, wonderful as investments, and surprisingly affordable to own.

3. 1955 doubled-die Lincoln cents graded Mint State-63 Red.

In 1955, popular music wasn't the only area of American life that was undergoing major change. Coin collecting, too, was beginning to rock and roll as millions of people with newfound leisure time on their hands began to immerse themselves in hobbies. Coin collecting was one of the principal beneficiaries of this cultural change—and in 1955, the U.S. Mint inadvertently gave this process a major boost by creating a new one-cent piece with a weird and very obvious error.

This coin is known to specialists as the "doubled-die" Lincoln cent. It's instantly recognizable even to novices, though, by the dramatic double images of the date and other features on the "heads" side (the reverse was not affected). This mint mistake came about because of misalignment in a process known as "hubbing" of dies at the Philadelphia Mint. A coin is produced by striking a *planchet*, or blank piece of metal, with two dies—one bearing the design for the head's side, or obverse, the other having the elements for the reverse. On each die, the design is in mirror image. A die, in turn, is produced by striking a piece of tempered steel with a hub—a harder piece of steel on which the design is positive, or exactly the way it will look on the finished coin. To sharpen the impression, workmen give each master die multiple blows with the hub. In rare instances, the hub and die become misaligned between blows—and when that happens, the die emerges with doubling of the images. That's what occurred in 1955.

The problem was discovered, but not before small but significant quantities of the misstruck cents—about 30,000, it's believed—had been mixed with normal coins. Inspectors decided to let the misstrikes go, rather than destroy the whole batch. Soon, the coins began turning up along the East Coast, especially in New England, and sharp-eyed collectors began to set them aside. Most were pulled from pocket change at a fairly early stage, but almost all did circulate at least to a modest extent. As a result, mint-state specimens are extremely elusive. At this writing, a fully red piece graded Mint State-63 might cost you $7,500. But this is a rare and coveted coin in a series that enjoys tremendous popularity with collectors. A few years from now, $7,500 may look, in retrospect, like a bargain.

4. Trade dollars graded Proof-64 or Proof-65.

After the Civil War, the U.S. government turned its attention abroad and sought to expand its trade with foreign nations. As part of this effort, Congress created a new silver coin called the Trade dollar. This coin was similar in size and appearance to the regular silver dollar, but contained a bit more silver. It was meant for use in the Orient, where merchants preferred to be paid with precious-metal coins.

The Trade dollar was a short-lived and essentially unsuccessful innovation: It remained in production for little more than a decade, from 1873 to 1885, and during the last seven years it was minted only in proof form, for sale at a premium to the public. However, it's a high-priced and highly prized collectible.

Trade dollars graded Proof-64 and Proof-65 are sleepers. Once again, there's a gap between the market prices in Proof-64 and Proof-65. As this is written, a Proof-64 example has a fair market retail value of $ 6,500, while a Proof-65 is worth $11,000.

Caution: Be careful in purchasing "raw" (or uncertified) proof Trade dollars. Many of these coins have been certified and encapsulated and then removed from their plastic holders because their owners felt the assigned grades were too low. You may be misled into grading such a coin optimistically and thus paying too much for it.

5. **Proof-64 Variety 3 Liberty Head double eagles (1877–1907).**
    The double eagle, or $20 gold piece, is the largest gold coin the U.S. Mint ever made for use in commerce. Each of these coins contains nearly one full ounce of gold, giving it a value of several hundred dollars just as metal. But many double eagles are much more than merely pieces of metal: They're beautiful, desirable collectibles that often command premiums of tens, or even hundreds, of thousands of dollars.

The double eagle made its first appearance in 1849, so it is, quite literally, a "Forty-Niner." It was, in fact, the California Gold Rush that gave rise to the issuance of this coin. It remained an important part of U.S. coinage for more than eighty years before being discontinued in 1933, at a time when Americans were mired in the Great Depression.

The first double eagle produced by the Mint is known as the Coronet or Liberty Head type because its design depicts a crowned figure of Liberty. This type, in turn, is divided into three different varieties because of small but important differences in the inscriptions. Double eagles minted from 1877 to 1907 are denoted as Variety 3 because they bear the inscription *IN GOD WE TRUST* and have the words *TWENTY DOLLARS* spelled out at the base of the reverse.

Very few proof double eagles were produced: In most years, the total proof mintage was less than one hundred. Proof-64 examples of the Variety

3 Liberty Head double eagle are almost unknown—yet they can be acquired for about $40,000 each. This sounds like a lot of money, and it is. But it's really quite a bargain—in fact, it's an absolutely phenomenal value—because these coins are so rare and so desirable. In Proof-65, the same coin would probably cost upwards of $75,000, and sometimes there's really little difference in the way the two coins look.

In buying proof double eagles, acquire only coins with cameo contrast—that is, a strong contrast between the devices (the raised portions of the design) and the fields (the flat background areas). Ideally, the devices should be frosted and the fields should have a lovely mirror-like sheen.

You can expect cameo proofs to cost a little more than regular ones; they generally sell for 10 to 15 percent, or even 20 percent, above the cost of their counterparts without the cameo contrast. But the difference in price is negligible compared with the increased value this eye-catching feature will impart to your spectacular coin.

Double eagles are very large coins with exceptional appeal to non-collectors. Never underestimate the importance of size as a selling point with such buyers. Investors are smitten with large, bold-looking coins—especially when they're made from gold or silver. That's why silver dollars are so popular with investors, and double eagles enjoy the same kind of popularity.

As the coin market expands and more and more noncollectors enter the field, interest in coins such as proof double eagles will almost surely grow by leaps and bounds. Many of these newcomers will have large sums of money to spend, and many will be drawn to big, beautiful coins made of gold and silver.

The Proof-64 Variety 3 Liberty double eagle is rare. Its aesthetic appeal is awesome. And it has a rock-solid collector base. Add up all these elements and what you have is a coin with almost unlimited potential. We may very well see this coin command a six-figure price tag in the not-too-distant future if the coin market expands as I expect it to.

6. **Proof-63 to Proof-66 "type" coins.**

Proof gold isn't the only proof coinage that makes my secret list. Gem proofs in other older series—Barber and Liberty Seated dimes, quarters and halves, for example—also have captivating beauty and attract attention interest in a bull market, and hold their values in a bear market. These coins are very strong collector coins, and as we see more of the newly

minted collectors progressing from modern coins into more established series, the spillover effect should be significant.

We have been seeing much more interest in proof-type coins in the Barber
and Liberty Seated series over the last several years. People realize that
these are great values and very underrated. Coins with minuscule proof
mintages are available in the $1,200 to $1,500 range. Some can even be had
for $500 to $600 if you go down to grades such as Proof-63. I recommend
these coins in grades from 63 to 66, but I suggest that you use your common
sense in buying the best value for the grade. If a Proof-66 is available for
$2,000, and its Proof-63 counterpart is priced at $1,750, I suggest you
stretch for the higher grade.

**7. Proof-66 nickel three-cent pieces, Shield nickels, and Liberty Head
nickels.**

Nickel coins never have enjoyed the same kind of respect as their gold
and silver cousins, but often they're rarer—and should be more valuable—
in very high grades and with very sharp strikes. Being a harder metal, nickel
doesn't yield crisp design details as readily as gold and silver when struck.
And nickel coins are more prone to environmental damage over long periods of time, so fewer survive in pristine levels of preservation.

Surviving populations of nineteenth-century nickel coins are quite small
in Proof-66, and at the height of the coin market's boom in 1989 some of
these coins were bringing many thousands of dollars. Today, those same
coins change hands for a great deal less. A coin that sold at auction for
$8,000 in 1989 might well be available now for $1,500. And it's still every
bit as rare.

Caution: Even though they may have been certified by one of the leading
grading services, Proof-66 three-cent nickels, Shield nickels, and Liberty
Head nickels should be free of carbon spots—that is, intense toning areas
which appear to be black. If a coin has any of these spots, you should reject
it, no matter how high the grade at which it has been certified.

8. 1909-S V.D.B. Lincoln head cent grading MS-65 Red.

This "king of Lincoln cents"—a perennial favorite with collectors of all
kinds—seems likely to enjoy an especially strong run for years to come.

Lincoln cents are spending lots of time in the limelight these days. In
one respect, all this attention is good: The U.S. Mint made four special
cents in 2009 to mark the bicentennial of Abraham Lincoln's birth and the

100th anniversary of the cent that bears his image. In another way, however, the publicity has been negative, focusing on the fact that rising metal prices have made the cost of producing cents more than a "penny" apiece. That has many Americans calling for a halt to further production.

No news may be good news, but this time just the opposite is true for the popular "S-V.D.B." All of the news—including the bad news regarding metal prices—is pumping up interest in putting together sets of Lincoln cents. And as the longtime centerpiece of the series, the 1909-S V.D.B. in Gem condition is drawing the greatest attention.

When I was a guest on NBC-TV's *Today Show*—ostensibly to discuss the chances that the cent might be discontinued, it turned out the subject everyone wanted to talk about was scarcer, more valuable Lincoln cents. I got to show the world's favorite U.S. coin: A 1909-S V.D.B. cent graded Mint State-65 Red by PCGS. NBC displayed close-ups of this coin, and I was later told that the segment had generated tremendous interest, with hundreds of e-mails pouring in.

I recommend the S-V.D.B. in all grades, but for this special list, the honor goes to the Gem MS-65 Red example. It's a wonderful coin to own—and with all the ongoing news about the Lincoln anniversary and possible discontinuation of the cent, it will remain in the limelight for years to come.

9. Franklin half dollars graded Proof-66 or Mint State-66 or higher.

For several years, knowledgeable coin market insiders, including some of the nation's leading dealers, have been quietly acquiring superbly toned Franklin half dollars in very high grades—Proof-66 or Mint State-66 and above.

You would think that if you went to a coin show and walked from table to table trying to find nice Franklin halves, they'd be plentiful. These are, after all, modern coins—coins produced as recently as 1963. And their mintage levels certainly weren't small by comparison with previous U.S. half dollars. Judging from their modest values in some of the price guides, you'd probably figure you ought to be able to find hundreds of these coins—maybe even buy them by the bag. You might expect to go up to Harry J. Forman, a highly regarded Philadelphia dealer who specializes in late-date U.S. coins, ask him for a roll of 1950 Franklin halves in Mint State-66, and have him produce not only a roll of 20 coins but a bag of 100 rolls.

This is one case, however, where even Harry Forman wouldn't be able to help you—for despite their seemingly plentiful mintage figures and despite what any price guides may say, high-grade Franklin halves are surprisingly scarce. And they're just not available in quantity.

It's true that the prices are modest. At this writing, a 1950 Franklin half dollar graded Mint State-66 by an independent grading service is priced at only about $700 sight-unseen. The problem is, hardly any 1950 halves are available in Mint State-66—at this price or even a higher price.

While insider dealers are aware of this situation and are seeking to benefit from it, collectors and investors as a whole haven't yet caught on. Thus, while the supply is low, the demand so far has also been relatively low. That has served to hold down the prices, at least on paper. Once additional people start looking for these coins and trying to obtain them, I look for the prices to rise dramatically. And since the present levels are so affordable, making these coins potentially attractive to such a broad spectrum of buyers, the price increase could be amazingly sharp.

I wouldn't be surprised to see high-grade Franklin halves that currently sell for $600 apiece soar in value to $1,500 each within a relatively short time. I wouldn't be at all surprised to see those 1950 halves in Mint State-66, now worth $600, skyrocket to the $2,000 range within the next ten years.

I don't expect this type of huge price increase to happen in the short term—within the next two years; I see it coming a little bit farther down the road. Therefore, if quick profit is your goal, you're probably better off buying something else. But if you can wait ten years, or even fifteen or twenty years, this is a great growth area.

10. Draped Bust dollars.

Silver dollars hold powerful appeal for investors. They're big, attractive coins with precious-metal content—assets that are quintessentially tangible. Early silver dollars, those produced in the nation's formative years, provide the added bonus of great rarity. Many of these coins had very low mintages, and the number of surviving examples is exceedingly small, especially in very high grades. Some are all but unknown even in the lowest Mint State levels.

Most of the very earliest U.S. silver dollars belong to a group known as the Draped Bust type. These coins bear a right-facing bust portrait of Miss Liberty with a garment draped over her shoulder, hence the name. The most famous of all U.S. silver dollars, the 1804, belongs to this group. Only fifteen specimens of this highly publicized rarity are known to exist, and all are accounted for as of this writing. One of them was sold at public auction in 1999 for $4,140,000, the highest price ever paid at auction up to that time for a single coin.

Unless you're a person of very substantial wealth, you probably can't expect to ever become the owner of an 1804 silver dollar. But the other Draped Bust dollars, from 1795 to 1803, are also highly desirable—and those can be obtained for significantly less than their world-renowned 1804 cousin.

None of these coins is cheap; all carry six-figure price tags in Mint State grades. But all have great potential to move up in value—perhaps to the seven-figure range—within the coming years as more and more institutional money enters the coin market. This is the type of coin that holds the greatest appeal for affluent members of the baby-boom generation, and the type that institutional investors will be seeking and acquiring with the greatest dedication.

Draped Bust dollars come with two different designs on the reverse. On the earliest examples, from 1795 to 1798, the reverse depicts a small eagle. In Mint State-67, one of these coins would cost more than $300,000 at the present time. From 1798 to the end of the series in 1804, the reverse portrayed a heraldic eagle.

The heraldic-eagle dollars from 1798 to 1803 strike me as particularly good investments at this time. The sight-unseen price is just $225,000 for a piece certified as Mint State-67 by one of the leading independent grading services, and you could probably get a super premium-quality specimen for not much more than $300,000. These are coins that may very well be trading for close to a million dollars a few years from now. Again, let me stress that you should buy only coins that are certified in these grades by one of the leading independent grading services.

These are very definitely not pocket-change rarities; they're about as far removed from that as anything in all of U.S. coinage. But they're coins that every collector dreams about owning someday—and coins that are dreams-come-true for a fortunate few.

Draped Bust dollars are exceedingly scarce even in the higher circulated grades. But specimens in Extremely Fine and Very Fine condition are findable treasures; Bust dollars in these grades are much more likely to turn up in your attic or cookie jar than a pristine Mint State example. You probably won't discover a Mint State piece unless it was purchased by someone in your family over the years.

If you do come across a Draped Bust dollar, don't sell it. These are coins with enormous investment potential and you should keep them.

11. Seated Liberty dollars graded AU-50 to AU-55.

Seated Liberty coins have always been special favorites of mine. They held sway in Americans' pocket change for more than half a century, from the late 1830s through the early 1890s, and they seem to me especially evocative of that period in U.S. history—one that saw a battle to the death between the North and South, a westward migration toward the nation's "manifest destiny," and the country's first tentative steps as a prime-time player on the international stage. These coins are distinctly nineteenth-century in appearance, and yet they embody a level of competence—in terms of both design and quality of production—not fully achieved on the nation's earliest coinage. Best of all, from a coin collector's standpoint, they include many issues that are scarce or even rare.

The Seated Liberty portrait appeared on five different U.S. coins, from the half cent through the silver dollar, but the dollar had by far the lowest mintages, typically below 100,000 and occasionally even below 10,000. The coin was produced on a regular annual basis from 1840 until it was discontinued in 1873, but it saw little use in circulation except in the West, where hard money enjoyed a special status.

In mint condition, Seated dollars can be very pricey. Their price tags are more reasonable, though, in grades just slightly lower. Circulated specimens certified in grades such as About Uncirculated-50 or AU-55 are available for just a few hundred dollars, and some of these possess even greater eye appeal than pieces that, while technically uncirculated, don't have much pizzazz. They're just as historic, with mintages just as low, and they're very attractive additions to any collection.

12. Common-date Barber silver coins in Mint State-64 or 65, or Proof-64 or 65.

The Barber silver coins, which replaced the Seated Liberty half dollar, quarter, and dime in 1892, brought continued uniformity to Americans' spending money. All three had the same design on the "head's" side, and the half dollar and quarter were virtually identical on the reverse as well. These are also known as Liberty Head coins, but many collectors today refer to them by the name of their designer, Mint chief sculptor-engraver Charles E. Barber.

The Barber coins had something else in common with their Seated Liberty predecessors: They wore well in circulation, remaining serviceable for decades. As evidence of this, they still could be found occasionally in circulation as late as the 1950s—some forty years after the Mint discontinued their production. People *did* use them for years and years, and the great majority ended up in well-worn condition. As a corollary of this, relatively few were preserved in mint condition, or even in the highest circulated grades. Unlike Morgan dollars, which saw only limited use, the Barber coins served the nation long and well in commerce, but collectors are paying the price for this today. You can expect to pay thousands of dollars for Barber coins in upper-level mint-state grades—MS-66 or higher—and in corresponding Proof grades. They're more reasonable, however, in the mid-level grades of MS-64 and 65 and Proof-64 and 65. You'll pay hundreds of dollars even for common-date examples, but they're worth it. These coins are genuinely scarce, and growing numbers of hobbyists are pursuing them. Remember, too, that proof Barber coins seldom were made in quantities exceeding 1,000.

Warning: The rare coin marketplace can be volatile. As this is written, all twelve coin types described in this chapter are excellent values. However, rapid changes in the marketplace could alter that situation; any or all of these coins may very well have experienced dramatic price increases (or decreases) by the time you read this. For that reason, you should check their prices carefully before making a purchase, and compare them to the prices listed here. In fact, you should do this before buying coins of any kind.

If any of these coins are selling for prices substantially higher than those listed here, use caution in considering their purchase. They may have already enjoyed the appreciation anticipated in this chapter, and thus may no longer be "sleepers." In that case, they will be removed from this special list in future editions of this book.

CHAPTER 9

THE DAZZLE OF GOLD,
THE SPARKLE OF SILVER

This stunning coin, produced by the U.S. Mint in 2009, is a replica of the Ultra High Relief 1907 double eagle, or $20 gold piece, designed by famed sculptor Augustus Saint-Gaudens. It was struck in limited numbers for sale to collectors as a premium, and strong demand has kept its resale value high. (Photo courtesy U.S. Mint)

Gold!

From time immemorial, that word has been a clarion call summoning mankind to pursue dreams of fortune embedded in shallow streams or buried beneath the surface of the earth.

Once recovered and refined, the metal has been fashioned into objects of consummate beauty and singular value—necklaces, bracelets, diadems, rings—and gloriously glittering coins. The first of those coins were minted more than 25 centuries ago in an Asia Minor kingdom known as Lydia. They were readily accepted as units of exchange by tradesmen who were limited prior to that time to the cumbersome practice of barter.

The gold in the earliest coins was mixed with silver in a natural amalgam known as *electrum*. Before long, however, ancient artisans learned how to separate the metals so that coins containing just gold or silver could be struck. Then as now, silver was perceived as precious and desirable in its own right but not as rare and valuable as gold.

Throughout the intervening centuries, gold in particular has played a prominent role in helping to determine the course of human events. It has triggered wars, sustained civilizations, decided which nations would survive and even thrive—and, unfailingly, fired up mankind's imagination. Silver, too, has changed the face of history. In 1193, for example, it literally was worth a king's ransom when England paid the enormous sum of 150,000 silver Cologne marks to secure the release of Richard the Lionheart after he was captured by an Austrian duke while returning home from the Third Crusade. The ransom—three tons of silver—represented three years' income for the British Crown. Several centuries later, the discovery of gold and silver in the Americas accelerated the New World's development by European powers.

GOLD'S HISTORIC ROLE

Gold's chief function is to serve as a store of value, and it has fulfilled that purpose exceedingly well for more than 5,000 years. There have been numerous experiments with fiat currency over the centuries and they have all failed. Right now, as we look around the world, we see nothing but fiat currencies, without any backing from precious metals—and it's only a question of time until they, too, will fail. The last man standing will be gold.

If we just go back to the creation of the Federal Reserve in December 1913, the dollar has lost from 95 to 98 percent of its value and purchasing power during the last century. One of the mandates of the Fed was to preserve the value of the dollar, so it's been a dismal failure in that regard. In 1913, the official value of gold was fixed at $20.67 an ounce. Since then, its value has risen to about 80 times that amount, and pretty much matches the 1913 value of the dollar, before that 95 to 98 percent loss of value—so gold, unlike the dollar, has preserved the purchasing power it enjoyed 100 years ago.

Going back 5,000 years, the big picture has been the same. You can point to specific periods when gold lagged a bit for 25 or 50 years or possibly even a century. You can make a case, for instance, that from 1980 to 2000, gold didn't provide protection against loss of purchasing power because during those 20 years, its value fell from over $800 to less than $250. It's unfair to pick your starting and ending points like that. It's undeniable, though, that from the year 2000 until now, gold has certainly made up for the previous 20 years' lack of performance.

Gold's value is based partly on its beauty, partly on its indestructibility, partly on its malleability—and mostly on its rarity. It is generally accepted that over the entire span of human history, only about 170,000 tons of gold have been mined. That comes to about 5.5 billion ounces. With the world's population currently totaling about 7 billion, that comes to less than four-fifths of an ounce for every individual on the planet. And that doesn't take into account the millions of ounces that have been lost through the centuries in shipwrecks and other disasters. The new mine production, or flow rate, is roughly 75 to 80 million ounces per year—so the world's gold supply is rising at the rate of only 1.5 percent a year.

INSURANCE OR INVESTMENT?

Should gold be viewed as insurance or an investment?

Each case is different, and every individual's approach will be guided by his or her financial situation. First and foremost, though, gold should be regarded as insurance—a time-tested form of financial protection against unforeseen setbacks in other assets' value. It's insurance against losses sustained because of government gone wrong.

The value of this insurance has been all too apparent during the economic crisis that has gripped the nation—and, indeed, the world—in recent years. Just as the recession was beginning, gold finished 2007 at $636 an ounce. From that point, it started a long, relentless climb that took it within hailing distance of $2,000 an ounce. On Aug. 22, 2011, it soared to an all-time high of $1,908— exactly three times its 2007 close. The price receded thereafter, but was still above $1,600 well into 2012.

From a low of $248 an ounce at the start of the twenty-first century, gold has seen an increase of more than 500 percent. During the same time, the stock market, NASDAQ and the housing market all have suffered major losses—and all are struggling even now to climb out of the deep hole in which they find themselves.

Gold has been a wonderful investment for those who acquired it before and during its steep ascent. That is still the case for people who buy it today. Above all, however, it has served as an invaluable insurance policy for those farsighted— and fortunate enough—to be holding it. And that's the way the average gold buyer should regard it. It's always good insurance, and at times it can be an excellent investment as well.

Like anything else, gold rises in value at times and goes down in value at other times. When the trend is up, you should be a buyer if you're looking at gold as an investment. When the primary long-term trend is down, your investment position should be reduced or eliminated. The important thing is to retain your insurance position. You should own gold—and silver, too—as insurance to offset possible losses in your other financial assets. If you can afford to buy more, and choose to do so for profit-making purposes, precious metals can be a great investment at times—as I believe they are right now.

GOLD, AMERICAN-STYLE

It can be argued that dollars should be priced in terms of their value as gold, rather than the other way around. The Founding Fathers embraced that view, though they broadened it to include silver as well. The Coinage Act of 1792, which created the U.S. monetary system, defined the dollar as 371.25 grains of pure silver or 24.75 grains of pure gold. Thus, the nation entered the world with a bimetallic system of currency with a fixed 15-to-1 exchange rate between silver and gold. In other words, 15 ounces of silver were equivalent to one ounce of gold—and the monetary system was based on both.

The American Eagle gold bullion coin, issued annually since 1986, is sold to collectors in a proof version priced substantially higher than the value of the bullion it contains. Its obverse design is based on that of the Saint-Gaudens double eagle. Its reverse depicts a family of eagles. (Photo courtesy U.S. Mint)

This system effectively ended in 1853, when the silver content of most U.S. coins was reduced and gold became the primary underpinning of the nation's monetary system. The demise of bimetallism was confirmed legislatively in 1873. And in 1900, the nation formally adopted the gold standard, tying the dollar officially to a designated market value of gold. Just a third of a century later, in 1933, the government not only abandoned the gold standard but ordered U.S. citizens to abandon virtually all of the gold in their possession (except for coins of numismatic value and up to $100 in ordinary gold pieces deemed to have no special value as collectors' items). These steps were part of the radical recovery plan initiated by newly elected President Franklin D. Roosevelt as he sought to jolt the prostrate U.S. economy out of the worst crisis in its history. Roosevelt saw the need for fundamental changes in the nation's fiscal policies, and feared that private hoards of gold could have an adverse impact on these policies.

Soon after buying up private citizens' gold at the then-official rate of $20.67 an ounce, the government raised the rate to $35 an ounce—pocketing a healthy profit in the process on the gold that had just been "surrendered" (some would say "confiscated"). That rate remained in effect until 1971, when President Richard Nixon allowed the price of gold to float—which it did, in an upward direction. Since 1971, there has been no official link between the U.S. monetary system and either gold or silver.

GOLD AND THE NATIONAL DEBT

In practical terms, there's no way the nation could return to a 100-percent gold standard, where the currency issued by the government is backed by gold of equivalent value. If the government issued $15 trillion worth of currency, an amount roughly equal to the current national debt, there would have to be $15 trillion worth of gold in the Treasury to back that enormous sum—and right now there's less than half a trillion dollars' worth of gold in Fort Knox. Rarely have we had 100-percent backing of our currency by gold. We need a stable currency, and we haven't had one in decades. That's the reason for the problems that beset us today.

Another point to remember is that while the national debt was reported to be $15.1 trillion at the end of 2011, that figure did not include the debt obligations of Fannie Mae and Freddie Mac, which own or guarantee the great majority of the housing loans in the United States. That debt totaled about $5 trillion—so the national debt was really $20 trillion at the time. Beyond that, the federal government also is responsible for $120 trillion in unfunded liabilities, including future benefits for Social Security, Medicare, and Medicaid.

The United States claims to own 261 million ounces of gold, but some observers are dubious of that figure—and even if they accept it, they question the fineness of the gold. Is it 24-karat (.9999)? Is it .900? If we accept that the gold is there, and multiply the 261 million ounces by today's gold price, we come up with a current market value of about $410 billion. That's only about 2 percent of the national debt and an even smaller percentage of the nation's unfunded liabilities—a fraction of about 1 over 300. Put another way, for every dollar of gold we have, we owe more than $300. To me, that's unsustainable;

we can get away with it for a while, but if we keep kicking the can down the road, sooner or later the pavement will end. That's a powerful argument for individual Americans to acquire gold today and keep it as a lifeboat in some future economic storm that dwarfs what we've experienced in recent years.

Over the years, gold has been perceived at various times as a commodity, a currency—and sometimes both. Actually, it is the *ultimate* currency, even when it is treated more as a commodity. At times it has been officially embraced as a currency and at other times it hasn't. It hasn't been considered a currency by the U.S. government domestically since 1934 and internationally since 1971, when the gold window was closed by President Nixon.

BACK IN PRIVATE HANDS

More than four decades would pass before Americans regained the right to buy, sell and own gold bullion, coins and other items deemed to be primarily forms of bulk gold, rather than collectible objects. That right was restored on Dec. 31, 1974, after critics persuaded Congress and President Gerald Ford that the actions taken in 1933 had outlived their usefulness—if, indeed, they were justified and legitimate in the first place.

Far from releasing pent-up demand and sparking a modern "gold rush" by liberated buyers exploring new investment opportunities, the lifting of restrictions on privately owning gold left many Americans confused and uncertain whether—or how—to act upon the options now available to them. After 40 years in the wilderness, much of the populace had lost its institutional memory of gold ownership and looked upon the just-opened door not as the gateway to a bright promised land, but rather as the portal to a marketplace fraught with risk. As a consequence, demand for gold was relatively modest at the start, and its price never rose above $195 an ounce until the middle of 1978, when it began a steady ascent that would peak at $887.50 in January 1980. Meanwhile, silver was also on the move, rising from the low single digits to $11 an ounce in November 1979—then surging to $50 two months later.

Precious metals' rocket ride was followed by a sudden plunge to earth. Overnight, gold and silver both lost much of the value they had gained—and when the dust settled, both were worth a fraction of what they had brought at the market's top. For the next two decades, stagnation was the norm for both metals, with occasional upticks soon giving way to prolonged inactive periods. As the twenty-first century opened, gold was trading for just $248 an ounce and silver for only $4.60. Both trended upward for five years thereafter—then, in

2006, they began moving higher more sharply. The economic crisis that started in late 2007 intensified demand for precious metals, and gold and silver's market value picked up still more momentum. By 2011, gold had topped $1,900 an ounce and silver had tested its 1980 high of $50—though both underwent corrections thereafter and ended the year somewhat lower.

BULLISH ON BULLION

Americans today are far more aware of the asset protection and investment potential of gold—and, to a lesser extent, silver—than their parents and grandparents were in the mid-1970s. That's obvious from the strong and growing demand for coins and other objects made of precious metals. The surprising thing is that it took them so long to grasp these advantages fully and add greater quantities of both gold and silver to their rainy-day funds and investment portfolios. Gold, after all, has been humankind's most coveted store of value for thousands of years, and silver has been esteemed and desired just as long.

Donald J. Trump (left), president and chairman of the Trump Organization, accepts a commercial rent security deposit for 40 Wall Street in the form of gold bars from bullion dealer and tenant Michael R. Haynes. (Photo courtesy Michael R. Haynes)

Critics warn prospective buyers of the metals' volatility and point to what happened during the 1980s as evidence that their value can go down as quickly—and sharply—as it goes up, and stay low for protracted periods of time. They also note that investments in precious metals earn no interest, although that's not a very persuasive argument at a time when certificates of deposit, savings accounts and other traditional wealth-preserving vehicles earn little more. But the length and severity of the economic slump in recent years have exposed the basic weakness of paper dollars and made it crystal clear that the bullion market's staying power is far greater now than it was 30 years ago.

Of course, the value of gold transcends 30-year cycles and has to be viewed through the prism of centuries, not decades. Gold has been the ultimate money, and ultimate wealth, throughout recorded history. When people distrust their government and their currency, they turn to gold. That's what we're seeing today: People's confidence in the dollar has eroded, and they're turning to gold and silver as safe havens that will preserve their wealth and serve as money, if need be, should the government's paper currency and base-metal coins continue to lose their already diminished buying power.

THE SCOTT TRAVERS 5-STEP PLAN FOR MANAGING GOLD, SILVER, AND YOUR FINANCES

Gold and silver in physical form should be held as a solid form of protection against financial loss—even financial disaster—in the perilous economy confronting us today. Before doing so, though, it would be prudent to map a plan for minimizing the risks and maximizing the potential rewards.

The Silver American Eagle contains one ounce of silver. Like the Gold Eagle, it's available both as a business-strike bullion coin and in a proof version, like the one shown here, offered to collectors at a premium. Its obverse bears the same design as the much-admired Walking Liberty half dollar. Its reverse features a heraldic eagle. (Photo courtesy U.S. Mint)

Here's my 5-point plan for achieving these objectives:

• Acquire enough gold and silver to cover the financial needs that you would face if your other assets lost significant value. Look at precious metals as a form of insurance for those assets—much as you routinely purchase accident insurance when you buy a car.

- Limit your discretionary spending for luxuries and other non-essential purchases and preserve as much cash as you can.

- Reduce or eliminate as much consumer debt as you can. Don't get in over your head.

- Consider acquiring other hard assets, such as rare coins, because historically these have yielded excellent returns during times of high inflation and the kind of rising gold price trend I see in the future.

- Understand that at some point, gold may become a bubble.

When I refer to a "bubble" in gold, I am referring to the period during which a euphoric bull market turns into an irrational, out-of-control mania where there are no underlying fundamentals supporting the increase, other than emotion and momentum. At some point, every bull market comes to an end. At this point, however, I don't see such a bubble developing for gold and other precious metals in the foreseeable future, as gold in 2012, as this is written, is still substantially underheld. This assessment is based on historical precedent. We've seen a number of bubbles burst in recent years, including the housing bubble and, before that, the dot-com bubble in technology stocks. Overextension and wild speculation were evident on those occasions. Similar conditions aren't apparent today in the gold market. We've actually seen a relatively quiet bull market. Fewer than 1 percent of adult Americans have gold or silver bullion in their possession, and less than 1 percent of global financial assets are in gold. Those figures don't add up to a bubble.

IF IT'S NOT IN YOUR POSSESSION, YOU DON'T OWN IT

There are a number of cutting-edge ways to purchase gold and silver in today's fast-paced marketplace. Shares of mining stock and Exchange Traded Funds (ETFs) are two important options. There's no good substitute, however, for the old-fashioned way: physical possession of the metal. There's something reassuring about holding gold or silver in your hand, feeling the substantial heft and admiring the rich glitter that has mesmerized monarchs and commoners alike throughout history. More importantly, mining stocks and ETFs are paper investments, and can carry significant risk—certainly far more so than buying physical gold or silver. You don't actually hold the precious metal represented by these paper financial instruments. What you own is a *claim* on that metal—and that's an important distinction. In a real global financial emergency, a claim on a metal could be difficult, if not impossible, to redeem.

A mining stock can be a very sound investment if the price of gold or silver goes up, since the value of the stock is leveraged to the price of the ore a mine produces. Still, it is also subject to gain or loss determined by the ability and success of the mine's management. The fortunes of a mine—and the value of its stock—could well decline even if the market price of gold or silver increased. Thus, it's much riskier than owning the actual metal, since it relies on the complexities of a company.

A prospectus offers shares in a gold Exchange Traded Fund (ETF). ETFs enable investors to purchase a stake in gold or silver without taking physical possession of the metal.

ETFs are short-term investments. Do not take a heavy position in gold ETFs over any extended period. Typically, when you buy shares in a gold or silver ETF, you "own" an undivided interest in the ounces of gold or ounces of silver held by the fund. The actual metal is stored by a custodian, usually a large bank, but all you really own is a paper representation showing how much of that metal constitutes your share. The value of each share is eroded over time, partly because the fund must sell part of the metal periodically to pay for its expenses. Some of the ETFs hold "unallocated" gold or silver, meaning that the ETF holds a promise from someone else to deliver the physical gold or silver as opposed to holding "allocated" gold or silver that is physically present, in the vaults, at all times. So there is some concern about whether all of the gold or silver purportedly held by ETFs could be delivered physically if there was a squeeze on physical deliveries.

COINS OR BULLION?

Gold and silver can be purchased in a variety of forms—bars, ingots, coins and jewelry, to name some of the most common. For investment purposes, bullion and coins make the most sense for buyers with limited budgets, since these normally offer the most precious metal per dollar spent. Jewelry, by contrast, usually requires a greater percentage outlay for fabrication. Bars and ingots are considered forms of bullion, but coins can be either bullion-related or numismatic.

"Bullion coins" are coins whose price is tied at any given time directly to the value of the metal they contain. This category includes gold and silver American Eagles, gold American Buffalos, gold and silver Canadian Maple Leafs and gold South African Krugerrands, to cite a few of the coins with the highest sales internationally. The prices of these coins include the value of their bullion content plus small premiums—generally well under 10 percent—to cover the costs of manufacturing, handling, and distribution. The premium is greater, percentagewise, for smaller bullion coins because it generally requires the same amount of manufacturing cost to make, for example, a half ounce coin as it does to make a one ounce coin and accordingly, the same manufacturing cost is allocated to a half ounce, in the case of the smaller bullion coin, as to a one ounce coin. Bullion coins rise or fall in value directly in response to market fluctuations in the price of the metal they contain.

Best-selling U.S. bullion coins include:

- Gold American Eagles ("Gold Eagles," for short), which contain .900-fine gold and come in a basic one-ounce size and three fractional sizes with one-half, one-quarter and one-tenth of an ounce of gold. Their obverse ("heads") design is based on the obverse of the majestic Saint-Gaudens $20 gold piece of 1907–1933.

- Gold American Buffalos, which contain one ounce of .9999-fine (24-karat) gold and bear a design based upon that of the popular Buffalo nickel of 1913–1938.

- Silver American Eagles ("Silver Eagles," for short), which contain one ounce of .999-fine silver and carry the same obverse design as the Liberty Walking half dollar of 1916–1947.

American Eagles offer U.S. citizens a very important advantage over bullion coins produced by other nations. Unlike those foreign competitors, they can be included in Individual Retirement Accounts, enabling Americans who buy and hold these coins to do so tax-free until they reach retirement age. This can represent a significant savings.

This 1913 Saint-Gaudens double eagle was certified as Mint State-65 by the Professional Coin Grading Service, confirming its status as a desirable uncirculated specimen. Its grade is the midpoint of the 60-to-70 range for mint-state coins. (Photo courtesy PCGS)

"Numismatic coins" are coins with added worth—beyond their metal value—as collectibles. A numismatic gold coin can be worth far more as a collector's item than as just a piece of precious metal. This premium is based upon rarity, condition and demand. Numismatic U.S. coins include precious-metal coins such as Saint-Gaudens and Liberty Head double eagles ($20 gold pieces) and Morgan silver dollars. But they also include many base-metal issues, such as large cents and Buffalo nickels. Despite their low intrinsic value, some base-metal coins have changed hands for millions of dollars as collectibles. Various examples of the rare 1913 Liberty Head nickel have brought seven-figure prices in recent years, and a 1793 Chain cent recently brought nearly $1.4 million at auction.

The 1-ounce American Buffalo proof bullion coin, first issued in 2006, is the first U.S. coin made of .9999-fine (24-karat) gold. Its design is based on that of the beloved Buffalo nickel. (Photo courtesy U.S. Mint)

Because of the overwhelming emphasis on the high market value of gold and silver bullion during the last few years, the added premium traditionally enjoyed by numismatic coins containing these metals has shrunk considerably in many cases. This is especially true of common-date $20 gold pieces, which contain just under an ounce of gold. In the past, these coins were worth hundreds of dollars more than one-ounce American Eagles in lower uncirculated grades such as Mint State-63. In 2011, however, that bonus value all but disappeared. In fact, there were occasions when the bullion coins were selling for more than their numismatic cousins. This is an anomaly; fully expect the numismatic premium to re-establish itself once we see greater normalcy in the marketplace.

THE IMPACT OF INFLATION

Inflation increases demand for gold, because it causes people to seek ways to protect their assets from losing value. Even in the absence of actual inflation, the same effect can often be produced by fear—or expectation—that inflation could be just around the corner. That is happening now. Inflation has been very low during recent years, but more and more people have been growing apprehensive that it could return soon and cause even greater problems for the economy. That's one reason for the continuing strength of precious metals—especially gold. People see gold as a safeguard against the inroads of inflation, a time-tested way to offset erosion of more traditional assets—and even, in worst-case scenarios, a reliable source of sustenance in meeting everyday needs.

Inflation is inevitable if politicians continue to spend too much money and the government pays its bills by printing more. Without much fanfare, inflation was already creeping back into the marketplace as 2011 came to a close. If this stirring becomes an all-out trend, it will further diminish Americans' already reduced confidence in paper money and traditional financial assets and stoke the fire even higher under unconventional assets—notably precious metals.

A possible preview of things to come can be viewed right now in India and China. During 2011, inflation hit 9 percent in India and 6 percent in China. The result has been greatly increased demand for gold—especially in China, where the government removed a ban on personal gold ownership in 2002 and clamor for the metal has grown ever more feverish since the tail-off of an economic boom.

HOW HIGH THE MOON?

The economic circumstances in 2012 as this is written are actually much worse than they were in the 1970s, in the lead-up to the last big boom in gold and silver. Back then, the United States was generally in good financial shape. Our debt position was quite manageable—just the opposite of where we are today. Even in 1980, with gold up to $887.50, the national debt was only about $845 billion. Since that time, gold has nearly doubled in price, but the debt has gone up nearly 20 times and the nation's money supply has gone up at least 10 times. Gold's potential is much higher today.

How high? Maurice H. Rosen, an astute and prize-winning market analyst, is on record as predicting that by 2020, gold will be selling for between $5,000 and $10,000 an ounce, and I agree with him. He has further stated that if this forecast is wrong, it will be because he set the bar too low—that is to say, because the price is much higher than $10,000 by 2020 or it reaches $10,000 even sooner.

Rosen sees silver doing even better, percentagewise. Noting that gold has been selling for roughly 54 times as much as gold, he sees that ratio narrowing to perhaps 25 to 1 by 2020. Thus, if gold were worth $10,000 an ounce, silver would then be worth $400 an ounce.

Gold and silver have never glowed as brightly as they do in the otherwise dark economic world of the twenty-first century. And their dazzle and sparkle will help many prudent Americans see even brighter light at the end of the tunnel.

It's not a case of "Time will tell." For thousands of years, time has already told.

PRECIOUS METALS AND RARE COINS: SIMILARITIES AND DIFFERENCES

Bullion coins contain a relatively high amount of precious metal. Rare coins often contain little or none. Bullion coins' value comes from the metal itself. These coins are purely an investment in precious metal. Rare coins derive their value from collector demand—and this demand, in turn, stems from such factors as the coins' design and date. Rare coins can be partly a bullion investment, but they're mainly an investment in collector taste.

With bullion coins, the margin is very small between a dealer's bid and ask prices; with rare coins, the margin is much higher. The margin is the spread between what a dealer will pay for a coin and what he'll sell it for. With bullion coins, this spread may be only 3 or 4 percent, and sometimes even less. With rare coins, a spread of 15 or 20 percent is quite routine.

Bullion coins are standardized, and it isn't important to grade them; rare coins aren't standardized, and subtle differences between two similar coins can translate into a major variation in value. With bullion coins, you can buy ten, fifteen, or twenty pieces and they'll all be the same; you won't need a magnifying glass to inspect them. That's not true with rare coins. Even if a rare coin comes in a holder from a leading grading service, with an insert tab indicating its grade, that doesn't mean the coin is exactly the same as another coin in the same kind of holder with the same grade written on its tab. It also doesn't mean that the coin won't be graded differently if it is submitted again to the same service.

Bullion and bullion coins are subject to government regulation, but at present, collector coins are not. Any time a person buys or sells bullion coins, the dealer has to fill out a Form 1099-B naming that person. A person buying or selling collector coins is entering into a relatively private transaction, as this book is written. The exception to this is the record-keeping requirements associated with the Patriot Act. Ask your gold coin dealer for details.

Bullion enjoys a much wider market than rare coins; the rare coin market is composed of thinly capitalized entrepreneurs. The market for gold is global and ranks among the world's most fully developed. It's also the most liquid of all the commodity markets. The rare coin marketplace is dramatically smaller. A few big investment firms tested the waters—Kidder, Peabody and Merrill Lynch, among them. But at this writing, the rare coin industry doesn't yet enjoy the full participation of companies such as this.

COIN SPECIFICATIONS

HALF CENTS

Diameter: 23.5 millimeters ($\frac{15}{16}$ of an inch)

Weight: 6.739 grams (0.238 ounce) in 1793–94 and part of 1795, 5.443 grams (0.192 ounce) thereafter

Composition: All-copper

Edge: Lettered (TWO HUNDRED FOR A DOLLAR) in 1793 and part of 1797, gripped in part of 1797, plain in all other cases

Designers: Henry Voight (1793), Robert Scot (1794–1808), John Reich (1809–1836), Christian Gobrecht (1840–1857)

LARGE CENTS

Diameter: 25–28 millimeters (about $1\frac{1}{16}$ inches) in 1793, 27–30 millimeters (about $1\frac{1}{8}$ inches) in 1794, 28–29 millimeters (about $1\frac{1}{8}$ inches) thereafter

Weight: 13.478 grams (0.475 ounce) in 1793, 1794, and part of 1795, 10.886 grams (0.384 ounce) thereafter

Composition: All-copper

Edge: Vine and bars in part of 1793, lettered (ONE HUNDRED FOR A DOLLAR) in 1793–1794 and part of 1795, gripped in part of 1797, plain in all other cases

Designers: Henry Voight (1793 Chain and Wreath cents), Joseph Wright, Robert Scot, and John Smith Gardner (1793–1796 Liberty Cap), Robert Scot (1796–1807), John Reich (1808–1814), John Reich (1816–1835), Christian Gobrecht (1835–1857)

FLYING EAGLE CENTS

Diameter: 19 millimeters ($\frac{3}{4}$ of an inch)

Weight: 4.666 grams (0.165 ounce)

Composition: 88 percent copper, 12 percent nickel

Edge: Plain

Designer: James B. Longacre

INDIAN HEAD CENTS

Diameter: 19 millimeters ($\frac{3}{4}$ of an inch)

Weight: 4.666 grams (0.165 ounce) from 1859 to 1863 and part of 1864, 3.110 grams (0.110 ounce) in the rest of 1864 and thereafter

Composition: 88 percent copper, 12 percent nickel from 1859 to 1863 and part of 1864; 95 percent copper, 5 percent zinc and tin in the rest of 1864 and thereafter

Edge: Plain

Designer: James B. Longacre

LINCOLN CENTS

Diameter: 19 millimeters (¾ of an inch)
Weight: 3.110 grams (0.110 ounce) from 1909 to 1981 and part of 1982, except for 1943; 2.689 grams (0.095 ounce) in 1943; 2.5 grams (0.088 ounce) for part of 1982 and thereafter
Composition: 95 percent copper, 5 percent zinc and tin from 1909 to 1961 and part of 1962, except for 1943–1946; zinc-plated steel in 1943; 95 percent copper, 5 percent zinc in 1944–1946, 1963–1981 and parts of 1962 and 1982; 97.5 percent zinc, 2.5 percent copper (copper-plated zinc) for part of 1982 and thereafter
Edge: Plain
Designers: Victor D. Brenner (obverse from 1909 to date and reverse from 1909 to 1958), Frank Gasparro (reverse from 1959 to date)

TWO-CENT PIECES

Diameter: 23 millimeters (%₀ of an inch)
Weight: 6.221 grams (0.219 ounce)
Composition: 95 percent copper, 5 percent zinc and tin
Edge: Plain
Designer: James B. Longacre

SILVER THREE-CENT PIECES

Diameter: 14 millimeters (%₆ of an inch)
Weight: 0.802 grams (0.026 ounce) from 1851–1853, 0.746 grams (0.024 ounce) thereafter
Composition: 75 percent silver, 25 percent copper from 1851–1853; 90 percent silver, 10 percent copper thereafter
Edge: Plain
Designer: James B. Longacre

NICKEL THREE-CENT PIECES

Diameter: 17.9 millimeters (%₀ of an inch)
Weight: 1.944 grams (0.069 ounce)
Composition: 75 percent copper, 25 percent nickel
Edge: Plain
Designer: James B. Longacre

HALF DIMES

Diameter: 16.5 millimeters (about ⅝ of an inch) from 1792 to 1805, 15.5 millimeters (%₀ of an inch) thereafter
Weight: 1.348 grams (0.0434 ounce) from 1792 to 1836, 1.336 grams (0.04295 ounce) from 1837 to part of 1853, 1.244 grams (0.040 ounce) for part of 1853 and thereafter
Composition: 89.25 percent silver, 10.75 percent copper for 1792; 90 percent silver and 10 percent copper for 1794 and part of 1795; 89.25 percent silver, 10.75 percent copper for part of 1795 through 1836; 90 percent silver and 10 percent copper for 1837 and thereafter
Edge: Reeded
Designers: William Russell Birch (1792), Robert Scot (1794–1805)

SHIELD NICKELS

Diameter: 20.5 millimeters (¹³⁄₁₆ of an inch)
Weight: 5 grams (0.176 ounce)

Composition: 75 percent copper, 25 percent nickel
Edge: Plain
Designer: James B. Longacre

LIBERTY HEAD NICKELS

Diameter: 21.2 millimeters (⅚ of an inch)
Weight: 5 grams (0.176 ounce)
Composition: 75 percent copper, 25 percent nickel
Edge: Plain
Designer: Charles E. Barber

"BUFFALO" NICKELS

Diameter: 21.2 millimeters (⅚ of an inch)
Weight: 5 grams (0.176 ounce)
Composition: 75 percent copper, 25 percent nickel
Edge: Plain
Designer: James E. Fraser

JEFFERSON NICKELS

Diameter: 21.2 millimeters (⅚ of an inch)
Weight: 5 grams (0.176 ounce)
Composition: 75 percent copper, 25 percent nickel except for 1943–1945 and part of 1942; 56 percent copper, 35 percent silver and 9 percent manganese during those years
Edge: Plain
Designer: Felix Schlag

DRAPED BUST DIMES

Diameter: About 19 millimeters (²⁵⁄₃₂ of an inch)
Weight: 2.696 grams (0.087 ounce)
Composition: 89.25 percent silver, 10.75 percent copper
Edge: Reeded
Designer: Robert Scot

CAPPED BUST DIMES

Diameter: About 18.8 millimeters (¾ of an inch) from 1809 to 1827 and part of 1828; 18.5 millimeters (⁷⁄₁₀ of an inch) for part of 1828 and thereafter
Weight: 2.696 grams (0.087 ounce) from 1809 through 1836 and 2.673 grams (0.086 ounce) for 1837
Composition: 89.25 percent silver, 10.75 percent copper for 1809 to 1836; 90 percent silver and 10 percent copper for 1837 and 1838
Edge: Reeded
Designer: John Reich

SEATED LIBERTY DIMES

Diameter: 17.9 millimeters (⁷⁄₁₀ of an inch)
Weight: 2.673 grams (0.086 ounce) from 1837 to 1852 and part of 1853; 2.488 grams (0.080 ounce) for parts of 1853 and 1873 and from 1854 to 1872; 2.50 grams (0.084 ounce) from 1874 to 1891

Composition: 90 percent silver, 10 percent copper
Edge: Reeded
Designer: Christian Gobrecht

BARBER DIMES

Diameter: 17.9 millimeters (⁷⁄₁₀ of an inch)
Weight: 2.50 grams (0.084 ounce)
Composition: 90 percent silver, 10 percent copper
Edge: Reeded
Designer: Charles E. Barber

"MERCURY" DIMES

Diameter: 17.9 millimeters (⁷⁄₁₀ of an inch)
Weight: 2.50 grams (0.084 ounce)
Composition: 90 percent silver, 10 percent copper
Edge: Reeded
Designer: Adolph A. Weinman

ROOSEVELT DIMES

Diameter: 17.9 millimeters (⁷⁄₁₀ of an inch)
Weight: 2.50 grams (0.084 ounce) from 1946 to 1964, 2.27 grams (0.080 ounce) from 1965 to date
Composition: 90 percent silver, 10 percent copper from 1946 to 1964; 75-percent-copper, 25-percent-nickel alloy bonded to pure copper core thereafter
Edge: Reeded
Designer: John R. Sinnock

TWENTY-CENT PIECES

Diameter: 22 millimeters (⅞ of an inch)
Weight: 5 grams (0.161 ounce)
Composition: 90 percent silver, 10 percent copper
Edge: Plain
Designer: William Barber

DRAPED BUST QUARTER DOLLARS

Diameter: About 27.5 millimeters (1½ inches)
Weight: 6.739 grams (0.217 ounce)
Composition: 89.25 percent silver, 10.75 percent copper
Edge: Reeded
Designer: Robert Scot

CAPPED BUST QUARTER DOLLARS

Diameter: 27 millimeters (1¼ inches) from 1815 to 1828, 24.3 millimeters (¹⁹⁄₂₀ of an inch) from 1831 to 1838
Weight: 6.739 grams (0.217 ounce) from 1815 through 1836 and 6.68 grams (0.215 ounce) for 1837 and 1838
Composition: 89.25 percent silver, 10.75 percent copper for 1815 to 1836; 90 percent silver and 10 percent copper for 1837 through 1838
Edge: Reeded
Designer: John Reich

SEATED LIBERTY QUARTER DOLLARS

Diameter: 24.3 millimeters (¹⁹⁄₂₀ of an inch)
Weight: 6.68 grams (0.215 ounce) from 1838 to 1852 and part of 1853; 6.221 grams (0.2 ounce) from 1854 to 1872 and part of 1873; 6.25 grams (0.201 ounce) in part of 1873 and from 1874 to 1891
Composition: 90 percent silver, 10 percent copper
Edge: Reeded
Designer: Christian Gobrecht

BARBER QUARTER DOLLARS

Diameter: 24.3 millimeters (¹⁹⁄₂₀ of an inch)
Weight: 6.25 grams (0.201 ounce)
Composition: 90 percent silver, 10 percent copper
Edge: Reeded
Designer: Charles E. Barber

STANDING LIBERTY QUARTER DOLLARS

Diameter: 24.3 millimeters (¹⁹⁄₂₀ of an inch)
Weight: 6.25 grams (0.201 ounce)
Composition: 90 percent silver, 10 percent copper
Edge: Reeded
Designer: Hermon A. MacNeil

WASHINGTON QUARTER DOLLARS

Diameter: 24.3 millimeters (¹⁹⁄₂₀ of an inch)
Weight: 6.25 grams (0.201 ounce) from 1932 to 1964; 5.670 grams (0.200 ounce) from 1965 to date
Composition: 90 percent silver, 10 percent copper from 1932 to 1964; 75-percent-copper, 25-percent-nickel alloy bonded to pure copper core thereafter
Edge: Reeded
Designer: John Flanagan
Note: The State quarter dollars have the same specifications (except for the designer) as the Washington quarters of 1965–1998

FLOWING HAIR HALF DOLLARS

Diameter: About 32.5 millimeters (1⁵⁄₃₂ of an inch)
Weight: 13.48 grams (0.433 ounce)
Composition: 90 percent silver and 10 percent copper for 1794 and 1795
Edge: Lettered (FIFTY CENTS OR HALF A DOLLAR)
Designer: Robert Scot

DRAPED BUST HALF DOLLARS

Diameter: 32.5 millimeters (1⁵⁄₃₂ of an inch)
Weight: 13.48 grams (0.433 ounce)
Composition: 89.25 percent silver, 10.75 percent copper
Edge: Lettered (FIFTY CENTS OR HALF A DOLLAR)
Designer: Robert Scot

CAPPED BUST HALF DOLLARS

Diameter: 32.5 millimeters (1 9/32 of an inch)
Weight: 13.48 grams (0.433 ounce)
Composition: 89.25 percent silver, 10.75 percent copper
Edge: Lettered (FIFTY CENTS OR HALF A DOLLAR)
Designer: John Reich

CAPPED BUST HALF DOLLARS (REEDED EDGE)

Diameter: 30.6 millimeters (1 2/10 of an inch)
Weight: 13.48 grams (0.433 ounces) for 1836, 13.36 grams (0.430 ounce) thereafter
Composition: 89.25 percent silver, 10.75 percent copper for 1836; 90 percent silver and 10 percent copper 1837 through 1839
Edge: Reeded
Designer: Christian Gobrecht (after John Reich)

SEATED LIBERTY HALF DOLLARS

Diameter: 30.6 millimeters (1 2/10 of an inch)
Weight: 13.36 grams (0.430 ounce) from 1839 to 1852 and part of 1853; 12.44 grams (0.4 ounce) in part of 1853 and 1873 and from 1854 to 1872; 12.5 grams (0.402 ounce) in part of 1873 and from 1874 to 1891
Composition: 90 percent silver, 10 percent copper
Edge: Reeded
Designer: Christian Gobrecht

BARBER HALF DOLLARS

Diameter: 30.6 millimeters (1 2/10 of an inch)
Weight: 12.5 grams (0.402 ounce)
Composition: 90 percent silver, 10 percent copper
Edge: Reeded
Designer: Charles E. Barber

WALKING LIBERTY HALF DOLLARS

Diameter: 30.6 millimeters (1 2/10 of an inch)
Weight: 12.5 grams (0.402 ounce)
Composition: 90 percent silver, 10 percent copper
Edge: Reeded
Designer: Adolph A. Weinman

FRANKLIN HALF DOLLARS

Diameter: 30.6 millimeters (1 2/10 of an inch)
Weight: 12.5 grams (0.402 ounce)
Composition: 90 percent silver, 10 percent copper
Edge: Reeded
Designer: John R. Sinnock

KENNEDY HALF DOLLARS

Diameter: 30.6 millimeters (1 2/10 of an inch)
Weight: 12.5 grams (0.402 ounce) in 1964; 11.5 grams (0.370 ounce) from 1965 to 1970; 11.34 grams (0.400 ounce) from 1971 to date

Composition: 90 percent silver, 10 percent copper in 1964; 40 percent silver from 1965 to 1970 (80-percent-silver, 20-percent-copper alloy bonded to a 20.9-percent-silver, 79.1-percent-copper core); 75-percent-copper, 25-percent-nickel alloy bonded to pure copper core from 1971 to date
Edge: Reeded
Designers: Gilroy Roberts (obverse) and Frank Gasparro (reverse)

FLOWING HAIR SILVER DOLLARS

Diameter: About 39 to 40 millimeters (1⅝₆ inches)
Weight: 26.96 grams (0.867 ounce)
Composition: 90 percent silver, 10 percent copper
Edge: Lettered (HUNDRED CENTS ONE DOLLAR OR UNIT)
Designer: Robert Scot

DRAPED BUST SILVER DOLLARS

Diameter: 39.5 millimeters (1⅝ inches)
Weight: 26.96 grams (0.867 ounce)
Composition: 89.25 percent silver, 10.75 percent copper
Edge: Lettered (HUNDRED CENTS ONE DOLLAR OR UNIT)
Designer: Robert Scot

GOBRECHT SILVER DOLLARS

Diameter: 39.5 millimeters (1⅝ inches)
Weight: Issue of 1836, 26.96 grams (0.867 ounce); issue of 1836 (struck in 1837) and 1838–1839, 26.73 grams (0.859 ounce)
Composition: 416 grain standard, 1836 only: 89.25 percent silver, 10.75 percent copper; 412.5 grain standard, 1836 (coined in 1837) and 1838–1839, 90 percent silver, 10 percent copper
Edge: Plain in 1836, reeded in 1839
Designer: Christian Gobrecht

SEATED LIBERTY SILVER DOLLARS

Diameter: 38.1 millimeters (1½ inches)
Weight: 26.73 grams (0.859 ounce)
Composition: 90 percent silver, 10 percent copper
Edge: Reeded
Designer: Christian Gobrecht

MORGAN SILVER DOLLARS

Diameter: 38.1 millimeters (1½ inches)
Weight: 26.73 grams (0.859 ounce)
Composition: 90 percent silver, 10 percent copper
Edge: Reeded
Designer: George T. Morgan

PEACE SILVER DOLLARS

Diameter: 38.1 millimeters (1½ inches)
Weight: 26.73 grams (0.859 ounce)
Composition: 90 percent silver, 10 percent copper
Edge: Reeded
Designer: Anthony de Francisci

TRADE DOLLARS

Diameter: 38.1 millimeters (1½ inches)
Weight: 27.216 grams (0.875 ounce)
Composition: 90 percent silver, 10 percent copper
Edge: Reeded
Designer: William Barber

EISENHOWER DOLLARS

Diameter: 38.1 millimeters (1½ inches)
Weight: 22.68 grams (0.800 ounce)
Composition: 75-percent-copper, 25-percent-nickel alloy bonded to pure copper core
Edge: Reeded
Designer: Frank Gasparro

SUSAN B. ANTHONY DOLLARS

Diameter: 26.5 millimeters (1⁄20 inch)
Weight: 8.1 grams (0.286 ounce)
Composition: 75-percent-copper, 25-percent-nickel alloy bonded to pure copper core
Edge: Reeded
Designer: Frank Gasparro

SACAGAWEA AND PRESIDENTIAL DOLLARS

Diameter: 26.5 millimeters (1⁄20 inches)
Weight: 8.1 grams (0.286 ounce)
Composition: 50 percent copper (core); clad layers are 4 percent nickel, 77 percent copper, 12 percent zinc, 7 percent manganese. Net alloy is 6 percent zinc, 3.5 percent manganese, 2 percent nickel, and 88.5 percent copper
Edge: Plain
Designers: Glenna Goodacre (obverse) and Thomas D. Rogers, Sr. (reverse)

GOLD DOLLARS

Diameter: 13 millimeters (½ inch) from 1849 to 1853 and part of 1854; 14.86 millimeters (⁹⁄₁₀ of an inch) for part of 1854 and thereafter
Weight: 1.672 grams (0.054 ounce)
Composition: 90 percent gold, 10 percent copper and silver
Edge: Reeded
Designer: James B. Longacre

CAPPED BUST FACING RIGHT QUARTER EAGLES ($2.50 GOLD PIECES)

Diameter: About 20 millimeters (⁹⁄₁₀ of an inch)
Weight: 4.374 grams (0.141 ounce)
Composition: 91.67 percent gold, 8.33 percent copper and silver
Edge: Reeded
Designer: Robert Scot

CAPPED BUST FACING LEFT QUARTER EAGLES

Diameter: About 20 millimeters (⁹⁄₁₀ of an inch)
Weight: 4.374 grams (0.141 ounce)

Composition: 91.67 percent gold, 8.33 percent copper and silver
Edge: Reeded
Designer: John Reich

CAPPED HEAD QUARTER EAGLES

Diameter: 18.5 millimeters (¾ inch) from 1821 to 1827, 18.2 millimeters (⁷⁄₁₀ inch) from 1829 to 1834
Weight: 4.374 grams (0.141 ounce)
Composition: 91.67 percent gold, 8.33 percent copper and silver
Edge: Reeded
Designer: Robert Scot and John Reich

CLASSIC HEAD QUARTER EAGLES

Diameter: 18.2 millimeters (⁷⁄₁₀ of an inch)
Weight: 4.18 grams (0.134 ounce)
Composition: 89.92 percent gold, 10.08 percent copper and silver from 1834 to 1836; 90 percent gold, 10 percent copper and silver from 1837 to 1839
Edge: Reeded
Designer: William Kneass

CORONET QUARTER EAGLES

Diameter: 18.2 millimeters (⁷⁄₁₀ of an inch)
Weight: 4.18 grams (0.134 ounce)
Composition: 90 percent gold, 10 percent copper
Edge: Reeded
Designer: Christian Gobrecht

INDIAN HEAD QUARTER EAGLES

Diameter: 18 millimeters (⁷⁄₁₀ of an inch)
Weight: 4.18 grams (0.134 ounce)
Composition: 90 percent gold, 10 percent copper
Edge: Reeded
Designer: Bela Lyon Pratt

$3 GOLD PIECES

Diameter: 20.5 millimeters (⁸⁄₁₀ of an inch)
Weight: 5.015 grams (0.161 ounce)
Composition: 90 percent gold, 10 percent copper
Edge: Reeded
Designer: James B. Longacre

"STELLAS" ($4 GOLD PIECES)

Diameter: 22 millimeters (⅞ of an inch)
Weight: 7 grams (0.225 ounce)
Composition: 85.71 percent gold, 4.29 percent silver, 10 percent copper
Edge: Reeded
Designers: Charles E. Barber and George T. Morgan

CAPPED BUST HALF EAGLES
($5 GOLD PIECES)

Diameter: 25 millimeters (1 inch)
Weight: 8.748 grams (0.281 ounce)
Composition: 91.67 percent gold, 8.33 percent copper and silver
Edge: Reeded
Designer: Robert Scot

CAPPED DRAPED BUST FACING
LEFT HALF EAGLES

Diameter: 25 millimeters (1 inch)
Weight: 8.748 grams (0.281 ounce)
Composition: 91.67 percent gold, 8.33 percent copper and silver
Edge: Reeded
Designer: John Reich

CAPPED HEAD HALF EAGLES

Diameter: 25 millimeters (1 inch) from 1813 to 1828 and part of 1829; 23.8 millimeters (¹⁵⁄₁₆ of an inch) for part of 1829 and thereafter
Weight: 8.748 grams (0.281 ounce)
Composition: 91.67 percent gold, 8.33 percent copper and silver
Edge: Reeded
Designer: John Reich

CLASSIC HEAD HALF EAGLES

Diameter: 22.5 millimeters (⅞ of an inch)
Weight: 8.36 grams (0.269 ounce)
Composition: 89.92 percent gold, 10.08 percent copper from 1834 to 1836; 90 percent gold, 10 percent copper and silver in 1837 and 1838
Edge: Reeded
Designer: William Kneass

CORONET HALF EAGLES

Diameter: 22.5 millimeters (⅞ of an inch) in 1839 and part of 1840; 21.6 millimeters (¹⁷⁄₂₀ of an inch) for part of 1840 and thereafter
Weight: 8.36 grams (0.269 ounce)
Composition: 90 percent gold, 10 percent copper
Edge: Reeded
Designer: Christian Gobrecht

INDIAN HEAD HALF EAGLES

Diameter: 21.6 millimeters (¹⁷⁄₂₀ of an inch)
Weight: 8.36 grams (0.269 ounce)
Composition: 90 percent gold, 10 percent copper
Edge: Reeded
Designer: Bela Lyon Pratt

CAPPED BUST EAGLES ($10 GOLD PIECES)

Diameter: 33 millimeters (1³⁰⁄₁₀ inches)
Weight: 17.496 grams (0.563 ounce)
Composition: 91.67 percent gold, 8.33 percent copper and silver
Edge: Reeded
Designer: Robert Scot

CORONET EAGLES

Diameter: 27 millimeters (1¹⁄₁₆ inches)
Weight: 16.718 grams (0.538 ounce)
Composition: 90 percent gold, 10 percent copper and silver from 1838 to 1872 and part of 1873; 90 percent gold, 10 percent copper for part of 1873 and thereafter
Designer: Christian Gobrecht

INDIAN HEAD EAGLES

Diameter: 27 millimeters (1¹⁄₁₆ inches)
Weight: 16.718 grams (0.538 ounce)
Composition: 90 percent gold, 10 percent copper
Edge: Starred (46 raised stars from 1907 to 1911, 48 raised stars thereafter; each star represents one of the states in the Union, and two new states—New Mexico and Arizona—joined the Union in 1912)
Designer: Augustus Saint-Gaudens

LIBERTY HEAD DOUBLE EAGLES ($20 GOLD PIECES)

Diameter: 34.2 millimeters (1⅛ inches)
Weight: 33.436 grams (1.075 ounce)
Composition: 90 percent gold, 10 percent copper and silver from 1849 to 1872 and part of 1873; 90 percent gold, 10 percent copper for part of 1873 and thereafter
Edge: Reeded
Designer: James B. Longacre

SAINT-GAUDENS DOUBLE EAGLES ($20 GOLD PIECES)

Diameter: 34.2 millimeters (1⅛ inches)
Weight: 33.436 grams (1.075 ounce)
Composition: 90 percent gold, 10 percent copper
Edge: Lettered (E PLURIBUS UNUM, with stars dividing the words)
Designer: Augustus Saint-Gaudens

NOTE: The weight in ounces is given in avoirdupois for base metals and troy standard for gold and silver.

APPENDIX B

WHERE TO LOOK FOR MINT MARKS

Mint marks appear in a number of different locations on U.S. coins. Today, the standard location on regular-issue coins—the five coins made for use in commerce—is the obverse, or "heads" side. In earlier times, however, most coins carried these letters on the reverse.

Following is a list of where to look for mint marks on various U.S. coins:

- **Lincoln cents (1909–present)**—on the obverse, below the date.
- **Indian Head cents (1908 and 1909 only)**—on the reverse, below the wreath.
- **Jefferson nickels (1938–1964)**—on the reverse, to the right of Monticello, except on part-silver war nickels of 1942–1945; there, a large mint mark appears above Monticello.
- **Jefferson nickels (1968–present)**—on the obverse, below the date.
- **"Buffalo" nickels (1913–1938)**—on the reverse, below the words FIVE CENTS.
- **Liberty Head nickels (1912 only)**—on the reverse, to the left of the word CENTS.
- **Roosevelt dimes (1946–1964)**—on the reverse, to the left of the torch's base.
- **Roosevelt dimes (1968–present)**—on the obverse, above the date.
- **"Mercury" dimes (1916–1945)**—on the reverse, to the left of the fasces.
- **Barber dimes (1892–1916)**—on the reverse, below the wreath.
- **Washington quarters (1932–1964)**—on the reverse, below the wreath.
- **Washington quarters (1968–present)**—on the obverse, to the right of George Washington's pigtail.
- **Standing Liberty quarters (1916–1930)**—on the obverse, to the left of the date.
- **Barber quarters (1892–1916)**—on the reverse, below the eagle.
- **Kennedy half dollars (1964)**—on the reverse, to the left of the eagle's tail feathers.
- **Kennedy half dollars (1968–present)**—on the obverse, below John F. Kennedy's neck.
- **Walking Liberty half dollars (1916–1917)**—on the obverse, below IN GOD WE TRUST.
- **Walking Liberty half dollars (1917–1947)**—on the reverse, above and to the left of HALF DOLLAR. (Half dollars dated 1917 come in both mint-mark varieties.)
- **Barber half dollars (1892–1915)**—on the reverse, below the wreath.
- **Susan B. Anthony dollars (1979–1981)**—on the obverse, above Susan B. Anthony's right shoulder.

- **Eisenhower dollars (1971–1978)**—on the obverse, below Dwight D. Eisenhower's neck.
- **Peace silver dollars (1921–1935)**—on the reverse, below the word ONE.
- **Morgan silver dollars (1878–1921)**—on the reverse, below the wreath.
- **Saint-Gaudens double eagles (1907–1933)**—on the obverse, above the date.
- **Liberty Head $20 double eagles**—on the reverse, below the eagle.

EPILOGUE

Rare coins provide rare opportunities. Although they are only pocket-size, they possess enormous attractions: historical significance . . . beautiful art . . . high value . . . great collector appeal . . . and, in some instances, investment potential.

The Insider's Guide to U.S. Coin Values, 20th Edition has given you all the knowledge you need to harness these assets and make them work for you.

I've shown you how to find a fortune in your pocket change—how to sift through the ordinary coins in your pocket and purse and discover the extraordinary coins that lie hidden there, totally overlooked by most people.

I've shown you what to look for in that long-forgotten cigar box in your attic, or that cookie jar filled with coins on a kitchen shelf—how to identify coins that are worth a small fortune among these seemingly humble family hoards.

Venturing into the far-flung coin marketplace, where rare coins are bought and sold by thousands of entrepreneurs, I've given you vital insights into how to measure the market's current mood—how to size up its psychology—and how to make this knowledge work to your advantage. I've stressed the importance of not simply following the crowd. Remember this advice: When everyone seems to be buying, you should be selling, and when everyone seems to be selling, you should be buying.

I've told you how coins are graded, and how a coin's grade directly affects its market value. I've demonstrated why an improperly graded coin could be just as devastating to you financially as one that is overpriced.

I've told you how you can make big profits from small coins and shown you how to cash in those profits. I've even supplied a secret list of twelve "sleeper" coins—coins with high potential to increase in value dramatically.

I've explained how rare coins are related to precious metals, and discussed both the similarities and the differences between rare coins and "bullion" coins.

Back in the 1970s, many investors didn't know how to deal with rampant inflation. The strategies they employed were unsophisticated and smacked of excessive trial and error. Today, the investment market is more mature—and rare coins and bullion have assumed an increasingly important role in many investors' plans and portfolios.

Some economic forecasters are predicting that inflation will return in coming years with a vengeance. If inflation does come raging back, rare coins and precious metals would surely soar in value.

This time people would know how to protect themselves against the ravages of inflation, and that protection would certainly include massive purchases of gold and silver bullion as well as heavy emphasis on rare coins as time-proven hedges.

But many coins have excellent potential for appreciation in value—irrespective of inflation or any other economic variable.

Follow the blueprint in *The Insider's Guide to U.S. Coin Values, 20th Edition* and you'll be prepared for any marketplace. You'll be ready and able to protect both yourself and your coins.

Reread the book, and enjoy it. Then use it like the expert you've become!

INVITATION FOR CORRESPONDENCE

The author welcomes reports of your pocket-change finds and your questions about coin investing at: Scott Travers Rare Coin Galleries, LLC, P.O. Box 1711, F.D.R. Station, New York, NY 10150. Telephone: 212-535-9135. E-mail: travers@USGoldExpert.com.

ABOUT THE AUTHOR

Scott A. Travers ranks as one of the most influential coin dealers in the world. His name is familiar to readers everywhere as the author of six bestselling books on coins: *How to Make Money in Coins Right Now*, *The Coin Collector's Survival Manual®*, *Travers' Rare Coin Investment Strategy*, *Scott Travers' Top 88 Coins to Buy and Sell*, *The Insider's Guide to U.S. Coin Values*, and *The Investor's Guide to Coin Trading*. All of them have won awards from the prestigious Numismatic Literary Guild (NLG). In 2002, NLG awarded him its highest bestowable honor, the lifetime achievement Clemy. He was elected vice-president (1997–1999) of the American Numismatic Association, a congressionally chartered, nonprofit educational organization. He is contributing editor to *COINage* magazine and a regular contributor to other numismatic periodicals, and has served as a coin valuation consultant to the Federal Trade Commission. His opinions as an expert are often sought by publications such as *Barron's*, *Business Week*, and the *Wall Street Journal*. A frequent guest on radio and television programs, Scott Travers has won awards and gained an impressive reputation not only as a coin expert but also as a forceful consumer advocate for the coin-buying public. He serves as numismatic advisor to a number of major investment funds and has coordinated the liquidation of numerous important coin collections. He is president and member of Scott Travers Rare Coin Galleries, LLC, in New York City.